W9-BBG-383

My Soul's High Song

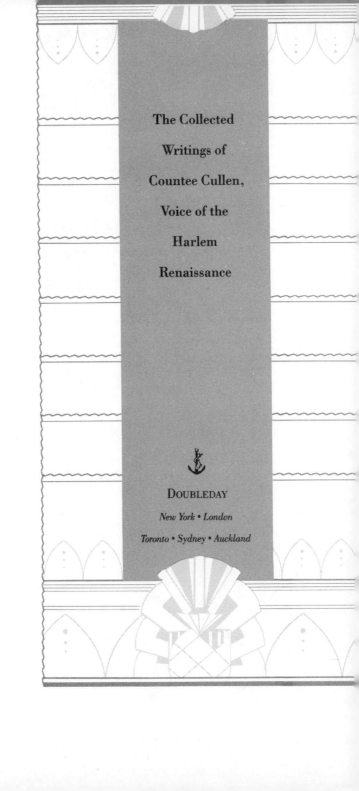

The Collected

Writings of

Countee Cullen,

Voice of the

Harlem

Renaissance

DOUBLEDAY

New York • London

Toronto • Sydney • Auckland

My Soul's High Song

Edited and with an
Introduction by
GERALD EARLY

PUBLISHED BY DOUBLEDAY
a division of Bantam Doubleday Dell Publishing Group, Inc.
666 Fifth Avenue, New York, New York 10103

DOUBLEDAY and the portrayal of an anchor with a dolphin are trademarks of Doubleday, a division of Bantam Doubleday Dell Publishing Group, Inc.

My Soul's High Song is published simultaneously in a trade paperback edition by Anchor Books, a division of Bantam Doubleday Dell Publishing Group, Inc.

BOOK DESIGN BY GUENET ABRAHAM

Library of Congress Cataloging-in-Publication Data
Cullen, Countee, 1903–1946.
    My soul's high song : the collected writings of Countee Cullen, voice of the Harlem Renaissance / edited with an introduction by Gerald Early.
        p.   cm.
    Includes bibliographical references.
    1. Afro-Americans—Literary collections.   2. Harlem Renaissance.
I. Early, Gerald Lyn.   II. Title.
PS3505.U287A6   1991
811′.52—dc20   90-40926
                                                                              CIP

ISBN 0-385-41758-6 (HC)
ISBN 0-385-41295-9 (pbk.)
Special thanks to the Estate of Ida M. Cullen

January 1991
1   3   5   7   9   10   8   6   4   2
First Edition

TO IDA, MY DEAREST FRIEND

ACKNOWLEDGMENTS

I would like to thank the interlibrary loan staffs of Washington University in St. Louis and Randolph-Macon Woman's College in Lynchburg, Virginia, where this book was completed while I was there as writer-in-residence. I would also like to thank my research assistant Marie Saunders and Jim McLeod, Director of African and Afro-American Studies at Washington University, for all their help. I would, finally, like to extend a note of appreciation to Christopher Brown and Joseph Brown, S.J., both of the University of Virginia.

CONTENTS

CONTENTS

CONTENTS

My
Soul's
High
Song

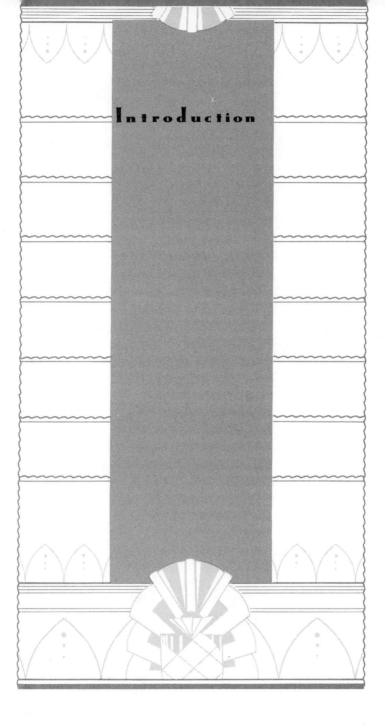

Introduction

I. BOY WONDER, MYSTERIOUS CHILD

I am borne darkly, fearfully, afar

—Shelley, "Adonais"

Till all the world was sea, and I a boat
Unmoored, on what strange quest I willed to float
—Countee Cullen, "The Shroud of Color"

There is not much to say about these earlier years
of Cullen—unless he himself should say it.
—James Weldon Johnson, The Book of American Negro Poetry

The Harlem Renaissance—that storied era principally occurring during the 1920s, when black letters in America reached their first real flowering—produced several significant writers whose works are now essential to the American literary canon. Poet, novelist, translator, journalist Langston Hughes; novelist, anthropologist, and playwright Zora Neale Hurston; and novelist, anthologist, historian, and poet James Weldon Johnson come to mind immediately as major stars associated with the era. Jamaican novelist and poet Claude McKay stands, perhaps, only slightly below Hughes, Hurston, Johnson, and, doubtless, Jean Toomer, who in 1923 gave the world the era's most distinguished novel, *Cane.* Even lesser-known writers of the period whose work is not as stellar—novelists Wallace Thurman, Nella Larsen, and Jessie Fauset, and poet Georgia Douglas Johnson—have been subjects of a revived critical, scholarly, and even popular interest. Yet the one who was once felt to have the most promise and whose name was on everyone's lips has been strangely and sadly neglected in recent years, when the Harlem Renaissance has otherwise enjoyed a kind of intellectual vogue in the classroom and a romantic vogue with the public. In 1925 Countee Cullen, at the age of twenty-two, was the most celebrated and probably the most famous black writer in America.[1] The 1924 publication of his poem "The Shroud of Color" in H. L. Mencken's *American Mercury* was the talk of the intellectual and artistic black community. Few books by a black writer were more eagerly anticipated by the white and black public than Cullen's first collection of poems, *Color,* in 1925. Few writers had won as many literary prizes at such a young age as Cullen. He was, indeed, a boy wonder, a young handsome black Ariel ascending, a boyish, bronze-skinned titan who, in the early and midtwenties, embodied many of the hopes, aspirations, and maturing expressive possibilities of his people. It was once a commonplace for all educated black people to have memorized lines from Countee Cullen's work or even whole works themselves. Once everyone knew such lines as:

> What is Africa to me:
> Copper sun or scarlet sea,
> Jungle star or jungle track,
> Strong bronzed men, or regal black
> Women from whose loins I sprang
> When the birds of Eden sang.
> One three centuries removed
> From the scenes his fathers loved,
> Spicy grove, cinnamon tree,
> What is Africa to me?

---

[1] Headlines such as "Countee Cullen, Young Negro Poet Aids Understanding of His Race," " 'Black Pan' Sings Again," "A Young Poet of Death and African Beauty," "Young Negro Poet Guest of Woman's Club," "Harvard Negro Poet Wins Another Prize," and "A Negro Shropshire Lad" were common both in the black and white press. Indeed, Cullen was sufficiently famous that when his poem "Black Majesty," inspired by a book on Africa of the same title by John Vandercook, appeared in *The Black Christ and Other Poems* (it had first been published in the May 1928 issue of *The Crisis*), Vandercook's grandmother wrote Cullen a gushing letter requesting a copy of the poem. Letter from Mrs. Vandercook to Cullen, April 10, 1929.

Or this closing couplet:

>   Yet do I marvel at this curious thing:
>   To make a poet black, and bid him sing.

Or this well-known poem:

>   Once riding in old Baltimore,
>   Heart-filled, head-filled with glee,
>   I saw a Baltimorean
>   Keep looking straight at me.
>
>   Now I was eight and very small,
>   And he was no whit bigger,
>   And so I smiled, but he poked out
>   His tongue, and called me, "Nigger."
>
>   I saw the whole of Baltimore
>   From May until December;
>   Of all the things that happened there
>   That's all that I remember.[2]

On September 12, 1951, five years after his death, Cullen was still highly esteemed enough to have the 135th Street Branch of the New York Public Library named in his honor. Few black writers can claim the eminence of having a public building named for them. In this regard, only Paul Laurence Dunbar exceeds Cullen.

---

[2]In an open letter in *Opportunity* magazine in July 1927, Carl Van Vechten remarked about Cullen's quotability: "I might say a word or two apropos of the quotableness of Countee Cullen. Suffice to say that the fact is that he is quoted more frequently, with two or three exceptions, than any other American poet. . . . I think the concluding lines of his beautiful sonnet, 'Yet Do I Marvel,' I have seen printed more often (in periodicals in other languages than English, moreover) than any other two lines by any contemporary poet." Bruce Kellner, *"Keep A-Inchin' Along": Selected Writings of Carl Van Vechten About Black Art and Letters* (Westport, Conn.: Greenwood Press, 1979), p. 237.

So what happened to this extraordinarily gifted young man? What diminished the astonishing start of what seemed a fabulous career? Or did Cullen really fall off as much as critics claim he did as he grew older? He certainly wrote less after the age of twenty-six and one is forced again to ask why? Why has his work been neglected and his books out of print for so many years? To be sure, Cullen's most famous poems continue to be anthologized and this perhaps has become the problem. He remains, in many senses, a mere school-house poet who is not conceptualized holistically as a working artist but as a remote figure in a mist—like Longfellow or Lanier or Bryant—whom one knows through a few overly familiar works disembodied from a corpus. Cullen has ceased to be real and so has his work which, aside from often being complex and troubling, has the added burden of being written in strict metrical forms like the ballad, the Spenserian stanza, the Shakespearean sonnet, and the Petrarchan sonnet (Longfellow's favorite form). All of this, to many modern readers and, alas, modern free-verse poets, seems quaint and old-fashioned. We no longer desire poetic diction but only poorly conceived prose bizarrely spread out on a page. In answering questions about Cullen hangs a profound tale of the dynamics and politics of the making of a black literary reputation.

Perhaps Countee Cullen was never fully understood as a poet or a writer because he has never been understood fully as a man. There is, and always has been, a quality of unknowableness, sheer inscrutability, that surrounds Cullen and is no more better symbolized, in a small yet telling way, than by the official, but varied accounts of his height. His passport of both 1934 and 1938 gives his height as 5′3″, his selective service registrant card of 1942 lists him as 5′10″ and his war ration book number 3, issued when Cullen was forty years old, gives his height as 5′7″.

We still do not know where Cullen was born. In James W. Tuttleton's extremely useful essay "Countee Cullen at 'The Heights,' " which provides a detailed account of Cullen's undergraduate years at New York University, we learn that Cullen's college transcript, for which he himself provided the information, lists his place of birth as Louisville, Kentucky.[3] This transcript was dated 1922. In the biographical headnote which Cullen wrote for his selections of poetry—contained in his own anthology of black poetry, *Caroling Dusk*—Cullen says he was born in New York City. This anthology appeared in 1927, three years after the publication of "The Shroud of Color" in the *American Mercury*, two years after the critically and commercially successful publication of his first book of poems, *Color*, two years after having won first prize in the Witter Bynner Poetry contest, the *Poetry* magazine John Reed Memorial Prize for "Threnody for a Brown Girl," the Amy Spingarn Award of *The Crisis* magazine for "Two Moods of Love," second prize in *Opportunity* magazine's first poetry contest for "To One Who Said Me Nay," after having been elected to Phi Beta Kappa, and second-prize winner in the poetry contest of *Palms* for "Wisdom Cometh with the Years." Cullen was to continue to state publicly that New York City was his place of birth for the rest of his life, as did his 1934 and 1938 passports, his 1928 French Identity Card, and James Weldon Johnson's headnote about Cullen in the 1931 edition of his anthology *The Book of American Negro Poetry*. Whatever the reasons for Cullen changing the place of his birth, one inescapable fact is that in 1922 he was a relatively obscure but well-regarded black student with some poetic inclination and ability. By 1927 only Edna St. Vincent Millay surpassed him in American poetry circles in critical and press attention. Here with the whole business of birthplaces, we have the difference between the public and private Cullen. Ida Mae Roberson Cullen, Countee Cullen's second wife (they married in 1940 and remained happily so until Cullen's death in 1946)[4], insisted to various biographers

---

[3]Tuttleton, "Countee Cullen at 'The Heights,' " in Amrijit Singh, William S. Shiver, and Stanley Brodwin, eds., *The Harlem Renaissance: Revaluations* (New York: Garland Publishing, 1989), p. 117.

[4]"Countee's wife Ida is quite lovely: petite, dainty, very friendly, very devoted to Countee. . . ." letter from Langston Hughes to Arna Bontemps, dated November 5, 1941, in

and scholars that Cullen was indeed born in Louisville. Langston Hughes and Harold Jackman, both of whom Cullen knew well, particularly Jackman, also voiced the opinion that he was born in Louisville. Around the time of Cullen's death, stories began to circulate that he was born in Baltimore (one writer even says that Mrs. Cullen confirms this). But there is little evidence for this— except, one supposes, the famous Cullen poem "Incident," which uses Baltimore as a setting. Also, Cullen's foster father was reared in Baltimore and that fact may have contributed to this new confusion. Oddly Beulah Reimherr, who had done the most extensive research into Cullen's childhood and young life, finds no record of anything about him in either the Louisville or Baltimore Bureau of Vital Statistics.[5] There is, moreover, no birth record for Cullen in New York City. The mystery remains unsolved.

Charles H. Nichols, ed., *Arna Bontemps–Langston Hughes Letters, 1925–1967* (New York: Dodd, Mead and Company, 1980), p. 95.

[5] It is Beulah Reimherr who says that Mrs. Cullen told her that her husband was born in Baltimore. See Beulah Reimherr, "Countee Cullen: A Biographical and Critical Study" (M.A. thesis, University of Maryland, 1960), p. 20. Jean Wagner, in his *Black Poets of the United States: From Paul Lawrence Dunbar to Langston Hughes*, trans. by Kenneth Douglas (Champaign-Urbana: University of Illinois Press, 1973), states that "according to the poet's widow . . . Countee Cullen was born in Louisville, Kentucky," p. 285. In Alan Shucard's *Countee Cullen* (Boston: Twayne Publishers, 1984), Mrs. Cullen is quoted in this way: "I have never been under the impression that Countee Cullen was born in Baltimore. In 1940 shortly after Countee and I married, I was told by him that he was born in Louisville, Kentucky," p. 6. Blanche E. Ferguson in her juvenile *Countee Cullen and the Negro Renaissance* (New York: Dodd, Mead and Co., 1966) avoids the issue of Cullen's birth entirely. For her, Cullen's life begins neither with conception nor birth, but with his "adoption" by the Reverend and Mrs. Cullen at, according to her, the age of eleven. Ferguson, on the whole, suggests some connections between Cullen and Kentucky, p. 11. The connection between Cullen and Baltimore is actually a curious one. On May 4, 1926, he was scheduled to address the Baltimore Civic Club at the Emerson Hotel. When the management learned that the speaker was black, it refused to allow the meeting to be held there. Unable to reach him before Cullen left Harvard, the club's treasurer met him at the train station and explained the situation which so deeply upset Cullen that despite the fact that he had two other commitments in Baltimore he simply returned to Boston. When the affair was reported in the New York *Daily News*, "Incident" was quoted as if what happened in the poem had actually occurred. In the June 3, 1926 issue of *The Advocate*, Cullen said, "That incident

And what of Cullen's assertion, in his anthology *Caroling Dusk,* that he was "reared in the conservative atmosphere of a Methodist parsonage." The implication here is that his adoptive parents, the Reverend Dr. Frederick A. and Carolyn Belle (Mitchell) Cullen of the Salem Methodist Episcopal Church in Harlem, were, in fact, his real parents. But Cullen supposedly was not "adopted" until 1918, when he was fifteen years old; and it would certainly overstate the case to claim that he was reared by a conservative Methodist pastor when, in fact, he lived with someone else for the first fifteen years of his life. In the somewhat unreliable biography *Countee Cullen and the Negro Renaissance,* Blanche E. Ferguson states that "Countee Cullen, eleven years, began a new life in the Salem parsonage.[6] This would mean that he was adopted in 1914. Harold Jackman, Cullen's closest friend, said that the adoption of Cullen was never made official. So it could have occurred in 1918, as is most commonly believed, or as early as 1914, or even as early as Cullen's infancy, which was what the second Mrs. Cullen told French scholar Jean Wagner.[7] Yet Cullen wrote an epitaph, "For My Grandmother," which appeared in *Color* and is generally considered not to be about the mother of either of his adoptive parents. If that is so, it would indicate that someone else, perhaps the grandmother, played a significant role in rearing Cullen and that, probably, at least the first ten or eleven years of his childhood were spent outside the influence of the Salem parsonage. Or perhaps it was an obese woman relative who died, leaving Cullen an

---

[referring to the poem] has been outstanding in my memory all these years. But once I had given expression to it—once I had put it into verse—it seemed to lose its sting." But in 1939 Cullen described "Incident" as poetry, as an account of a child's reaction, and not as a biographical fact. Cullen also suggests validation of his origins through another poem, "The Ballad of the Brown Girl," which he said he first heard while growing up in Kentucky. A poem that serves as an interesting gloss of Cullen's view of his natural parents and his birth is "Saturday's Child." Cullen, apparently, was born on a Saturday.

[6]Ferguson, p. 12.

[7]Wagner, p. 285.

orphan, according to accounts by Wagner and Reimherr.[8] Or as another account goes, Cullen's mother, Elizabeth Lucas, reappeared in his life in the 1920s, when Cullen had achieved his fame, and Cullen helped her financially for the rest of her life and even attended her funeral in Kentucky in 1940. Or was Cullen reared by a Mrs. Porter, his grandmother, who brought him to New York City at the age of nine.[9]

In the end we do not know where Countee Cullen was born; we do not know who his natural parents were; we do not know when he was adopted or when he started living with the Reverend and Mrs. Cullen; we do not know the source in his childhood of his intense Christian consciousness: it may have been his mother, his grandmother, the Reverend and Mrs. Cullen, or someone else—or some combination of influences. We also do not know from all of this exactly how or why, what complex of biological or environmental elements made him want to be a writer generally, and, in particular, a great lyric poet. The shifts in identity are indicated by the changes in his name: he signed his earliest published works in 1918 as "Countee L. Porter," although by the time he was writing for his high school literary magazine, *The Magpie*, in 1920 and 1921, he had become "Countee P. Cullen." (This would give credence to the assumption that he was adopted by the Cullens in some sort of formal manner around 1918 and that gradually he began to use their name as his own.)[10] By the time of his first book, *Color*, he was known simply as Countee Cullen.

[8]Wagner, p. 285, suggests it is Cullen's mother; Reimherr, p. 22, insists it is not his mother but probably his grandmother.

[9]See Shucard, p. 6; Reimherr, p. 21; Wagner p. 285; and Shirley Lumpkin, the "Countee Cullen" entry in the *Dictionary of Literary Biography, Vol. 48: American Poets, 1880–1945, Second Series*, Peter Quartermain, ed., (Detroit: Gale Research Co., 1986), p. 110.

[10]One of Cullen's earliest poems, "To the Swimmer," published in *The Modern School: A Monthly Magazine Devoted to Libertarian Ideas in Education* in May 1918, was signed "Countee L. Porter" (p. 142). This would seem to call into question Blanche Ferguson's assertion that Cullen received a writing certificate on May 15, 1915, which said in part,

Ample evidence exists that Cullen enjoyed a close relationship with his foster parents. The Shakespearean sonnet "Tribute (To My Mother)," which appeared in *The Black Christ and Other Poems* (1929) and was written while Cullen was in France on a Guggenheim Fellowship in 1928 and 1929, suggests the influence of his mother's moral presence:

> Because man is not virtuous in himself,
> Not kind, nor given to sweet charities,
> Save goaded by the little kindling elf
> Of some dear face it pleasures him to please;
> Some men who else were humbled to the dust,
> Have marveled that the chastening hand should stay,
> And never dreamed they held their lives in trust
> To one the victor loved a world away.

The phrase "a world away" not only implies that Cullen is writing this poem abroad, far from his mother, but also that he and his mother are, not surprisingly, different, of separate worlds, if you will. Despite this, she continues to be conjured up by the poet; her image haunts him in a way that is conventional yet not sentimental, perhaps somewhat to his own surprise. Cullen's mother seems to have inspired the poet in another way besides being the subject of a poem. He once said: "My mother sings . . . It is wonderful . . . But I . . . I cannot sing. I do not know one note from another. My poetry, I should think, has become the way of my giving out what music is within me."[11] Carolyn Cullen was, for many years, a leading soprano in her husband's church choir. Cullen, who loved music, heard her every week for many years. Also, he probably heard some of the choir rehearsals and his mother singing around

---

"issued to Countee Porter Cullen" (p. 17). As Ferguson provides no citations in her book, it is impossible to check her sources.

[11] *The Christian Science Monitor*, October 23, 1925, p. 6.

the house. She was an able pianist as well. In this sense Cullen saw his poetry as songs of singing, and we might say that his mother exercised some influence over him in his becoming a poet or at least provided significant inspiration.

But it was apparently with his foster father, Frederick A. Cullen, that the poet enjoyed his closest relationship. Dr. Cullen certainly was a man who deserved admiration for his accomplishments. The elder Cullen was born in Somerset County, Maryland, the eleventh child of a couple who had been slaves.[12] Frederick endured a childhood of terrible deprivation and poverty. His father died when Dr. Cullen was only two months old and his mother's life, with eleven children, was a constant struggle. At the age of twelve, Dr. Cullen went to live in Baltimore and apparently by this time his brother and sisters "having grown large left home, leaving only myself and my mother."[13] Dr. Cullen attended the State Normal School in Baltimore and completed college and theological studies at Morgan State College in Baltimore. He was called to the ministry and became a Methodist pastor. He was later granted an honorary degree from Gammon Theological Seminary, Atlanta, Georgia. He arrived in New York City in 1902 after having spent two years pastoring small churches in the Baltimore area. He was assigned to the Salem Methodist Episcopal Church, then a storefront mission. Dr. Cullen collected nineteen cents in his first offering. As one newspaper account goes, "With newspapers stuffed into his shoes for sole, and a bun and coffee his only food, he visited fifty homes a day, giving encouragement and assistance all along the way. Before the year was out, the little store was found too small and the little mission moved to a private house. A fire broke out, destroying all the furniture and the precious little library. Here again Dr. Cullen refused to recognize defeat. Narrowly escaping with his life, the

---

[12]The source of information on Frederick Cullen's life is his privately printed autobiography *From Barefoot Town to Jerusalem* (New York: n.p., n.d.).

[13]From an early draft of Dr. Cullen's autobiography found in the Countee Cullen Papers.

minister made a tour of the neighborhood, collecting boxes to be used for seats—and the services went on."[14]

By the mid-1920s, the church could boast a membership of over 2,500 members; a large educational program that included subjects such as French, Latin, typewriting, shorthand, and math, five large choirs and a full orchestra, as well as a highly competitive youth athletic club, including a particularly notable amateur boxing program of which Dr. Cullen seemed quite proud. It was with youth that Frederick Cullen felt his ministry ought to be particularly concerned. Theologically he was quite conservative and his sermons tended to dwell on the evils that most beset the urban black poor: gambling, drinking, and prostitution, sins of conduct that tend to break up families and lead to social irresponsibility. Yet by the time Salem Methodist moved to Harlem in 1924, Dr. Cullen was the head of one of the most powerful, socially active, and committed institutions in the black community.[15] Countee Cullen's father was active in the NAACP all his life (Countee himself never expressed much political activism in his life and seemed either uninterested

---

[14]Berta Gilbert, "Young Poet Inspired by Father," *Bronx Journal*, November 26, 1929.

[15]There was perhaps a certain tradition of political activism among both black and white ministers in New York in the 1910s. The Reverend Reverdy Casius Ransom, who came to New York in 1907 and eventually started a mission in "New York's black Tenderloin," had been an outspoken member of the Niagra movement from which the NAACP was formed. Ransom became editor of the *AME Church Review* in 1912 and we may assume that it took on a decidedly activist tone as a result. It must be assumed as well that the *AME Church Review* was probably read by black ministers who were not AME simply because, over the years, a good many noted black writers and thinkers, including Paul Laurence Dunbar, Edward Blyden, and Alice Dunbar, had work that appeared in its pages. It was always a very Pan-Africanist journal.

Adam Clayton Powell, Sr., from the time of his arrival in New York to head the Abyssinian Baptist Church in 1912, was a social activist preacher as well, fighting particularly prostitution in the black community. Also, the Reverend Walter Rauschenbush had a ministry among the white poor of New York's Hell's Kitchen and wrote many books during this time—*Christianity and the Social Crisis* (1912), *Christianizing the Social Order* (1912), and his most famous treatise, *A Theology for the Social Gospel* (1917)—about the importance of social mission in a Christian society.

in politics or to have purposely eschewed it) and served for many years as president of the Harlem branch. He assisted James Weldon Johnson and W. E. B. Du Bois in the organizing of the famous silent protest parade of July 28, 1917, in which nearly ten thousand women and children dressed in white and men in dark clothing marched silently down Fifth Avenue to the beat of muffled drums to protest the bloody East St. Louis riot in which hundreds of blacks were killed. He also accompanied Johnson to Washington after the Houston affair in which a regiment of black soldiers on rather scant evidence was accused of shooting several white policemen in a melee.[16] From this we can assume a certain political and racial self-consciousness and a real spirit of militancy on the part of Dr. Cullen since he was a member of the NAACP during the First World War when it was still considered to be a fairly radical organization by many, both black and white (at least before Du Bois's "closed ranks" editorial in *The Crisis* in 1917, which angered many black nationalists). The Reverend Cullen met his wife, Carolyn, when she sang at a concert he attended while vacationing in Atlantic City.

That Cullen was closer to his father than his mother is undeniable. For twelve summers, from 1926 to 1938, Dr. Cullen traveled abroad to Europe and the Middle East with his adopted son as a companion on all the trips save one. Dr. Cullen's wife, who died in 1932, never accompanied her husband and son on any of the trips. On March 13, 1926, Countee Cullen enjoyed one of his greatest triumphs when he heard a chamber orchestra conducted by Alexander Smallens play *Saturday's Child*, a song cycle of his poems "Saturday's Child," "To One Said Me Nay," and "A Song of Praise," set to music by Emerson Whithorne, whose composi-

[16]See James Weldon Johnson, *Along This Way* (New York: Viking Press, 1933), pp. 319–22, 325; Cullen, *From Barefoot Town to Jerusalem*, pp. 52–54; and Eugene Levy, *James Weldon Johnson: Black Leader, Black Voice*, (Chicago: University of Chicago Press, 1973), pp. 190–91, 188–89. Dr. Cullen officiated at Johnson's funeral. Johnson died in June 1938.

tions had been featured as part of Vincent Lopez's Carnegie Hall symphonic jazz concert in November 1924. Cullen's father was present but not his mother. In the summer of 1945, while Cullen was in Los Angeles working with cowriter Arna Bontemps and others on the production of *St. Louis Woman,* his father fell extremely ill. Cullen's letters to his wife often contain touching and anxious displays of concern for his father. His wife's response to one of his letters reveals the closeness between father and son to be of such magnitude that even Cullen's wife was deeply moved by it:

> Countee, your father is the most amazing person that anyone could ever know. It is indeed a privilege to have the fortune and honor to know and be with him at a time like this. His courage and faith is just something one does not have the fortune to see very much in this life. And do you know that through all of this, this week he has been in the hospital, every thought of his has been for you. Just wanting everything to be right for you. Oh, he is wonderful.[17]

Cullen also wrote three poems for his father during the course of his career—"Dad," which first appeared in *The Magpie* in 1922; "Fruit of the Flower," (also containing stanzas about his mother), which was first published in *Harper's* in 1924 and is included in *Color;* and "Lines for My Father," which appeared in *Copper Sun,* Cullen's second collection of poetry, published in 1927. Comparing the earliest with the last published poem is instructive in understanding how Cullen saw his father:

> His ways are circumspect and bound
> With trite simplicities;
> His is the grace of comforts found

---

[17]Letter from Ida Cullen to Countee Cullen, July 24, 1945.

In homely hearthside ease.
His words are sage and fall with care,
Because he loves me so;
And being his, he knows, I fear,
The dizzy path I go.
For he was once as young as I,
As prone to take the trail,
To find delight in the sea's low cry,
And a lone wind's lonely wail.
It is his eyes that tell me most
How full his life has been;
There lingers there the faintest ghost
Of some still sacred sin.
So I must quaff Life's crazy wine,
And taste the gall and dregs;
And I must follow, follow, follow
The lure of a silver horn,
That echoes from a leafy hollow,
Where the dreams of youth are born.
Then when the star has shed its gleam,
The rose its crimson coat;
When Beauty flees the hidden dream,
And Pan's pipes blow no note;
When both my shoes are worn too thin,
My weight of fire to bear,
I'll turn like dad, and like him win
The peace of a snug arm-chair.[18]

We see here clearly that Cullen has begun the process of obscuring his origins by suggesting in this poem that Frederick Cullen is his natural father; for the poem is meant to say, to declare really,

---

[18]The four italicized lines are used verbatim in Cullen's second poem about his father, "Fruit of the Flower."

that Cullen is indeed his father's son, that the "sacred sin," the oxymoron which for Cullen was always sensuality and an obsession with the delights of the carnal, has its origins in his father. (That a theological and metaphorical reading of this as the relation of human—Christian God—original sin would be problematical is obvious.) The rest of the poem is nothing more than a kind of standard *carpe diem* theme that youth must be served in the end, and, thus, the father becomes in this way much the same figure as the old man in William Wordsworth's "Animal Tranquility and Decay." "Lines for My Father" is a more mature assessment of the father:

> Now ushered regally into your own,
> Look where you will, as far as eye can see,
> Your little seeds are to a fullness grown,
> And golden fruit is ripe on every tree.
>
> Yours is no fairy gift, no heritage
> Without travail, to which weak wills aspire;
> This is a merited and grief-earned wage
> From One Who holds His servants worth their hire.

This is a much more theologically considered (and dogmatically sound) evaluation of his father, an evaluation from which Cullen has removed himself so that, ultimately, his assessment of his father does not become, in some respects, merely a complexly dimensioned way to examine himself. Nonetheless, because Cullen was an orphan, to think about his character in relation to his foster father, for whom he bore much respect, is not surprising. Yet there must have been some tension between the two men; the father was a strict fundamentalist while Cullen experienced intellectual doubts and often expressed a kind of ongoing quarrel with Christianity in many of his poems. The father had a certain Puritan demeanor and Cullen, even as an adult, kept the occasional episodes of wild carousing with drink, dancing, and gambling away from him. In many inescapable ways, Cullen had to realize that he was not his father's son or at least not all the time *that* particular father's son. But the bond between Cullen and his adoptive parents was a very strong one, perhaps because he was adopted and so grateful to be in a loving home with a couple who had no children of their own (this fact too made it easier for Cullen to be devoted to his parents; there was no rivalry with any other children, especially any other children to whom the Cullens could have been natural parents); perhaps this made him want to be worthy of that love. As Arna Bontemps so perceptively wrote:

> He paid his adopted parents a devotion, one is almost inclined to say a submission, only rarely rendered by natural sons. But it was all a part of his choice. He did not stand in fear of his foster parents. He simply preferred pleasing them to having his own way.[19]

Countee Cullen excelled at every school he ever attended. And if excelling in school is a way for a child, particularly an orphan, to win a parent's favor, then surely Cullen played the role of an overachiever to his best advantage. On February 4, 1918, he enrolled in DeWitt Clinton High School. It was then located at Fifty-ninth Street and Tenth Avenue, which was a considerable distance from his home, but it was, and continued to be after Cullen's graduation, a highly regarded boys' school.[20] At the time Cullen attended, the school was almost exclusively white. (Ironically, considering the racial composition of the student body, it should be noted that it was while Cullen was at DeWitt Clinton that he made

---

[19]Arna Bontemps, "The Harlem Renaissance," *The Saturday Review of Literature*, March 22, 1947, p. 12.

[20]Among some of DeWitt Clinton's outstanding graduates are Cullen, Richard Rodgers, Louis Untermeyer, Waldo Frank, Paul Gallico, Richard Avedon, James Baldwin, George Sokolsky, and Paddy Chayefsky.

the most important and enduring friendship of his life, with a hand-some West Indian boy named Harold Jackman, to whom he would eventually dedicate a number of his works, give his handwritten copy of "The Ballad of the Brown Girl" as a Christmas gift in 1923, travel to Europe several times in the 1930s, and leave a good portion of his papers when he died.[21]) Cullen was an active student serving as vice president of the senior class; associate editor of the 1921 *Magpie*, the school's literary magazine; and editor of the *Clinton News*. He also won the Douglas Fairbanks Oratorical Contest and the Magpie Cup. It was in high school that Cullen received significant recognition as a poet by winning first prize in a citywide poetry contest sponsored by the Empire Federation of Women's Clubs. His winning entry was entitled "I Have a Rendezvous with Life."[22] This acclaim had many people talking about Cullen as having a future as a major poet and was fraught with significance, suggesting things to come.

In some real sense, it was this initial success by Cullen and not the September 1923 publication of Jean Toomer's *Cane* that really kicked off the literary movement called the Harlem Renaissance; for if anyone was being groomed, being intellectually and culturally conditioned and bred, first by whites and then by blacks, to be a major black crossover literary figure, it was this thin, shy black boy. America has always loved precocious children and Cullen's was the race's first honest-to-goodness child literary star. Perhaps

---

[21]It is appropriate to address here the issue of homosexuality as at least three major scholars have asserted that Cullen was homosexual. David Lewis in *When Harlem Was in Vogue*, Jean Wagner in *Black Poets of the United States*, and Arnold Rampersad in *The Life of Langston Hughes, Vol. 1: 1902–1941*. There is, however, no evidence that Cullen and Jackman were lovers. There is no evidence that Cullen was engaged in any homosexual relations with any other figures of the Renaissance. Some scholars have read letters and poems that seem suggestive in this regard but have offered nothing conclusive.

[22]There are two versions of this poem, both included in this volume. The shorter version is a revision of the longer, more wordy one. The wordy version is the one for which Cullen won the award. The poem was inspired or suggested by Alan Seeger's "I Have a Rendezvous With Death," which was published in 1916.

much of what happened to Cullen in his subsequent career might be better understood if we see him precisely in the light of being a child star, understanding as we do the inability of young gifted performers to sustain themselves over the long stretch of an adult career when the bloom and wonder of early achievement has rather lost its hypnotic, charismatic tint.

Cullen continued to "knock them in the aisles," when he went to New York University, which he attended on a New York State Regents Scholarship. He attended NYU from 1922 to 1925 and while there forged his substance and style as a poet. As James W. Tuttleton informs us, he took the traditional courses in English, French, Latin, math, physics, geology, philosophy, Greek, and physical science while writing most of the poems for which he was to become famous when *Color* and *Copper Sun* appeared.[23] Cullen took most of his English courses with Hyder E. Rollins, who wrote several treatises on the ballad during Cullen's stay at NYU. Rollins also fell in love with Keats at this time, a love that was to become an undying passion as he eventually became a leading Keats scholar. That Rollins was a big influence on Cullen's development, as Professor Tuttleton argues, can scarcely be gainsaid: Cullen took most of his English from Rollins, wrote his undergraduate thesis on Edna St. Vincent Millay for him, and, finally, had him write in support of his successful 1928 application for a Guggenheim. "Is it any wonder, then," writes Professor Tuttleton, "that Cullen's first three volumes—*Color* (1925), *Copper Sun* (1927), and *The Ballad of the Brown Girl* (1927)—were full of ballad settings, characters, and stylistic features?"[24] Is it any wonder too that the first two books show the strong influence of Keats and Millay? Many of the poems Cullen wrote as an undergraduate appeared in the university literary magazine *The Arch*, including two major ones, "Spirit Birth," which became "The Shroud of Color" and "The

[23]Tuttleton, "Countee Cullen at 'The Heights,' " p. 118.

[24]Tuttleton, p. 119, 123, 124, 125, 127.

Ballad of the Brown Girl." (Cullen also wrote "Heritage" while he was an undergraduate.) Generally he was very highly regarded and apparently well liked by other undergraduates. When *Color* was published in 1925, Cullen's senior year, he was heartily congratulated by both faculty and students, including a handwritten note of appreciation from the chancellor.[25] Tuttleton assesses Cullen's undergraduate education as particularly well rounded and rigorous:

> Cullen's program of studies and his manifest distinction as a student, then, indicate that he received a solid liberal arts education with a strong emphasis on languages and literature, history, and philosophy. He was well prepared for graduate study at Harvard in either English or French, both of which he later taught in New York City.[26]

Cullen went to Harvard after graduating Phi Beta Kappa from NYU. It seemed the proper place to bring one phase of his education to an end. He received his Master of Arts from Harvard in 1926 and in December of that year began to write a column entitled "The Dark Tower" for *Opportunity*, the magazine the National Urban League had started just a few years earlier. Perhaps it was so that Cullen was not the leader of the Harlem Renaissance; he had neither the personality nor the vision to lead. (Among the younger writers, Wallace Thurman served that role, and James Weldon Johnson of the NAACP was the overall drum major, with Charles S. Johnson of the Urban League and W. E. B. Du Bois serving as chiefs of staff.) But Cullen had left his stamp on the era more than anyone else. The title of his column, "The Dark Tower," became the name of the literary salon that A'Lelia Walker, daugh-

---

[25]Tuttleton, p. 120, 121, 129.

[26]Tuttleton, p. 119.

ter of Madame C. J. Walker and heiress of the Walker "beauty culture" fortune, started in 1928 in her fashionable townhouse at 108 West 136th Street in Harlem. It was the place for the black intelligentsia and slumming whites who sought something exotic, a place where on the walls one could read Cullen's poetry as well as the poetry of Langston Hughes. In the era of Marcus Garvey, Cullen, in his poem "Heritage," had posed the central question: "What is Africa to me?" And finally in his "Yet Do I Marvel" he produced, according to James Weldon Johnson, "the two most poignant lines in American literature"[27]:

> Yet do I marvel at this curious thing:
> To make a poet black, and bid him sing!

As Owen Dodson wrote so appropriately in his eulogy for Cullen:

> If you asked any Negro what he found in Cullen's poetry, he would say: all my dilemmas are written here. . . .[28]

More than any other presence of the time, including Langston Hughes, Cullen defined his age and, in that sense, dominated it as much as a man of Cullen's temperament could dominate anything. Alas, what he defined was not the triumphs of being black and not even its anguish but the conundrum of blackness which, shaped as it is centrally in the black mind, ought to, in some ways, be centrally poised in the wider cultural discourse itself. When Cullen wrote the line, "Let it be allowed," he meant exactly what he said—that the divided black psyche was the single most riveting riddle of the twentieth-century Western world and it was time for

---

[27]James Weldon Johnson, *Black Manhattan* (Salem, N.H.: Ayer Co., 1988), p. 267.

[28]Owen Dodson, "Countee Cullen (1903–1946)," *Phylon* (First Quarter, 1946), p. 20.

the white Western world to recognize it as such. Cullen said in 1924:

> If I am going to be a poet at all, I am going to be POET and not NEGRO POET. That is what has hindered the development of artists among us. Their one note has been the concern with their race. That is all very well, none of us can get away from it. I cannot at times. You will see it in my verse. The consciousness of this is too poignant at times. I cannot escape it. But what I mean is this: I shall not write of negro subjects for the purpose of propaganda. That is not what a poet is concerned with. Of course, when the emotion rising out of the fact that I am a negro is strong, I express it. But that is another matter.[29]

But the other matter really is the whole of the point: how to express one's blackness without being trapped by it or merely seeing it as a convenient pose. This is the black writer's inviolate anxiety: to be free to be yourself and to be free to be anything but yourself. It must always be kept in mind that Cullen was a great poet. To paraphrase T. S. Eliot's sentence on Keats and Shelley, Cullen would not have been as great as he was but for the limitations which prevented him from being greater than he was. That sums up the paradoxical weight of his blackness as well as anything and comes close enough to explicating the last two lines of "Yet Do I Marvel."[30] In his review of *Color* that appeared in the March 31, 1926 issue of *The New Republic*, Eric Walrond wrote that "Countee Cullen is a fulfilment of one of the pregnant promises of

---

[29]Margaret Sperry, "Countee P. Cullen, Negro Boy Poet, Tells His Story," *Brooklyn Daily Eagle*, February 10, 1924.

[30]T. S. Eliot, *The Use of Poetry and the Use of Criticism* (London: Faber and Faber, 1933), p. 100.

the New World." Walrond was partly wrong and absolutely right.
Childe Countee to the Dark Tower Came . . .

II. THE HARLEM RENAISSANCE AND THE NEW NEGRO

The American Negro of today believes intensely in America.
            —*Eric Walrond, "The New Negro Faces America," 1923*

*I was there. I had a swell time while it lasted. But I thought it
wouldn't last long . . . For how long could a large enthusiastic
number of people be crazy about Negroes forever? But some Harlemites thought the millennium had come. . . . I don't know what
made any Negroes think that—except that they were mostly intellectuals doing the thinking. The ordinary Negroes hadn't heard
of the Negro Renaissance. And if they had, it hadn't raised their
wages any.*
                —*Langston Hughes, The Big Sea, 1940*

The Negro is America's metaphor.
            —*Richard Wright, "The Literature of the Negro
                        in the United States," 1957*

*For we are not Republicans, Democrats, or Socialists any longer.
We are Negroes first.*
            —*Hubert H. Harrison, When Africa Awakes, 1920*

It has been a mistake to understand the Harlem Renaissance as
being the same as the New Negro Movement. Despite some slight
differences among scholars, the Harlem Renaissance is largely conceived to have run from roughly 1915, or around the First World
War, when blacks began to migrate from the rural South to either
the more urban South or Midwest or the urban North, to 1929 or
1930 when the Depression began. This designation is useful
enough, but it must be understood that the Harlem Renaissance
was only a phase, a kind of peak moment, of what I call the New
Negro Movement. I date the New Negro Movement from exactly

1908 to 1938. In order to understand the Harlem Renaissance
and Countee Cullen's role in it, it is necessary to understand the
larger New Negro Movement that made the Renaissance ideologi-
cally possible. It is also necessary to understand that black pugilists
play a central role in a major phase in the development of twentieth-
century American and African-American culture.

Jack Johnson,[31] the first black heavyweight boxing champion,
was an early archetype of the New Negro. It is easy to see why:
he was different from any other black who had ever come to prom-
inence in America before. To be sure, there were blacks who were
boxing champions before Johnson (George Dixon, Joe Walcott, and
Joe Gans), but none had ever been heavyweight champion, the
most significant title in sports in the United States. There were
blacks who had beaten white men in the ring but none who did it
with such glee and disdain. There were black men who had had
sexual relations with white women before (boxing champion George
Dixon was married to a white woman; it caused him no problem),
but none had so flaunted their sexuality and sexual prowess as did
Johnson. Indeed, Johnson was the first black whose sex life became a cause of national scrutiny and national scandal, making
him a truly modern, media-invented star. Johnson won the heavyweight title in December 1908 from Tommy Burns in a fight that
did not receive much press attention. Few were particularly outraged or concerned that a black had won the title; in fact, the
National Police Gazette, the leading sports publication of the day
and certainly not noted for its liberalism if its antimiscegenation

---

[31]For more on Jack Johnson see Jeffrey Sammons, *Beyond the Ring* (Urbana: University of
Illinois Press, 1988), pp. 34–47; Al-Tony Gilmore, *Bad Nigger! The National Impact of
Jack Johnson* (Port Washington, N.Y.: Kennikat Press, 1975); John D. McCallum, *The
World Heavyweight Boxing Championship, A History* (Radnor, Pa.: Chilton Book Co., 1974),
pp. 65–80; Randy Roberts, *Papa Jack: Jack Johnson and the Era of White Hopes* (New
York: The Free Press, 1983), Bert Randolph Sugar, *The 100 Greatest Boxers of All Time*,
pp. 48–49; Rayford W. Logan, *The Betrayal of the Negro: From Rutherford B. Hayes to
Woodrow Wilson* (New York: Collier Books, 1965), pp. 357, 364, 384.

stories are any indication, had actually campaigned for Johnson, saying he deserved a shot at the title. It was not until Johnson's personality became more known and his liaisons with white women more publicized and Jack London's hysterical newspaper columns whipped the public into a frenzy that the calls for a "white hope" to beat Johnson went up throughout the land.

Johnson's career had two distinct public peaks: first, the July 4, 1910 fight in Reno, Nevada, against former champion Jim Jeffries, which Johnson won quite easily, leading to small race riots around the country. It was the most publicized sporting event in American history up to that time. People who normally paid no attention to sports generally or to prizefighting particularly were anxiously awaiting to hear word of the outcome. Johnson's victory made him more unpopular than ever, at least with whites, and certainly many middle-class blacks and several members of the black leadership elite felt uneasy about him. But most blacks felt gladdened by Johnson's success, particularly so because race relations at the time were so strained and blacks were generally forced to suffer the indignity of Jim Crow laws and rampant institutionalized segregation. The Reverend Reverdy Ransom spoke for many blacks when he said before the Johnson-Jeffries fight: "What Jack Johnson seeks to do to Jeffries in the roped arena will be more the ambition of Negroes in every domain of human endeavor."[32] This became the basic idea of the New Negro—the black who asserted his rights and his manhood, who wanted to best the white, who was "reckless, independent, bold, and superior in the face of whites."[33]

The second peak for Johnson was his highly publicized trial and subsequent conviction under the Mann Act in 1913. This prosecution occurred largely because Johnson's first white wife committed suicide in his Chicago nightclub in September 1912 and

---

[32]Quoted in Sammons, *Beyond the Ring*, p. 38.

[33]Sammons, *Beyond the Ring*, p. 42.

because in December of the same year he married another white woman whom the federal government had, at first, tried to use to construct a possible case against Johnson for violation of the Mann Act. In a country that was slowly but inexorably moving toward Prohibition and where a kind of racist, backwater Protestant, small-town morality prevailed, Johnson, who owned a nightclub and played jazz—both nefarious activities, as far as many middle-class whites were concerned—had, through his association with white women, simply tried the country's patience once too often. Johnson fled the country after his conviction.

Although Johnson was not liked by many blacks—especially race leaders like W. E. B. Du Bois, who disapproved of intermarriage— he was, to a large extent, the famous black badman of blues songs and folktales raised to a national icon, no longer the local terrorist of some black community. The black badman was now, through Johnson, bestowed with a political and cultural meaning, and his defiance was no longer simply psychopathic. Middle-class blacks, who in large measure were responsible for the nationalistic formation of the concept of the New Negro, rejected many aspects of Johnson—notwithstanding, his simple act of assertion, his refusal to accept his place became an element of the New Negro. Johnson forced the nation to submit to, or at least tolerate, his dominance. His name blared from the headlines of white newspapers (he was clearly the most written-about black man of his day, even more famous than Booker T. Washington). He showed that a display of assertion commanded both the respect and the fear of whites.

To understand fully how Jack Johnson functioned as an archetype for the New Negro, one must understand the forces that came into play to make it possible, of course, for not only did the New Negro create himself, he was also created by his circumstances. This is important in understanding, finally, how Countee Cullen became the representative New Negro poet by the mid-1920s and what sort of modifications the idea of the New Negro underwent. First, Johnson was born in Galveston, Texas, and he moved, ultimately, to Chicago: like the migration movement, which was to occur around World War I and which made the concept of New Negro the rallying cry for a new cultural movement among blacks. He was not, however, a product of the rural South as Galveston was, in fact, a town. Therefore, he was not a product of the more submissive system of discipline and correction that was usual with black rural workers of the day. His father was a preacher and a school janitor. Also, Johnson was born in 1878, part of that post-slavery generation that came to adulthood at the turn of the century. Johnson became a boxer, a sport that required harsh physical training, great tenacity, a highly disciplined pursuit of improvement, an ability to withstand pain, and a willingness to move around from place to place to fight. While black fighters of Johnson's day were not expected to be as aggressive when boxing against white fighters as they were against each other, aggression was and is the *sine qua non* of boxing, especially if one is ambitious and wishes to get ahead in the sport as Johnson did.

By the 1890s there was a highly developed black sporting society that included jockeys, bicycle racers, boxers, runners, walkers—sports in which a significant number of blacks participated as well as blacks from the world of the stage and popular music.[34] By the time Johnson became a noted boxer at the turn of the century, he was part of a relatively small, but privileged and moneyed world of black performers and entertainers. And America at the time was rapidly beginning to develop the huge entertainment machinery that would be firmly in place by the 1920s. Without the growth of this entertainment machine, the Harlem Renaissance, which was largely a kind of entertainment-based movement when one considers its musical and stage connections, would not have been possible.

What is ironic is that Johnson was permitted to fight for the

---

[34]See James Weldon Johnson, *The Autobiography of an Ex-Colored Man* (New York: Penguin, 1990), and Paul Laurence Dunbar, *The Sport of the Gods* (Miami: Mnemosyne Publishing, 1969).

heavyweight championship (no black had been permitted to do so since the days of the Regency in England) in an era when race relations were very bad and jingoism, imperialism, and strongly racist practices were all part of the accepted American cultural and social expression. Yet it makes perfect sense that Johnson was permitted to do so, because, first, there was such an interest among whites to demonstrate symbolically and graphically that they were the superior race; second, as sports developed there was an ideology of fair play that seemed to demand that blacks be given a chance. There were several black contemporaries of Johnson who were more or less equal in skill and could have fought for the title: Sam McVey, Joe Jeanette, and Sam ("Boston Tarbaby") Langford. The fact that it was ultimately Johnson who won it was simply fortuitous. In the development of the New Negro there is an incredible conjunction of a particular temperament and a set of special cultural circumstances. Moreover, the New Negro idea was masculine. This should certainly not be surprising as, of course, at the time and for a long time following, the idea that black women may have a separate set of political or cultural concerns based on their sex was seen as nonsense by the black male leadership. Also, among the oppressed it is the expression of manhood that is most important politically because for the oppressor male, it is the oppressed male who is the greatest danger to him and who must be particularly and harshly shamed and diminished. In virtually every society, manhood is a precarious attainment. Men worry about being men, realizing their manhood. No one thinks that women must become women in the same way that men must become men. Women simply are.

The sexist preoccupation of the New Negro idea was to be particularly problematic during the Renaissance as men tended to control the movement and to promote male writers over women writers. (Jessie Fauset was a major presence during the Renaissance but largely worked under Du Bois's shadow as literary editor of *The Crisis*. It is often forgotten that she wrote more novels, between 1924 and 1933, than any black male novelist of the period.) Anne Spencer, one of the fine poets of the Renaissance, certainly felt this to be so, and in truth it was. Johnson's reign as champion occurred when Du Bois was an established black leader and James Weldon Johnson was on the verge of becoming one. Charles S. Johnson, another major leader of the Renaissance, was fifteen when Jack Johnson became champion. So the entire elder leadership of the Harlem Renaissance lived through the Johnson era and had memories of it. Claude McKay was nineteen when Johnson became champion. Countee Cullen, Langston Hughes, Eric Waldron, and Wallace Thurman were all little boys when Johnson became champion and most likely heard much from their elders about the black champion as they grew up since Johnson was the subject of much debate and eventually became a part of black folklore.[35] Jack Johnson's influence on the New Negro Movement simply cannot be denied.

As we learn from Daniel Bell, the period around 1912 and 1913, the time when Johnson's name was almost constantly in the papers in connection with the suicide death of his wife and his Mann Act trial, was when white American intellectuals launched their frontal cultural assault on Puritanism and reactionism. It was essentially a two-front attack: first, for a more inclusive and representative culture, and second, for sexual freedom. (Johnson, as a cultural icon, symbolized both.) As Bell writes:

> The exuberance of life was summed up in a series of catchwords. One of them was "New." There was the New Democracy, the New Nationalism, the New Freedom, the New Poetry, and even the *New Republic* (which was started in 1914).[36]

---

[35]See Lawrence W. Levine, *Black Culture and Black Consciousness: Afro-American Folk Thought from Slavery to Freedom* (New York: Oxford University Press, 1977), pp. 429–33, passim.

[36]Daniel Bell, *The Cultural Contradictions of Capitalism*, (New York: Basic Books), p. 62.

So with the presence of Jack Johnson and the emergence of a movement of white intellectuals who desired to reshape the culture and create it anew is it a surprise that around the time of the outbreak of the First World War, blacks, particularly middle-class blacks, began to formulate the idea of a New Negro? The outbreak of the War and blacks' subsequent experience in it; the general movement of the black population away from a rural to an urban way of life (a trend of the entire American population and not just unique to blacks); the armed invasion of Haiti by U.S. Marines in 1915, an occupation that was to last until 1934; the death of Booker T. Washington in 1915; the formation of the Association for the Study of Negro Life and History and the *Journal of Negro History* by Carter G. Woodson in 1915; the emergence of Marcus Garvey as a major race leader by 1918 and the increasing popularity of black nationalism and Pan-Africanism; the swift development of jazz and blues music as, if only in a derivative manner, a significant element of American popular music—all of these historical circumstances conspired to give us, by 1920, a true ideological concept called a New Negro, or the racially conscious Negro. As early as 1909 the term was used in an article on ragtime by J. Rosamond Johnson, brother of James Weldon Johnson.[37] By 1920 there were already apparently at least three poems entitled "The New Negro"—by Reverend Reverdy Ransom, Will Sexton, and L. B. Watkins—as well as a monthly publication by that name edited by black nationalist intellectual and Garveyite Hubert H. Harrison. It was, by 1920, a

---

[37]J. Rosamond Johnson, "Why They Call American Music Ragtime," *The Colored American Magazine*, January 1909, p. 638. William Pickens, Dean of Morgan State College (now Morgan State University) and after 1920 a leader in the NAACP, published in 1916 *The New Negro: His Political, Civil, and Mental Status*. Apparently, the earliest use of the term "New Negro" in any publication occurred in Sutton Griggs's 1899 novel, *Imperium in Imperio*. Booker T. Washington also wrote a book entitled *A New Negro for a New Century* (Chicago: American Publishing House, 1900). See Wilson J. Moses's "The Lost World of the Negro, 1895–1919: Black Literary and Intellectual Life Before the 'Renaissance,' " *Black American Literature Forum* Nos. 1–2, Spring–Summer 1987, pp. 61–84.

term that had been bandied about in the black press quite a bit. Definitions were not exact, but blacks understood that the term represented some independent spirit, some politicized sense of selfhood, some notion of self-determination. This is how Hubert H. Harrison described the mood in the introduction of his very popular book that inaugurated the black 1920s, *When Africa Awakes* (1920):

> The tenseness of this new situation has been reflected here in the United States in the mental attitude of the Negro people. They have developed new ideas of their own place in the category of races and have evolved new conceptions of their powers and destiny. These ideas have quickened their race-consciousness and they are making new demands on themselves, on their leaders, and on the white people in whose midst they live. These new demands apply to politics, domestic and international, to education and culture, to commerce and industry.[38]

"New situation," "new ideas," "new conceptions," "new demands"—whatever all of this might be (and Harrison, to some degree, goes on to explain them in the body of the text), certainly the post–World War I era is being defined by the African-American's "newness." What Harrison does make clear is that whatever the new race consciousness means for the African-American's future, it, at least in part, means a radically new reunderstanding of the tradition and history of his past.

> Now, what is the knowledge which the New Negro needs most? He needs above all else a knowledge of the wider world and of the long past. But that is history,

[38]Hubert H. Harrison, *When Africa Awakes: The "Inside Story" of the Stirrings of the New Negro in the Western World* (New York: Porro Press, 1920), p. 6.

modern and ancient. . . . The Negro needs also the knowledge of the best thought; but that is literature as conceived, not as a collection of flowers from the tree of life, but as its garnered fruit. And, finally, the Negro needs a knowledge of his own kind. . . .[39]

Thus the book that really kicked off the phase of the New Negro Movement known as the Harlem Renaissance[40]—the phase that tried to produce a school or an identifiable discipline of black American letters—was not Jean Toomer's *Cane* (1923) or Claude McKay's *Spring in New Hampshire* (1922), it was James Weldon Johnson's 1922 anthology *The Book of American Negro Poetry*, the first collection of its type but surely not the last to display a considerable obsession in anthologizing the Negro.[41] (The book that made Johnson's book possible was Arthur A. Schomburg's *A Bibliographical Checklist of American Negro Poetry*, published in 1916.) Johnson, a noted songwriter (along with his brother J. Rosamond Johnson and Bob Cole), novelist (*The Autobiography of an Ex-Colored Man*, 1912), poet (*Fifty Years and Other Poems*,

---

[39]Harrison, *When Africa Awakes*, p. 133.

[40]Perhaps the biggest criticism that can be made against the Renaissance was that it seemed to be nothing more than a series of beginnings: Claude McKay's *Spring in New Hampshire*, or *Harlem Shadows*, as the book was entitled when published in the United States in 1922, Johnson's anthology in 1922, *Cane* in 1923. The dinner that brought together white publishers and black writers in celebration of Jessie Fauset's novel, *There Is Confusion* in 1924, Cullen's *Color* in 1925, Hughes's *The Weary Blues* in 1926, Alain Lock's *The New Negro* in 1925. It seemed to be a movement that was always getting started but never going anywhere.

[41]Among the more important anthologies of black life and art produced in the 1920s are: Robert T. Kerlin, *Negro Poets and Their Poems* (Washington, D.C.: Associated Press, 1923); Newman Ivey White and Walter Clinton Jackson, *An Anthology of Verse by American Negroes* (Durham, N.C.: Trinity College Press, 1924); James Weldon Johnson and J. Rosamond Johnson, *The Book of American Negro Spirituals* (New York: Viking, 1925); J. Weldon Johnson and J. Rosamond Johnson, *The Second Book of American Negro Spirituals* (New York: Viking, 1926); Alain Locke, *Four Negro Poets* (New York: Simon and Schuster, 1927). For an interesting analysis of black anthologies, see John S. Lash "The Anthologist and the Negro Author," *Phylon* (First Quarter, 1947), pp. 68–76.

1917), newspaper publisher (he published, from 1895 to 1896, the *Daily American* out of Jacksonville, Florida, one of the earliest black daily papers, the *New Orleans Creole* being the first such paper), U.S. consul to Venezuela and Nicaragua, grade school principal, and field secretary of the NAACP, the man called by Cullen, "the Dean of American Negro writers,"[42] was one of the most respected blacks in the country and the ideal person—being something of a Renaissance (no pun intended) man—to espouse the position of the New Negro. His anthology was, in truth, both a cultural history and a cultural manifesto. One might even argue that the poetry that follows serves as nothing more than an excuse for the extraordinary and lengthy essay that functioned as the introduction and seems to be the real reason for the book. Johnson, in effect, announces that the coming decade is the period of the Negro's coming of age in the renovating and reconstruction of his culture through the self-conscious creation of virtuosic art:

> A people may become great through many means, but there is only one measure by which greatness is recognized and acknowledged. The final measure of the greatness of all people is the amount and standard of the literature and art they have produced. The world does not know that a people is great until that people produces great literature and art. No people that has produced great literature and art has ever been looked upon by the world as distinctly inferior.
>
> The status of the Negro in the United States is more a question of national mental attitude toward the race

---

[42]Cullen's headnote to James Weldon Johnson's "The Creative Negro," in Fred J. Ringel, ed., *America as Americans See It* (New York: Harcourt, Brace, and Co., 1932), p. 160.

than of actual conditions. And nothing will do more to change that mental attitude and raise his status than a demonstration of intellectual parity by the Negro through the production of literature and art.[43]

Johnson continues with a specific charge for black poets as they must transcend the use of dialect:

What the colored poet in the United States needs to do is something like what Synge did for the Irish; he needs to find a form that will express the racial spirit by symbols from within rather than by symbols from without, such as the mere mutilation of English spelling and pronunciation. He needs a form that is freer and larger than dialect, but which will still hold the racial flavor; a form expressing the imagery, the idioms, the peculiar turns of thought, and the distinctive humor and pathos, too, of the Negro, but which will also be capable of voicing the deepest and highest emotions and aspirations, and allow of the widest range of subjects and the widest scope of treatment.[44]

What is extremely important about Johnson's statements is that he has further refined the concept of the New Negro and race consciousness that was earlier formulated by Harrison. He has no real disagreement with Harrison on one level as the New Negro concept is, by necessity, at least somewhat nationalistic. Johnson only wishes to make clear the ultimate bourgeois aims of the New Negro Movement: to produce a self-conscious high art that emanates from the particular and remarkable awareness that the black artist has of his racialness. Both Harrison and Johnson are the

---

[43]James Weldon Johnson, *The Book of American Negro Poetry* (New York: Harcourt, Brace, and World, 1931), p. 9.

[44]James Weldon Johnson, *The Book of American Negro Poetry*, p. 41.

bourgeois and intellectual refinements of Jack Johnson, who still remains the original, crude archetype of New Negro consciousness, a kind of ur-black consciousness. But filtered through the bourgeois black mind, New Negro consciousness not only aims to produce a culture but a new type of cultured and acculturated person.

In their own distinct ways, both Countee Cullen and Langston Hughes followed Johnson's prescription and produced a striking and powerful new black poetry; one through suffusing essentially English poetry with race consciousness as Cullen wrote in fact little explicitly nonracial poetry, and the other through elevating black folk forms with a kind of ingenious self-consciousness, without resorting to old-fashioned dialect, in effect escaping the creative trap that so frustrated Johnson's good friend, Paul Laurence Dunbar. Cullen's task was, in some respects, the more difficult, although the more likely to be turned "outdoors," to borrow an old black folk expression, when blacks themselves, both as a mass—and Cullen in his heyday had a mass black audience—and as an intellectual elite were no longer impressed by a black man's manipulation of white poetic forms for not only his personal ends but for the race's. Houston Baker writes that "Countee Cullen . . . served a national need in a time of 'forced' institution building and national projection. He gained white American recognition for 'Negro poetry' at a moment when there was little encouraging recognition in the United States for *anything* Negro."[45]

Two extremely suggestive occurrences took place during the Harlem Renaissance, both involving anthologies, that placed Cullen at the heart and center of the movement. First, in 1925, when Cullen enjoyed his watershed year of recognition with the publication of *Color* and with the winning of several literary prizes, Alain Locke's *The New Negro* was published. It was the most celebrated and storied anthology of black culture ever produced (based on the famous March 1925 special Harlem issue of *Survey Graphic*,

[45]Houston A. Baker, *Modernism and the Harlem Renaissance* (Chicago: University of Chicago Press, 1987), p. 86.

which Locke edited), with Locke's own title essay offering the final bourgeois refinement of the definition of the New Negro and race consciousness. "The intelligent Negro of to-day is resolved," Locke argues, "not to make discrimination an extenuation for his short-comings in performance, individual or collective; he is trying to hold himself at par, neither inflated by sentimental allowances nor depreciated by current social discounts. For this he must know himself and be known for precisely what he is. . . ."[46] And later in the essay Locke writes: "Subtly the conditions that are molding a New Negro are molding a new American attitude."

The conjunction of the publication of this book and this essay with the year of Cullen's great success was a very fortunate happenstance as each tended to validate the other. The New Negro idea had swung away from anything explicitly nationalistic in Locke's view. He argued that the Negro must learn to define the shape of his ethnicity within the larger cultural framework of American life and not within a framework purely of his own creation. In other words, the Negro's nationalism was now no more than a typical American ethnic nationalism: namely, a kind of race pride and a sense of group identification that made one a distinct flavor in the American melting pot. To define themselves within the framework of American life meant that blacks were almost unavoidably defining themselves according to the terms that whites had constructed about them.

In short, the New Negro Movement, by the time Locke became its spokesman and Cullen its exemplar, ceased to be a search purely for a race-conscious ideology and certainly ceased to have any meaningful teleological pretensions for a New Africa, although some vague, largely condescending sense of mission to the darker people of the world still existed, but this scarcely differed from the African mission idea that was popular with some black intellectuals and black leaders in the mid-nineteenth century. The New Negro

---

[46]Alain Locke, "The New Negro" in *The New Negro*, ed. by Alain Locke (New York: Atheneum, 1970), p. 8.

Movement had become purely a movement where the Negro, like
the white immigrants before him, could construct a migratory myth
of freedom, so that he could become an American by, in effect,
being reborn and having a new past that would free him from the
burdens of slavery. What was being espoused was a mere reworking of Booker T. Washington's ideas about the Americanization of
the Negro in his autobiography *Up from Slavery.* In 1920 black
nationalist Hubert H. Harrison said to blacks, "We are Negroes
first!" In 1925 Countee Cullen, to the white and black press, said,
"I am not a Negro poet!" So the New Negro Movement split in
the 1920s into distinct, though not necessarily antagonistic, groups:
the chiliastic, nationalistic, visionary remnant of Garveyites, many
of whom were to become followers of Father Divine in the 1930s;
and the secular, modernist, assimilationist elite.

Of course, there was overlap between the two camps and the goals
of both sometimes coincided. This is especially true of some of Du
Bois's views which seemed, at times, a contradictory mixture of both.
In some of his poems, notably "Heritage," Cullen himself seemed
torn between both constellations of sentiments. The union between
Locke, the certifier of the New Negro, and Cullen reached an apogee
when we read the opening sentences of Locke's review of *Color:*

> Ladies and gentlemen! A genius! Posterity will laugh
> at us if we do not proclaim him now. COLOR tran-
> scends all of the limiting qualifications that might be
> brought forward if it were merely a work of talent. . . .
> it is the work of a Negro poet writing for the most part
> out of the intimate emotional experience of race, but
> the adjective is for the first time made irrelevant, so
> thoroughly has he poeticized the substance and fused it
> with the universally human moods of life.[47]

[47]Alain Locke, "Color: A Review," *Opportunity,* January 1926, p. 14.

The New Negro had arrived and his name was Countee Cullen.
The other occurrence was the 1927 publication of Cullen's own
black poetry anthology, *Caroling Dusk*. He had a kind of dress
rehearsal for this sort of thing when he was guest editor of the
Negro issue of *Palms* (October 1926), a poetry magazine. In that
issue, Walter White provided an overview essay, "The Negro Renaissance," and Alain Locke favorably reviewed Langston Hughes's
The Weary Blues. But in *Caroling Dusk*, Cullen delivers his own
artistic manifesto in his introduction:

> I have called this collection an anthology of verse by
> Negro poets rather than an anthology of Negro verse,
> since this latter designation would be more confusing
> than accurate. Negro poetry, it seems to me, in the
> sense that we speak of Russian, French, or Chinese
> poetry, must emanate from some country other than
> this, in some language other than our own. Moreover,
> the attempt to corral the outbursts of the ebony muse
> into some definite mold to which all poetry by Negroes
> will conform seems altogether futile and aside from the
> facts. This country's Negro writers may here and there
> turn some singular facet toward the literary sun, but in
> the main, since theirs is also the heritage of the English
> language, their work will not present any serious aber-
> ration from the poetic tendencies of their times. The
> conservatives, the middlers, and the arch heretics will
> be found among them as among the white poets; and
> to say that the pulse beat of their verse shows generally
> such a fever, or the symptoms of such an ague, will
> prove on closer examination merely the moment's ex-
> aggeration of a physician anxious to establish a new
> literary ailment. As heretical as it may sound, there is
> the probability that Negro poets, dependent as they are
> on the English language, may have more to gain from
> the rich background of English and American poetry

MY SOUL'S HIGH SONG

than from any nebulous atavistic yearnings towards an African inheritance. Some of the poets herein represented will eventually find inclusion in any discriminatingly ordered anthology of American verse, and there will be no reason for giving such selections the needless distinction of a separate section marked Negro verse.[48]

We now see with Cullen the complete reification of the idea of the New Negro and racial consciousness, completely estranged from its beginnings as a merging of American popular culture and black folklore culture in the person of Jack Johnson, and, more importantly, completely estranged from the idea of a militant black nationalism since blacks have no separate language that defines them as a distinct cultural or national group. The goal ultimately is that there will be no need for anthologies of black poets because, eventually, they will be included in standard American anthologies. After nearly twenty years or a generation since Jack Johnson and after nearly eight years since *When Africa Awakes,* in Cullen's introduction we have the view that the manifestation of race consciousness is only so that the Negro and his white countrymen can understand the uniqueness of the Negro not as a function of his blackness, but as a function of his being an American.

This, of course, is nothing more than a variation of the bourgeois manifestoes of James Weldon Johnson and Alain Locke. Through

---

[48]Countee Cullen, ed., *Caroling Dusk: An Anthology of Verse by Negro Poets* (New York: Harper and Brothers, 1927), pp. xi–xii. The subtitle for Cullen's book is nearly the same as the title used by Newman Ivey White and Walter Clinton Jackson (white editors) for their anthology of black verse published a few years earlier (*An Anthology of Verse by American Negroes,* published in 1924 in North Carolina). Cullen's subtitle was *An Anthology of Verse by Negro Poets.* Obviously the White and Jackson title has a bit more clinical and sociological ring to it. Nonetheless Cullen was not the only one thinking along those lines of not wishing to describe writing by blacks as black writing, nor was that thinking confined to blacks. Moreover, as we see with Cullen's response to critics like Langston Hughes and Frank Mott that he must have had those who wanted a more consciously racial aesthetic associated with the writing of blacks in mind when he wrote the poem, "To Certain Critics."

the line of James Weldon Johnson, Alain Locke, and Countee Cullen, racial consciousness leads, ironically, to racelessness or to a world where color will be depoliticized. Racial consciousness thus leads to deracination. "A variety within a uniformity" is the way Cullen expressed it, and this idea of multiplicity within a union is a constant throughout his writing, from "The Shroud of Color" in 1924, where his narrator wears "a many-colored coat of dreams," to his novel *One Way to Heaven* in 1932, where he ultimately condemns orthodoxy and mindless uniformity as the worst sort of deception on to his children's book, *The Lost Zoo* in 1940, with its wild menagerie of animals joining together on Noah's ark. Cullen once wrote about Helen Keller: "Her impediments have given her a kindred feeling for all oppressed peoples, for all in any way handicapped. She speaks of the people of the earth in a biblically symbolic way, telling us that Joseph's coat had many colors, all of which contributed to the beauty of that coveted mischief-working garment."[49] This thematic preoccupation anticipates Ralph Ellison's *Invisible Man* (1952) and Ishmael Reed's *Mumbo Jumbo* (1971), in which the same concern with multiplicity is evidenced. It simply cannot be overemphasized how central Cullen was to the entire concept of the Harlem Renaissance and the formation of a national black literature.

Cullen established his credentials as the Renaissance's new leading young man of letters in three ways. He authenticated and certified his poetic knowledge and abilities by going to and graduating from white schools (DeWitt Clinton High, New York University, and Harvard). This meant that he had legitimate training, something virtually

---

[49] Countee Cullen, "The Dark Tower," *Opportunity*, February 1928. Ironically, Keller herself was aware of the strong race feeling in Cullen's work. She said this about *Color* in a letter to Cullen dated April 6, 1928:

I find the poems intensely race-conscious; but I cannot agree with the criticism I read sometime ago, I think in *The Nation*, that this is a fault. A man must write out of his deepest experience, or there will be no individual tang [sic] to what he writes. Indeed, the more saturated a poet is with the heritage of his race—its sufferings, its aspirations, its defeats and victories—the more sincere and poignant his self-expression must be.

no black poet had had before. Dunbar, the race's greatest poet before the Renaissance, had only finished high school.[50] Next, Cullen put together an anthology, which meant that he was exercising his judgment about a black literary canon and a black poetic tradition. Finally, and most important, he became a rigorous critic. The preface to his anthology was simply one of a long line of critical pronouncements. Starting with the League of Youth address in 1923, he provided his definition of the New Negro as essentially the Negro youth who was now "going in strong for education; [realizing] its potentialities for combating bigotry and blindness," and was less religiously passive, realizing "that religious fervor is a good thing for many people, and while . . . it and the Negro are fairly inseparable . . . where it exists in excess it breeds stagnation, and passive acquiescence, where a little active resistance would work better results." He ended by making a plea for the races to come together, quoting the very Booker T. Washington-esque poem "To America" by James Weldon Johnson.[51] (This poem, incidentally, was also quoted in Alain Locke's essay "The New Negro.") Cullen's use of the poem, which was published in 1917, signifies how relevant and imposing a figure Washington was in the whole New Negro Movement. In effect, in this speech Cullen makes himself the model for the New Negro: young, educated, less fundamentalist and messianic in religious orientation,

---

[50]William Stanley Braithwaite, the nationally known anthologist, critic, professor, and conservative poet, never finished grade school. Of course, it must be noted that the three major black American poets produced before the Second World War—Cullen, Hughes, and Dunbar—were all "star" poets in high school.

[51]Cullen, League of Youth Address, *The Crisis*, August 1923, p. 167, 168. Cullen admired Johnson greatly and obviously thought that Johnson had successfully solved the problem of creating a universal poetry from black folk material. Johnson as a model was instrumental in the development of Cullen's critical creed. Cullen said this in his review of Johnson's *God's Trombones*, which appeared in *The Bookman* in October 1927: "There is a universality of appeal and appreciation in these poems that raises them, despite the fact that they are labeled 'Seven Negro Sermons in Verse,' and despite the persistent racial emphasis of Mr. [Aaron] Douglas' beautiful illustration, far above a relegation to any particular group or people."

seeking to come together with the whites. This, of course, was largely the message of the less militantly nationalistic bourgeois black intellectuals of the 1920s. When Cullen became assistant editor of *Opportunity* in 1926, he developed his line of criticism more fully in his "Dark Tower" columns, which ran fairly regularly through 1927 and 1928. Even before he began the column, Cullen makes his critical position clear when he responds to an NAACP questionnaire which was used as a feature entitled "The Negro in Art—How Shall He Be Portrayed—A Symposium," which ran in *The Crisis* in 1926 and 1927.

> I should be the last person to vote for any infringement of the author's right to tell a story, to delineate a character, or to transcribe an emotion in his own way, and in the light of the truth as he sees it. . . . I do believe, however, that the Negro has not yet built up a large enough body of sound, healthy race literature to permit him to speculate in abortions and aberrations which other people are all too prone to accept as legitimate. . . . For Negroes to raise a hue and cry against . . . misrepresentations without attempting, through their artists, to reconstruct the situation seems futile as well as foolish. Negro artists have a definite duty to perform in this matter, one which should supersede their individual prerogatives, without denying those rights. We must create types that are truly representative of us as a people. . . .[52]

This call for the creation of respectable, bourgeois, "more representative" race literature was to be reiterated in his March 1928 "Dark Tower" column:

---

[52]Cullen, "The Negro in Art," *The Crisis*, August 1926, p. 193.

Perhaps a bit of the Browning philosophy practiced by
some of our present day Negro writers and journalists
might improve race relations more than the wholesale
betrayal of racial idiosyncrasies and shortcomings which
seems so rampant. Every house worthy of the name has
an attic or a bin or an out-of-the way closet where one
may hide the inevitable family skeleton. But who inviting
a prominent guest to tea, or dinner, and hoping to make
even the slightest of good impressions, feels called upon
to guide the guest sedulously through every nook and
corner of the house, not omitting attic, bin, and the dusty
retreat of the skeleton? In most well-regulated house-
holds one's guest would not get further than the parlor.

American life is so constituted, the wealth of power
is so unequally distributed that whether they relish the
situation or not, Negroes should be concerned with
making good impressions. . . . Every phase of Negro life
should not be the white man's concern. The parlor
should be large enough for his entertainment and instruction.[53]

In another "Dark Tower" column he complains about Wallace
Thurman's essay on Harlem which affects "that sharp staccato
writing" probably of H. L. Mencken and which presented Harlemites as "human checkers automatically moving on a huge crazy-
quilt and getting nowhere at all."[54] The house metaphor—a
properly bourgeois image of rectitude and respectability—in his
first essay is especially noteworthy as it suggests that the African-
American now had, first, an edifice of traditions in need of protec-
tive definition and, second, that he had a place to which he can
invite whites and expect them to come. Although Cullen himself

---

[53]Cullen, The Dark Tower, *Opportunity*, March 1928, p. 90.

[54]Cullen, The Dark Tower, *Opportunity*, June 1927, p. 180.

was not above satirically critiquing the black middle class in his novel *One Way to Heaven*, he seems to have found Thurman's approach unappealing and grating, as if it were all being done for effect, simply to be iconoclastic. He was to have an ongoing quarrel with Thurman.

The other corollary of Cullen's critical creed was that the black artist should not be bound by his race or restricted to race matters simply because he or she is black. In the same "Dark Tower" column where he criticized Thurman's article on Harlem, he also criticized Frank L. Mott's article on Harlem poets that appeared in *Midland* because it seemed that Mott was suggesting that black artists ought to stick to racial material, the implications of which Cullen politely but pointedly resented. In the same column, Cullen writes of a related matter:

> Without in the least depreciating the beauty of Negro spirituals or the undeniable fact that Negro singers do them, as it were, to the manner born, we have always resented the natural inclination of most white people to demand spirituals the moment it is known that a Negro is about to sing. So often the request has seemed to savor of the feeling that we could do this and this alone.[55]

In another column, Cullen takes Alain Locke to task for stating in the introduction of his new anthology, *Four Negro Poets*, that the "Negro poet regard his racial heritage as a more precious endowment than his own personal genius. . . ."[56] Cullen, whose work is included in the volume, along with poems by Claude McKay, Langston Hughes, and Jean Toomer, responds:

---

[55]Cullen, "The Dark Tower," column, *Opportunity*, June 1927, p. 181.

[56]Quoted in Cullen, "The Dark Tower," column, *Opportunity*, July 1927, p. 210.

As one, to a slight extent, in on the know of things, we have serious doubts that Negro poets feel themselves more strongly obligated to their race than to their own degree of personal talent. Two of the poets herein represented might subscribe to Dr. Locke's tenets; two we think are less racially altruistic.[57]

The latter two are, of course, Jean Toomer and Cullen himself.

Cullen's critical creed did not go unchallenged. Wallace Thurman was particularly critical of the idea of creating a respectable bourgeois race literature "of the parlor." In both his "Negro Artists and the Negro," which appeared in the August 31, 1927 issue of the *New Republic*, and in "Negro Poets and their Poetry," an article from *The Bookman*, Thurman lashes out at philistine black taste as well as the pretensions of black literature itself, which, from its history, he felt was scarcely deserving of the name. In the essay on black poets he writes:

> Not only was [Paul Laurence Dunbar] the first Negro to write poetry which had real merit and could be considered as having more than merely sentimental or historical value, but he was also the first Negro poet to be emancipated from Methodism, the first American Negro poet who did not depend on a Wesleyan hymn-book for inspiration and vocabulary. Most of the poets preceding him were paragons of piety.[58]

---

[57]Cullen, "The Dark Tower," *Opportunity*, July 1927, p. 210.

[58]Thurman, "Negro Poets and Their Poetry," *The Bookman*, July 1928, p. 557. In the special Negro issue of *Palms* (October 1926), which Cullen edited, Walter White in his essay entitled "The Negro Renaissance" gave a nearly identical assessment of Negro poetry before Dunbar.

But Thurman asserts that "Dunbar was far from being a great poet," and that after him, the sum total of the achievement of other black dialect poets was zero.[59] Finally, he gets to the contemporary big three: Cullen, McKay, and Hughes. About Cullen he writes, bestowing left-handed praise, that "there is hardly anyone writing poetry in America today who can make the banal sound as beautiful as does Mr. Cullen. . . . Technically, he is almost precocious, and never, it may be added, far from the academic. . . ."[60] Yet Cullen is a deeply flawed poet: "Mr. Cullen's love poems are too much made to order. His race poems, when he attempts to paint a moral, are inclined to be sentimental and stereotyped. It is when he gives vent to the pagan spirit and lets it inspire and dominate a poem's form and context that he does his most impressive work. His cleverly turned rebellious poems are also above the ordinary. But there are not enough of these in comparison to those poems which are banal, though beautiful."[61] Thurman's bottom line is: "All of us do know that as yet the American Negro has not produced a great poet."[62]

But Thurman is even harsher in his essay "Negro Artists and the Negro," in which he gives direct answer to Cullen's assertions about the need for a bourgeois black literature:

> The American Negro feels that he has been misinterpreted and caricatured so long by insincere artists that once a Negro gains the ear of the public he should expend his spiritual energy feeding the public honeyed manna on a silver spoon. The mass of Negroes, like the mass of whites, seem unable to differentiate between sincere art and insincere art. They seem unable to

---

[59]Thurman, "Negro Poets and Their Poetry," *The Bookman*, July 1928, p. 557.

[60]Thurman, "Negro Poets and Their Poetry," *The Bookman*, July 1928, p. 559.

[61]Thurman, "Negro Poets and Their Poetry," column, *The Bookman*, July 1928, p. 560.

[62]Thurman, "Negro Poets and Their Poetry," column, *The Bookman*, July 1928, p. 561.

fathom the innate differences between a dialect farce committed by Octavus Roy Cohen to increase the gaiety of Babbitts, and a dialect interpretation done by a Negro writer to express some abstract something that burns within his people and sears him.[63]

And Thurman is severer still in his criticism of Cullen here, calling his work, "conventional in theme and manner." Cullen, for Thurman, is a thoroughly bourgeois poet who "never will seek the so-called lower elements of Negro life for his poetic rhythms and material, and since he, too, assumes the conventional race attitude toward his people rather than an artistic one, he will probably remain endeared to both bourgeois black American and sentimental white America. . . ."[64]

Langston Hughes also inveighed against the Cullen critical standard in his famous essay "The Negro Artist and the Racial Mountain," which appeared in *The Nation* on June 23, 1926, ostensibly as a reply to George Schuyler's essay "The Negro Art Hokum," which appeared a week earlier in the same magazine. Actually, as a reply to Schulyer the Hughes essay makes little sense since Hughes starts out assuming the validity of a concept which Schulyer argued did not exist. As a response to Cullen, the Hughes essay is amazingly clear. The opening of Hughes's essay is directly about Cullen:

One of the promising of the young Negro poets said to me once, 'I want to be a poet—not a Negro poet,' meaning, I believe, 'I want to write like a white poet';

---

[63]Thurman, "Negro Artists and the Negro," column, *The New Republic*, August 31, 1927, p. 38.

[64]Thurman, "Negro Artists and the Negro," column, *The New Republic*, August 31, 1927, p. 39.

meaning subconsciously, 'I would like to be a white poet'; meaning behind that, 'I would like to be white.'[65]

While Hughes's logic is not necessarily convincing, it is a very effective and damning assertion against what everyone in the Harlem Renaissance knew was the Cullen credo. There is a particularly interesting defense that Hughes gives of his position as a racially conscious poet:

> Most of my own poems are racial in theme and treatment from the life I know. In many of them I try to grasp and hold some of the meaning and rhythms of jazz. I am [as] sincere as I know how to be in these poems and yet after every reading I answer question like these from my own people: Do you think Negroes should always write about Negroes? I wish you wouldn't read some of your poems to white folks. How do you find anything interesting in a place like a cabaret? Why do you write about black people? You aren't black. What makes you do so many jazz poems?
>
> But jazz to me is one of the inherent expressions of Negro life in America: the eternal tom-tom beating in the Negro soul—the tom-tom of revolt against weariness in a white world, a world of subway trains, and work, work, work; the tom-tom of joy and laughter, and pain swallowed in a smile. Yet the Philadelphia clubwoman is ashamed to say that her race created it and she does not like me to write about it. The old subconscious "white is best" runs through her mind.[66]

---

[65]Hughes, "The Negro Artist and the Racial Mountain," *The Nation*, June 23, 1926, p. 692.

[66]Hughes, "The Negro Artist and the Racial Mountain," *The Nation*, p. 694.

But this passage on jazz, poetry, and bourgeois criticism makes a vital if troubling connection—troubling because it is stereotypical and has become a virtual cliché—between jazz and the natural world, the world of the African American which stands opposed to the white American world of endless work and dehumanizing machines. This assertion, which says in effect that the black, at least the poor, uncorrupted black (of whom Hughes was inordinately fond), is naturally antibourgeois, even antimodernist, in his or her values, only makes sense when we consider that in February 1926, when Cullen reviewed Hughes's first collection of poetry, *The Weary Blues*, he criticized him on the very ground of attempting to make a natural-supernatural totemic utterance of jazz:

> Never having been one to think all subjects and forms proper for poetic consideration, I regard these jazz poems as interlopers in the company of the truly beautiful poems in other sections of the book. They move along with the frenzy and electric heat of a Methodist or Baptist revival meeting, and affect me in much the same manner. The revival meeting excites me, cooling and flushing me with alternate chills and fevers of emotion; so do these poems. But when the storm is over, I wonder if the quiet way of communing is not more spiritual for the God-seeking heart; and in the light of reflection I wonder if jazz poems really belong to that dignified company, that select and austere circle of high literary expression which we call poetry.[67]

---

[67]Cullen, "Poet on Poet," *Opportunity*, February 1926, p. 73. Despite what might be considered a conservative or at least reserved attitude about jazz and despite his reluctance in wishing to be identified as a black poet, Cullen could be vehemently prideful in a racial way, especially when the miscegenation taboo was mentioned. As Gunnar Myrdal pointed out in his seminal *An American Dilemma* (New York: Harper and Row, 1944), blacks and whites tended to see the issue of assimilation in diametrically opposite ways: whites fearing intermarriage the most and thinking that blacks most desired sexual unions with them while

The problem Cullen had with jazz poetry is that he believed jazz to be an insufficiently developed, insufficiently permanent art form to use as an aesthetic for poetry. Because he connects the effects of jazz with the effects of Holiness religious services, the piece becomes a bourgeois attack against lower-class aesthetic preoccupations which have emotion but little else. For Cullen, this means, in effect, that race identification and race consciousness become nothing more than an exhibitionistic display of emotion that makes the person so expressing him- or herself more natural and freer than a white who is unable to do so. It is not that Cullen did not believe this rather dubious idea; actually at times he expressed a great affinity for it. It was unavoidable that he should because race consciousness in this culture, for the black, has become a firm belief in his or her superior naturalness. But Cullen did not think it proper to construct poetry entirely on this idea. The question for Cullen is not one of morals or even finally of taste. It is a matter

---

blacks most wanted economic and political parity and least desiring intermarriage (pp. 60–61). It is immediately obvious in Cullen's poetry that he, like other black male Harlem Renaissance writers, overly praised the pulchritude of black women. (This indicates, among other things, that there was a rudimentary black aesthetic and a strong sense of a politicized and propagandistic black literary art long before the 1960s and that this aesthetic necessity was, as in the 1960s, a largely gender-based and gender-oriented response to the complexities of interracial sex.) In a poem such as "Song of Praise," Cullen was a downright racial nationalist and chauvinist, extolling the sexual superiority of the black woman over the white woman. All of this is helpful in understanding a fundamental contradictory intellectual and artistic impulse in Cullen that was and is far from being unique to Cullen. In a letter to the editor that appeared in the *New York University Daily News* in 1926, Cullen responded to a white male southern reader who disliked the intermarriage theme of Eugene O'Neill's *All God's Chillun Got Wings:* "The vast majority of Negroes, and I am happy to count myself among that number, could never entertain the idea of marriage outside our race. We hang together, of different shades though we are (and perhaps Mr. Loeb can account for that, being a Southerner), proud to belong to a race which in sixty short years of emancipation has made progress unparalleled in world history. . . .

"For me to be the social equal of Mr. Loeb does not mean that I should care to eat dinner at his table; I am too fond of home cooking for that. Nor does it mean that I would want to marry any of his relatives or friends; there are too many beautiful girls of my own race for that, if only the white boys would cease worrying them with their attentions."

of substituting one thing for another; in this case, a temporary, perishable pose for something which is supposed to represent some other, higher, more sublime, more demanding, more difficult experience. Cullen believed that jazz was not poetry and ought not to be substituted for it.

Cullen further solidified his position as a leading light of the Harlem Renaissance socially by marrying the daughter of W. E. B. Du Bois, Nina Yolande, on April 9, 1928, in his foster father's church. "The wedding of the leading lyric poet of the Negro Renaissance to Yolande Du Bois, the daughter and only child of the leading old-guard Negro writer, Dr. W. E. B. Du Bois,"[68] was the biggest social event in the history of the Renaissance. Du Bois himself saw a great deal of significance in the wedding: "The symbolism of that procession was tremendous. It was not the mere marriage of a maiden. It was not simply the wedding of a fine young poet. It was the symbolic march of young and black America—America, because there was Harvard, Columbia, Smith, Brown, Howard, Chicago, Syracuse, Penn, and Cornell. There were three masters of arts and fourteen bachelors. There were poets and teachers, actors, artists, and students. . . . it was a new race, a new thought, a new thing rejoicing in a ceremony as old as the world."[69]

The entire world of the Talented Tenth was there; it was a showcase, according to Du Bois, of the New Negro. The wedding was huge, with virtually everyone connected with the Renaissance playing a role—Langston Hughes as an usher, James Weldon Johnson as a special guest. The huge church was packed to capacity. Few marriages have begun with such fanfare and ended so disastrously. The couple divorced in 1930, although the actual time they spent together only amounted to several months.[70] Why in the world did

[68]Hughes, *The Big Sea* (New York: Hill and Wang, 1975), p. 274.

[69]W. E. B. Du Bois, "So the Girl Marries," *The Crisis*, June 1928, pp. 208–9.

[70]From the letters that Du Bois sent to Cullen during September and October 1928, it seems

Cullen marry a woman with whom he must have known he would be incompatible? He may have been fond of Yolande, but she was not terribly intellectual or in any way much in synch with his temperament. Moreover, he was clearly the most eligible bachelor of the Renaissance and could have had his pick of nearly any middle-class or upper-middle-class black woman. I speculate that he married Yolande because she was Du Bois's daughter, and this gave him a particular pedigree and status, not only socially but in polite circles of black literary culture which he wanted. It was ultimately a merger of a young conservative poet laureate and an old conservative literary giant, for despite some of his radical political views, Du Bois was by temperament a conservative, even a Victorian. At a time when Cullen was revising his biography and altering his origins, it seemed that the Du Bois connection would be very appealing to him.

But the New Negro Movement did not end with the stock market crash and the Depression. Certainly, black writers did not stop writing or find it impossible to find publishers. In fact, more books by black writers were published in the thirties than in the twenties. James Weldon Johnson, Langston Hughes, J. A. Rogers, William Attaway, W. E. B. Du Bois, Zora Neale Hurston, Arna Bontemps, Claude McKay, Richard Wright, Wallace Thurman, George Schuyler, and even Countee Cullen himself all produced major work in the 1930s. But the writers themselves were less interested in the New Negro or felt the idea to be less central to the development of black literature. Yet it was, ironically, with the emergence of a

---

as though the father-in-law certainly did not blame the groom for the failure. Du Bois thought his daughter was spoiled and shy about sex. Du Bois advises: "Do not interpret your wife's love in terms of sexual response. Wait until she learns and re-adjusts body and soul." Du Bois goes on in a fatherly way: "Forgive the plain talk but it's built on the experience of 30 married years. I shall never forget my own consternation when my wife refused what I thought it was my right to demand. . . . Since that first refusal over a quarter a century ago I made it a rule never to have sexual intercourse except with a willing wife." Letter from Du Bois to Cullen, October 11, 1928.

new black heavyweight champion, Joe Louis,[71] in 1937 that the New Negro concept achieved its fulfillment. In 1938, when Louis fought and defeated the German Max Schmeling in the most publicized fight in history, dwarfing the Johnson-Jeffries match, we see the supercession of Jack Johnson; for when Johnson fought a white, all whites wanted to see Johnson defeated, but Louis fought Schmeling as the favorite among the whites as well as the blacks. Louis was the American hero, the symbolic integration of the black folk hero with the American popular hero. Nor did Louis have to give up or compromise the one aspect of his craft that made him a hero to blacks: the fact that he could pulverize white men with impunity. Naturally, because of his profession, Louis was a black hero with nationalistic dimensions for blacks; this was especially true when he fought Primo Carnera in 1935, shortly after Italy threatened to invade Ethiopia. After the 1938 Schmeling fight, Marcus Garvey wrote an editorial in his publication *The Black Man*, which talks about Louis's "responsibility to his race." "Giant-like, he rose in the American stadium on the 22nd [of] June and delivered the punches to Schmeling that are typical of our race in true action," wrote Garvey.[72]

After the Johnson-Jeffries fight, the interstate transporting of fight films was banned for fear that showing films of a black beating a

---

[71]For more on Joe Louis, see Wilson J. Moses, *Black Messiahs and Uncle Toms: Social and Literary Manipulations of a Religious Myth* (University Park: The Pennsylvania State University Press, 1982), pp. 155–82; Bert Randolph Sugar, *The 100 Greatest Boxers of All Time*, pp. 24–27; John D. McCallum, *The World Heavyweight Boxing Championship, A History*, pp. 198–217; Lawrence Levine, *Black Culture and Black Consciousness: Afro-American Folk Thought from Slavery to Freedom*, pp. 433–38; Chris Mead, *Champion: Joe Louis, Black Hero in White America* (New York: Scribner, 1985).

[72]Marcus Garvey, "Joe Louis," editorial in *The Black Man: A Monthly Magazine of Negro Thought and Opinion*, Vol. 3, July 1938. Further proof of the extent and intensity of Joe Louis's nationalistic heroism among blacks can be found in accounts of Louis's popularity given in *The Autobiography of Malcolm X* (New York: Ballantine Books, 1989), pp. 23–24 and passim, and Maya Angelou's *I Know Why the Caged Bird Sings* (New York: Bantam Books, 1973), pp. 111–15.

white would cause race riots; this ban was not lifted until Louis became champion. The emergence of Louis effectively ended the New Negro Movement. Neither race consciousness nor black nationalism were really quite the ends or quite served the needs of blacks. Blacks achieved a satisfaction with discharging a certain tense preoccupation they had with having a reshaped or more positive involvement with the national mythology and having a more compelling and powerful image in American popular culture, which is what the New Negro Movement was really all about.

III. CHRISTIAN HERITAGE

I want to hear the chanting
Around a heathen fire
Of a strange black race.

—*Gwendolyn Bennett, "Heritage"*

Poetry is a potent and dangerous vehicle just because it is always
and inevitably religious in its ultimate nature.
—*Amos N. Wilder,* The Christian Tradition: A Study in the
Relation of Christianity to Culture

It is unjust to Christianity to call our civilization Christian; it is
unjust to our civilization to call it unchristian. It is semi-Christian.
—*Walter Rauschenbush,* Christianizing the Social Order

"I find you this time writing a book which almost any one might have written. Temporarily, something has happened to you. You have fallen into other people's language, you have lapsed from your own swift simplicities. . . . Kick out hard, whatever influence is impeding. Don't let yourself be crucified on a Guggenheim cross, . . ." wrote Witter Bynner, one of Cullen's biggest boosters just a few years earlier, in a letter dated November 22, 1929. He was responding to Cullen's new collection *The Black Christ and Other Poems.* This was the way the thirties were to greet Cullen, with the unwavering and brutal intention of waking him from a dream. The new decade started with a bang and a whimper. With the publication of *The Black Christ and Other Poems* in 1929, a phase of Countee Cullen's literary career was over. In the thirties Cullen was to experience life differently; he was no longer the black literary wonder boy. He divorced Yolande in 1930, surely a kind of disillusioning and uncomfortable experience, even if not bitter or acrimonious. His novel, *One Way to Heaven*, was not to be reviewed in *The Crisis* and was treated with about fifteen other books by and about blacks in Alain Locke's round-up review in *Opportunity*, January 1933. These leading black magazines had previously been lavish in the attention and care they paid to Cullen's works. By the end of the decade, while working with Arna Bontemps on *St. Louis Woman*, he was to be attacked by the black literary establishment that had once so staunchly supported him on the very tenets of his own critical creed: producing a literary work that was degrading to blacks. In the thirties and through to the end of his life in 1946, he was to write much less.

Many have speculated on Cullen's reduced output. Part of it may have been writer's block, lack of inspiration, or sheer laziness, but a part of it must have been that after 1929, when Cullen's Guggenheim Fellowship ended, he no longer quite had the time to write that he had before. This was especially true after publication of *One Way to Heaven* in 1932. Shortly after that he was to become a certified public school teacher, a job he was to keep until his death. In the 1920s, Cullen had been a student and, although he worked hard, a rather indulged one. He had time, even as a hardworking student, to write, especially when one considers the fact that several of the poems he produced in the 1920s were written for classes in lieu of paper assignments. If today professors at major research institutions who spend only six hours a week in the classroom feel justified in complaining about the amount of time class preparation and grading take away from their scholarly pursuits, how much more so was Cullen, who had to teach for six hours a day.

By the age of twenty-six, virtually all of his major poems, all the poems for which he was to be known to posterity, were published. In the 1930s, Cullen explored avenues other than *tour de force* lyric poetry: namely, the novel, translation, drama, song lyrics for musical comedy, and children's literature in both poetry and prose. It was not that Countee Cullen was no longer interested in writing or could not write, it seems more likely that he was no longer interested or could not write lyric poetry of the sort that made him famous, so he cast about for some other form. This is not unusual as lyric poets often do their greatest work when quite young. Drama seems to have held a particular fascination for him; not only did he translate *The Medea,* but he also wrote at least two dramatic adaptations of his novel and worked with Arna Bontemps on a musical adaption of Bontemps's novel *God Sends Sunday,* the aforementioned *St. Louis Woman.* He also coauthored with Owen Dodson a choreo-musical called *The Third Fourth of July,* his only published play. He seemed to have found his niche in children's literature and had he lived may have gone on to write considerably more in this genre. At the time of his death he had already completed a manuscript called "The Monkey Baboon" and a prose version of his earlier "The Lost Zoo," called "The Little Lost Zoo."[73]

There are two related things that must be understood about Cullen's major poetry: first, most of it is racial and, second, all of it is Christian or could only have been produced by a Christian consciousness. This is his dilemma, which, of course, became his pose: to wit, as he wrote, his "chief problem has been that of

---

[73]Cullen received letters dated February 18, 1943, and March 6, 1943, from Eugene F. Saxton of Harper and Brothers, the first stating that because of material shortages, undoubtedly caused by the Second World War, the company was not likely to publish either "The Monkey Baboon" or a prose version of "The Lost Zoo;" the second, however, is an acceptance of the prose version of "The Lost Zoo." However, Saxton died on June 26, 1943 and his death may have affected publication, for no prose version of "The Lost Zoo" was ever published.

reconciling a Christian upbringing with a pagan inclination."[74] In poems such as "Heritage," "The Black Christ," "The Shroud of Color," "The Litany of the Dark People," and "Pagan Prayer," this is manifested by understanding that the poetry is the product of a black Christian who cannot reconcile two things. First, he cannot reconcile his blackness, which he refers to as his paganism, and his Christianity. However, this fact has little to do exclusively with a race consciousness and a great deal to do with an overbearing and overburdened Christian one. What Cullen finds attractive as a writer is the basic ambiguity that exists in the meaning of his being a black Christian. That ambiguity is there, to borrow an idea from Clifford Geertz,[75] because being a black Christian has both religious and political significance, a kind of uneasy meshing of the sacred and secular. To be a black Christian is to be caught always between ideology and theology, to be unsure whether one's major concern is eschatology or a power struggle.

That disjuncture is for Cullen something that he must, in truth, have had no real interest in wanting to reconcile as it was the resulting fictive tension, the resulting dramatic functionalism, that enabled Cullen to write so well. The threat on every page that his personality would simply break apart, would absolutely defy integration was a rich, though not necessarily singular, vein for a black writer to work. But this is only one disjuncture; the other theme that preoccupies Cullen is the inherent rationalization with theodicy that every black Christian must make. The Jew, as another long-suffering former slave, knew better than to devise a religion that would tell him that the only way he can transcend his tragedy is to remain a tragic figure. But Cullen, as an intellectual black, easily saw that black Christianity must ultimately accept that the Negro's humanity must forever be his tragic suffering: this is precisely what his greatest religious poems—"The Litany of the Dark People,"

[74]Cullen, *Caroling Dusk*, p. 179.

[75]Clifford Geertz, *The Interpretation of Cultures* (New York: Basic Books, 1973), pp. 165ff.

"The Shroud of Color," "The Black Christ"—say. He is constantly condemned to be entrapped by the myth of his victimization, and whether he rages against it or submits to it, he ultimately confesses that he is helpless before it. This is precisely what the poems "Pagan Prayer" and "Mood" question.

It is a curious observation that in "Heritage," considered by everyone to be Cullen's finest poem, his masterpiece, he uses the phrase "So I lie . . ." five times. It seems there is a great deal of lying going on in the poem, not only lying as in the sense of reposing, à la some of the narrators of Poe and Browning, but also lying in the sense of dishonesty and duplicity. Cullen was very taken with the art of lying or why else did he have his cat tell tall tales in *The Lost Zoo* and in *My Lives and How I Lost Them*, or why else did he translate *The Medea*, which is all about the lying of two lovers, or why write a novel where the central character lies about his conversion? The entire scope of Cullen's 1930s career seems a long philosophical and aesthetic examination of the many creative and nefarious dimensions of lying, deception, and hypocrisy. Also the interest in lying as art explains the character Sam Lucas in *One Way to Heaven*. Many critics have felt that Cullen named the character Lucas because his own real name may have been Lucas. What makes a great deal more sense is that the con man character of Cullen's novel is named after the great black stage minstrel of the same name who was very popular in the early 1900s. As the novel turns on Lucas's ability to act, to play out a conversion that he does not feel convincingly, both in the beginning of the novel and at the novel's end, we see instantly that the book centers on the art of lying, and what black person was a better professional liar than a minstrel with his degrading, low, stereotypical comedy? In fact, the connection between the novel's character and the minstrel is made even more explicit by the symbols of the playing cards and razor, which Sam tosses away at every conversion. These are of course the props of the stereotypical black minstrel.

Some readers have criticized "Heritage" for not offering more realistic images of Africa, decrying Cullen's ignorance but that is one of the levels on which the poem, the narrator is lying. These images of Africa are lies; certainly Cullen knew that. But is the poem also lying when it suggests that Africa means nothing to the narrator? Or is the poem lying when it suggests that Africa means anything to the narrator? Or is this very interiorized speech-act, speech-event poem nothing more than the system of lies that the impotent black intellectual uses to heal his own sickness of alienation and despair? The poem deals with the black narrator's own trinity: body ("the dark blood dammed within" and the word "dammed" of course is a pun), mind ("Africa? A book one thumbs / listlessly, till slumber comes"), and heart/spirit ("Lord, forgive me if my need / Sometimes shapes a human creed"), which has been thoroughly "civilized" or acculturated, trapped in language and reflection, a room of nothing but sound. But that whole business might be lies as well. The poem does not solve anything as the speaker can neither experience true conversion—the only act that can save him—nor deny it.

In typical romantic terms, Cullen is not simply concerned with the perfectability of the black Christian but the perfectability of the black Christian's God. "The Black Christ" is the only Cullen poem that is centrally concerned with conversion. In fact, the poem is about precisely the absolute politicization of conversion, for in the poem Cullen wishes to reverse the tradition of liberal Christian redemption. Evil is removed from the providential history of the self and deposited into the providential history of mankind. What the atheistic narrator of the poem demands is recognition from God that blacks do indeed exist in His sight. The recognition comes in the form of a miracle— the resurrection of his lynched brother, Jim. And it is this resurrection that makes Jim the Black Christ, not simply the fact that he is lynched. Indeed, in reworking the entire Christ idea, we find Cullen has totally politicized the crucifixion or made the political significance of Christ for a black believer completely *explicit.* Jim, a militant handsome black boy, kills a white man who insults him and his white girlfriend while they are enjoying the coming of spring. The white man is accused of threatening to harm spring:

His vile and puny fingers churned
Our world about that sang and burned
A while as never world before.
He had unlatched an icy door,
And let the winter in once more.
To kill a man is a woeful thing,
But he who lays a hand on spring
Clutches the first bird by its throat
And throttles it in the midst of a note;
Whose breath upon the leaf-proud tree
Turns all that wealth to penury. . . .

Here, as has been pointed out, Cullen combines his standard romantic/poetic conceit (spring and nature) with the American politics of race and sex. Note how Jim the rebel kills the white man not for any violent acts on his part, but merely for his speech:

I had gone on unheeding but
He struck me down, he called her slut,
And black man's mistress, bawdy whore,
And such like names, and many more,
. . . My right
I knew could not outweigh his might
Who had the law for satellite—
Only I turned to look at her,
The early spring's first worshipper,
(Spring, what have you to answer for?)
The blood had fled from either cheek
And from her lips; she could not speak,
But she could only stand and stare
And let her pain stab through the air.
I think a blow to heart or head
Had hurt her less than what he said.
A blow can be so quick and kind,
But words will feast upon the mind

And gnaw the heart down to a shred,
And leave you living, yet leave you dead.

This is an absolute reversal of Christ, for it was Christ himself
who died for his speech, his blasphemous claims of being the
Messiah and being able to forgive sins. Here it is not the Christ
figure who dies for his speech but rather who kills because he has
been victimized by the speech of his oppressor, defined, trapped,
degraded, and belittled by it. Since Jim represents the spirit of the
New Negro, the little drama played out is surprisingly like the life
of the archetypal New Negro, Jack Johnson, insulted and taunted
by white men because of his white wives and girlfriends (and they
themselves insulted as well, as we know that Johnson's first wife
committed suicide because she found being a black man's wife a
hard lot) and who takes revenge by calmly beating white men in
the ring, the white opponents who have come to restore the order
of things, the proper political balance (the equivalent of the poetic
threat "to murder spring"). Thus "The Black Christ" is not simply
a case of making a sacrificial black lamb into a Christ figure but
rather of reinventing the entire myth of disobedience to authority,
which is the cornerstone of Christian theology, so that it is *that*
disobedience which is understood as the expression, the assertion
of political and moral right. That disobedience to the white man's
authority which is so central to the poem goes counter to the prevailing social myth of blacks and Christianity—namely, that the
religion made them passive and, indeed, obedient. Certainly that
element is represented in the poem by Jim and the narrator's
mother, but it is not ultimately what the poem is suggesting that
being a black Christian means, although in poems like "Litany of
the Dark People," "Shroud of Color," and "Judas Iscariot," where
Judas's burden is clearly akin to the accursedness of color, Cullen
seems attracted to Christianity as the mystification of black suffering and trial, a reworking of the Uncle Tom, blacks-as-natural-
Christian idea. In a poem like "The Black Christ," Cullen is

obviously looking for the liberationist and nationalistic impulses inherent in this cultural stereotype.

I have said earlier that all of Cullen's poems are Christian, and this statement might puzzle some readers, who think of the many love poems, frankly sensual poems, and *carpe diem* poems that Cullen wrote as indicative that Cullen was just as attracted to something pagan as to something Christian. But paganism as an attraction (and all of those "pagan" poems finally assert that paganism is just that, an attraction) is not possible in a pagan mind but only in a Christian mind that has been taught to see paganism as an attractive alternative to the rigors of Christianity. Kierkegaard expresses this compellingly and convincingly in his *Either/Or:*

> To assert that Christianity has brought sensuousness into the world may seem boldly daring. But as we say that a bold venture is half the battle, so also here; and my proposition may be better understood if we consider that in positing one thing, we also indirectly posit the other which we exclude. Since the sensuous generally is that which should be negatived, it is clearly evident that it is posited first through the act which excludes it, in that it posits the opposite positive principle. As principle, as power, as a self-contained system, sensuousness is first posited in Christianity; and in that sense it is true that Christianity brought sensuousness into the world. Rightly to understand this proposition, that Christianity has brought sensuousness into the world, one must apprehend it as identical with the contrary proposition, that it is Christianity which has driven sensuousness out, has excluded it from the world. As principle, as power, as a self-contained system, sensuousness was first posited by Christianity. . . . This is quite natural for Christianity is spirit, and spirit is the positive principle which Christianity has brought into

the world. But when sensuousness is understood in its relationship to spirit [i.e., as its contrary], it is clearly known as a thing that must be excluded, it is determined as a principle, as a power; for that which spirit—itself a principle—would exclude must be something which is also a principle, although it first reveals itself as a principle in the moment of its exclusion.[76]

So Christianity has, in effect, created its own antithesis which makes possible both sin and guilt (both of which are located in Christianity but generated by the realization or actualization of paganism), but which is, in truth, a reflection of a unitary mind. This unitary mind in terms of understanding the Christian's thinking about paganism is quite true of Cullen. But Cullen has particularized the case of the black Christian in another way. In effect, from the point of view of theodicy, God did not invent evil but rather made available the consciousness that realized, through its own demented necessity, the existence of evil as an attraction. Cullen's own version of racial theodicy is this: Why did God make a racist world—which for Cullen, as for James Baldwin, was the absolute degeneracy and debasement of paganism and sensualism, the absolute repression of it as "The Black Christ" clearly show—for blacks to suffer in? The answer must exceed the simplistic: so that they might suffer exquisitely according to His will. That might be, to some degree, the belief of his father, but it was not Cullen's. Once again like Baldwin, Cullen was not a Calvinist and the central quarrel he has with Christianity is why there is an elect or a consciousness—racism—which demands that there must be an elect. So, on one level, Cullen surely has the pagan/Christian split-in-unity of which Kierkegaard speaks, but what has been posited as

---

[76]Søren Kierkegaard, "The Immediate Stages of the Erotic or the Musical Erotic" in *Either/Or*, Vol. 1, translated by David F. Swenson and Lillian Marvin Swenson (Princeton: Princeton University Press, 1959), pp. 59–60.

a principle and a power in opposition to Christianity, while having reached its highest expression of perfection through Christianity, for Cullen, is the idea of the elect. Therefore, Cullen must be understood as a Christian poet.

IV. THE ONE REMAINS, THE MANY CHANGE AND PASS

> *Though faint with weariness he must possess*
> *Some fragment of the sunset's majesty . . .*
> —*Amy Lowell, "The Poet"*

> *The descent beckons*
>   *as the ascent beckoned.*
>   —*William Carlos Williams, "The Descent"*

"He taught me French" was apparently all James Baldwin had to say of Countee Cullen when he was being interviewed by Fern Marja Eckman for her biography of the younger star writer of the civil rights era.[77] Yet, as she points out, Cullen was the faculty supervisor of the Douglass Junior High literary club and Baldwin was a prominent member of that club. Cullen must have told the young Baldwin and the other black boys stories of his beloved France, stories that perhaps inspired Baldwin to go abroad which Baldwin did after graduating from high school, winning a Eugene F. Saxton Fellowship. In retrospect, perhaps for Baldwin a certain familiarity bred a certain contempt. Both were adopted sons of fundamentalist ministers, both attended the DeWitt Clinton High School and became editors of the school's literary magazine, *The Magpie,* and both went on to become noted writers. In high school, Baldwin interviewed Cullen for *The Magpie* at the time of the publication of Cullen's *The Lost Zoo*. It is a delightful interview and is

[77]Fern Marja Eckman, *The Furious Passage of James Baldwin* (New York: M. Evans and Co., 1966), pp. 49–50.

included in the appendix of this volume. It is one of the paradoxes of life that two men who seemed such kindred spirits may not have gotten on well. But Cullen was a good and conscientious teacher.[78]

After he returned from nearly a two-year stay in France during 1928 and 1929, Cullen finished his novel, *One Way to Heaven,* by October 1931 and apparently had been receiving offers of professorships from black colleges and universities at that time and throughout the early thirties. Cullen received his teacher's certificate from the New York Board of Education in December 1931, which certified him to teach French in junior high. He started teaching in the New York schools as a substitute teacher in 1932. Yet he was making inquiries about teaching jobs at both Atlanta University and Lincoln University, and the Atlantic City Public Schools, and at Straight College in New Orleans in 1934. He also received job offers in 1934 from Dillard University, Sam Huston College in Austin, Texas,[79] and West Virginia State College. Cullen, however, who really wanted to stay in New York, received his official appointment to the New York public schools on December 3, 1934, and his interest in other jobs diminished.

In 1935 *The Medea and Some Poems* was published, making Cullen the first black American writer to do a major Greek drama translation in prose. He wrote the choruses as lyric poems which, through a commission from actor John Houseman, were set to music by Virgil Thomson[80] in 1935 for women's choir and percussion. A women's chorus premiered the work on December 16, 1942, in New York City. A 1967 version for mixed chorus by

---

[78]There are a number of letters from former students in the Countee Cullen Papers which amply support the assertion.

[79]Pianist Teddy Wilson's father was dean of men at Sam Huston College back in the early part of the twentieth century. (The spelling "Huston" is correct.)

[80]After receiving a copy of *The Lost Zoo*, Virgil Thomson suggested to Cullen that "it has musical possibilities, too." He made a date to talk to Cullen about the possibility of adapting *The Lost Zoo* but apparently nothing came of it. Letter from Virgil Thomson to Countee Cullen, February 5, 1941.

Daniel Pinkham was premiered on June 13, 1967, at Cambridge, Massachusetts. In thinking about the shape of Cullen's career, the romantic and traditionalist models he had, it is easy to see why he would translate *The Medea:* It simply authenticated his own traditionalist and classical credentials. Paradoxically, he was attracted for much the same reason he was attracted to "The Ballad of the Brown Girl"; once again, his creative racial misreading made him think of *The Medea* in racial terms, a woman of color betrayed.

He married for a second time in 1940. The union with the sister of a good friend, Ida Roberson, proved to be much more successful than his first, more celebrated marriage. He wrote two children's books about "Christopher Cat," his own house pet, entitled *The Lost Zoo* (1940) and *My Lives and How I Lost Them* (1942), the first in verse, the second in prose, and while many thought the writing of children's books showed that Cullen was losing his powers, Langston Hughes, who wrote a number of children's books himself, thought Cullen seemed reengaged in the forties and said the children's books showed that Cullen had revived his poetic interests and abilities.[81] Cullen seemed fully motivated for his readings and apparently was delivering his most racial poems with real bite, if this excerpt from a letter to his wife in 1944 is any indication:

> Everybody was gracious and complimentary. There were far more white than colored present. Many of the students from the surrounding white universities were on hand, and although I read some very bitter things, they took it very well.[82]

---

[81]In a letter to Arna Bontemps, after complimenting Cullen's wife as the source for Cullen's renewed energy, Hughes writes, "As a result Countee is writing as of old. Another book about a cat (this one in prose) is due in the spring, and he is actively planning his next." Letter from Hughes to Bontemps, November 5, 1941, in Charles H. Nichols, *Arna Bontemps–Langston Hughes Letters, 1925–1967,* p. 95.

[82]Letter from Countee Cullen to Ida Roberson Cullen, July 17, 1944.

Cullen began to compile the poems that were to make up *On These I Stand* in 1945 as his health was deteriorating. He had been battling with the "St. Louis Woman," receiving letters such as this from Walter White:

> Let me say quite frankly that my impression after hearing the play is stronger than it was when I read it myself. I wholly disagree with the argument that because plays like PORGY AND BESS and ANNA LUCASTA have appeared on the stage a play like SAINT LOUIS WOMAN written by two Negroes is justified. ANNA LUCASTA at least has some decent characters; SAINT LOUIS WOMAN has virtually none.[83]

Or this from actress/journalist Fredi Washington, who attacked "St. Louis Woman" in her column in the *People's Voice,* an attack which angered and disturbed Cullen very much:

> It grieves me deeply that you refused to talk with me on the phone this morning for I had just previously spoken at length to Owen Dodson concerning *St. Louis Woman.* He told me that he had just finished reading the revised script and is of the opinion that, if directed with sympathy, the story will come through with a great deal of charm and sympathetic understanding.
>
> This was indeed welcome news to me for that is exactly what I hoped would happen. And, it was for this reason that I called to ask if I might be allowed to see the latest version of the script. It was and still is my intention, if allowed, to do another column in which I will relate the revisions which have been made.[84]

---

[83]Letter from Walter White to Countee Cullen, February 19, 1945.

[84]Letter from Fredi Washington to Countee Cullen, August 21, 1945.

INTRODUCTION

Despite the fact that Cullen was distressed to the point of rage over these attacks, there is no indication that he considered abandoning his writing. Moreover, there is no particular reason to think that he felt his career was over because he was engaged in making a comprehensive statement about his career by putting together a representative volume of his work. Poets periodically put out Selected Poems volumes as a way of reassessing, recontextualizing, and revising their work. Also, it was a way for him to clear the decks if he was about to enter a new phase of his work. Song lyric writing, drama, and children's literature interested him, and there is no reason to think that, at least, in the immediate future, he did not intend to continue writing in those genres. Moreover, despite the fact that Cullen's health was bad, he certainly did not think he was going to die soon. He was, during his last months, more concerned about his father's health than his own. He died of high blood pressure and uremic poisoning on January 9, 1946, at the age of forty-two.

Do we really know, after all this, who Countee Cullen really was? What made him what he was? And are we now quite ready to accept that he was the finest black American lyric poet, one of the finest lyric poets in America? Or does everything shift uneasily as we come to the awareness that he did indeed write some bad poems? As if every great poet does not mostly write mediocre poems except for the six, eight, or ten by which he or she is known? So we still cannot locate Countee Cullen. "What happened to Countee?"[85] Langston Hughes exclaimed in a letter to Arna Bontemps when he heard that Cullen had died. What has happened and how have we ever understood the Harlem Renaissance or twentieth-century African-American literature without his works being placed in the center of the heap?

Is it that inability to locate or fix Cullen's origins that has made

---

[85]Letter from Langston Hughes to Arna Bontemps, January 14, 1946, in Charles H. Nichols, ed., *Arna Bontemps–Langston Hughes Letters, 1925–1967*, p. 203.

locating and fixing his identity such a contradictory task? In Ishmael Reed's 1971 satiric novel about the Harlem Renaissance,
Mumbo Jumbo (largely based on James Weldon Johnson's preface
to *The Book of American Negro Poetry*, Johnson's autobiography
Along This Way, his articles on the U.S. invasion of Haiti, and his
Black Manhattan), we have Countee Cullen presented, more sym-
pathetically and in more detail than with any other Harlem Renaissance writer, as Nathan Brown. The novel's hero PaPa LaBas
ruminates on Brown in this vein: "the young poet Nathan Brown
. . . was serious about his Black Christ, however absurd that may
sound. . . . Yes, Brown was serious, but the rest were hucksters
who had invented this Black Christ, this fraud, simply in order to
avoid an honest day's sweat."[86]

Later in the book, Brown is harshly criticized at a party by
Hinckle Von Vampton[87] as being "so arid and stuffy with his material that [his] Phi Beta Kappa key must have gone to his head."
But Brown is defended during the conversation by another black
writer as being "a very accomplished poet."[88] In another scene,
Von Hinckle, a member of a secret white society that wants to
disarm and disrupt the growth of black art symbolized by a virus
called "jes' grew,"[89] approaches Brown, "slight-of-build, wiry, sin-

[86]Ishmael Reed, *Mumbo Jumbo* (New York: Avon Books, 1972), p. 111.

[87]Hinckle Von Vampton is a satiric portrait of Carl Van Vechten, one of the major white
promoters of the Harlem Renaissance, whose 1926 novel, *Nigger Heaven*, caused quite a
stir among black intellectuals and writers. Van Vechten's articles on black music and black
theater, which appeared in *Vanity Fair* in 1925, exposed artistic happenings among high-
brow whites. Indeed, Van Vechten was responsible for getting *Vanity Fair* to take some of
Cullen's poems for their June 1925 issue. In Van Vechten's introduction to Cullen's poetry,
he noted that "all his poetry is characterized by a suave, unpretentious, brittle, intellectual
elegance. . . ." See Bruce Kellner, ed., *"Keep A-Inchin' Along: Selected Writings of Carl
Van Vechten About Black Art and Letters* (Westport, Conn.: Greenwood Press, 1979), p.
140.

[88]Reed, *Mumbo Jumbo*, p. 116.

[89]In the preface to James Weldon Johnson's *The Book of American Negro Poetry*, he called
old ragtime by unschooled black musicians "jes' grew" songs, p. 12. One wonders about

ewy and melancholy,"[90] who [resembles] "the drawings of Charles Cullen"[91], as he is leaving the "Salem African Methodist Episcopal [church], where he comes to meditate about the Black Christ," and offers him a position on his magazine the *Benign Monster* because his poetry is "solidly in the Western tradition and convinces me that you are the foremost bard of your race." In turning down the offer, Brown mutters the song title "All Coons Look Alike To Me" and then clarifies his meaning by saying, "I think that when people like you, Mr. Von Vampton, say 'the Negro Experience,' you are saying that all Negroes experience the world the same way. In that way you can isolate the misfits who could propel them into penetrating the ceiling of this bind you and your assistants have established in this country. . . ."[92] Brown here is ultimately for the freedom of multiplicity over the oppressive falsity of the unitary. That is, as I have argued, what Cullen stood for, and it is indeed what Reed himself strenuously argues for throughout his novel.

But if Cullen is seen as an admirable figure, indeed, the Harlem Renaissance's most representative figure and most important purveyor of the creative African-American impulse in a recent black satirical novel, he was not seen to such an advantage in a novel by one of his own contemporaries, Wallace Thurman's *Infants of the Spring* (1932), a much more cutting thrust against the black writers

---

the whole Uncle Tom connection: one of Count Basie's big hits of the 1930s was called "Topsy."

[90]Reed makes Cullen an almost literal black John Keats.

[91]Charles Cullen was Countee Cullen's illustrator for several of his books and is known for his sensual yet tasteful nude drawings of beautiful men and women. The two men were not related.

[92]Reed, pp. 132–34. Incidentally, "All Coons Look Alike to Me" was written by Ernest Hogan, a black minstrel, who died on May 20, 1909. *The Colored American Magazine* (May 1909, p. 308) wrote: "In the death of Ernest Hogan, the stage loses one of its foremost and veteran characters. Though fifty years of age, Mr. Hogan seemed in the midst of his career. He did much for the advancement of the Negro on the stage. Aggressive, unselfish, ever proud of his race, the Negro race sustains a genuine loss in his death."

of the Harlem Renaissance than Reed's novel. Here is how Thurman draws Cullen and his close friend, Harold Jackman:

> DeWitt Clinton, the Negro poet Laureate, was there, too, accompanied, as usual, by his fideles achates, David Holloway. David had been acclaimed the most handsome Negro in Harlem by a certain group of whites. He was in great demand by artists who wished to paint him. He had become a much touted romantic figure. In reality he was a fairly intelligent school teacher, quite circumspect in his habits, a rather timid beau, who imagined himself to be bored with life.[93]

As the scene develops, Dr. Parkes (Alain Locke) presides over a meeting of the writers of the Renaissance:

> "Come, come, now," Dr. Parkes urges somewhat impatiently, "I'm not to do all the talking. What have you to say, DeWitt?"
>
> All eyes sought out the so-called Negro poet laureate. For a moment he stirred uncomfortable in his chair, then in a high pitched, nasal voice proceeded to speak.
>
> "I think, Dr. Parkes, that you have said all there is to say. I agree with you. The young Negro artist must go back to his pagan heritage for inspiration and to the old masters for form."
>
> Raymond could not suppress a snort. For DeWitt's few words had given him a vivid mental picture of that poet's creative hours—eyes on a page of Keats, fingers on typewriter, mind frantically conjuring African scenes. And there would of course be a Bible nearby.[94]

---

[93]Wallace Thurman, *Infants of the Spring* (New York: The Macaulay Co., 1932), p. 232.

[94]Thurman, *Infants of the Spring,* p. 236.

Thurman's bitter portrait of the Renaissance, as the scene finally disintegrates into chaos, is more a reflection of his frustrations as a failed writer and his disappointment in a movement that often failed to provide the writers with the proper discipline to be able to produce the work that their talent promised. Langston Hughes described Thurman as "a strangely brilliant black boy who had read everything." Thurman "wanted to be a very great writer, like Gorki or Thomas Mann, and he felt that he was merely a journalistic writer. . . . Wallace Thurman laughed a long bitter laugh."[95] I have spoken earlier of the disagreement between Cullen and Thurman, and so this satirical thrust should hardly be surprising. Yet it seems simply pique, in the end, an attempt to diminish a more successful writer, a better writer.

So we have two conflicting portraits of Cullen, but the evidence of Cullen's work would suggest that Reed's view will win out. The reading public has too long been denied the work; as we slowly begin to reassemble all the missing pieces of the black literary canon, a new perspective of the common intellectual and artistic heritage shared by blacks and whites will make itself clear. It is a great privilege to present Cullen to the public—the poet, the novelist, the essayist, the dramatist. Our American horizons, our American selves seem to harmonize and radiate with such singing as this. Tenor saxophonist Sonny Rollins was right: music is an open sky. Perhaps Amy Lowell's tribute to John Keats, the favorite poet of both her and Cullen, is fitting as parting words for Cullen himself.

> A youth who trudged the highroad we tread now
> Singing the miles behind him; so may we
> Faint throbbings of thy music overhear.

—Amy Lowell, "To John Keats"

GERALD EARLY

---

[95] Langston Hughes, *The Big Sea* (New York: Hill and Wang, 1975), pp. 234, 235, 238.

A note about the collection

This collection includes all the poems that make up *On These I Stand* except the excerpts from *The Lost Zoo*. I felt that what Cullen felt to be his best and most representative work should be left intact. In addition, his translation of the *Medea* is included. Apparently, he had intended to include it in an original draft of a table of contents for *On These I Stand* but probably decided to omit it and make the volume more unified as an all-poetry collection. I have also included a few additional poems from each of Cullen's books, with the exception of *The Medea and Some Poems*, where I stuck to Cullen's selections exclusively. The additions were made because I felt either that the poems were good or that they helped to more fully elucidate Cullen's art. The section of uncollected poems includes all that Cullen had chosen for *On These I Stand*. I have added "Apostrophe for the Land," which appeared in *Phylon* in 1942 and which Cullen originally penciled in as a selection for *On These I Stand*. Other uncollected poems here are some of Cullen's earliest famous poems, "To the Swimmer" and both versions of "I Have a Rendezvous With Life." I have also included an earlier version of "Judas Iscariot." In this way, the reader can see how Cullen developed as a poet by seeing how he made revisions in his work. The other uncollected poems are "Singing in the Rain," "The Poet," "Night Rain," and "From Life to Love." The complete texts of *The Ballad of the Brown Girl* and *One Way to Heaven* are included. Finally, there is a section of prose writing, including an essay by Cullen about his experiences as a teacher of creative writing which I think is particularly valuable in helping the reader understand how Cullen saw the enterprise of teaching. The other prose pieces are four travel pieces Cullen did for *The Crisis* in 1929, a "Dark Tower" column in which Cullen describes a trip to Talladega College in Alabama, and his 1923 League of Youth speech. There is a bit of sparse annotation here and there but nothing obtrusive or excessive. The works are meant to be read and enjoyed, not burdened with a lot of scholarly minutiae.

The appendix includes both the prologue and the epilogue for the *Medea*. When Cullen finished the entire translation, he called it "Byword for Evil" and intended to publish the whole in *On These I Stand*. Also included is the interview of Cullen by a youthful James Baldwin, which appeared in *The Magpie* in 1942.

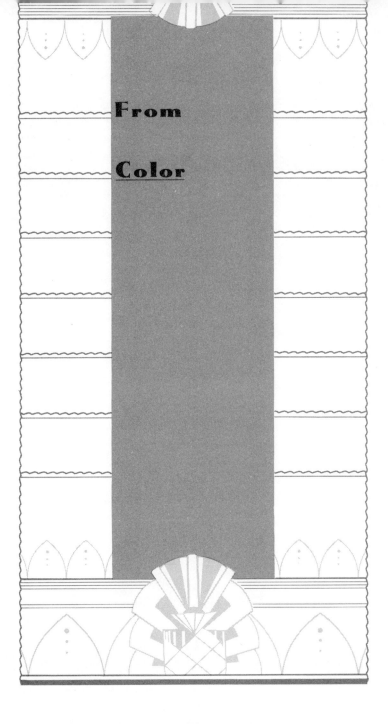

From

Color

YET DO I MARVEL

I doubt not God is good, well-meaning,
    kind,
And did He stoop to quibble could tell
    why
The little buried mole continues blind,
Why flesh that mirrors Him must some day
    die,
Make plain the reason tortured Tantalus[1]
Is baited by the fickle fruit, declare
If merely brute caprice dooms Sisyphus[2]
To struggle up a never-ending stair.
Inscrutable His ways are, and immune
To catechism by a mind too strewn
With petty cares to slightly understand
What awful brain compels His awful hand.
Yet do I marvel at this curious thing:
To make a poet black, and bid him sing!

---

[1]Tantalus was a king of Sispylus in Lydia, the father of Niobe and Pelops, and a friend of
the gods, who was punished for the crime of either: (1) killing his son Pelops and serving
him to the gods; (2) stealing nectar and ambrosia, the gods' food; or (3) revealing the
secrets he learned from the gods. He was dispatched to Hades, where he stood up to his
neck in water which would recede whenever he tried to drink. The fruit just above his head
would ascend whenever he tried to reach for it.

[2]Sisyphus was a king of Corinth who was punished in Hades by having to roll a huge stone
up a hill, only to have the stone roll down again as soon as he brought it to the top.

A SONG OF PRAISE

(For one who praised his lady's being fair.)

You have not heard my love's dark throat,
    Slow-fluting like a reed,
Release the perfect golden note
    She caged there for my need.

Her walk is like the replica
    Of some barbaric dance
Wherein the soul of Africa
    Is winged with arrogance.

And yet so light she steps across
    The ways her sure feet pass,
She does not dent the smoothest moss
    Or bend the thinnest grass.

My love is dark as yours is fair,
    Yet lovelier I hold her
Than listless maids with pallid hair,
    And blood that's thin and colder.

You-proud-and-to-be-pitied one,
    Gaze on her and despair;
Then seal your lips until the sun
    Discovers one as fair.

BROWN BOY TO BROWN GIRL

(Remembrance on a hill) (For Yolande)[1]

"As surely as I hold your hand in mine,
As surely as your crinkled hair belies
The enamoured sun pretending that he dies
While still he loiters in its glossy shine,
As surely as I break the slender line
That spider linked us with, in no least wise
Am I uncertain that these alien skies
Do not our whole life measure and confine.
No less, once in a land of scarlet suns
And brooding winds, before the hurricane
Bore down upon us, long before this pain,
We found a place where quiet water runs;
I held your hand this way upon a hill,
And felt my heart forebear, my pulse grow still."

---

[1]This is one of several poems that Cullen dedicated to women he knew. Yolande was the daughter of W. E. B. Du Bois and Cullen's first wife. They were married on April 9, 1928. She died in Baltimore in March 1960 (or 1961, according to some accounts).

A BROWN GIRL DEAD

With two white roses on her breasts,
   White candles at head and feet,
Dark Madonna of the grave she rests;
   Lord Death has found her sweet.

Her mother pawned her wedding ring
   To lay her out in white;
She'd be so proud she'd dance and sing
   To see herself tonight.

TO A BROWN GIRL

(For Roberta)[1]

What if his glance is bold and free,
   His mouth the lash of whips?
So should the eyes of lovers be,
   And so a lover's lips.

What if no puritanic strain
   Confines him to the nice?
He will not pass this way again,
   Nor hunger for you twice.

Since in the end consort together
   Magdalen and Mary,
Youth is the time for careless weather:
   Later, lass, be wary.

---

[1]This poem is dedicated to Roberta Bosley, who was a friend of Cullen's and a bridesmaid at his first wedding.

BLACK MAGDALENS

These have no Christ to spit and stoop
    To write upon the sand,
Inviting him that has not sinned
    To raise the first rude hand.

And if he came they could not buy
    Rich ointment for his feet,
The body's sale scarce yields enough
    To let the body eat.

The chaste clean ladies pass them by
    And draw their skirts aside,
But Magdalens have a ready laugh;
    They wrap their wounds in pride.

They fare full ill since Christ forsook
    The cross to mount a throne,
And Virtue still is stooping down
    To cast the first hard stone.

ATLANTIC CITY WAITER[1]

With subtle poise he grips his tray
  Of delicate things to eat;
Choice viands to their mouths half way,
  The ladies watch his feet

Go carving dexterous avenues
  Through sly intricacies;
Ten thousand years on jungle clues
  Alone shaped feet like these.

For him to be humble who is proud
  Needs colder artifice;
Though half his pride is disavowed,
  In vain the sacrifice.

Sheer through his acquiescent mask
  Of bland gentility,
The jungle flames like a copper cask
  Set where the sun strikes free.

---

[1]This poem is based on actual experience Cullen had as a waiter in an Atlantic City hotel during one of his undergraduate summers.

TABLEAU
(For Donald Duff)[1]

Locked arm in arm they cross the way,
  The black boy and the white,
The golden splendor of the day,
  The sable pride of night.

From lowered blinds the dark folk stare,
  And here the fair folk talk,
Indignant that these two should dare
  In unison to walk.

Oblivious to look and word
  They pass, and see no wonder
That lightning brilliant as a sword
  Should blaze the path of thunder.

---

[1]Donald Duff was a pacifist and a literary-fringe type who, apparently, was friendly with a number of artists. He died on December 7, 1942 (Pearl Harbor day).

SIMON THE CYRENIAN SPEAKS[1]

He never spoke a word to me,
  And yet He called my name;
He never gave a sign to me,
  And yet I knew and came.

At first I said, "I will not bear
  His cross upon my back;
He only seeks to place it there
  Because my skin is black."

But He was dying for a dream,
  And He was very meek,
And in His eyes there shone a gleam
  Men journey far to seek.

It was Himself my pity bought;
  I did for Christ alone
What all of Rome could not have wrought
  With bruise of lash or stone.

---

[1]In response to an inquiry, Cullen explained that seeing Simon the Cyrenian as a black is a tradition among African-Americans. Ridgely Torrence's 1917 play *Simon the Cyrenian* (part of his collection *Plays for a Negro Theater*) probably popularized the idea. The Reverend Reverdy Ransom called his first New York A.M.E. mission the Church of Simon the Cyrenian.

TWO WHO CROSSED A LINE

(She Crosses)

From where she stood the air she craved
  Smote with the smell of pine;
It was too much to bear; she braved
  Her gods and crossed the line.

And we were hurt to see her go,
  With her fair face and hair,
And veins too thin and blue to show
  What mingled blood flowed there.

We envied her a while, who still
  Pursued the hated track;
Then we forgot her name, until
  One day her shade came back.

Calm as a wave without a crest,
  Sorrow-proud and sorrow-wise,
With trouble sucking at her breast,
  With tear-disdainful eyes,

She slipped into her ancient place,
  And, no word asked, gave none;
Only the silence in her face
  Said seats were dear in the sun.

TWO WHO CROSSED A LINE

(He Crosses)

He rode across like a cavalier,
  Spurs clicking hard and loud;
And where he tarried dropped his tear
  On heads he left low-bowed.

But, "Even Stephen," he cried, and struck
  His steed an urgent blow;
He swore by youth he was a buck
  With savage oats to sow.

To even up some standing scores,
  From every flower bed
He passed, he plucked by threes and fours
  Till wheels whirled in his head.

But long before the drug could tell,
  He took his anodyne;
With scornful grace, he bowed farewell
  And retraversed the line.

INCIDENT

(For Eric Walrond)[1]

Once riding in old Baltimore,
  Heart-filled, head-filled with glee,
I saw a Baltimorean
  Keep looking straight at me.

Now I was eight and very small,
  And he was no whit bigger,
And so I smiled, but he poked out
  His tongue, and called me, "Nigger."

I saw the whole of Baltimore
  From May until December;
Of all the things that happened there
  That's all that I remember.

---

[1]Eric Walrond (1898–1966) was one of the touted young West Indian writers of the Harlem Renaissance. His collection of stories *Tropic Death* is uneven but contains good work. He worked for Garvey's publications on and off in the twenties and the thirties. He was impressed with Cullen's *Color* and gave it a very favorable review in *The New Republic*. Walrond won a Guggenheim in the same year as Cullen (1928).

SATURDAY'S CHILD[1]

Some are teethed on a silver spoon,
  With the stars strung for a rattle;
I cut my teeth as the black raccoon—
  For implements of battle.

Some are swaddled in silk and down,
  And heralded by a star;
They swathed my limbs in a sackcloth gown
  On a night that was black as tar.

For some, godfather and goddame
  The opulent fairies be;
Dame Poverty gave me my name,
  And Pain godfathered me.

For I was born on Saturday—
  "Bad time for planting a seed,"
Was all my father had to say,
  And, "One mouth more to feed."

Death cut the strings that gave me life,
  And handed me to Sorrow,
The only kind of middle wife
  My folks could beg or borrow.

---

[1]Some consider this an autobiographical poem. Cullen, apparently, was born on a Saturday.

PAGAN PRAYER

Not for myself I make this prayer,
But for this race of mine
That stretches forth from shadowed places
Dark hands for bread and wine.

For me, my heart is pagan mad,
My feet are never still,
But give him hearths to keep them warm
In homes high on a hill.

For me, my faith lies fallowing,
I bow not till I see,
But these are humble and believe;
Bless their credulity.

For me, I pay my debts in kind,
And see no better way,
Bless these who turn the other cheek
For love of you, and pray.

Our Father, God, our Brother, Christ—
So are we taught to pray;
Their kinship seems a little thing
Who sorrow all the day.

Our Father, God; our Brother, Christ,
Or are we bastard kin,
That to our plaints your ears are closed,
Your doors barred from within?

Our Father, God; our Brother Christ,
   Retrieve my race again;
So shall you compass this black sheep,
   This pagan heart. Amen.

WISDOM COMETH WITH THE YEARS

Now I am young and credulous,
  My heart is quick to bleed
At courage in the tremulous
  Slow sprouting of a seed.

Now I am young and sensitive,
  Man's lack can stab me through;
I own no stitch I would not give
  To him that asked me to.

Now I am young and a fool for love,
  My blood goes mad to see
A brown girl pass me like a dove
  That flies melodiously.

Let me be lavish of my tears,
  And dream that false is true;
Though wisdom cometh with the years,
  The barren days come, too.

FRUIT OF THE FLOWER

My father is a quiet man
　With sober, steady ways;
For simile, a folded fan;
　His nights are like his days.

My mother's life is puritan,
　No hint of cavalier,
A pool so calm you're sure it can
　Have little depth to fear.

And yet my father's eyes can boast
　How full his life has been;
There haunts them yet the languid ghost
　Of some still sacred sin.

And though my mother chants of God,
　And of the mystic river,
I've seen a bit of checkered sod
　Set all her flesh aquiver.

Why should he deem it pure mischance
　A son of his is fain
To do a naked tribal dance
　Each time he hears the rain?

Why should she think it devil's art
　That all my songs should be
Of love and lovers, broken heart,
　And wild sweet agony?

Who plants a seed begets a bud,
   Extract of that same root;
Why marvel at the hectic blood
   That flushes this wild fruit?

THE SHROUD OF COLOR

(For Llewellyn Ransom)[1]

"Lord, being dark," I said, "I cannot bear
The further touch of earth, the scented air;
Lord, being dark, forewilled to that despair
My color shrouds me in, I am as dirt
Beneath my brother's heel; there is a hurt
In all the simple joys which to a child
Are sweet; they are contaminate, defiled
By truths of wrongs the childish vision fails
To see; too great a cost this birth entails.
I strangle in this yoke drawn tighter than
The worth of bearing it, just to be man
I am not brave enough to pay the price
In full; I lack the strength to sacrifice.
I who have burned my hands upon a star,
And climbed high hills at dawn to view the far
Illimitable wonderments of earth,
For whom all cups have dripped the wine of mirth,
For whom the sea has strained her honeyed throat
Till all the world was sea, and I a boat
Unmoored, on what strange quest I willed to float;
Who wore a many-colored coat of dreams,
Thy gift, O Lord—I whom sun-dabbled streams
Have washed, whose bare brown thighs have held the sun

---

[1] As Cullen almost never dedicated a poem to anyone living he did not know personally, it is fairly certain that Llewellyn Ransom was a personal acquaintance or friend. It is possibly a pseudonym, although most of the time Cullen did not disguise his dedications. Ransom was neither a high school nor college classmate nor a teacher of Cullen's. He may have been simply a neighbor. There is, apparently, no connection between Llewellyn Ransom and the Reverend Reverdy Ransom.

Incarcerate until his course was run,
I who considered man a high-perfected
Glass where loveliness could lie reflected,
Now that I sway athwart Truth's deep abyss,
Denuding man for what he was and is,
Shall breath and being so inveigle me
That I can damn my dreams to hell, and be
Content, each new-born day, anew to see
The steaming crimson vintage of my youth
Incarnadine the altar-slab of Truth?

Or hast Thou, Lord, somewhere I cannot see,
A lamb imprisoned in a bush for me?

Not so? Then let me render one by one
Thy gifts, while still they shine; some little sun
Yet gilds these thighs; my coat, albeit worn,
Still hold its colors fast; albeit torn,
My heart will laugh a little yet, if I
May win of Thee this grace, Lord: on this high
And sacrificial hill 'twixt earth and sky,
To dream still pure all that I loved, and die.
There is no other way to keep secure
My wild chimeras; grave-locked against the lure
Of Truth, the small hard teeth of worms, yet less
Envenomed than the mouth of Truth, will bless
Them into dust and happy nothingness.
Lord, Thou art God; and I, Lord, what am I
But dust? With dust my place, "Lord, let me die."

Across the earth's warm, palpitating crust
I flung my body in embrace; I thrust
My mouth into the grass and sucked the dew,
Then gave it back in tears my anguish drew;
So hard I pressed against the ground, I felt

The smallest sandgrain like a knife, and smelt
The next year's flowering; all this to speed
My body's dissolution, fain to feed
The worms. And so I groaned, and spent my strength
Until, all passion spent, I lay full length
And quivered like a flayed and bleeding thing.

So lay till lifted on a great black wing
That had no mate nor flesh-apparent trunk
To hamper it; with me all time had sunk
Into oblivion; when I awoke
The wing hung poised about two cliffs that broke
The bowels of the earth in twain, and cleft
The seas apart. Below, above, to left,
To right, I saw what no man saw before:
Earth, hell, and heaven; sinew, vein, and core.
All things that swim or walk or creep or fly,
All things that live and hunger, faint and die,
Were made majestic then and magnified
By sight so clearly purged and deified.
The smallest bug that crawls was taller than
A tree, the mustard seed loomed like a man.
The earth that writhes eternally with pain
Of birth, and woe of taking back her slain,
Laid bare her teeming bosom to my sight,
And all was struggle, gasping breath, and fight.
A blind worm here dug tunnels to the light,
And there a seed, racked with heroic pain,
Thrust eager tentacles to sun and rain;
It climbed; it died; the old love conquered me
To weep the blossom it would never be.
But here a bud won light; it burst and flowered
Into a rose whose beauty challenged, "Coward!"
There was no thing alive save only I
That held life in contempt and longed to die.

And still I writhed and moaned, "The curse, the curse,
Than animated death, can death be worse?"

"Dark child of sorrow, mine no less, what art
Of mine can make thee see and play thy part?
The key to all strange things is in thy heart."

What voice was this that coursed like liquid fire
Along my flesh, and turned my hair to wire?

I raised my burning eyes, beheld a field
All multitudinous with carnal yield,
A grim ensanguined mead whereon I saw
Evolve the ancient fundamental law
Of tooth and talon, fist and nail and claw.
There with the force of living, hostile hills
Whose clash the hemmed-in vale with clamor fills,
With greater din contended fierce majestic wills
Of beast with beast, of man with man, in strife
For love of what my heart despised, for life
That unto me at dawn was now a prayer
For night, at night a blood heart-wrung tear
For day again; for *this,* these groans
From tangled flesh and interlocked bones.
And no thing died that did not give
A testimony that it longed to live.
Man, strange composite blend of brute and god,
Pushed on, nor backward glanced where last he trod.
He seemed to mount a misty ladder flung
Pendant from a cloud, yet never gained a rung
But at his feet another tugged and clung.
My heart was still a pool of bitterness,
Would yield nought else, nought else confess.
I spoke (although no form was there
To see, I knew an ear was there to hear),
"Well, let them fight; they *can* whose flesh is fair."

Crisp lightning flashed; a wave of thunder shook
My wing; a pause, and then a speaking, "Look."

I scarce dared trust my ears or eyes for awe
Of what they heard, and dread of what they saw;
For, privileged beyond degree, this flesh
Beheld God and His heaven in the mesh
Of Lucifer's revolt, saw Lucifer
Glow like the sun, and like a dulcimer
I heard his sin-sweet voice break on the yell
Of God's great warriors: Gabriel,
Saint Clair and Michael, Israfel and Raphael.[1]
And strange it was to see God with His back
Against a wall, to see Christ hew and hack
Till Lucifer, pressed by the mighty pair,
And losing inch by inch, clawed at the air
With fevered wings; then, lost beyond repair,
He tricked a mass of stars into his hair;
He filled his hands with stars, crying as he fell,
"A star's a star although it burns in hell."
So God was left to His divinity,
Omnipotent at that most costly fee.

[1]Gabriel (literally "man of God")—an archangel and messenger of God who announced the birth of Jesus. He is part of both Christian and Islamic tradition.

Raphael (literally "God has healed")—an archangel of both Christian and Islamic tradition who figures prominently in the Book of Tobit in the Apocrypha, where he takes human form.

Israfel, or Israfil—in Islam the archangel who, on God's orders, will sound the trumpet from the holy rock in Jerusalem to signal the Day of Resurrection. Israfel tutored Muhammad for three years to prepare him to receive the recitations that make up the Koran.

Michael (literally "like God")—one of the archangels of Islamic and Christian tradition, leader of the heavenly host. This is the fiery warrior who symbolizes war against the heathen. He was the voice who spoke to Moses on Mount Sinai.

Saint Clair (French for "Clarus")—there are several saints by this name, and it is difficult to determine if Cullen was referring to any of these. More likely, Cullen was referring to Uriel (literally "God is my light"), the angel of thunder and earthquakes who drove Adam and Eve from the Garden.

There was a lesson here, but still the clod
In me was sycophant unto the rod,
And cried, "Why mock me thus? Am I a god?"

"One trial more: this failing, then I give
You leave to die; no further need to live."

Now suddenly a strange wild music smote
A chord long impotent in me; a note
Of jungles, primitive and subtle, throbbed
Against my echoing breast, and tom-toms sobbed
In every pulse-beat of my frame. The din
A hollow log bound with a python's skin
Can make wrought every nerve to ecstasy,
And I was wind and sky again, and sea,
And all sweet things that flourish, being free.

Till all at once the music changed its key.

And now it was of bitterness and death,
The cry the lash extorts, the broken breath
Of liberty enchained; and yet there ran
Through all a harmony of faith in man,
A knowledge all would end as it began.
All sights and sounds and aspects of my race
Accompanied this melody, kept pace
With it; with music all their hopes and hates
Were charged, not to be downed by all the fates.
And somehow it was borne upon my brain
How being dark, and living through the pain
Of it, is courage more than angels have. I knew
What storms and tumults lashed the tree that grew
This body that I was, this cringing I
That feared to contemplate a changing sky,
This that I grovelled, whining, "Let me die,"
While others struggled in Life's abattoir.
The cries of all dark people near or far

Were billowed over me, a mighty surge
Of suffering in which my puny grief must merge
And lose itself; I had no further claim to urge
For death; in shame I raised my dust-grimed head,
And though my lips moved not, God knew I said,
"Lord, not for what I saw in flesh or bone
Of fairer men; not raised on faith alone;
Lord, I will live persuaded by mine own.
I cannot play the recreant to these;
My spirit has come home, that sailed the doubtful seas."
With the whiz of a sword that severs space,
The wing dropped down at a dizzy pace,
And flung me on my hill flat on my face;
Flat on my face I lay defying pain,
Glad of the blood in my smallest vein,
And in my hands I clutched a loyal dream,
Still spitting fire, bright twist and coil and gleam,
And chiselled like a hound's white tooth.
"Oh, I will match you yet," I cried, "to truth."
Right glad I was to stoop to what I once had spurned,
Glad even unto tears; I laughed aloud; I turned
Upon my back, and though the tears for joy would run,
My sight was clear; I looked and saw the rising sun.

HERITAGE

(For Harold Jackman)[1]

What is Africa to me:
Copper sun or scarlet sea,
Jungle star or jungle track,
Strong bronzed men, or regal black
Women from whose loins I sprang
When the birds of Eden sang?
One three centuries removed
From the scenes his fathers loved,
Spicy grove, cinnamon tree,
What is Africa to me?

So I lie, who all day long
Want no sound except the song
Sung by wild barbaric birds
Goading massive jungle herds,
Juggernauts[2] of flesh that pass
Trampling tall defiant grass
Where young forest lovers lie,
Plighting troth beneath the sky.
So I lie, who always hear,
Though I cram against my ear
Both my thumbs, and keep them there,

---

[1]Harold Jackman (1900–1960) was Cullen's best friend. Of West Indian descent, Jackman was quite handsome and his portrait by Winold Reiss became a noted icon of the Renaissance. He was largely a fringe player, but his journals and letters contain a great deal of gossipy information about Harlem happenings. He was the recipient of most of Cullen's papers when Cullen died.

[2]Among the Hindus in India, the juggernaut is a sacred idol conveyed on a huge cart in the path of which believers often throw themselves.

Great drums throbbing through the air.
So I lie, whose fount of pride,
Dear distress, and joy allied,
Is my somber flesh and skin,
With the dark blood dammed within
Like great pulsing tides of wine
That, I fear, must burst the fine
Channels of the chafing net
Where they surge and foam and fret.

Africa? A book one thumbs
Listlessly, till slumber comes.
Unremembered are her bats
Circling through the night, her cats
Crouching in the river reeds,
Stalking gentle flesh that feeds
By the river brink; no more
Does the bugle-throated roar
Cry that monarch claws have leapt
From the scabbards where they slept.
Silver snakes that once a year
Doff the lovely coats you wear,
Seek no covert in your fear
Lest a mortal eye should see;
What's your nakedness to me?
Here no leprous flowers rear
Fierce corollas[3] in the air;
Here no bodies sleek and wet,
Dripping mingled rain and sweat,
Tread the savage measures of
Jungle boys and girls in love.
What is last year's snow to me,

---

[3]Corollas—the petals that form the inner envelope of a flower.

Last year's anything? The tree
Budding yearly must forget
How its past arose or set—
Bough and blossom, flower, fruit,
Even what shy bird with mute
Wonder at her travail there,
Meekly labored in its hair.
One three centuries removed
From the scenes his fathers loved,
Spice grove, cinnamon tree,
What is Africa to me?

So I lie, who find no peace
Night or day, no slight release
From the unremittant beat
Made by cruel padded feet
Walking through my body's street.
Up and down they go, and back,
Treading out a jungle track.
So I lie, who never quite
Safely sleep from rain at night—
I can never rest at all
When the rain begins to fall;
Like a soul gone mad with pain
I must match its weird refrain;
Ever must I twist and squirm,
Writhing like a baited worm,
While its primal measures drip
Through my body, crying, "Strip!
Doff this new exuberance.
Come and dance the Lover's Dance!"
In an old remembered way
Rain works on me night and day.

Quaint, outlandish heathen gods
Black men fashion out of rods,

Clay, and brittle bits of stone,
In a likeness like their own,
My conversion came high-priced;
I belong to Jesus Christ,
Preacher of humility;
Heathen gods are naught to me.

Father, Son, and Holy Ghost,
So I make an idle boast;
Jesus of the twice-turned cheek,
Lamb of God, although I speak
With my mouth thus, in my heart
Do I play a double part.
Ever at Thy glowing altar
Must my heart grow sick and falter,
Wishing He I served were black,
Thinking then it would not lack
Precedent of pain to guide it,
Let who would or might deride it;
Surely then this flesh would know
Yours had borne a kindred woe.
Lord, I fashion dark gods, too,
Daring even to give You
Dark despairing features where,
Crowned with dark rebellious hair,
Patience wavers just so much as
Mortal grief compels, while touches
Quick and hot, of anger, rise
To smitten cheek and weary eyes.
Lord, forgive me if my need
Sometimes shapes a human creed.

All day long and all night through,
One thing only must I do:
Quench my pride and cool my blood,
Lest I perish in the flood.

Lest a hidden ember set
Timber that I thought was wet
Burning like the dryest flax,
Melting like the merest wax,
Lest the grave restore its dead.
Not yet has my heart or head
In the least way realized
They and I are civilized.

FOR A POET

(To John Gaston Edgar)[1]

I have wrapped my dreams in a silken
    cloth,
And laid them away in a box of gold;
Where long will cling the lips of the moth,
I have wrapped my dreams in a silken cloth;
I hide no hate; I am not even wroth
Who found earth's breath so keen and cold;
I have wrapped my dreams in a silken cloth,
And laid them away in a box of gold.

---

[1]John Gaston Edgar was probably another personal friend from Cullen's youth as, most likely, Llewellyn Ransom was. Professor Walter Fisher of the then Morgan State College described Edgar as "a white friend" in his liner notes to the album "To Make a Poet Black: The Best Poems of Countee Cullen," read by Ossie Davis and Ruby Dee (Caedmon TC 1400), released in 1971.

FOR MY GRANDMOTHER

This lovely flower fell to seed;
Work gently, sun and rain;
She held it as her drying creed
That she would grow again.

FOR A LADY I KNOW

She even thinks that up in heaven
Her class lies late and snores,
While poor black cherubs rise at seven
To do celestial chores.

FOR AN ATHEIST

Mountains cover me like rain,
Billows whirl and rise;
Hide me from the stabbing pain
In His reproachful eyes.

FOR AN EVOLUTIONIST AND HIS OPPONENT

Showing that our ways agreed,
Death is proof enough;
Body seeks the primal clay,
Soul transcends the slough.

FOR AN ANARCHIST

What matters that I stormed and swore?
Not Samson with an ass's jaw,
Not though a forest of hair he wore,
Could break death's adamantine law.

FOR A PESSIMIST

He wore his coffin for a hat,
    Calamity his cape,
While on his face a death's-head sat
    And waved a bit of crape.

FOR DAUGHTERS OF MAGDALEN

Ours is the ancient story:
  Delicate flowers of sin,
Lilies, arrayed in glory,
  That would not toil nor spin.

FOR A MOUTHY WOMAN

God and the devil still are wrangling
   Which should have her, which repel;
God wants no discord in his heaven;
   Satan has enough in hell.

FOR JOHN KEATS, APOSTLE OF BEAUTY[1]

Not writ in water, nor in mist,
  Sweet lyric throat, thy name;
Thy singing lips that cold death kissed
Have seared his own with flame.

---

[1]John Keats (1795–1821) was Cullen's principal influence. Although Keats wrote several long poems, his reputation as one of the greatest lyric poets in English is built on a series of astonishingly beautiful and powerful odes.

FOR PAUL LAURENCE DUNBAR[1]

Born of the sorrowful of heart,
Mirth was a crown upon his head;
Pride kept his twisted lips apart
In jest, to hide a heart that bled.

---

[1]Paul Laurence Dunbar (1872–1906) was an important model for Cullen. Dunbar was a lyric poet, although he became known mostly through his dialect poems. He also wrote several novels and short stories. He was the most famous and accomplished black American poet before Cullen and Langston Hughes.

FOR JOSEPH CONRAD[1]

Not of the dust, but of the wave
His final couch should be;
They lie not easy in a grave
Who once have known the sea.
How shall earth's meagre bed enthrall
The hardiest seaman of them all?

---

[1]Joseph Conrad (1857–1924), born of a land-owning Polish family in a Ukrainian province in Poland, became one of the greatest novelists in the English language, which was not his native tongue. Among his works are *Lord Jim*, *Heart of Darkness*, and *Nostromo*.

FOR MYSELF

What's in this grave is worth your tear;
There's more than the eye can see;
Folly and Pride and Love lie here
Buried alive with me.

IF YOU SHOULD GO

Love, leave me like the light,
  The gently passing day;
We would not know, but for the night,
  When it has slipped away.

Go quietly; a dream,
  When done, should leave no trace
That it has lived, except a gleam
  Across the dreamer's face

SPRING REMINISCENCE

"My sweet," you sang, and, "Sweet," I sang,
  And sweet we sang together,
Glad to be young as the world was young,
  Two colts too strong for a tether.

Shall ever a spring be like that spring,
  Or apple blossoms as white;
Or ever clover smell like the clover
  We lay upon that night?

Shall ever your hand lie in my hand,
  Pulsing to it, I wonder;
Or have the gods, being jealous gods,
  Envied us our thunder?

SHE OF THE DANCING FEET SINGS

(To Ottie Graham)[1]

"And what would I do in heaven, pray,
  Me with my dancing feet,
And limbs like apple boughs that sway
  When the gusty rain winds beat?

And how would I thrive in a perfect place
  Where dancing would be sin,
With not a man to love my face,
  Nor an arm to hold me in?

The seraphs and the cherubim
  Would be too proud to bend
To sing the faery tunes that brim
  My heart from end to end.

The wistful angels down in hell
  Will smile to see my face,
And understand, because they fell
  From that all-perfect place."

---

[1]Ottie Graham was a girl Cullen dated.

JUDAS ISCARIOT

I think when Judas' mother heard
   His first faint cry the night
That he was born, that worship stirred
   Her at the sound and sight.
She thought his was as fair a frame
   As flesh and blood had worn;
I think she made this lovely name
   For him—"Star of my morn."

As any mother's son he grew
   From spring to crimson spring;
I think his eyes were black, or blue,
   His hair curled like a ring.
His mother's heart-strings were a lute
   Whereon he all day played;
She listened rapt, abandoned, mute,
   To every note he made.

I think he knew the growing Christ,
   And played with Mary's son,
And where mere mortal craft sufficed,
   There Judas may have won.
Perhaps he little cared or knew,
   So folly-wise is youth,
That He whose hand his hand clung to
   Was flesh-embodied Truth;

Until one day he heard young Christ,
   With far-off eyes agleam,
Tell of a mystic, solemn tryst
   Between Him and a dream.

And Judas listened, wonder-eyed,
  Until the Christ was through,
Then said, "And I, though good betide,
  Or ill, will go with you."

And so he followed, heard Christ preach,
  Saw how by miracle
The blind man saw, the dumb got speech,
  The leper found him well.
And Judas in those holy hours
  Loved Christ, and loved Him much,
And in his heart he sensed dead flowers
  Bloom at the Master's touch.

And when Christ felt the death hour creep
  With sullen, drunken lurch,
He said to Peter, "Feed my sheep,
  And build my holy church."
He gave to each the special task
  That should be his to do,
But reaching one, I hear him ask,
  "What shall I give to you?"

Then Judas in his hot desire
  Said, "Give me what you will."
Christ spoke to him with words of fire,
  "Then, Judas, you must kill
One whom you love, One who loves you
  As only God's son can:
This is the work for you to do
  To save the creature man."

"And men to come will curse your name,
  And hold you up to scorn;
In all the world will be no shame
  Like yours; this is love's thorn.

It takes strong will of heart and soul,
  But man is under ban.
Think, Judas, can you play this role
  In heaven's mystic plan?"

So Judas took the sorry part,
  Went out and spoke the word,
And gave the kiss that broke his heart,
  But no one knew or heard.
And no one knew what poison ate
  Into his palm that day,
Where, bright and damned, the monstrous weight
  Of thirty white coins lay.

It was not death that Judas found
  Upon a kindly tree;
The man was dead long ere he bound
  His throat as final fee.
And who can say if on that day
  When gates of pearl swung wide,
Christ did not go His honored way
  With Judas by His side?

I think somewhere a table round
  Owns Jesus as its head,
And there the saintly twelve are found
  Who followed where He led.
And Judas sits down with the rest,
  And none shrinks from His hand,
For there the worst is as the best,
  And there they understand.

And you may think of Judas, friend,
  As one who broke his word,
Whose neck came to a bitter end
  For giving up his Lord.
But I would rather think of him

As the little Jewish lad
Who gave young Christ heart, soul, and limb,
And all the love he had.

THE WISE

(For Alain Locke)[1]

> Dead men are wisest, for they know
> How far the roots of flowers go,
> How long a seed must rot to grow.
>
> Dead men alone bear frost and rain
> On throbless heart and heatless brain,
> And feel no stir of joy or pain.
>
> Dead men alone are satiate;
> They sleep and dream and have no weight,
> To curb their rest, of love or hate.
>
> Strange, men should flee their company,
> Or think me strange who long to be
> Wrapped in their cool immunity.

---

[1]Alain Locke (1886–1954) was one of the primary promoters of the Harlem Renaissance. A Rhodes Scholar, Harvard graduate, and philosophy professor at Howard, he edited the famous Renaissance anthology *The New Negro* (1925).

TO JOHN KEATS, POET. AT SPRING TIME*

(For Carl Van Vechten)[1]

I cannot hold my peace, John Keats;
There never was a spring like this;
It is an echo, that repeats
My last year's song and next year's bliss.
I know, in spite of all men say
Of Beauty, you have felt her most.
Yea, even in your grave her way
Is laid. Poor, troubled, lyric ghost,
Spring never was so fair and dear
As Beauty makes her seem this year.

I cannot hold my peace, John Keats,
I am as helpless in the toil
Of Spring as any lamb that bleats
To feel the solid earth recoil
Beneath his puny legs. Spring beats
Her tocsin call to those who love her,
And lo! the dogwood petals cover
Her breast with drifts of snow, and sleek
White gulls fly screaming to her, and hover
About her shoulders, and kiss her cheek,

---

*Spring, 1924. [This footnote was in the original text.]

[1]Carl Van Vechten (1880–1964) was a noted novelist, photographer, and essayist who was one of the leading white promoters of the Harlem Renaissance. His 1926 novel *Nigger Heaven* was the center of much controversy. Among the several important collections Van Vechten established was the James Weldon Johnson Memorial Collection of Negro Arts and Letters at Yale University in 1941.

While white and purple lilacs muster
A strength that bears them to a cluster
Of color and odor; for her sake
All things that slept are now awake.

And you and I, shall we lie still,
John Keats, while Beauty summons us?
Somehow I feel your sensitive will
Is pulsing up some tremulous
Sap road of a maple tree, whose leaves
Grow music as they grow, since your
Wild voice is in them, a harp that grieves
For life that opens death's dark door.
Though dust, your fingers still can push
The Vision Splendid to a birth,
Though now they work as grass in the hush
Of the night on the broad sweet page of the earth.

"John Keats is dead," they say, but I
Who hear your full insistent cry
In bud and blossom, leaf and tree,
Know John Keats still writes poetry.
And while my head is earthward bowed
To read new life sprung from your shroud,
Folks seeing me must think it strange
That merely spring should so derange
My mind. They do not know that you,
John Keats, keep revel with me, too.

SONG OF PRAISE

Who lies with his milk-white maiden,
Bound in the length of her pale gold hair,
Cooled by her lips with the cold kiss laden,
He lies, but he loves not there.

Who lies with his nut-brown maiden,
Bruised to the bone by her sin-black hair,
Warmed with the wine that her full lips trade in,
He lies, and his love lies there.

HARSH WORLD THAT LASHEST ME

(For Walter White)[1]

Harsh World that lashest me each day,
  Dub me not cowardly because
I seem to find no sudden way
  To throttle you or clip your claws.
No force compels me to the wound
  Whereof my body bears the scar;
Although my feet are on the ground,
  Doubt not my eyes are on a star.

You cannot keep me captive, World,
  Entrammeled, chained, spit on, and spurned.
More free than all your flags unfurled,
  I give my body to be burned.
I mount my cross because I will,
  I drink the hemlock which you give
For wine which you withhold—and still,
  Because I will not die, I live.

I live because an ember in
  Me smoulders to regain its fire,
Because what is and what has been

---

[1]Walter White (1893–1955), a Southerner, was assistant to James Weldon Johnson of the
NAACP during the Harlem Renaissance. Publicist, lobbyist, *bon vivant*, and researcher on
the phenomenon of lynching, White wrote several important books in the twenties including
The Fire in the Flint (1924) and *Rope and Faggot* (1929). He was a big promoter of Cullen
in the twenties, but the men were more distant at the end of Cullen's career when White
criticized Cullen for writing *St. Louis Woman.*

Not yet have conquered my desire.
I live to prove the groping clod
  Is surely more than simple dust;
I live to see the breath of God
  Beatify the carnal crust.

But when I will, World, I can go,
  Though triple bronze should wall me round,
Slip past your guard as swift as snow,
  Translated without pain or sound.
Within myself is lodged the key
  To that vast room of couches laid
For those too proud to live and see
  Their dreams of light eclipsed in shade.

REQUIESCAM

I am for sleeping and forgetting
  All that has gone before;
I am for lying still and letting
  Who will beat at my door;
I would my life's cold sun were setting
  To rise for me no more.

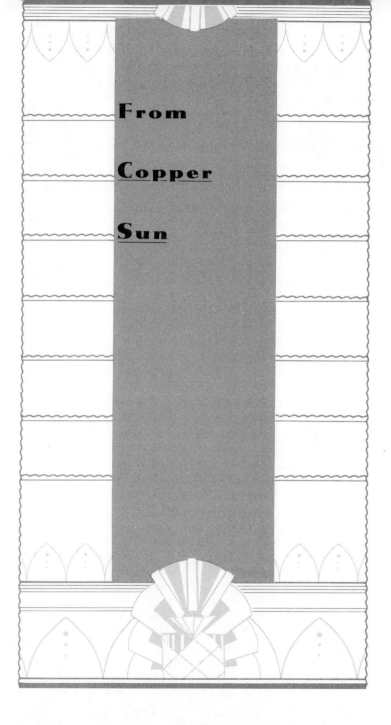

From

Copper

Sun

FROM THE DARK TOWER

(To Charles S. Johnson)[1]

We shall not always plant while others
   reap
The golden increment of bursting fruit,
Not always countenance, abject and mute,
That lesser men should hold their brothers
   cheap;
Not everlastingly while others sleep
Shall we beguile their limbs with mellow
   flute,
Not always bend to some more subtle brute;
We were not made eternally to weep.

The night whose sable breast relieves the
   stark,
White stars is no less lovely being dark,
And there are buds that cannot bloom at all
In light, but crumple, piteous, and fall;
So in the dark we hide the heart that bleeds,
And wait, and tend our agonizing seeds.

---

[1]Charles S. Johnson (1893–1956) was a major promoter of the Harlem Renaissance. A noted sociologist, Johnson was Executive Director of Research and Publicity for the National Urban League and the founder of *Opportunity*, the League's official organ. Most of the important black writers of the period had their work featured in *Opportunity*.

THRENODY FOR A BROWN GIRL[1]

Weep not, you who love her;
What rebellious flow
Grief undams shall recover
Whom the gods bid go?
Sorrow rising like a wall,
Bitter, blasphemous,
What avails it to recall
Beauty back to us?

Think not this grave shall keep her,
This marriage-bed confine;
Death may dig it deep and deeper;
She shall climb it like a vine.
Body that was quick and sentient,
Dear as thought or speech,
Death could not with one trenchant
Blow snatch out of reach.

She is nearer than the word
Wasted on her now,
Nearer than the swaying bird
On its rhythmic bough.
Only were our faith as much
As a mustard seed,
Aching, hungry hands might touch
Her as they touch a reed.

---

[1]A threnody is a lamentation or dirge.

Life who was not loth to trade her
Unto death, has done
Better than he planned, has made her
Wise as Solomon.
Now she knows the Why and Wherefore,
Troublous Whence and Whither,
Why men strive and sweat, and care for
Bays that droop and wither.

All the stars she knows by name,
End and origin thereof,
Knows if love be kin to shame,
If shame be less than love.
What was crooked now is straight,
What was rough is plain;
Grief and sorrow have no weight
Now to cause her pain.

Plain to her why fevered blisters
Made her dark hands run,
While her favored, fairer sisters
Neither wrought nor spun;
Clear to her the hidden reason
Men daily fret and toil,
Staving death off for a season
Till soil return to soil.

One to her are flame and frost;
Silence is her singing lark;
We alone are children, lost,
Crying in the dark.
Varied feature now, and form,
Change has bred upon her;
Crush no bug nor nauseous worm
Lest you tread upon her.

Pluck no flower lest she scream;
Bruise no slender reed,
Lest it prove more than it seem,
Lest she groan and bleed.
More than ever trust your brother,
Read him golden, pure;
It may be she finds no other
House so safe and sure.

Set no poet carving
Rhymes to make her laugh;
Only live hearts starving
Need an epitaph.
Lay upon her no white stone
From a foreign quarry;
Earth and sky be these alone
Her obituary.

Swift as startled fawn or swallow,
Silence all her sound,
She has fled; we cannot follow
Further than this mound.
We who take the beaten track
Trying to appease
Hearts near breaking with their lack,
We need elegies.

UNCLE JIM

"White folks is white," says uncle Jim;
"A platitude," I sneer;
And then I tell him so is milk,
And the froth upon his beer.

His heart walled up with bitterness,
He smokes his pungent pipe,
And nods at me as if to say,
"Young fool, you'll soon be ripe!"

I have a friend who eats his heart
Always with grief of mine,
Who drinks my joy as tipplers drain
Deep goblets filled with wine.

I wonder why here at his side,
Face-in-the-grass with him,
My mind should stray the Grecian urn
To muse on uncle Jim.

COLORED BLUES SINGER

Some weep to find the Golden Pear
Feeds maggots at the core,
And some grow cold as ice, and bear
Them prouder than before.

But you go singing like the sea
Whose lover turns to land;
You make your grief a melody
And take it by the hand.

Such songs the mellow-bosomed maids
Of Africa intone
For lovers dead in hidden glades,
Slow rotting flesh and bone.

Such keenings tremble from the kraal,
Where sullen-browed abides
The second wife whose dark tears fail
To draw him to her sides.

Somewhere Jeritza[1] breaks her heart
On symbols Verdi[2] wrote;
You tear the strings of your soul apart,
Blood dripping note by note.

---

[1]Maria Jeritza, a Czech-born soprano who was a major opera star of the twenties and thirties.

[2]Giuseppe Verdi (1813–1901), Italian composer of some of the most famous operas in the world, including *Aïda* (1871), *Otello* (1887), *Il Trovatore* (1853), and *La Traviata* (1853).

COLORS
(To Leland)[1]

(Red)

She went to buy a brand new hat,
And she was ugly, black, and fat:
"This red becomes you well," they said,
And perched it high upon her head.
And then they laughed behind her back
To see it glow against the black.
She paid for it with regal mien,
And walked out proud as any queen.

(Black)

1

The play is done, the crowds depart; and see
That twisted tortured thing hung from a tree,
Swart victim of a newer Calvary.

2

Yea, he who helped Christ up Golgotha's track,
That Simon who did *not* deny, was black.

---

[1]Leland B. Pettit was the organist of the All Saints Cathedral Choir and, apparently, a good friend of Cullen during the mid-twenties. In 1925 he organized a reading for Cullen at the Athenaeum in Milwaukee.

(The Unknown Color)

I've often heard my mother say,
When great winds blew across the day,
And, cuddled close and out of sight,
The young pigs squealed with sudden fright
Like something speared or javelined,
"Poor little pigs, they see the wind."

THE LITANY OF THE DARK PEOPLE

Our flesh that was a battle-ground
Shows now the morning-break;
The ancient deities are downed
For Thy eternal sake.
Now that the past is left behind,
Fling wide Thy garment's hem
To keep us one with Thee in mind,
Thou Christ of Bethlehem.

The thorny wreath may ridge our brow,
The spear may mar our side,
And on white wood from a scented bough
We may be crucified;
Yet no assault the old gods make
Upon our agony
Shall swerve our footsteps from the wake
Of Thine toward Calvary.

And if we hunger now and thirst,
Grant our withholders may,
When heaven's constellations burst
Upon Thy crowning day,
Be fed by us, and given to see
Thy mercy in our eyes,
When Bethlehem and Calvary
Are merged in Paradise.

PITY THE DEEP IN LOVE

(To Fiona)[1]

Pity the deep in love;
They move as men asleep,
Traveling a narrow way
Precipitous and steep.
Tremulous is the lover's breath
With little moans and sighs;
Heavy are the brimming lids
Upon a lover's eyes.

---

[1]Fiona Braithwaite was the sister of literary critic, anthologist, and poet William Stanley Braithwaite. She was one of several women Cullen was interested in before his marriage.

ONE DAY WE PLAYED A GAME

(Yolande: Her Poem)[1]

One day we lay beneath an apple tree,
Tumultuous with fruit, live with the bee,
And there we played a gay, fantastic game
Of our own making, called Name me a Name.
The grave was liberal, letting us endow
Ourselves with names of lovers who by now
Are dust, but rarer dust for loving high
Than they shall be who let the red flame die. . . .
Crouched sphinx-wise in the grass, you hugged your knees,
And called me "Abelard"; I, "Heloise,"[2]
Rejoined, and added thereto, "Melisande";
Then "Pelleas,"[3] I heard, and felt a hand
Slide into mine; joy would not let us speak
Awhile, but only sit there cheek to cheek,
Hand clasping hand. . . . till passion made us bold;

---

[1] See the earlier note on Nina Yolande Du Bois, p. 81.

[2] Pierre Abelard (1079–1142) was a French theologian and philosopher. He fell in love with Heloise while she was his student. They married secretly and had a son. Her uncle, Canon Fulbert, one of the clergy of the cathedral of Paris, once he discovered the marriage, had Abelard castrated. Heloise went into the convent. Abelard became a monk.

[3] Claude Debussy's opera *Pelleas et Melisande*, based on a play by Maurice Maeterlinck, was premiered in Paris in 1902. It is, in essence, the story of Pelleas, who falls in love with Melisande, his half-brother's wife.

"Tristan," you purred to me. . . . I laughed, "Isolde."[4]
"King Ninus, I," I cried; snared in a kiss
You named yourself my dark Semiramis.[5]
"Queen Guinevere," I sang; you, "Lancelot."[6]
My heart grew big with pride to think you'd not
Cried "Arthur," whom his lovely queen forgot
In loving him whose name you called me by. . . .
We two grew mad with loving then, and I
With whirlpool rapture strained you to my breast;
"First love! First love!" I urged, and "Adam!" blessed
My urgency. My lips grew soft with "Eve,"
And round with ardor purposing to leave
Upon your mouth a lasting seal of bliss. . . .
But midway of our kissing came a hiss
Above us in the apple tree; a sweet
Red apple rolled between us at our feet,
And looking up we saw the glide and dip,
Cold supple coils among the branches slip.
"Eve! Eve!" I cried, "Beware!" Too late. You bit
Half of the fruit away. . . . The rest of it
I took, assuring you with misty eyes,
"Fare each as each, we lose no Paradise."

---

[4]Tristan and Isolde were two lovers whose story is part of the Arthurian cycle of tales. Tristan and Isolde accidentally fall in love with each other after drinking a love potion which was intended for Isolde and King Mark. Isolde, also known as Isolde of Cornwall, marries King Mark and Tristan eventually marries Isolde of the White Hands. Neither is happy and both die tragically.

[5]King Ninus was the king of ancient Babylon. Semiramis was his queen. Ninus's tomb was the meeting place for two tragic lovers, Pyramus and Thisbe. At their meeting place, Pyramus, who is late, thinks Thisbe has been killed by a lioness. He then kills himself, and Thisbe, realizing what has happened, kills herself.

[6]Lancelot of the Lake was the lover of Queen Guinevere, the wife of King Arthur. She is seduced by Modred, her husband's nephew, and, as a result of war, Modred is killed and Arthur mortally wounded. Guinevere becomes a nun and Lancelot a monk.

VARIATIONS ON A THEME

(The Loss of Love)

I

This house where Love a little while
   abode,
Impoverished completely of him now,
Of every vestige bare, drained like a bough
Wherefrom the all-sustaining sap has flowed
Away, yet bears upon its front bestowed
A cabalistic legend telling how
Love for a meagre space deigned to allow
It summer scent before the winter snowed.
Here rots to ruin a splendor proudly calm,
A skeleton whereof the clean bones wear
Their indigence relieved of any qualm
For purple robes that once were folded there.
The mouldy Coliseum draws upon
Our wonder yet . . . no less Love's Parthenon.

2

All through an empty place I go,
And find her not in any room;
The candles and the lamps I light
Go down before a wind of gloom.

Thick-spraddled lies the dust about,
A fit, sad place to write her name
Or draw her face the way she looked
That legendary night she came.

The old house crumbles bit by bit;
Each day I hear the ominous thud
That says another rent is there
For winds to pierce and storms to flood.

My orchards groan and sag with fruit;
Where, Indian-wise, the bees go round;
I let it rot upon the bough;
I eat what falls upon the ground.

The heavy cows go laboring
In agony with clotted teats;
My hands are slack; my blood is cold;
I marvel that my heart still beats.

I have no will to weep or sing,
No least desire to pray or curse;
The loss of love is a terrible thing;
They lie who say that death is worse.

A SONG OF SOUR GRAPES

I wish your body were in the grave,
Deep down as a grave may be,
Or rotting under the deepest wave
That ever ploughed the sea.

I wish I never had seen your face,
Or the sinuous curve of your mouth,
Dear as a straw to a man who drowns
Or rain to a land in drouth.

I would that your mother had never borne,
Your father's seed to fruit,
That meadow rats had gnawed his corn
Before it gathered root.

LAMENT

Now let all lovely things embark
Upon the sea of mist
With her whose luscious mouth the dark,
Grim troubadour has kissed.

The silver clock that ticked away
Her days, and never knew
Its beats were sword thrusts to the clay
That too much beauty slew.

The pillow favored with her tears
And hallowed by her head;
I shall not even keep my fears,
Now their concern is dead.

But where shall I bury sun and rain,
How mortalise the stars,
How still the half-heard cries of pain
That seared her soul with scars?

In what sea depths shall all the seeds
Of every flower die?
Where shall I scatter the broken reeds,
And how erase the sky?

And where shall I find a hole so deep
No troubled ghost may rise?
There will I put my heart to sleep
Wanting her face and eyes.

THE LOVE TREE

Come, let us plant our love as farmers
    plant
A seed, and you shall water it with tears,
And I shall weed it with my hands until
They bleed. Perchance this buried love of
    ours
Will fall on goodly ground and bear a tree
With fruit and flowers; pale lovers chancing
    here
May pluck and eat, and through their veins a
    sweet
And languid ardor play, their pulses beat
An unimagined tune, their shy lips meet
And part, and bliss repeat again. And men
Will pilgrimage from far and wide to see
This tree for which we two were crucified,
And, happy in themselves, will never know
'Twas break of heart that made the Love Tree
    grow.

THE WIND BLOWETH WHERE IT LISTETH

"Live like the wind," he said, "unfettered,
  And love me while you can;
And when you will, and can be bettered,
  Go to the better man.

"For you'll grow weary, maybe, sleeping
  So long a time with me;
Like this there'll be no cause for weeping;
  The wind is always free.

"Go when you please," he would be saying,
  His mouth hard on her own;
That's why she stayed and loved the staying,
  Contented to the bone.

And now he's dust, and he but twenty,—
  Frost that was like a flame;
Her kisses on the head death bent, he
  Gave answer to his name.

And now he's dust and with dust lying
  In sullen arrogance;
Death found it hard, for all his trying,
  To shatter such a lance.

She laid him out as fine as any
  That had a priest and ring;
She never spared a silver penny
  For cost of anything.

Her grief is crowned with his child sucking
  The milk of her distress,
As if his father's hands were plucking
  Her buds of bitterness.

He may grow tall as any other,
 Blest with his father's face,
And yield her strength enough to smother
 What some will call disgrace.

He may be cursed and be concerned
 With thoughts of right and wrong,
And brand with "Shame" these two that burned
 Without the legal thong.

Her man would say they were no rabble
 To love like common clay,—
But Christian tongues are trained to babble
 In such a bitter way.

Still, she's this minted gold to pour her,
 This from her man for a mark:
It was no law that held him for her,
 And moved his feet in the dark.

THOUGHTS IN A ZOO

They in their cruel traps, and we in ours,
Survey each other's rage, and pass the hours
Commiserating each the other's woe,
To mitigate his own pain's fiery glow.
Man could but little proffer in exchange
Save that his cages have a larger range.
That lion with his lordly, untamed heart
Has in some man his human counterpart,
Some lofty soul in dreams and visions wrapped,
But in the stifling flesh securely trapped.
Gaunt eagle whose raw pinions stain the bars
That prison you, so men cry for the stars!
Some delve down like the mole far underground,
(Their nature is to burrow, not to bound),
Some, like the snake, with changeless slothful eye,
Stir not, but sleep and smoulder where they lie.
Who is most wretched, these caged ones, or we,
Caught in a vastness beyond our sight to see?

TWO THOUGHTS OF DEATH

I

When I am dead, it will not be
Much matter of concern to me
Who folds my hands, or combs my hair,
Or, pitying their sightless stare,
Draws down the blinds across my eyes.
I shall not have the least surmise
Which of the many loves I had
Weeps most the passing of her lad.
Not what these give, nor what they keep,
Shall gladden or disturb my sleep,
If only one who never guessed
How ever tremor in her breast
Reverberated in my own.
In that last hour come and bend down
To kiss my long-expectant mouth
Still curved, in death, to meet her mouth.

2

I am content to play the martyr,
To wear the dunce cap here at school;
For every tear I shed I'll barter
To Death; I'll be no more a fool
When that pale rider reaches down
His hand to me. He'll beat a crown
From all the aches my shoulders bore,
And I shall lord one regal hour
Illumined in all things before
His sickle spears another flower.

While still his shears snarl through my thread,
Dismembering it strand by strand,
While I hang poised between the dead
And quick, into omniscience fanned,
My mind shall glow with one rich spark
Before it ends in endless dark.
These straining eyes, clairvoyant then,
Shall probe beneath the calloused husk
That hides the better selves of men.
And as my day throbs into dusk,
This heart the world has made to bleed,
While all its red stream deathward flows,
Shall comprehend just why the seed
Must agonize to be the rose.

LOVE'S WAY

Love is not love demanding all, itself
Withholding aught; love's is the nobler way
Of courtesy, that will not feast aware
That the beloved hungers, nor drink unless
The cup be shared down to the last sweet dregs.
Renunciatory never was the thorn
To crown love with, but *prodigal* and *proud!*
Too proud to rest the debtor of the one
Dear passion most it dotes upon, always
Love rehabilitates unto the end.
So let it be with us; the perfect faith
We each to other swear this moment leaves
Our scales harmonious, neither wanting found
Though weighed in such strict balances. So let
It be with us always. I am too proud
To owe you one caress; you must not drop
Beholden to my favor for one least
Endearing term. Should you reveal some stretch
Of sky to me, let me revive some note
Of music lost to you. This is love's way,
That where a heart is asked gives back a heart.

IN SPITE OF DEATH

All things confirm me in the thought that
    dust,
Once raised to monumental pride of breath,
To no extent affirms the right of death
To raze such splendor to an ancient crust.
"Grass withereth, the flower fadeth;" yea,
But in the violated seed exults,
The bleakest winter through, a deathless
    pulse,
Beating, "Spring wipes this sacrilege away."

No less shall I in some new fashion flare
Again, when death has blown my candles out;
Although my blood went down in shameful
    rout
Tonight, by all this living frame holds fair,
Though death should closet me tonight, I
    swear
Tomorrow's sun would find his cupboard
    bare.

COR CORDIUM*[1]

> *Cor cordium* is written there,
> But the heart of hearts is away;
> They could not fashion any bier
> To hold that burning clay.
>
> Imprisoned in the flesh, he wrought
> Till Death as Prospero,
> Pitied the spark that life had caught,
> Loosed him, and let him go.
>
> Look, a light like a sun-girt flask;
> Listen, and hear it sing.
> Light and song are what, you ask?
> Ariel off the wing!

---

*Written at the Shelley Memorial in Rome, August 1926. [This footnote appeared in the original edition.]

[1]Percy Bysshe Shelley (1792–1822) was another of the English Romantic poets who influenced Cullen but to a lesser extent than Keats. Shelley's principal poems are "Alastor," "Mont Blanc," "Prometheus Unbound,"and "The Witch of Atlas." Leigh Hunt inscribed "Cor Cordium" on Shelley's tomb in Rome where he was buried near to his young son and his good friend John Keats. Edward Trelawney added these lines from Ariel's song in *The Tempest* to the tomb:

> Nothing of him that doth fade,
> But doth suffer a sea change
> Into something rich and strange.

LINES TO MY FATHER

The many sow, but only the chosen reap;
Happy the wretched host if Day be brief,
That with the cool oblivion of sleep
A dawnless Night may soothe the smart of grief.

If from the soil our sweat enriches sprout
One meagre blossom for our hands to cull,
Accustomed indigence provokes a shout
Of praise that life becomes so bountiful.

Now ushered regally into your own,
Look where you will, as far as eye can see,
Your little seeds are to a fullness grown,
And golden fruit is ripe on every tree.

Yours is no fairy gift, no heritage
Without travail, to which weak wills aspire;
This is a merited and grief-earned wage
From One Who holds His servants worth their hire.

So has the shyest of your dreams come true,
Built not of sand, but of the solid rock,
Impregnable to all that may accrue
Of elemental rage: storm, stress, and shock.

PROTEST

(To John Trounstine)[1]

I long not now, a little while at least,
For that serene interminable hour
When I shall leave this Barmecidal[2] feast
With poppy for my everlasting flower;
I long not now for that dim cubicle
Of earth to which my lease will not expire,
Where he who comes a tenant there may dwell
Without a thought of famine, flood, or fire.

Surely that house has quiet to bestow—
Still tongue, spent pulse, heart pumped of its last throb,
The fingers tense and tranquil in a row,
The throat unwelled with any sigh or sob—
But time to live, to love, bear pain and smile,
Oh, we are given such a little while!

---

[1]John Trounstine was a student at Harvard during a part of Cullen's tenure there. He arranged a reading for Cullen at Harvard after Cullen had graduated. He also suggested to Cullen the idea of writing a novel and served in the capacity of an agent in helping to get the novel *One Way to Heaven* published.

[2]"Barmecidal"—unreal or illusive; a Barmecide feast is a banquet of no food.

AN EPITAPH

(For Amy Lowell)[1]

She leans across a golden table,
    Confronts God with an eye
Still puzzled by the standard label
    All flesh bears: Made to die—
And questions Him if He is able
    To reassure her why.

---

[1] Amy Lowell (1874–1925), noted American poet and critic and one of the leading members of the Imagist school. She completed a two-volume biography of John Keats just before her death. Although Keats was a major influence on Cullen, Lowell's biography of the great English poet (which Cullen read) figures prominently in the story of Langston Hughes's "discovery" by Vachel Lindsay, a white poet popular from 1910 through the 1920s. In exchange for receiving some of Hughes's poems and to serve as an inspiration for him, Lindsay gave Hughes a copy of the Lowell biography of Keats.

YOUTH SINGS A SONG OF ROSEBUDS

(To Roberta)¹

Since men grow diffident at last,
And care no whit at all,
If spring be come, or the fall be past,
Or how the cool rains fall,

I come to no flower but I pluck,
I raise no cup but I sip,
For a mouth is the best of sweets to suck;
The oldest wine's on the lip.

If I grow old in a year or two,
And come to the querulous song
Of "Alack and aday" and "This was true,
And that, when I was young,"

I must have sweets to remember by,
Some blossom saved from the mire,
Some death-rebellious ember I
Can fan into a fire.

¹See earlier note on Roberta Bosley, p. 83.

HUNGER

(To Emerson Whithorne)[1]

Break me no bread however white it be;
It cannot fill the emptiness I know;
No wine can cool this desert thirst in me
Though it had lain a thousand years in snow;
No swooning lotus flower's languid juice
Drips anodyne unto my restlessness,
And impotent to win me to a truce
Is every artifice of loveliness.
Inevitable is the way I go,
False-faced amid a pageant permeate
With bliss, yet visioning a higher wave
Than this weak ripple washing to and fro;
The fool still keeps his dreams inviolate
Till their virginity espouse the grave.

---

[1]Emerson Whithorne (1884–1958) was a composer who adapted several of Cullen's poems to music, including a song cycle, *Saturday's Child,* that premiered at New York's Town Hall in 1926.

MORE THAN A FOOL'S SONG

(To Edward Perry)[1]

Go look for beauty where you least
Expect to hear her hive;
Regale your belly with a feast
Of hunger till you thrive.

For honest treatment seek the thief;
For truth consult the liar;
Court pleasure in the halls of grief;
Find smoothness on a briar.

The worth impearled in chastity
Is known best of the harlot,
And courage throws her panoply
On many a native varlet.

In Christian practice those who move
To symbols strange to us
May reckon clearer of His love
Than we who own His cross.

The world's a curious riddle thrown
Water-wise from heaven's cup;
The souls we think are hurtling down
Perhaps are climbing up.

---

[1] Edward Perry was a good friend of Cullen's who worked at the New York *Amsterdam News*.

ADVICE TO A BEAUTY
(To Sydonia)[1]

Of all things, lady, be not proud;
Inter not beauty in that shroud
Wherein the living waste, the dead,
Unwept and unrememberéd,
Decay. Beauty beats so frail a wing;
Suffer men to gaze, poets to sing
How radiant you are, compare
And favor you to that most rare
Bird of delight: a lovely face
Matched with an equal inner grace.
Sweet bird, beware the Fowler, Pride;
His knots once neatly crossed and tied,
The prey is caged and walked about
With no way in and no way out.

---

[1]Sydonia Byrd was apparently from Indianapolis but attended school in Boston. Cullen dated her occasionally.

ULTIMATUM

I hold not with the fatalist creed
Of what must be must be;
There is enough to meet my need
In this most meagre me.

These two slim arms were made to rein
My steed, to ward and fend;
There is more gold in this small brain
Than I can ever spend.

The seed I plant is chosen well;
Ambushed by no sly sweven,
I plant it if it droops to hell,
Or if it blooms to heaven.

AT THE WAILING WALL IN JERUSALEM[1]

Of all the grandeur that was Solomon's
High testament of Israel's far pride,
Shedding its lustre like a sun of suns,
This feeble flicker only has not died.
This wall alone reminds a vanquished race,
This brief remembrance still retained in stone,
That sure foundations guard their given place
To rehabilitate the overthrown.

So in the battered temple of the heart,
That grief is harder on than time on stone,
Though three sides crumble, one will stand apart,
Where thought may mourn its past, remembrance groan,
And hands now bare that once were rich with rings
Rebuild upon the ancient site of things.

[1]Written as a result of a Middle Eastern trip taken with his father in 1926.

TO ENDYMION*[1]

Endymion, your star is steadfast now,
Beyond aspersion's power to glitter down;
There is no redder blossom on the bough
Of song, no richer jewel in her crown;
Long shall she stammer forth a broken note,
(Striving with how improvident a tongue)
Before the ardor of another throat
Transcends the jubilate you have sung.

High as the star of that last poignant cry
Death could not stifle in the wasted frame,
You know at length the bright immortal lie
Time gives to those detractors of your name,
And see, from where you and Diana[2] ride,
Your humble epitaph—how misapplied!

---

*Rome, August 1926, after a visit to the grave of Keats. [This footnote was part of original text.]

[1]"Endymion" is the title of John Keats's long 1817 poem of the quest of the shepherd-prince Endymion. There are echoes of "Endymion" in Cullen's "The Black Christ."

[2]Diana—the Roman goddess of the forests and of childbirth.

EPILOGUE

The lily, being white not red,
  Contemns the vivid flower,
And men alive believe the dead
  Have lost their vital power.

Yet some prefer the brilliant shade,
  And pass the livid by;
And no man knows if dead men fade
  Or bloom, save those that die.

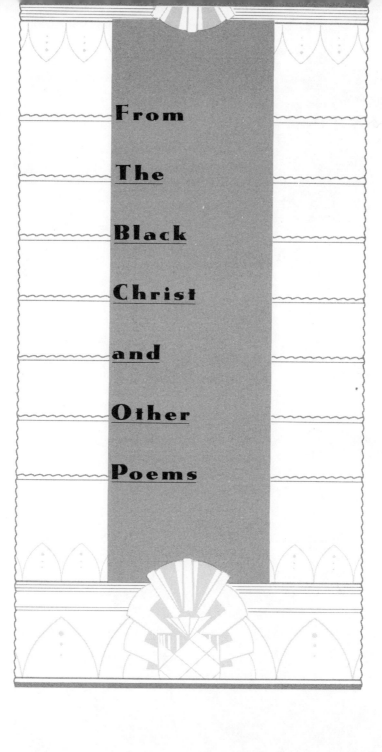

From

The

Black

Christ

and

Other

Poems

TO THE THREE FOR WHOM THE BOOK[1]

Once like a lady
In a silken dress,
The serpent might eddy
Through the wilderness,
Billow and glow
And undulate
In a rustling flow
Of sinuous hate.
Now dull-eyed and leaden,
Of having lost
His Eden
He pays the cost.
He shuns the tree
That brought him low
As grown to be
Domestic; no
Temptations dapple,
From leaf to root,
The modern apple
Our meekest fruit.
Dragon and griffin
And basilisk
Whose stare could stiffen,
And the hot breath whisk
From the overbold
Braving a gaze
So freezing cold,

---

[1]The three to whom Cullen dedicated *The Black Christ* are Roberta Bosley, Harold Jackman, and Edward Perry. See earlier notes, pp. 83, 104, and 169.

Who sings their praise
These latter days?
That venomous head
On a woman fair,—
Medusa's dead
Of the hissing hair.
No beasts are made
Meet for the whir
Of that sunken blade
Excalibur.[2]
No smithies forge
A shining sword
Fit for the gorge
Of a beast abhorred.
Pale Theseus
Would have no need,
Were he with us,
Of sword or thread;
For long has been set
The baleful star
Of Pasiphaë's pet,
The Minotaur.[3]
Though they are dead,
Those ancient ones,
Each bestial head

---

[2]In the Arthurian legend, the name of King Arthur's sword which, as a boy, he was able to extract from a stone in which it was fixed. Another story states that the sword was given to Arthur by the Lady of the Lake and that, when he was mortally wounded, Arthur ordered the sword thrown into the water. An arm rose to catch the sword, twirled it three times, and disappeared.

[3]The Minotaur was a mythical monster with the body of a man and the head of a bull, the offspring of Pasiphaë, the wife of Minos, the king of Crete, and a bull given to Minos by Poseidon. The Minotaur was locked in the Labyrinth by Minos and every year was fed seven young women and seven young men. Theseus offered himself as a victim one year and, with the help of Ariadne, succeeded in killing the beast and escaping the Labyrinth.

Dust under tons
Of dust, new beasts
Have come, their heirs,
Claiming their feasts
As the old did theirs.
Clawless they claw,
Fangless they rend;
And the stony maw
Crams on without end.
Still are arrayed
(But with brighter eyes)
Stripling and maid
For the sacrifice.
We cannot spare
This toll we pay
Of the slender, the fair,
The bright and the gay!
Gold and black crown,
Body slim and taut,
How they go down
'Neath the juggernaut!
Youth of the world,
Like scythèd wheat,
How they are hurled
At the clay god's feet!
Hear them cry Holy
To stone and to steel,
See them bend lowly,
Loyal and leal,
Blood rendered and bone,
To steel and to stone.
They have forgot
The stars and the sun,
The grassy plot,
And waters that run

From rock to rock;—
Their only care
Is to grasp a lock
Of Mammon's[4] hair.

But you three rare
Friends whom I love
(With rhymes to swear
The depths whereof)
A book to you three
Who have not bent
The idolatrous knee,
Nor worship lent
To modern rites,
Knowing full well
How a just god smites
The infidel;
Three to whom Pan[5]
Is no mere myth,
But a singing Man
To be reckoned with;—
Witness him now
In the mist and dew;
Lean and hear how
He carols to you:
"Gather as a flower
Living to your heart;
Let the full shower

---

[4]Mammon—the Aramaic (Jesus Christ's language) word for riches, found in the Greek version of Matthew 6:24 and Luke 16:9–13.

[5]Pan—god of the shepherds and flocks in Greek mythology. He was depicted as half man, half animal with a reed pipe, a shepherd's crook, and a branch of pine or a crown of pine leaves. He was also a deity of considerable sexual prowess who pursued both nymphs and boys with equal passion.

Rankle and smart;
Youth is the coffer
Where all is hid;
All age may offer
Youth can outbid.
Blind with your beauty
The ranks of scorn,
Take for a duty
Pleasure; you were born
Joy to incur.
Ere the eyes are misted
With a rheumy blur,
Ere the speech is twisted
To a throaty slur,
Ere the cheeks are haggard;
Ere the prick of the spur
Finds you lame or laggard,
Do not demur!
When Time advances
Terrible and lone,
Recall there were dances
Though they be flown.
When Death plys the riddle
To which all are mute,
Remember the fiddle,
The lyre and the flute."

To three who will heed
His song, nor brook
That a god should plead
In vain, a book.

TRIBUTE
(To My Mother)

Because man is not virtuous in himself,
Nor kind, nor given to sweet charities,
Save goaded by the little kindling elf
Of some dear face it pleasures him to please;
Some men who else were humbled to the dust,
Have marveled that the chastening hand should stay,
And never dreamed they held their lives in trust
To one the victor loved a world away.
So I, least noble of a churlish race,
Least kind of those by nature rough and crude,
Have at the intervention of your face
Spared him with whom was my most bitter feud
One moment, and the next, a deed more grand,
The helpless fly imprisoned in my hand.

THAT BRIGHT CHIMERIC BEAST
(For Lynn Riggs)[1]

That bright chimeric beast
Conceived yet never born,
Save in the poet's breast,
The white-flanked unicorn,
Never may be shaken
From his solitude;
Never may be taken
In any earthly wood.

That bird forever feathered,
Of its new self the sire,
After aeons weathered,
Reincarnate by fire,
Falcon may not nor eagle
Swerve from his eerie,
Nor any crumb inveigle
Down to an earthly tree.

That fish of the dread regime
Invented to become
The fable and the dream
Of the Lord's aquarium,
Leviathan, the jointed
Harpoon was never wrought
By which the Lord's anointed
Will suffer to be caught.

[1]Lynn Riggs was a performing artist who particularly impressed Cullen.

Bird of the deathless breast,
Fish of the frantic fin,
That bright chimeric beast
Flashing the argent skin,—
If beasts like these you'd harry,
Plumb then the poet's dream;
Make it your aviary,
Make it your wood and stream.
There only shall the swish
Be heard, of the regal fish;
There like a golden knife
Dart the feet of the unicorn,
And there, death brought to life,
The dead bird be reborn.

TO AN UNKNOWN POET

"Love is enough," I read somewhere;
Lines some poor poet in his pride
And poverty wrote on the air
To ease his heart, and soothe his bride.

Something in me, child of an age
Cold to the core, undeified,
Warmed to my brother bard, this sage;
And I too leaned upon my pride.

But pride I found can blind our eyes,
And poverty is worse than pride.
Love's breed from both is a nest of lies;
And singer of sweet songs, you lied.

LITTLE SONNET TO LITTLE FRIENDS

Let not the proud of heart condemn
Me that I mould my ways to hers,
Groping for healing in a hem
No wind of passion ever stirs;
Nor let them sweetly pity me
When I am out of sound and sight;
They waste their time and energy;
No mares encumber me at night.

Always a trifle fond and strange,
And some have said a bit bizarre,
Say, "Here's the sun," I would not change
It for my dead and burnt-out star.
Shine as it will, I have no doubt.
Some day the sun, too, may go out.

MOOD

I think an impulse stronger than my mind
May some day grasp a knife, unloose a vial,
Or with a little leaden ball unbind
The cords that tie me to the rank and file.
My hands grow quarrelsome with bitterness,
And darkly bent upon the final fray;
Night with its stars upon a grave seems less
Indecent than the too complacent day.

God knows I would be kind, let live, speak fair,
Requite an honest debt with more than just,
And love for Christ's dear sake these shapes that wear
A pride that had its genesis in dust,—
The meek are promised much in a book I know
But one grows weary turning cheek to blow.

COUNTER MOOD

Let this be scattered far and wide, laid low
Upon the waters as they fall and rise,
Be caught and carried by the winds that blow,
Nor let it be arrested by the skies:
I who am mortal say I shall not die;
I who am dust of this am positive,
That though my nights tend toward the grave, yet I
Shall on some brighter day arise, and live.

Ask me not how I am oracular,
Nor whence this arrogant assurance springs.
Ask rather Faith the canny conjurer,
(Who while your reason mocks him mystifies
Winning the grudging plaudits of your eyes)—
How suddenly the supine egg has wings.

MINUTELY HURT

Since I was minutely hurt,
Giant griefs and woes
Only find me staunchly girt
Against all other blows.

Once an atom cracks the heart
All is done and said;
Poison, steel, and fiery dart
May then be buffeted.

THE FOOLISH HEART

Be still, heart, cease those measured strokes;
Lie quiet in your hollow bed;
This moving frame is but a hoax
To make you think you are not dead."

Thus spake I to my body's slave,
With beats still to be answerèd;
Poor foolish heart that needs a grave
To prove to it that it is dead.

FOR HELEN KELLER[1]

Against our puny sound and sight
In vain the bells of Heaven ring,
The Mystic Blossoms red and white
May not intrigue our visioning.

For lest we handle, lest we touch,
Lest carnally our minds condone,
Our clumsy credence may not clutch
The under or the overtone.

Her finer alchemy converts
The clanging brass to golden-pealed,
And for her sight the black earth spurts
Hues never thought there unrevealed.

---

[1]Helen Keller (1880–1968) was a blind, deaf, and mute lecturer and writer whose childhood education was the subject of the famous play and film *The Miracle Worker*.

NOT SACCO AND VANZETTI[1]

These men who do not die, but send to death,
These iron men whom mercy cannot bend
Beyond the lettered law; what when their breath
Shall suddenly and naturally end?
What shall their final retribution be,
What bloody silver then shall pay the tolls
Exacted for this legal infamy
When death indicts their stark immortal souls?

The day a slumbering but awful God,
Before Time to Eternity is blown,
Examines with the same unyielding rod
These images of His with hearts of stone,
These men who do not die, but death decree,—
These are the men I should not care to be.

---

[1]Nicola Sacco and Bartolomeo Vanzetti were two Italian-born anarchists accused of robbery and murder. Their case became a *cause célèbre* among intellectuals and liberals in the 1920s. Despite doubts about their guilt and strenuous protests, they were executed in 1927.

SELF CRITICISM

Shall I go all my bright days singing,
(A little pallid, a trifle wan)
The failing note still vainly clinging
To the throat of the stricken swan?

Shall I never feel and meet the urge
To bugle out beyond my sense
That the fittest song of earth is a dirge,
And only fools trust Providence?

Than this better the reed never turned flute,
Better than this no song,
Better a stony silence, better a mute
Mouth and a cloven tongue.

A THORN FOREVER IN THE BREAST

A hungry cancer will not let him rest
Whose heart is loyal to the least of dreams;
There is a thorn forever in his breast
Who cannot take his world for what it seems;
Aloof and lonely must he ever walk,
Plying a strange and unaccustomed tongue,
An alien to the daily round of talk,
Mute when the sordid songs of earth are sung.

This is the certain end his dream achieves:
He sweats his blood and prayers while others sleep,
And shoulders his own coffin up a steep
Immortal mountain, there to meet his doom
Between two wretched dying men, of whom
One doubts, and one for pity's sake believes.

THE PROUD HEART

That lively organ, palpitant and red,
Enrubied in the staid and sober breast,
Telling the living man, "You are not dead
Until this hammered anvil takes its rest,"
My life's timepiece wound to alarm some day
The body to its need of box and shroud,
Was meant till then to beat one haughty way;
A crimson stroke should be no less than proud.

Yet this high citadel has come to grief,
Been broken as an arrow drops its bird,
Splintered as many ways as veins in a leaf
At a woman's laugh or a man's harsh word;
But being proud still strikes its hours in pain;
The dead man lives, and none perceives him slain.

THEREFORE, ADIEU

Now you are gone, and with your unreturning goes
All I had thought in spite of you would stay;
Now draws forever to its unawakening close
The beauty of the bright bandanna'd day.

Now sift in ombrous flakes and revolutions slow
My dreams descending from my heady sky.
The balm I kept to cool my grief in (leaves of snow)
Now melts, with your departure flowing by.

I knew, indeed, the straight unswerving track the sun
Took to your face (as other ecstasies)
Yet I had thought some faith to me in them; they run
From me to you as fly to honey, bees.

Avid, to leave me neither fevered joy nor ache,
Only of soul and body vast unrest.
Sun, moon, and stars should be enough; why must you take
The feeling of the heart out of the breast?

Now I who dreamed before I died to shoot one shaft
Of courage from a warped and crooked bow,
Stand utterly forsaken, stripped of that small craft
I had, watching with you all prowess go.

AT A PARTING

Let us not turn for this aside to die,
Crying a lover may not be a friend.
Our grief is vast enough without that lie;
All stories may not boast a happy end.
Love was a flower, sweet, and flowers fade;
Love was a fairy tale; these have their close.
The endless chronicle was never made,
Nor, save in dreams, the ever-scented rose.

Seeing them dim in passion's diadem,
Our rubies that were bright that now are dull,
Let them not fade without their requiem,
How they were red one time and beautiful,
And how the heart where once a ruby bled
May live, yet bear that mark till it is dead.

DICTUM

Yea, I have put thee from me utterly,
And they who plead thy cause do plead in vain;
Window and door are bolted, never key
From any ore shall cozen them again.
This is my regal justice: banishment,
That those who please me now may read and see
How self-sustained I am, with what content
I thrive alike on love or treachery.

God, Thou hast Christ, they say, at Thy right hand;
Close by Thy left Michael is straight and leal;
Around Thy throne the chanting elders stand,
And on the earth Thy feudal millions kneel.
Criest Thou never, Lord, above their song:
"But Lucifer was tall, his wings were long?"

BRIGHT BINDINGS

Your love to me was like an unread book,
Bright-backed, with smooth white pages yet unslit;
Fondly as a lover, foolishly, I took
It from its shelf one day and opened it.
Here shall I read, I thought, beauty and grace,
The soul's most high and awful poetry:—
Alas for lovers and the faith they place
In love, alas for you, alas for me.

I have but read a page or two at most,
The most my horror-blinded eyes may read.
I find here but a windy tapering ghost
Where I sought flesh gifted to ache and bleed.
Yet back you go, though counterfeit you be.
I love bright books even when they fail me.

BLACK MAJESTY

(After reading John W. Vandercook's chronicle of sable glory)[1]

These men were kings, albeit they were black,
Christophe and Dessalines and L'Ouverture;[2]
Their majesty has made me turn my back
Upon a plaint I once shaped to endure.
These men were black, I say, but they were crowned
And purple-clad, however brief their time.
Stifle your agony; let grief be drowned;
We know joy had a day once and a clime.

Dark gutter-snipe, black sprawler-in-the-mud,
A thing men did a man may do again.

---

[1] John W. Vandercook's *Black Majesty* was published in 1928. The figures which Cullen used to publish in *Opportunity* of the most widely requested books from the 135th Street Branch of the New York Public Library indicate that Vandercook's book was very popular with black readers.

[2] Henri Christophe (1767–1820) was born a slave in the British West Indies and became a lieutenant under Toussaint-L'Ouverture during the Haitian Revolution (1791–1804). He became king of northern Haiti in 1811. After his death, Haiti was reunited.

Jean-Jacques Dessalines (1758–1806) was the Emperor of Haiti who proclaimed the country's independence in 1804. A former slave who worked for a black master, Dessalines became a lieutenant under Toussaint during the Revolution. After Toussaint was deposed in 1802, Dessalines led a new revolt against the French when Napoleon made it clear that he was not going to honor his pledge to Toussaint not to reintroduce slavery in the island. Dessalines's reprisals against both the mulattoes and especially the whites on the island were particularly harsh.

François Dominique Toussaint-L'Ouverture (1743–1803) was leader of the Haitian revolution against France. Toussaint eventually became the governor of the island but was removed from power once Napoleon became emperor of France. Fearing that Toussaint would lead another revolt, Napoleon had him arrested and jailed in the French Alps where, under constant interrogation, Toussaint died.

What answer filters through your sluggish blood
To these dark ghosts who knew so bright a reign?
"Lo, I am dark, but comely," Sheba sings.
"And we were black," three shades reply, "but kings."

GHOSTS

Breast under breast when you shall lie
  With him who in my place
Bends over you with flashing eye
  And ever nearing face;

Hand fast in hand when you shall tread
  With him the springing ways
Of love from me inherited
  After my little phase;

Be not surprised if suddenly
  The couch or air confound
Your ravished ears upbraidingly,
  And silence turn to sound.

But never let it trouble you,
  Or cost you one caress;
Ghosts are soon sent with a word or two
  Back to their loneliness.

SONG IN SPITE OF MYSELF

Never love with all your heart,
  It only ends in aching;
And bit by bit to the smallest part
  That organ will be breaking.

Never love with all your mind,
  It only ends in fretting;
In musing on sweet joys behind,
  Too poignant for forgetting.

Never love with all your soul,
  For such there is no ending,
Though a mind that frets may find control,
  And a shattered heart find mending.

Give but a grain of the heart's rich seed,
  Confine some under cover,
And when love goes, bid him God-speed.
  And find another lover.

NOTHING ENDURES

Nothing endures,
Not even love,
Though the warm heart purrs
Of the length thereof.

Though beauty wax,
Yet shall it wane;
Time lays a tax
On the subtlest brain.

Let the blood riot,
Give it its will;
It shall grow quiet,
It shall grow still.

Nirvana[1] gapes
For all things given;
Nothing escapes,
Love not even.

---

[1] Nirvana (literally meaning in Sanskrit "extinction") is, in Buddhism, the final and supreme goal of the disciplines of meditation where the self and the ego are transcended and the individual consciousness and desire are extinguished.

THE STREET CALLED CROOKED

(Le Havre, August 1928)

"Bon soir, monsieur," they called to me;
  And, *"Venez voir nos femmes."*
"Bon soir, mesdames," they got from me,
  And, *"J'ai une meilleure dame."*

"To meet strange lips and foreign eyes
  I did not cross the foam,
I have a dearer, fairer prize
  Who waits for me at home."

"Her eyes are browner, lips more red
  Than any lady's light;
'Twould grieve her heart and droop her head
  If I failed her tonight."

"Bon soir, mesdames; que Dieu vous garde;
  And catch this coin I throw;
The ways of life are bleak and hard,
  Ladies, I think you know."

A bright and crooked street it gleamed
  With light and laughter filled;
All night the warm wine frothed and streamed
  While souls were stripped and killed.

TO CERTAIN CRITICS

Then call me traitor if you must,
Shout treason and default!
Say I betray a sacred trust
Aching beyond this vault.
I'll bear your censure as your praise,
For never shall the clan
Confine my singing to its ways
Beyond the ways of man.

No racial option narrows grief,
Pain is no patriot,
And sorrow plaits her dismal leaf
For all as lief as not.
With blind sheep groping every hill,
Searching an oriflamme,
How shall the shepherd heart then thrill
To only the darker lamb?

THE BLACK CHRIST[1]

(Hopefully dedicated to White America)

I

God's glory and my country's shame,
And how one man who cursed Christ's name
May never fully expiate
That crime till at the Blessed Gate
Of Heaven He meet and pardon me
Out of His love and charity;
How God, who needs no man's applause,
For love of my stark soul, of flaws
Composed, seeing it slip, did stoop
Down to the mire and pick me up,
And in the hollow of His hand
Enact again at my command
The world's supremest tragedy,
Until I die my burthen be;
How Calvary in Palestine,
Extending down to me and mine,
Was but the first leaf in a line
Of trees on which a Man should swing
World without end, in suffering
For all men's healing, let me sing.

---

[1]Similarities between "The Black Christ" and Herman Melville's *Billy Budd* have been noticed by readers of both works. *Billy Budd* was published in 1924 and, although there is no proof that Cullen read it, it is known that he had read other books by Melville and that Cullen was generally a very well-read poet. The themes of Christian resignation, revolution, and the necessity of order are apparent in both works. The speech of the principal characters is important as well: Billy Budd stutters, Jim in "The Black Christ" shifts his diction from youthful slang to a heroic poetic language. Interestingly, *Billy Budd* emerged from the poetry that Melville had been working on in his later years. Cullen's interest in Christianity, conversion, and race led him from poetry to his novel, *One Way to Heaven* (1932).

O world grown indolent and crass,
I stand upon your bleak morass
Of incredulity and cry
Your lack of faith is but a lie.
If you but brushed the scales apart
That cloud your eyes and clench your heart
There is no telling what grace might
Be leveled to your clearer sight;
Nor what stupendous choir break
Upon your soul till you should ache
(If you but let your fingers veer,
And raised to heaven a listening ear)
In utter pain in every limb
To know and sing as they that hymn.
If men would set their lips to prayer
With that delight with which they swear,
Heaven and earth as bow and string,
Would meet, would be attuned and sing.

We are diseased, trunk, branch, and shoot;
A sickness gathers at the root
Of us. We flaunt a gaudy fruit
But maggots wrangle at the core.
We cry for angels; yet wherefore,
Who raise no Jacobs any more? . . .
No men with eyes quick to perceive
The Shining Thing, clutch at its sleeve,
Against the strength of Heaven try
The valiant force of men who die;—
With heaving heart where courage sings
Strive with a mist of Light and Wings,
And wrestle all night long, though pressed
Be rib to rib and back to breast,
Till in the end the lofty guest
Pant, "Conquering human, be thou blest."

As once they stood white-plumed and still,
All unobserved on Dothan's hill,
Now, too, the angels, stride for stride,
Would march with us, but are denied.
Did we but let our credence sprout
As we do mockery and doubt,
Lord Christ Himself would stand revealed
In every barren, frosty field
That we misname the heart. Belief
In something more than pain and grief,
In only earth's most commonplace,
Might yet illumine every face
Of wretchedness, every blinded eye,
If from the hermitage where nigh
These thousand years the world of men
Has hemmed her in, might come again
With gracious eyes and gentle breath
The still unconquered Lady, Faith.

Two brothers have I had on earth,
One of spirit, one of sod;
My mother suckled one at birth,
One was the Son of God.

Since that befell which came to me,
Since I was singled out to be,
Upon a wheel of mockery,
The pattern of a new faith spun;
I never doubt that once the sun
For respite stopped in Gibeon,
Or that a Man I could not know
Two thousand ageless years ago,
To shape my profit by His loss,
Bought my redemption on a cross.

2

"Now spring that heals the wounds of earth
Is being born; and in her birth
The wounds of men may find a cure.
By such a thought I may endure,
And of some things be no less sure.
This is a cruel land, this South,
And bitter words to twist my mouth,
Burning my tongue down to its root,
Were easily found; but I am mute
Before the wonder of this thing:
That God should send so pure a spring,
Such grass to grow, such birds to sing,
And such small trees bravely to sprout
With timid leaves first coming out.
A land spring yearly levies on
Is gifted with God's benison.
The very odor of the loam
Fetters me here to this, my home.
The whitest lady in the town
Yonder trailing a silken gown
Is less kin to this dirt than I.
Rich mistresses with proud heads high
This dirt and I are one to them;
They flick us both from the bordered hem
Of lovely garments we supply;
But I and the dirt see just as high
As any lady cantering by.
Why should I cut this bond, my son,
This tie too taut to be undone?
This ground and I are we not one?
Has it not birthed and grown and fed me:
Yea, if you will, and also bled me?
That little patch of wizened corn

Aching and straining to be born,
May render back at some small rate
The blood and bone of me it ate.
The weevil there that rends apart
My cotton also tears my heart.
Here too, your father, lean and black,
Paid court to me with all the knack
Of any dandy in the town,
And here were born, and here have grown,
His sons and mine, as lean and black.
What ghosts there are in this old shack
Of births and deaths, soft times and hard!
I count it little being barred
From those who undervalue me.
I have my own soul's ecstasy.
Men may not bind the summer sea,
Nor set a limit to the stars;
The sun seeps through all iron bars;
The moon is ever manifest.
These things my heart always possessed.
And more than this (and here's the crown)
No man, my son, can batter down
The star-flung ramparts of the mind.
So much for flesh; I am resigned,
Whom God has made shall He not guide?"

So spake my mother, and her pride
For one small minute in its tide
Bore all my bitterness away.
I saw the thin bent form, the gray
Hair shadowed in the candlelight,
The eyes fast parting with their sight,
The rough, brown fingers, lean with toil,
Marking her kinship to the soil.
Year crowding year, after the death

Of that one man whose last drawn breath
Had been the gasping of her name,
She had wrought on, lit with some flame
Her children sensed, but could not see,
And with a patient wizardry
Wheedled her stubborn bit of land
To yield beneath her coaxing hand,
And sometimes in a lavish hour,
To blossom even with a flower.
Time after time her eyes grew dim
Watching a life pay for the whim
Some master of the land must feed
To keep her people down. The seed
They planted in her children's breasts
Of hatred toward these men like beasts
She weeded out with legends how
Once there had been somewhere as now
A people harried, low in the dust;
But such had been their utter trust
In Heaven and its field of stars
That they had broken down their bars,
And walked across a parted sea
Praising His name who set them free.
I think more than the tales she told,
The music in her voice, the gold
And mellow notes she wrought,
Made us forbear to voice the thought
Low-buried underneath our love,
That we saw things she knew not of.
We had no scales upon our eyes;
God, if He was, kept to His skies,
And left us to our enemies.
Often at night fresh from our knees
And sorely doubted litanies
We grappled for the mysteries:

"We never seem to reach nowhere,"
Jim with a puzzled, questioning air,
Would kick the covers back and stare
For me the elder to explain.
As like as not, my sole refrain
Would be, "A man was lynched last night."
"Why?" Jim would ask, his eyes star-bright.
"A white man struck him; he showed fight.
Maybe God thinks such things are right."
"Maybe God never thinks at all—
Of us," and Jim would clench his small,
Hard fingers tight into a ball.

"Likely there ain't no God at all,"
Jim was the first to clothe a doubt
With words, that long had tried to sprout
Against our wills and love of one
Whose faith was like a blazing sun
Set in a dark, rebellious sky.
Now then the roots were fast, and I
Must nurture them in her despite.
God could not be, if He deemed right,
The grief that ever met our sight.

Jim grew; a brooder, silent, sheathed;
But pride was in the air he breathed;
Inside you knew an Aetna seethed.
Often when some new holocaust
Had come to undermine and blast
The life of some poor wretch we knew,
His bones would show like white scars through
His fists in anger's futile way.
"I have a fear," he used to say,
"This thing may come to me some day.
Some man contemptuous of my race
And its lost rights in this hard place,

Will strike me down for being black.
But when I answer I'll pay back
The late revenge long overdue
A thousand of my kind and hue.
A thousand black men, long since gone
Will guide my hand, stiffen the brawn,
And speed one life-divesting blow
Into some granite face of snow.
And I may swing, but not before
I send some pale ambassador
Hot footing it to hell to say
A proud black man is on his way."

When such hot venom curled his lips
And anger snapped like sudden whips
Of lightning in his eyes, her words,—
Slow, gentle as the fall of birds
That having strained to win aloft
Spread out their wings and slowly waft
Regretfully back to the earth,—
Would challenge him to name the worth
Contained in any seed of hate.
Ever the same soft words would mate
Upon her lips: love, trust, and wait.
But he, young, quick, and passionate,
Could not so readily conceal,
Deeper than acid-burns, or steel
Inflicted wounds, his vital hurt;
So still the bitter phrase would spurt:
"The things I've seen, the things I see,
Show what my neighbor thinks of me.
The world is large enough for two
Men any time, of any hue.
I give pale men a wide berth ever;
Best not to meet them, for I never

Could bend my spirit, never truckle
To them; my blood's too hot to knuckle."
And true; the neighbors spoke of him
As that proud nigger, handsome Jim.
It was a grudging compliment,
Half paid in jest, half fair intent,
By those whose partial, jaundiced eye
Saw each of us as one more fly,
Or one more bug the summer brings,
All shaped alike; antennae, wings,
And noxious all; if caught, to die.
But Jim was not just one more fly,
For he was handsome in a way
Night is after a long, hot day.
If blood flows on from heart to heart,
And strong men leave their counterpart
In vice and virtue in their seed,
Jim's bearing spoke his imperial breed.
I was an offshoot, crude, inclined
More to the earth; he was the kind
Whose every graceful movement said,
As blood must say, by turn of head,
By twist of wrist, and glance of eye,
"Good blood flows here, and it runs high."
He had an ease of limb, a raw,
Clean, hilly stride that women saw
With quickened throbbings of the breast.
There was a show of wings; the nest
Was too confined; Jim needed space
To loop and dip and interlace;
For he had passed the stripling stage,
And stood a man, ripe for the wage
A man extorts of life; his gage
Was down. The beauty of the year
Was on him now, and somewhere near

By in the woods, as like as not,
His cares were laid away, forgot
In hearty wonderment and praise
Of one of spring's all perfect days.

But in my heart a shadow walked
At beauty's side; a terror stalked
For prey this loveliness of time.
A curse lay on this land and clime.
For all my mother's love of it,
Prosperity could not be writ
In any book of destiny
For this most red epitome
Of man's consistent cruelty
To man. Corruption, blight, and rust
Were its reward, and canker must
Set in. There were too many ghosts
Upon its lanes, too many hosts
Of dangling bodies in the wind,
Too many voices, choked and thinned,
Beseeching mercy on its air.
And like the sea set in my ear
Ever there surged the steady fear
Lest this same end and brutal fate
March toward my proud, importunate
Young brother. Often he'd say,
" 'Twere best, I think, we moved away."
But custom and an unseen hand
Compelled allegiance to this land
In her, and she by staying nailed
Us there, by love securely jailed.

But love and fear must end their bout,
And one or both be counted out.
Rebellion barked now like a gun;
Like a split dam, this faith in one

Who in my sight had never done
One extraordinary thing
That I should praise his name, or sing
His bounty and his grace, let loose
The pent-up torrent of abuse
That clamored in me for release:
"Nay, I have done with deities
Who keep me ever on my knees,
My mouth forever in a tune
Of praise, yet never grant the boon
Of what I pray for night and day.
God is a toy; put Him away.
Or make you one of wood or stone
That you can call your very own,
A thing to feel and touch and stroke,
Who does not break you with a yoke
Of iron that he whispers soft;
Nor promise you fine things aloft
While back and belly here go bare,
While His own image walks so spare
And finds this life so hard to live
You doubt that He has aught to give.
Better an idol shaped of clay
Near you, than one so far away.
Although it may not heed your labors,
At least it will not mind your neighbors'.
'In His own time, He will unfold
You milk and honey, streets of gold,
High walls of jasper . . .' phrases rolled
Upon the tongues of idiots.
What profit *then*, if hunger gluts
Us *now?* Better my God should be
This moving, breathing frame of me,
Strong hands and feet, live heart and eyes;
And when these cease, say then God dies.

Your God is somewhere worlds away
Hunting a star He shot astray;
Oh, He has weightier things to do
Than lavish time on me and you.
What thought has He of us, three motes
Of breath, three scattered notes
In His grand symphony, the world?
Once we were blown, once we were hurled
In place, we were as soon forgot.
He might not linger on one dot
When there were bars and staves to fling
About, for waiting stars to sing.
When Rome was a suckling, when Greece was young,
Then there were Gods fit to be sung,
Who paid the loyal devotee
For service rendered zealously,
In coin a man might feel and spend,
Not marked 'Deferred to Journey's End.'
The servant then was worth his hire;
He went unscathed through flood and fire;
Gods were a thing then to admire.
'Bow down and worship us,' they said.
'You shall be clothed, be housed and fed,
While yet you live, not when you're dead.
Strong are our arms where yours are weak.
On them that harm you will we wreak
The vengeance of a God though they
Were Gods like us in every way.
Not merely is an honor laid
On those we touch with our accolade;
We strike for you with that same blade!' "
My mother shook a weary head—
"Visions are not for all," she said,
"There were no risings from the dead,
No frightened quiverings of earth

To mark my spirit's latter birth.
The light that on Damascus' road[2]
Blinded a scoffer never glowed
For me. I had no need to view
His side, or pass my fingers through
Christ's wounds.[3] It breaks like that on some,
And yet it can as surely come
Without the lightning and the rain.
Some who must have their hurricane
Go stumbling through it for a light
They never find. Only the night
Of doubt is opened to their sight.
They weigh and measure, search, define,—
But he who seeks a thing divine
Must humbly lay his lore aside,
And like a child believe;[4] confide
In Him whose ways are deep and dark,
And in the end perhaps the spark
He sought will be revealed. Perchance
Some things are hard to countenance,
And others difficult to probe;
But shall the mind that grew this globe,
And out of chaos thought a world,
To us be totally unfurled?
And all we fail to comprehend,
Shall such a mind be asked to bend
Down to, unravel, and untwine?
If those who highest hold His sign,
Who praise Him most with loudest tongue
Are granted no high place among

---

[2]A reference to the conversion of the Apostle Paul. See Acts 9:1–31.

[3]A reference to Doubting Thomas. See John 20:24–29.

[4]A reference to Jesus' imperative to his disciples. See Matthew 18:1–6.

The crowd, shall we be bitter then?
The puzzle shall grow simple when
The soul discards the ways of dust.
There is no gain in doubt; but trust
Is our one magic wand. Through it
We and eternity are knit,
Death made a myth, and darkness lit.
The slave can meet the monarch's gaze
With equal pride, dreaming to days
When slave and monarch both shall be,
Transmuted everlastingly,
A single reed blown on to sing
The glory of the only King."

We had not, in the stealthy gloom
Of deepening night, that shot our room
With queerly capering shadows through,
Noticed the form that wavered to
And fro on weak, unsteady feet
Within the door; I turned to greet
Spring's gayest cavalier, but Jim
Who stood there balanced in the dim
Half-light waved me away from him.
And then I saw how terror streaked
His eyes, and how a red flow leaked
And slid from cheek to chin. His hand
Still grasped a knotted branch, and spanned
It fiercely, fondling it. At last
He moved into the light, and cast
His eyes about, as if to wrap
In one soft glance, before the trap
Was sprung, all he saw mirrored there:
All love and bounty; grace; all fair,
All discontented days; sweet weather;
Rain-slant, snow-fall; all things together

Which any man about to die
Might ask to have filmed on his eye,
And then he bowed his haughty head,
"The thing we feared has come," he said;
"But put your ear down to the ground,
And you may hear the deadly sound
Of two-limbed dogs that bay for me.
If any ask in time to be
Why I was parted from my breath,
Here is your tale: I went to death
Because a man murdered the spring.
Tell them though they dispute this thing,
This is the song that dead men sing:
One spark of spirit God head gave
To all alike, to sire and slave,
From earth's red core to each white pole,
This one identity of soul;
That when the pipes of beauty play,
The feet must dance, the limbs must sway,
And even the heart with grief turned lead,
Beauty shall lift like a leaf wind-sped,
Shall swoop upon in gentle might,
Shall toss and tease and leave so light
That never again shall grief or care
Find long or willing lodgement there.
Tell them each law and rule they make
Mankind shall disregard and break
(If this must be) for beauty's sake.
Tell them what pranks the spring can play;
The young colt leaps, the cat that lay
In a sullen ball all winter long
Breaks like a kettle into song;
Waving it high like a limber flail,
The kitten worries his own brief tail;
While man and dog sniff the wind alike,

For the new smell hurts them like a spike
Of steel thrust quickly through the breast;
Earth heaves and groans with a sharp unrest.
The poet, though he sang of death,
Finds tunes for music in simple breath;
Even the old, the sleepy-eyed,
Are stirred to movement by the tide.
But oh, the young, the aging young,
Spring is a sweetmeat to our tongue;
Spring is the pean; we the choir;
Spring is the fuel; we the fire.
Tell them spring's feathery weight will jar,
Though it were iron, any bar
Upreared by men to keep apart
Two who when probed down to the heart
Speak each a common tongue. Tell them
Two met, each stooping to the hem
Of beauty passing by. Such awe
Grew on them hate began to thaw
And fear and dread to melt and run
Like ice laid siege to by the sun.
Say for a moment's misty space
These had forgotten hue and race;
Spring blew too loud and green a blast
For them to think on rank and caste.
The homage they both understood,
(Taught on a bloody Christless rood)
Due from his dark to her brighter blood,
In such an hour, at such a time,
When all their world was one clear rhyme,
He could not give, nor she exact.
This only was a glowing fact:
Spring in a green and golden gown,
And feathered feet, had come to town;
Spring in a rich habiliment

That shook the breath and woke the spent
And sleepy pulse to a dervish beat,
Spring had the world again at her feet.
Spring was a lady fair and rich,
And they were fired with the season's itch
To hold her train or stroke her hair
And tell her shyly they found her fair.
Spring was a voice so high and clear
It broke their hearts as they leaned to hear
In stream and grass and soft bird's-wing;
Spring was in them and they were spring.
Then say, a smudge across the day,
A bit of crass and filthy clay,
A blot of ink upon a white
Page in a book of gold; a tight
Curled worm hid in the festive rose,
A mind so foul it hurt your nose,
Came one of earth's serene elect,
His righteous being warped and flecked
With what his thoughts were: stench and smut. . . .
I had gone on unheeding but
He struck me down, he called her slut,
And black man's mistress, bawdy whore,
And such like names, and many more,—
(Christ, what has spring to answer for!)
I had gone on, I had been wise,
Knowing my value in those eyes
That seared me through and out and in,
Finding a thing to taunt and grin
At in my hair and hue. My right
I knew could not outweigh his might
Who had the law for satellite—
Only I turned to look at her,
The early spring's first worshiper,
(Spring, what have you to answer for?)

The blood had fled from either cheek
And from her lips; she could not speak,
But she could only stand and stare
And let her pain stab through the air.
I think a blow to heart or head
Had hurt her less than what he said.
A blow can be so quick and kind,
But words will feast upon the mind
And gnaw the heart down to a shred,
And leave you living, yet leave you dead.
If he had only tortured me,
I could have borne it valiantly.
The things he said in littleness
Were cheap, the blow he dealt me less,
Only they totalled more; he gagged
And bound a spirit there; he dragged
A sunlit gown of gold and green,—
(The season's first, first to be seen)
And feathered feet, and a plumèd hat,—
(First of the year to be wondered at)
Through muck and mire, and by the hair
He caught a lady rich and fair.
His vile and puny fingers churned
Our world about that sang and burned
A while as never world before.
He had unlatched an icy door,
And let the winter in once more.
To kill a man is a woeful thing,
But he who lays a hand on spring,
Clutches the first bird by its throat
And throttles it in the midst of a note;
Whose breath upon the leaf-proud tree
Turns all that wealth to penury;
Whose touch upon the first shy flower
Gives it a blight before its hour;

Whose craven face above a pool
That otherwise were clear and cool,
Transforms that running silver dream
Into a hot and sluggish stream
Thus better fit to countenance
His own corrupt unhealthy glance,
Of all men is most infamous;
His deed is rank and blasphemous.
The erstwhile warm, the short time sweet,
Spring now lay frozen at our feet.
Say then, why say nothing more
Except I had to close the door;
And this man's leer loomed in the way.
The air began to sting; then say
There was this branch; I struck; he fell;
There's holiday, I think, in hell."

Outside the night began to groan
As heavy feet crushed twig and stone
Beating a pathway to our door;
A thin noise first, and then a roar
More animal than human grew
Upon the air until we knew
No mercy could be in the sound.
"Quick, hide," I said. I glanced around;
But no abyss gaped in the ground.
But in the eyes of fear a twig
Will seem a tree, a straw as big
To him who drowns as any raft.
So being mad, being quite daft,
I shoved him in a closet set
Against the wall. This would but let
Him breathe two minutes more, or three,
Before they dragged him out to be
Queer fruit upon some outraged tree.

Our room was in a moment lit
With flaring brands; men crowded it—
Old men whose eyes were better sealed
In sleep; strong men with muscles steeled
Like rods, whose place was in the field;
Striplings like Jim with just a touch
Of down upon the chin; for such
More fitting a secluded hedge
To lie beneath with one to pledge
In youth's hot words, immortal love.
These things they were not thinking of;
"Lynch him! Lynch him!" O savage cry,
Why should you echo, "Crucify!"
One sought, sleek-tongued, to pacify
Them with slow talk of trial, law,
Established court; the dripping maw
Would not be wheedled from its prey.
Out of the past I heard him say,
"So be it then; have then your way;
But not by me shall blood be spilt;
I wash my hands clean of this guilt."
This was an echo of a phrase
Uttered how many million days
Gone by?[5]

    Water may cleanse the hands
But what shall scour the soul that stands
Accused in heaven's sight?

                  "The Kid."
One cried, "Where is the bastard hid?"
"He is not here."

      It was a faint

---

[5] A reference to Pontius Pilate, the Roman governor who tried and condemned Jesus Christ.
See Matthew 27:24.

And futile lie.

       "The hell he ain't;
We tracked him here. Show us the place,
Or else . . ."

         He made an ugly face,
Raising a heavy club to smite.
I had been felled, had not the sight
Of all been otherwise arraigned.
Each with bewilderment unfeigned
Stared hard to see against the wall
The hunted boy stand slim and tall;
Dream-born, it seemed, with just a trace
Of weariness upon his face,
He stood as if evolved from air;
As if always he had stood there. . . .
What blew the torches' feeble flare
To such a soaring fury now?
Each hand went up to fend each brow,
Save his; he and the light were one,
A man by night clad with the sun.
By form and feature, bearing, name,
I knew this man. He was the same
Whom I had thrust, a minute past,
Behind a door,—and made it fast.
Knit flesh and bone, had like a thong,
Bound us as one our whole life long,
But in the presence of this throng,
He seemed one I had never known.
Never such tragic beauty shone
As this on any face before.
It pared the heart straight to the core.
It is the lustre dying lends,
I thought, to make some brief amends
To life so wantonly cut down.
The air about him shaped a crown

Of light, or so it seemed to me,
And sweeter than the melody
Of leaves in rain, and far more sad,
His voice descended on the mad,
Blood-sniffing crowd that sought his life,
A voice where grief cut like a knife:
"I am he whom you seek, he whom
You will not spare his daily doom.
My march is ever to the tomb,
But let the innocent go free;
This man and woman, let them be,
Who loving much have succored me."
And then he turned about to speak
To me whose heart was fit to break,
"My brother, when this wound has healed,
And you reap in some other field
Roses, and all a spring can yield;
Brother (to call me so!) then prove
Out of your charity and love
That I was not unduly slain,
That this my death was not in vain.
For no life should go to the tomb
Unless from it a new life bloom,
A greater faith, a clearer sight,
A wiser groping for the light."
He moved to where our mother stood,
Dry-eyed, though grief was at its flood,
"Mother, not poorer losing one,
Look now upon your dying son."
Her own life trembling on the brim,
She raised woe-ravaged eyes to him,
And in their glances something grew
And spread, till healing fluttered through
Her pain, a vision so complete
It sent her humbly to his feet

With what I deemed a curious cry,
"And must this be for such as I?"
Even his captors seemed to feel
Disquietude, an unrest steal
Upon their ardor, dampening it,
Till one less fearful varlet hit
Him across the mouth a heavy blow,
Drawing a thin, yet steady flow
Of red to drip a dirge of slow
Finality upon my heart.
The end came fast. Given the start
One hound must always give the pack
That fears the meekest prey whose back
Is desperate against a wall,
They charged. I saw him stagger, fall
Beneath a mill of hands, feet, staves.
And I like one who sees huge waves
In hunger rise above the skiff
At sea, yet watching from a cliff
Far off can lend no feeblest aid,
No more than can a fragile blade
Of grass in some far distant land,
That has no heart to wrench, nor hand
To stretch in vain, could only stand
With streaming eyes and watch the play.
There grew a tree a little way
Off from the hut, a virgin tree
Awaiting its fecundity.
O Tree was ever worthier Groom
Led to a bride of such rare bloom?
Did ever fiercer hands enlace
Love and Beloved in an embrace
As heaven-smiled-upon as this?
Was ever more celestial kiss?
But once, did ever anywhere

So full a choir chant such an air
As feathered splendors bugled there?
And was there ever blinder eye
Or deafer ear than mine?
                                    A cry
So soft, and yet so brimming filled
With agony, my heart strings thrilled
An ineffectual reply,—
Then gaunt against the southern sky
The silent handiwork of hate.
Greet, Virgin Tree, your holy mate!

No sound then in the little room
Was filtered through my sieve of gloom,
Except the steady fall of tears,
The hot, insistent rain that sears
The burning ruts down which it goes,
The futile flow, for all one knows
How vain it is, that ever flows.
I could not bear to look at *her*
There in the dark; I could not stir
From where I sat, so weighted down.
The king of grief, I held my crown
So dear, I wore my tattered gown
With such affection and such love
That though I strove I could not move.
But I could hear (and this unchained
The raging beast in me) her pained
And sorrow-riven voice ring out
Above the spirit's awful rout,
Above the howling winds of doubt,
How she knew Whom she traveled to
Was judge of all that men might do
To such as she who trusted Him.
Faith was a tower for her, grim

And insurmountable; and death
She said was only changing breath
Into an essence fine and rare.
Anger smote me and most despair
Seeing her still bow down in prayer.
"Call on Him now," I mocked, "and try
Your faith against His deed, while I
With intent equally as sane,
Searching a motive for this pain,
Will hold a little stone on high
And seek of it the reason why.
Which, stone or God, will first reply?
Why? Hear me ask it. He was young
And beautiful. Why was he flung
Like common dirt to death? Why, stone,
Must he of all the earth atone
For what? The dirt God used was homely
But the man He made was comely.
What child creating out of sand,
With puckered brow and intent hand,
Would see the lovely thing he planned
Struck with a lewd and wanton blade,
Nor stretch a hand to what he made,
Nor shed a childish, futile tear,
Because he loved it, held it dear?
Would not a child's weak heart rebel?
But Christ who conquered Death and Hell
What has He done for you who spent
A bleeding life for His content?
Or is the white Christ, too, distraught
By these dark skins His Father wrought?"

I mocked her so until I broke
Beneath my passion's heavy yoke.
My world went black with grief and pain;

My very bitterness was slain,
And I had need of only sleep,
Or some dim place where I might weep
My life away, some misty haunt
Where never man might come to taunt
Me with the thought of how men scar
Their brothers here, or what we are
Upon this most accursèd star.
Not that sweet sleep from which some wake
All fetterless, without an ache
Of heart or limb, but such a sleep
As had raped him, eternal, deep;—
Deep as my woe, vast as my pain,
Sleep of the young and early-slain.
My Lycidas[6] was dead. There swung
In all his glory, lusty, young,
My Jonathan,[7] my Patrocles,[8]
(For with his death there perished these)
And I had neither sword nor song,
Only an acid-bitten tongue,
Fit neither in its poverty
For vengeance nor for threnody,
Only for tears and blasphemy.

---

[6]*Lycidas* was a pastoral elegy written by John Milton early in his career (1630s). It is a lament for a fellow Cambridge student, Edward King, who had drowned and who, in the poem, comes to symbolize all lost hope.

[7]In the books of I and II Samuel in the Old Testament, Jonathan appears as the loyal and steadfast friend of David and is one of the most admired figures in the Bible. He is killed in a battle against the Philistines at Mt. Gilboa.

[8]Patroclus or Patrocles, in Greek mythology, was the friend and companion of Achilles in the Trojan War. He borrowed Achilles' armor and led the Greeks into battle but was killed by the great Trojan warrior Hector.

Now God be praised that a door should creak,
And that a rusty hinge should shriek.
Of all sweet sounds that I may hear
Of lute or lyre or dulcimer,
None ever shall assail my ear
Sweet as the sound of a grating door
I had thought closed forevermore.
Out of my deep-ploughed agony,
I turned to see a door swing free;
The very door he once came through
To death, now framed for us anew
His vital self, his and no other's
Live body of the dead, my brother's.
Like one who dreams within a dream,
Hand at my throat, lest I should scream,
I moved with hopeful, doubting pace
To meet the dead man face to face.

"Bear witness now unto His grace";
I heard my mother's mounting word,
"Behold the glory of the Lord,
His unimpeachable high seal.
Cry mercy now before Him; kneel,
And let your heart's conversion swell
The wonder of His miracle."

I saw; I touched; yet doubted him;
My fingers faltered down his slim
Sides, down his breathing length of limb.
Incredulous of sight and touch,
"No more," I cried, "this is too much
For one mad brain to stagger through."
For there he stood in utmost view
Whose death I had been witness to;
But now he breathed; he lived; he walked;
His tongue could speak my name; he talked.

He questioned me to know what art
Had made his enemies depart.
Either I leaped or crawled to where
I last had seen stiff on the air
The form than life more dear to me;
But where had swayed that misery
Now only was a flowering tree
That soon would travail into fruit.
Slowly my mind released its mute
Bewilderment, while truth took root
In me and blossomed into light:
"Down, down," I cried, in joy and fright,
As all He said came back to me
With what its true import must be,
"Upon our knees and let the worst,
Let me the sinfullest kneel first;
O lovely Head to dust brought low
More times than we can ever know
Whose small regard, dust-ridden eye,
Behold Your doom, yet doubt You die;
O Form immaculately born,
Betrayed a thousand times each morn,
As many times each night denied,
Surrendered, tortured, crucified!
Now have we seen beyond degree
That love which has no boundary;
Our eyes have looked on Calvary."

No sound then in the sacred gloom
That blessed the shrine that was our room
Except the steady rise of praise
To Him who shapes all nights and days
Into one final burst of sun;
Though with the praise some tears must run

In pity of the King's dear breath
That ransomed one of us from death.

The days are mellow for us now;
We reap full fields; the heavy bough
Bends to us in another land;
The ripe fruit falls into our hand.
My mother, Job's dark sister,[9] sits
Now in a corner, prays, and knits.
Often across her face there flits
Remembered pain, to mar her joy,
At Whose death gave her back her boy.
While I who mouthed my blasphemies,
Recalling now His agonies,
Am found forever on my knees,
Ever to praise her Christ with her,
Knowing He can at will confer
Magic on miracle to prove
And try me when I doubt His love.
If I am blind He does not see;
If I am lame He halts with me;
There is no hood of pain I wear
That has not rested on His hair
Making Him first initiate
Beneath its harsh and hairy weight.
He grew with me within the womb;
He will receive me at the tomb.
He will make plain the misty path
He makes me tread in love and wrath,
And bending down in peace and grace

---

[9]Job is the Old Testatment figure in the biblical book of the same name who was forced, inexplicably, to suffer at the hands of God. As the book of Job deals with theodicy or the meaning of suffering and evil in the world, Cullen's reference illuminates one of the major concerns of the poem.

May wear again my brother's face.
Somewhere the Southland rears a tree,
(And many others there may be
Like unto it, that are unknown,
Whereon as costly fruit has grown).
It stands before a hut of wood
In which the Christ Himself once stood—
And those who pass it by may see
Nought growing there except a tree,
But there are two to testify
Who hung on it . . . we saw Him die.
Its roots were fed with priceless blood.
It is the Cross; it is the Rood.

Paris, January 31, 1929.

From The Medea and Some Poems

AFTER A VISIT

(At Padraic Colum's where there were Irish poets)[1]

Last night I lay upon my bed and would have slept;
But all around my head was wet with tears I wept,
As bitter dreams swarmed in like bees to sting my brain,
While others kissed like endless snakes forged in a chain,
Dull-eyed Euminedes[2] estranging me and sleep,
Each soft insidious caress biting me deep.
And I wept not what I had done but what let go,
Between two seasons, one of fire and one of snow.
I had known joy and sorrow I had surely known,
But out of neither any piercing note was blown.
Friends had been kind and surely friends had faithless been,
But long ago my heart was closed, panelled within.
And I had walked two seasons through, and moved among
Strange ways and folk, and all the while no line was wrung
In praise or blame of aught from my frost-bitten tongue.
Silence had sunned me with her hot, embalming mouth,
And indolence had watered me with drops of drouth.
Then I walked in a room where Irish poets were;
I saw the muse enthroned, heard how they worshiped her,
Felt men nor gods could ever so envenom them
That Poetry could pass and they not grasp her hem,
Not cry on her for healing; shaken off, still praise,

---

[1]Padraic Colum (1881–1972) was an Irish poet, playwright, biographer, novelist, short story writer, folklorist, and writer of children's literature. He was one of the leading figures of the Irish Renaissance. He was instrumental in shaping Irish theater. He lived for considerable periods of time in the United States.

[2]Eumenides (The Kindly Ones) were goddesses who ensured the fertility of the earth and were worshipped in various Greek cities. The spelling "Euminedes" (sic) is per the original text.

Not questioning her enigmatical delays.
And shame of my apostasy was like a coal
That reached my tongue and heart and far off frigid soul.
Melting myself into myself, making me weep
Regeneration's burning tears, preluding sleep.

MAGNETS

The straight, the swift, the debonair,
Are targets on the thoroughfare
For every kind appraising eye;
Sweet words are said as they pass by.
But such a strange contrary thing
My heart is, it will never cling
To any bright unblemished thing.
Such have their own security,
And little need to lean on me.
The limb that falters in its course,
And cries, "Not yet!" to waning force;
The orb that may not brave the sun;
The bitter mouth, its kissing done;
The loving heart that must deny
The very love it travels by;
What most has need to bend and pray,
These magnets draw my heart their way.

ANY HUMAN TO ANOTHER

The ills I sorrow at
Not me alone
Like an arrow,
Pierce to the marrow,
Through the fat
And past the bone.

Your grief and mine
Must intertwine
Like sea and river,
Be fused and mingle,
Diverse yet single,
Forever and forever.

Let no man be so proud
And confident,
To think he is allowed
A little tent
Pitched in a meadow
Of sun and shadow
All his little own.

Joy may be shy, unique,
Friendly to a few,
Sorrow never scorned to speak
To any who
Were false or true.
Your every grief
Like a blade
Shining and unsheathed

Must strike me down.
Of bitter aloes wreathed,
My sorrow must be laid
On your head like a crown.

ONLY THE POLISHED SKELETON

The heart has need of some deceit
  To make its pistons rise and fall;
For less than this it would not beat.
  Nor flush the sluggish vein at all.

With subterfuge and fraud the mind
  Must fend and parry thrust for thrust,
With logic brutal and unkind
  Beat off the onslaughts of the dust.

Only the polished skeleton,
  Of flesh relieved and pauperized,
Can rest at ease and think upon
  The worth of all it so despised.

TO FRANCE

Though I am not the first in English terms
To name you of the earth's great nations Queen;
Though better poets chant it to the worms
How that fair city perched upon the Seine
Is lovelier than that they traveled to;
While kings and warriors and many a priest
In their last hour have smiled to think of you,
Among these count me not the last nor least.

As he whose eyes are gouged craves light to see,
And he whose limbs are broken strength to run,
So have I sought in you that alchemy
That knits my bones and turns me to the sun;
And found across a continent of foam
What was denied my hungry heart at home.

MEDUSA[1]

I mind me how when first I looked at her
A warning shudder in the blood cried, "Ware!
Those eyes are basilisk's she gazes through,
And those are snakes you take for strands of hair!"
But I was never one to be subdued
By any fear of aught not reason-bred,
And so I mocked the ruddy word, and stood
To meet the gold-envenomed dart instead.

O vengeful warning, spiteful stream, a truce!
What boots this constant crying in the wind,
This ultimate indignity: abuse
Heaped on a tree of all its foliage thinned?
Though blind, yet on these arid balls engraved
I know it was a lovely face I braved.

---

[1]Medusa—the most famous of the Gorgons in Greek mythology, with the form of a young woman and a head of hair consisting of snakes. To look upon her would turn anyone into stone. She was slain by Perseus.

SONNET

I have not loved you in the noblest way
The human heart can beat, where what it loves
Is canonized and purged, outtops the day
To masquerade beneath itself,—as gloves
Upon a pilfering hand (sly fingers) laid,
Can make them move as something frank and kind,—
Yet in the curved-up palm is niched a blade;
Loved have I much, but I have not been blind.

The noblest way is fraught with too much pain;
Who travels it must drag a crucifix;
What hurts my heart hurts deep and to the grain;
My mother never dipped me in the Styx,[1]
And who would find me weak and vulnerable
Need never aim his arrow at my heel.[2]

---

[1]Styx—one of the rivers of the Underworld. It literally means "hateful."

[2]This is a reference to Achilles, the famous warrior of the *Iliad*. He was the son of Peleus, king of the Myrmidons, and a nereid or sea nymph. A non-Homeric legend is that Achilles' mother dipped him in the waters of the River Styx, which made him invulnerable, except for the part of his heel by which she held him.

SONNET

Some for a little while do love, and some for long;
And some rare few forever and for aye;
Some for the measure of a poet's song,
And some the ribbon width of a summer's day.
Some on a golden crucifix do swear,
And some in blood do plight a fickle troth;
Some struck divinely mad may only stare,
And out of silence weave an iron oath.

So many ways love has none may appear
The bitter best, and none the sweetest worst;
Strange food the hungry have been known to bear,
And brackish water slakes an utter thirst.
It is a rare and tantalizing fruit
Our hands reach for, but nothing absolute.

SONNET

I know now how a man whose blood is hot
And rich, still undiminished of desire,
Thinking (too soon), "The world is dust and mire,"
Must feel who takes to wife four walls, a cot,
A hempen robe and cowl, saying, "I'll not
To anything, save God and Heaven's fire,
Permit a thought; and I will never tire
Of Christ, and in Him all shall be forgot."

He too, as it were Torquemada's rack,[1]
Writhes piteously on that unyielding bed,
Crying, "Take Heaven all, but give me back
Those words and sighs without which I am dead;
Which thinking on are lances, and I reel."
Letting you go, I know how he would feel.

---

[1] Tomás de Torquemada (1420–98) was the first Grand Inquisitor in Spain, whose name came to represent the horror, cruelty, and bigotry of the Inquisition. He burned more than two thousand at the stake.

TO ONE NOT THERE

(For D. W.)[1]

This is a land in which you never were,
A land perchance which you may never see;
And yet the length of it I may not stir,
But your sweet spirit walks its ways with me.
Your voice is in these Gallic accents light,
And sweeter is the Rhenish wine I sip
Because this glass (a lesser Grail) is bright
Illumined by the memory of your lip.

Thus would I have it in the dismal day,
When I fare forth upon another ship,
The heart not warm as now; but cold, and clay;
The journey forced; not, sweet, a pleasure trip.
Thus would I take your image by the hand,
But leave you safe within a living land.

Paris, July 1933

---

[1] "D. W." is probably Dorothy West, who was a good friend of Cullen's and who wrote him many affectionate letters in the early 1930s. She is also the author of a well-regarded novel, *The Living Is Easy* (1948).

SONNET

What I am saying now was said before,
And countless centuries from now again,
Some poet warped with bitterness and pain,
Will brew like words hoping to salve his sore.
And seeing written he will think the core
Of anguish from that throbbing wound, his brain,
Squeezed out; and these ill humours gone, disdain,
Or think he does, the face he loved of yore.

And then he too, as I, will turn to look
Upon his instrument of discontent,
Thinking himself a Perseus,[1] and fit to brook
Her columned throat and every blandishment;
And looking know what brittle arms we wield,
Whose pencil is our sword, whose page our shield.

---

[1]Perseus—in Greek mythology the son of Zeus and Danaë, the slayer of the Medusa, and
the rescuer of Andromeda.

SONNET

These are no wind-blown rumors, soft say-sos,
No garden-whispered hearsays, lightly heard
I know that summer never spares the rose,
That spring is faithless to the brightest bird.
I know that nothing lovely shall prevail
To win from Time and Death a moment's grace;
At Beauty's birth the scythe was honed, the nail
Dipped for her hands, the cowl clipped for her face.

And yet I cannot think that this my faith,
My wingèd joy, my pride, my utmost mirth,
Centered in you, shall ever taste of death,
Or perish from the false, forgetting earth.
You are with time, as wind and weather are,
As is the sun, and every nailèd star.

SONNET DIALOGUE

I to My Soul:

Why this preoccupation, soul, with Death,
This servile genuflexion to the worm,
Making the tomb a Mecca where the breath
(Though still it rises vaporous, but firm,
Expelled from lungs still clear and unimpaired,
To plough through nostrils quivering with pride)
Veers in distress and love, as if it dared
Not search a gayer place, and there subside?

My Soul to Me:

Because the worm shall tread the lion down,
And in the end shall sicken at its feast,
And for a worm of even less renown
Loom as a dread but subjugated beast;
Because whatever lives is granted breath
But by the grace and sufferance of Death.

TO FRANCE[1]

I have a dream of where (when I grow old,
Having no further joy to take in lip
Or limb, a graybeard caching from the cold
The frail indignity of age) some ship
Might bear my creaking, unhinged bones
Trailing remembrance as a tattered cloak,
And beach me glad, though on their sharpest stones,
Among a fair, and kindly foreign folk.

There might I only breathe my latest days,
With those rich accents falling on my ear
That most have made me feel that freedom's rays
Still have a shrine where they may leap and sear,—
Though I were palsied there, or halt, or blind,
So I were there, I think I should not mind.

---

[1]Like many black Americans who, from the time of World War I through the 1960s, traveled in Europe, Cullen found France much more open and accepting. Although he was not an expatriate, Cullen felt a deep love and an abiding affection for France, which he visited almost yearly from the mid-twenties to late thirties.

DEATH TO THE POOR

(From the French of Baudelaire)[1]

In death alone is what consoles; and life
And all its end is death; and that fond hope
Whose music like a mad fantastic fife
Compels us up this ridged and rocky slope.
Through lightning, hail, and hurt of human look,
Death is the vibrant light we travel toward,
The mystic Inn forepromised in the Book
Where all are welcomed in to bed and board.

An angel whose star-banded fingers hold
The gift of dreams and calm, ecstatic sleep
In easier beds than those we had before,
Death is the face of God, the only fold
That pens content and ever-happy sheep,
To Paradise the only open door.

---

[1]Charles Pierre Baudelaire (1821–67) was a major French Symbolist poet.

THE CAT

(From the French of Baudelaire)

Come, lovely cat, to this adoring breast;
Over thy daggers silken scabbards draw;
Into thy beauty let me plunge to rest,
Unmindful of thy swift and cruel claw.
The while my fingers leisurely caress
Thy head and vaulted back's elastic arch,
And through each tip mysterious pleasures press
And crackle on their swift dynamic march,
I see revived in thee, felinely cast,
A woman with thine eyes, satanic beast,
Profound and cold as scythes to mow me down.
And from her feet up to her throat are massed
Strange aromas; a perfume from the East
Swims round her body, sinuous and brown.

CATS

(From the French of Baudelaire)

Lovers that burn and learnèd scholars cold
Dote equally in their appointed time
On subtle cats which do them both combine—
Quiet as scholars and as lovers bold.
Friendly alike to sage and sybarite,
They thrive on silence; shadow is their friend;
Earth's fittest runners for the Prine of Night,
Unto no other pride their own will bend.

In noble attitudes they sit and dream,
Small sphinxes miming those in lonelier lands,
In stony sleep eternal and afar.
With passion's seed their fruitful bodies teem,
While golden scintilla like burning sands
Their eyes with mystery and light bestar.

SCOTTSBORO, TOO, IS WORTH ITS SONG[1]
(A poem to American poets)

I said:
Now will the poets sing,—
Their cries go thundering
Like blood and tears
Into the nation's ears,
Like lightning dart
Into the nation's heart.
Against disease and death and all things fell,
And war,
Their strophes rise and swell
To jar
The foe smug in his citadel.

Remembering their sharp and pretty
Tunes for Sacco and Vanzetti,
I said:
Here too's a cause divinely spun
For those whose eyes are on the sun,
Here in epitome
Is all disgrace
And epic wrong,

---

[1] In Scottsboro, Alabama, nine black boys, ranging in age from thirteen to nineteen, were accused of raping two white prostitutes. Between 1931 and 1933 the case became a *cause célèbre* for blacks and the white liberal left after the boys were sentenced to death. As a result of public outcry and persistent legal appeals, the convictions, one by one, were overturned.

Like wine to brace
The minstrel heart, and blare it into song.

Surely, I said,
Now will the poets sing.
  But they have raised no cry.
  I wonder why

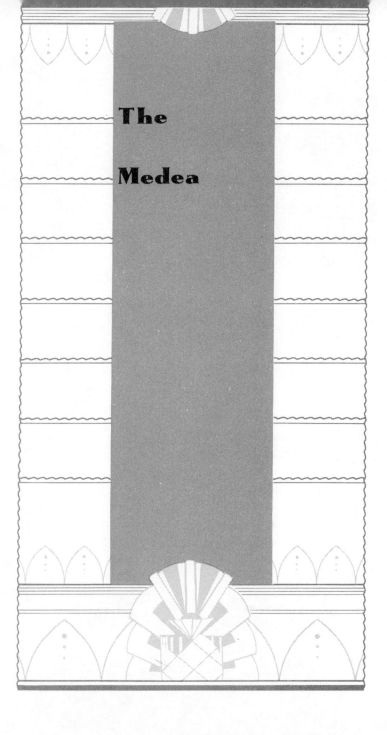

The

Medea

CHARACTERS

NURSE

TUTOR

TWO CHILDREN

FIRST WOMAN

SECOND WOMAN

MEDEA

CREON

JASON

AEGEUS

MESSENGER

THE CHORUS

THE MEDEA

The scene is laid outside Jason's house in Corinth. The stage is empty, except for the old NURSE *crouching on the steps before the door. The action is continuous.*

NURSE: Those Greeks! They should never have come to our country. The Argo should never have sailed, and the pines from which her oars were cut should still be standing in the Forest of Pelion. They should never have heard of the golden fleece, the cause of all our troubles.

For then Medea, my mistress, would never have followed Jason across the sea for love; old Pelias would not lie murdered by his daughters; and Medea would not have fled here to Corinth with Jason and their children, hiding from that bloody deed.

For a while all went well; this people welcomed them, and they were happy here, as man and woman are who love. But now all is changed and every vow lies broken. Jason has betrayed his wife and children. He has married the king's daughter. In vain Medea recalls his vows and whispered promises, and calls on the gods to witness what thanks she gets from Jason. She lies in there fasting; grief is her only food, and every hour goes by in weeping at Jason's treachery. She is ashamed; she will not lift her eyes from the ground, but lies there, cold as stone. In her loneliness she sometimes calls to mind all she gave up for this sad fate: home, father, country, all betrayed, all for this man who now betrays her. And in her grief all that she lost seems dearer and more lost.

The sight of her children is hateful to her; not even they can turn her from brooding on her dark designs. For I know her. She is proud, and not one to be hurt without vengeance. And I am afraid.

(She looks off in the distance)

Here come the children now, hot from their play, with no thought of their mother's grief; for they are young.

(The TUTOR *and the* CHILDREN *come in)*

TUTOR: Why do you sit out there, you old buzzard, mumbling and crying? Why aren't you inside with your mistress when she needs you?

NURSE: No good servant can be happy when her mistress is sad. Don't you know that? I feel her wrongs so deep I want to shout them out to heaven and earth.

TUTOR: Is she still grieving?

NURSE: You don't know her; her grief grows. It has no end.

TUTOR: And still she hasn't heard the worst!

NURSE: The worst? What is it now?

TUTOR: Nothing.

NURSE: What have you heard?

TUTOR: Nothing. I heard nothing.

NURSE: Don't be afraid to tell me. I can hold my tongue.

TUTOR: I was down by the fountain where the old men sit in the sun playing dice. I heard a man say they were going to send them away, Medea and the children, away from Corinth. Perhaps it isn't true, just fountain talk and public gossip.

NURSE: Of course, it isn't true. Jason wouldn't let them. He may hate her, but do you think he'd let his sons be treated so?

TUTOR: Jason has other things to think of now.

NURSE: Oh, it was bad enough as it was. If this is true, then there is no hope left for us, no hope . . .

TUTOR: Well, you know nothing of it yet. Let her hear it from her enemies, not from us.

NURSE: Poor little children, a fine father you have. He's my master and I shouldn't speak ill of him, but a man who betrays his own children, . . .

TUTOR: Don't you know that all men are alike, and selfish at such a time . . . all for themselves?

NURSE: Go into the house, children; and don't you worry.

(To the TUTOR)

You keep them out of her way. Don't let her see them in this wild mood of hers. A little while ago I caught her glaring at them, as if she saw too much of Jason in their faces. If she hadn't been their mother, I would have thought she hated them. She has some horrible thing in mind, I know, and I am afraid that in her anger she may hurt the innocent with the guilty.

MEDEA: *(From within the house)* O misery and shame! To be so despised and fallen! Would that I were dead and gone and laid in my grave.

NURSE: Do you hear how she raves? Go in children, go in quickly, and don't let her see you. Keep out of her way while her anger lasts. Go now; hurry. A wild storm will soon burst from these clouds of grief. It frightens me to think of what she may do in her despair.

The CHILDREN *and the* TUTOR *go into the house)*

MEDEA: *(Still within)* No woman should be made to suffer as I have suffered. And you that remind me of Jason, you with your father's eyes, would you and he were dead together and our whole house with you!

NURSE: What have they done, her own little boys, that she should hate them so? They aren't to blame for what their father does. How I tremble for you, my children!
Oh, our masters are violent and uncurbed in their passions. We who live humbly are better off than they. It is better to live contented than to be famous. Too much power brings ruin to men, and misery to whole families when the gods are aroused against them.

(Two WOMEN *draw near)*

FIRST WOMAN: I heard a voice. I heard her crying.

SECOND WOMAN: I heard a loud sound of grieving.

FIRST WOMAN: Is there bad news? Tell us. This family and we are friends.

NURSE: Family! There's no family here now! The head of this house has left us. He sleeps with the princess these days, while my poor mistress lies alone in her room, melting her life away, and won't be comforted.

MEDEA: *(Within)* May lightning strike me where I stand. Living is hateful to me now. I am tired; let death come and put an end to my suffering.

FIRST WOMAN: Do you hear her crying?

SECOND WOMAN: How she longs for death to soothe her pride!

FIRST WOMAN: Why does she waste herself in weeping? The gods are just; they will avenge.

MEDEA: *(Within)* Have you seen my suffering, you mighty gods, and how he breaks the solemn promises we made together before you? He has betrayed us all. Let these eyes see them suffer and die, him and his bride! Let their bones be broken and their flesh torn from their bodies! O my father and my native land that I left for him, see how he pays me now!

NURSE: Do you hear what she says, how she calls on the gods to avenge her? I tell you she will not rest until the blood runs down.

FIRST WOMAN: Let us persuade her to come out, so we who love her may reason with her. We may be able to cool her anger and set bounds to her awful fury.

SECOND WOMAN: *(To the* NURSE) Go on and bring her to us; she must not let despair get the best of her.

NURSE: I'll go. It will be of no use, but I will go. She has only hard words and evil looks for anyone who tries to comfort her.

(She goes into the house)

FIRST WOMAN: I heard her loud and bitter crying, wild speeches,—

SECOND WOMAN: And dark curses on Jason, the traitor to her bed, the faithless husband.

FIRST WOMAN: In her anguish she calls on the gods, who take
note of every broken pledge, who led her across the sea with
Jason, over the pathless waters.

(Enter MEDEA *from the house)*

MEDEA: I have come out to speak to you, women of Corinth. I
don't want you to think me proud or distant. You don't know
how difficult it can be for a stranger in a foreign land. One is
so easily misunderstood. And this thing has nearly driven me
mad. I am spiritless, and ready and willing to die.
I loved Jason with my whole heart and he has left me. What can
I do? We women are so helpless. . . . But a man is free to come
and go. When the children fret or cry, or when his supper rides
high in his throat, he can leave the house and go to some friend,
or to his dice, or to the wine-cup for comfort, but we have only
our husbands to go to. And if they fail us we are better off in
our grave! They imagine, just because . . .
Forgive me; I didn't mean to bore you with my troubles. This is
your own country, and was your father's country before you. All
life means is here for you, and the sweet companionship of
friends. I am alone, a stranger among you, wronged by my
husband, far from my native land, with neither father, nor
brother nor any friend to look to. And so I ask, a woman pleading with my kind, if I should find some way to avenge myself
on those who have wronged me, that you will keep my secret
with me and be silent.

FIRST WOMAN: We will be silent, Medea. Whatever happens, Jason will have brought it on himself. . . .

SECOND WOMAN: Here comes Creon now!

(Enter CREON)

CREON: I hereby sentence you, Medea, stubborn-browed sorceress and insubordinate wife, to instant exile from Corinth, you and your two children. I who rule this land and people banish you, and I have sworn not to return to my palace until I see you gone.

MEDEA: Shame on shame, and grief on top of grief is mine wherever I turn! My enemies surround me. Not one friendly hand is held out to me anywhere. But though I die for it, I must ask you, Creon, why do you banish me?

CREON: Frankly, because I fear you. I'm not one for beating about the bush, Medea. I fear for my daughter's life. That's why! And my fears are not groundless, as you well know. You are too wise a woman for the good of my house, too skilled in magic and evil knowledge, and you are desperate because you no longer sleep at Jason's side. I have heard of your threats against me, against my daughter and Jason. Forewarned is forearmed, Medea. I'd rather have your full enmity than live to repent my softness later!

MEDEA: Creon . . . Creon . . . you flatter me. I am only a poor, ignorant, unhappy woman. Believe me, Creon! You say you are afraid some harm may come to your house through me. Why, my pitiful fortunes could never disturb the peace of a great king like you. . . .
. . . Besides, in what way have you injured me? Your daughter's hand was yours to give, and you have given it where you wished. So be it. I hate Jason, I will not deny that. But I have no reason to hate you. I don't envy your house its happiness. Go marry your daughter off and my blessings on the union. Only let me remain here in Corinth with my sons, alone and apart, deeply injured, but accepting my fate in meekness and silence.

CREON: Your speech is glib. You have a soft and oily tongue, Medea, but these old ears are tough. Now I trust you even less than I did before. A man or woman who says his say in the first hot flush of anger can be guarded against, but never one that is sullen and roundabout. No, I'll not bandy more words with you. You are my sworn enemy. I have decreed your exile. I mean to hold to my word.

MEDEA: Have pity, Creon. By your love for your daughter, let me stay!

CREON: You are wasting your breath, as well as my time.

MEDEA: I am at your mercy, Creon, here on my knees before you. Will you refuse to hear a defenceless woman?

CREON: I must think of my own flesh and blood. Charity begins at home.

MEDEA: Ah, Jason, Jason, was it to be treated like this that I loved you so deeply?

CREON: When misfortune enters the door, child, love flies out of the window, they say. Love comes and goes.

MEDEA: O my native land, where there is peace and quiet, I wish I had never left you!

CREON: I'll not waste more words on you, Medea. You must leave Corinth. And with your going, my troubles will be over!

MEDEA: *You* talk of troubles! What do you know of troubles?

CREON: Oh enough! Must I have my servants drive you out with stones? Must I?

MEDEA: Would you do that to me, too?

CREON: Not willingly, but you drive me to it with your stubbornness.

271

MEDEA: *(As if resigned)* I'll go.

CREON: Then why, by Zeus, do you make such a fuss about it?

MEDEA: Only give me a day's grace, time in which to make my plans, to get some food ready for so long a journey with my little sons; since, even now, Jason has prepared nothing for them. Have pity on them, Creon. You say it is because you are a father, and love your daughter, and fear for her life that you are banishing me from Corinth. Then pity my little ones, if a father's tenderness is really in your heart. Give me time to get them ready. I have no thought for myself. I have suffered. I can suffer still. But my heart bleeds for them.

CREON: *(Taken in)* I'm not really a hard man, Medea. In fact I am just about my own worst enemy. Something tells me I shouldn't listen to you, that I'm making a great mistake. Still, I am going to grant your request. Take today to prepare for your journey, but if you or your sons are found in Corinth by tomorrow, you shall all be put to death. I swear it. Just one more day—I don't see how any harm can come of that!

(CREON *leaves*)

Unhappy Medea! Most wretched of women! Where can you go now? Who will befriend you? What country will give you refuge?

MEDEA: They have hemmed me in on every side, but the last word has not yet been said, neither by Creon, nor by Jason, nor by me! Do you think I would have stooped to beg the smallest favor of that man, except for his undoing? I would have scorned to speak one word to him, or to soil my hands in touching him. He had it in his power to banish me and to put an end to all my plans. But I have softened him with guile, and for heeding me, they shall die, he and his daughter and Jason. O I have killed them already so many times and in so many ways in my mind that now I don't know which death is most bitter for them to die.

(To herself)

But once I have destroyed them, what city will receive Medea then? What friend in all the world will grant me the shelter of his roof? None in all the world. But what have I to lose? I will kill them still, though the moment afterward should be my last. Why do you stand here plotting and debating? Have you forgotten who you are? Will you let these Corinthians laugh at you, daughter of the Sun? No man or woman can wrong Medea and live! Ah, they shall pay for their first sleep together and my long nights alone!

CHORUS: *(Sing)*
> O LOVING HEART, O NOBLE HEART,
>   O HEART OF GOLD AND FIRE,
> WHAT DESTINY COULD KEEP THAT HEART
>   FROM FINDING ITS DESIRE?
>
> THE RAGING SEA, THE MIGHTY TIDE
>   WERE CROSSED FOR JASON'S SAKE;
> REJECTED NOW AND CAST ASIDE,
>   FOR JASON LET IT BREAK!
>
> YE WHO SEEK VIRTUE HERE, PASS BY;
>   GREECE HAS FORGOTTEN VIRTUE'S NAME.
> HERE ONLY GRIEF, THE STONY LIE,
>   ARE FOUND, AND LUST AND SHAME.
>
> AND HERE WAILS ONE
>   WHO HAS NO HOME
> IN EARTH OR AIR
>   OR ANYWHERE.

(JASON *comes in*)

JASON: Are you satisfied now, Medea? Do you see what your tongue has brought you to? If you had been wise, if you had been willing to obey the king, you might have stayed here in peace, in this land and house. But no, you would not, but flashed out on all sides in your wild temper. And now you are banished forever. Say what you have a mind to say against me; let your worst word be too good for me; it doesn't matter. But you should be glad that you are getting off with exile only, after your mad threats against Creon and his family. Believe me or not, I spoke for you. I asked them to let you stay here. Still, you would not be silenced. You filled the town with your crying and cursing. What could they do but banish you?

Yet for what you were to me once, I have come to offer you money and whatever else you may need in your journey, so that neither you, nor our children, may want for anything. The road to exile is rough and stony, and I would make it as easy as possible for you. For hate me as you will, Medea, I cannot hate you.

MEDEA: Welcome, Jason! It sickens me even to speak your name! I thought I had some skill in speech, but not enough to tell you how I despise a coward like you! You have done well to come. For it will ease my heart a little to curse you, and hurt you a little to hear it. Let me remind you of what you should know only too well, but seem to have forgotten. You owe your very life to me. Ask any of those who sailed with you in the Argo, and not one man but will say I saved you. When you were sent to yoke the great bulls whose very breath is fire, and to sow the seed whose harvest is death to the sower, it was Medea that saved you. For love of you, I, a woman, killed the dragon that kept sleepless watch over the prize you hungered for. I held the light of safety up to your eyes that you might seize the fleece of gold. I betrayed my own father and my own country. I put them behind me forever to follow you. I loved you more than any woman should love a man. I brought Pelias to the most shameful death a man can die, to be killed by his own children. All this I did for you that nothing might stand in your way. And I am richly paid at last; betrayed by you, the father of my children who leaves me to climb into another woman's bed. I could find some excuse for you if it were not for the children. . . .

Let no one swear an oath again, Jason! For oaths are only made to be broken; the gods exist only for us to mock, and the old laws for us to laugh at.

Once you clung to this hand of mine, and whined for me to save you from death. Once you clasped your craven arms about these knees in fear. Now they are unclean, they are of no further use to you. If they are unclean, it is your touch that has made them so.

(Pause)

You say you come as a friend? Give me a friend's counsel then. Advise me. Where shall I go? Where *can* I go? Back to my father's house? Will he kill the fatted calf for the daughter who betrayed him and brought his gray hairs to shame? Or perhaps you think Pelias' daughters will welcome me in with open arms for the murder of their father? On every side I have made enemies, all through helping you. Those at home who might still be loving me, and the first strangers who took me in, to whom above all others I should have been loyal, I have betrayed them all for you.

There were many who envied me when I married you. Married to Jason, the brave warrior and the gentle lover! But now they know what a sorry prize I drew, a coward who stands idly by and sees me driven into exile with a helpless child of his in either arm. Perhaps it will add zest to your love-making in the palace to think of us wandering off friendless and alone and poverty-stricken? Oh, we can tell if a coin is good by its ring, but never a man's heart from his face!

A WOMAN: There are no foes so bitter as those who once were friends!

JASON: Lies, Medea, lies from beginning to end! As for your saving me, I owe my safety neither to man nor God, unless your own hot passion for me can be called a god. You saved me because you wanted me, and for no nobler reason. But enough of that; you saved me, and you have my thanks for the service. Yet it seems to me you have the better of the bargain at that. Instead of leaving you to waste your days in your own wild country, I brought you here to Greece, the queen of all the nations of the world. Here you have learned what justice is, and law and order, you who had seen nothing but violence and brute force. Throughout this land they have admired you for your wisdom. Who would have heard of you, living still in your own benighted country? And fame, Medea, is a sweet thing to have. So much for the good I may have done you. And I would not have mentioned this except to give the lie to your reproaches.

Now as to the real cause of all this—my marriage to Creon's daughter, though you will not see it in that light, I have been wise and far-seeing, I have acted for your own good and for that of our children, in entering into this marriage.

(MEDEA *makes as if to answer him*)

No, hear me out! After we had come here to Corinth, strangers with all our bloody past behind us, what better fortune could have come to me, than to marry a king's daughter? I did not seek this chance, as you accuse me of doing, either because I was tired of you or hot for new embraces. Nor God knows, because I wanted to make more brats. For those that I have by you are a full plenty. But the chance came of itself, and I took it. We both know how few friends a man without money has. In this way I thought to provide for our children, and to place them on an equal footing with any that might be born of this second marriage.

You already have children by me. You need no further proof of my affection for you; but if the king's daughter should give me sons, our two houses would be truly bound together.

In all this, what have I done to deserve your hate? You cannot give one clear reason. It is only the thought of sleeping alone that goads you on. For you women are all alike; your bed is everything to you. When your passion is satisfied the whole world is bright, but when you want a man nothing else on earth can please you. Truly, the gods should have made some other animal for men to couple with and to get children by, instead of women. Then we might have had more comfort and peace of mind.

FIRST WOMAN: A smooth speech, Jason, and yet, though you may not like to hear it—betrayal is not the just reward for love.

MEDEA: Careful, Jason, watch what you say—with those fine phrases; for one slip of the tongue may uncover all your treachery. If you really went into this marriage in good faith, why didn't you tell me of it in the beginning, and ask my help instead of leaving me to hear of it after it was done?

JASON: And you would have helped me, I suppose? From your wild tantrums now it is plain to see how you would have helped me!

MEDEA: You never gave a thought to how I would take it. You only knew that in me, the mother of your sons, you had a worn out baggage in which you took no further pleasure, while this new girl . . .

JASON: Once and for all, I tell you for sleeping with, she is no more to me than you! Only I thought that as she was Creon's daughter, my marriage with her would ensure your safety here and that of my sons.

MEDEA: What would we want with safety here without your love? Or peace bought with pain and misery?

JASON: You see only your side! Nothing I say can change you.

MEDEA: How can you hope to change me, you with a home to go to, while my sons and I are driven out into the night with only the sky to cover us?

JASON: You have only yourself to thank for that.

MEDEA: How, Jason? Were *you* the virgin, and did I seduce *you*, and then forsake you?

JASON: You ask me how? I'll tell you how! By your vicious tongue and your curses against Creon and his house.

MEDEA: Perhaps your own house, Jason, will not be free of my curses!

JASON: I see that I cannot reason with you, so I'll not argue with you further. But if anything of mine can help you and the children on your journey, it is yours for the asking. I am ready to give to the last penny, and to send you with gifts to friends of mine in other cities, who will take you in and shelter you. You will do well, Medea, to accept this offer. Let your foolish anger die. Come, meet me half-way.

MEDEA: No, Jason. Whatever I took from you would be as rank and evil as the hand that gave it.

JASON: Now I call on the gods to witness that I have tried my best to help this damned woman and her children. But nothing can change her savage heart. Like a viper she must sting herself to death!

MEDEA: Go leave me, Jason. Even now your cheeks are hot and your eyes are wild from wanting that other one. Quick, run to the palace. Go fornicate with her! Enjoy her while you can! I know a bride that will soon take her place!

(JASON *goes out*)

CHORUS: *(Sing)*
> LOVE LIKE A LEAF BEFORE THE WIND,
> LUST OF THE FLESH, CONSUMING FIRE,
> ON US, DREAD ARCHER, NEVER BEND
>   SUCH ARROWS OF DESIRE!
>
> THAT LOVE IN WHICH AN EQUAL PART
> TRUE WOMAN HOLDS WITH HONEST MAN,
> BORN OF THE MIND, AS OF THE HEART,
>   GRANT US, O CYPRIAN!
>
> O NATIVE LAND WHERE FIRST A RAY
> OF LIGHT BURST ON THE INFANT EYE,
> IF THOU MUST EVER PASS AWAY,
>   PASS ONLY WHEN WE DIE!
>
> WE KNOW THY SORROW, HOMELESS ONE,
> WHOM SHALT THOU CALL? OR WHITHER FLEE?
> WHAT HAVEN UNDER HEAVEN'S SUN,
>   O EXILE, WAITS FOR THEE?

(A middle-aged MAN *in King's Robes comes in)*

AEGEUS: Good day to you, and good luck with it, Medea. I can think of no better greeting to an old friend.

MEDEA: Aegeus, son of Pandion! From what far corner of the world have you come to this unhappy land?

AEGEUS: I have been on pilgrimage to Apollo's shrine.

MEDEA: To ask advice of the oracle?

AEGEUS: Yes, to ask how I might get children to carry on my name after me.

MEDEA: Then you have no sons yet, Aegeus?

AEGEUS: None. The gods have kept me barren!

MEDEA: Have you tried a wife? That might help.

AEGEUS: Oh, indeed, yes. I have tried *wives,* Medea, but not to any purpose.

MEDEA: What hope did the oracle give you?

AEGEUS: Like all oracles his words were incomprehensible.

MEDEA: Will you tell me what he said?

AEGEUS: To be sure. . . . You may be able to find some meaning in the thing. He said something about drawing the wine-skin tight, and saving the wine . . .

MEDEA: Until you did something, or until you came to some land?

AEGEUS: Until I came to my own country again . . . that's what he said.

MEDEA: May all go well with you, Aegeus. May you have your desire.

AEGEUS: But what has come over you, Medea? You are not as you used to be. There are tears in your eyes. . . .

MEDEA: Of all men alive, Aegeus, my husband is most false.

AEGEUS: Jason?

MEDEA: Yes, Jason, who never had anything from me but love, and help in all his troubles.

AEGEUS: We are old friends, Medea. You needn't hide anything from me.

MEDEA: One wife wasn't enough for him. He has taken another.

AEGEUS: Another wife?

MEDEA: Yes, and my children and me he loves no more.

AEGEUS: Does he really love this other woman, or has he simply grown tired of you?

MEDEA: Love her? No. Just lust and ambition to sleep with a princess!

AEGEUS: A princess? Tell me her name?

MEDEA: She is the daughter of Creon, king of Corinth.

AEGEUS: The king's daughter! Then you have reason to be sad!

MEDEA: I am to be banished from Corinth.

AEGEUS: Surely, it never rains but it pours! Has Jason so little manhood left that he will allow this? This does not sound like the Jason I once new.

MEDEA: He doesn't condone it in so many words, but in his heart he does.

(She kneels to him)

Oh, Aegeus, by all you hold sacred and by the memory of the woman who was your mother, I beg of you, kneeling to you in this hated Corinthian dust, have pity on me in my distress. Don't let them drive me out into aimless exile, but promise me a refuge and a welcome in your land. If you will do this for me, I swear by the gods that your prayer for children will be answered. You shall grow old and die in happiness with many sons to carry on your name. I can do what I promise, Aegeus. I know charms and magic words to give life even to your seed. Believe me, Aegeus, I can raise up children to you.

AEGEUS: *(Helping her to rise)* I'll help you, Medea. If once you come to my country, I will receive you and welcome you in all friendliness. I cannot raise a finger to help you here in Corinth where Creon is king, you understand that. . . . But in my own country I do as I please! Come there of your own free will, and I promise you shelter and safety, and no man shall drive you out, or come in and take you.

MEDEA: Let it be as you say. But swear to me that it shall be so. Give me a pledge of some sort on which to hope in my despair.

AEGEUS: Don't you trust me, Medea? What do we need with oaths and pledges?

MEDEA: I do trust you, but I have enemies, the daughters of Pelias and all their kin; and Creon too. If I had your sworn word

with some god's name to bind you to it, I should be sure that
you would never give me up to them, no matter how they pressed
you. I am alone and helpless; they are many and rich and powerful.

AEGEUS: By what god do you want me to swear?

MEDEA: Swear by the earth, and by the blazing majesty of my
kinsman, the mighty sun, and by all the gods men call upon.

AEGEUS: What shall I swear?

MEDEA: That you will never cast me out of your country, nor
surrender me to my enemies, as long as you have life and
strength.

AEGEUS: This I swear by the earth, and by the almighty light of
the sun, and by every god men call upon.

MEDEA: So much for the oath, but if you fail to keep it?

AEGEUS: If I fail to keep it, let me suffer that death which comes
to all those who take the names of the gods in vain.

MEDEA: *(Rejoicing)* Go your way, Ægeus, and my blessing go with
you. The goal I seek is in view. I will join you in your own
country as quickly as possible. I have a certain thing to do in
Corinth first and a fierce thirst to slake.

FIRST WOMAN: Farewell, Ægeus, the gods give you safe conduct
home.

SECOND WOMAN: And in the end, fulfillment of your desire.

(AEGEUS *goes out*)

MEDEA: Now by the great Zeus, and by his godly justice, and by the burning light of the sun, now I shall triumph over my enemies. The gods have shown me the very haven that I needed.

(She turns to the chorus)

Hear now, my dark and bloody purpose, and do not look for mercy or pity! I shall send one of my servants to ask Jason to come and speak to me again. I will word my request meekly, and when he has come, I will receive him meekly; I will beg his pardon. I will see nothing but honesty and decency in his every word and move. I will humble myself before him. Then I will beg him to let my sons stay here in Corinth with him. Not that I would ever leave them here as a prey to their enemies; they shall help me to kill Creon's daughter. I shall send my children to her, with presents in their innocent little hands, a fine robe woven of gold thread, and a shining crown for her hair—deadly in their beauty, steeped through and through with poison and fire.

(Pause)

Even then do not think all the horror told, for there is more. No woman ever had so hard a thing to do as I! I must kill my own children. Oh—since it must come, let it come quickly! What hope has life for me? I have no country, no home, nothing! Surely, I dealt my own death blow the day I left my father's house to follow Jason and his lying Grecian tongue. But he shall have his!
Never will you see your sons again, Jason, and for all your fine dreams she will not live to bear you one. For today my poison shall feed deep on her heart. And then having tumbled Jason's fine hopes about his ears, I will forever shake the dust of Corinth from my feet!

(To the chorus)

I'm no monster—only flesh and blood. As I loved Jason once to overflowing, so I hate him now!

A WOMAN: We pity you, Medea! Out of our love for you, we beseech you, do not do this bloody deed.

MEDEA: There is no other way. You have not been wronged as I have been. You cannot know my pain.

A WOMAN: You must not do this deed! You cannot murder your own babies.

MEDEA: It is my way to murder Jason.

A WOMAN: But the agony will be yours. You will be the most wretched woman in all the world.

MEDEA: I am that already. So let it come.

(She claps her hands and the NURSE *comes out of the house)*

Go tell your master I want to speak to him again, that I beg him to come and hear me. I have no one to trust but you.

(The NURSE *goes)*

CHORUS: *(Sing)*
OH, HAPPY WERE OUR FATHERS WHEN, TO MIGHTY GODS IN OLDEN DAYS AKIN, GREECE BORE THE MUSES NINE. OH, HAPPY LAND THAT VENUS SMILED UPON, THRICE HAPPY LAND BREATHED ON BY LOVE! THRICE HAPPY LAND OF ARCADY!
BUT THOU THAT WOULDST DESTROY THINE OWN, HOW SHALL THESE SACRED WATERS FERRY THEE, OR GENTLE BREEZES WAFT THEE HOME?
BY ALL THOU HOLDEST DEAR, THOU WILD ONE HEAR! HOW WILT

THOU STEEL THY HAND TO DEAL THE MURDEROUS BLOW? HOW WILT
THOU TURN THY HEART TO STONE?

(Enter JASON)

JASON: You sent for me, Medea, and here I am, as much as I
know you hate me. What is it now?

MEDEA: Forgive me, Jason, and let us bury the past if you will. I
am weary of beating against the wind. Forgive my bitter words
in memory of the sweeter ones we once spoke together. I have
wrestled with myself and I have come to my senses at last.
"Why," I reasoned, "why rage against the one man in all the
world who has your interests at heart? Why rebel against the
power of the king, and against the good judgment of your husband who has done all for the best, hoping to make royal brothers for your children? Shouldn't your first thought be for them?
As you set out in exile won't you need every friend, and
shouldn't you be grateful for even the least kind word?"
So I reasoned with myself, and these thoughts have opened my
eyes. And, now I give thanks for your wisdom. I was a fool,
Jason, I should have seen eye to eye with you from the first.
Yes, I should have been your friend and helped you with your
wooing, welcoming your bride with smiles and meekness. But I
am only a woman, and it takes us time to see these things. . . .
Don't stoop to my level now. Don't meet folly with folly! See, I
am in your hands. I have done wrong, I confess, but now I want
only peace between you and me.

(She claps her hands)

Come here, children, come out into the bright sun, and welcome
your father. Kiss him, and welcome him as mother does, as a
dear and a loving friend. There is no bad blood between us any

more. That's it; go up to him; take him by the hand. He won't
bite you. There!

(She places their hands in JASON'S. *As the* CHILDREN *stand looking
up at their father,* MEDEA *bursts into tears— Aside)*

Oh, my mind is full of shadows and horrors! How long will you
live, my sons, to reach up those little hands to your father?
Forgive me, all of you, I am so quick to tears today. I wanted so
to be at peace with you, Jason, and all I do is cry.

A WOMAN: My eyes, too, are wet. Oh, let this peace between you
be full and lasting.

JASON: You have done well to reconsider, Medea. I can't blame
you altogether. . . . It's only natural for a woman to go into a fit
if her husband so much as looks at another woman. She wouldn't
be a woman if she didn't. I'm glad it's all over now and that
you see as I do.

(He turns to the children)

As for you, my sons, your father has never neglected or forgotten
you. I'll see you numbered among the lords of this land, you
and your brothers to come. Just you grow strong and obedient,
and your father and the gods will do the rest. I shall live to see
you in the pride of your manhood, lording it high above my
enemies, Cock-of-the-Walks of Corinth! Medea, why do you stand
there like that, like some ghost or other? Why do you still weep
and wring your hands? Come, aren't you happy? Can't you smile
at the bright future I've just painted for our sons?

MEDEA: Don't pay me any mind, Jason. I was thinking of my little
ones.

JASON: Trust me, Medea! I'll take care of them.

MEDEA: I will. I will trust you to the utmost, Jason, but a woman cries so easily.

JASON: What are you crying for now?

MEDEA: I am their mother, Jason. And when you prayed just now that they might live long, a dark foreboding of horror swept over me, a wondering if long life would really be granted to them. But that is for the gods to decide. I sent for you to make my peace with you, and for another thing as well:— Since Creon will not let me stay in Corinth,—and I see that if I stayed I should only be in the way—I am ready and willing to leave. But, if I can help it, I don't want my sons to grow up without their father's care and advice. So go to Creon, Jason, and ask him to let them remain here with you.

JASON: He is a hard man to change, once he has made up his mind, but it is only right that I should try.

MEDEA: Ask the princess, out of her love for you, to persuade him.

JASON: Yes, I will ask her. If any one can persuade him, she can. And I believe she will do it; for she is kind at heart.

MEDEA: And I will help you to win her over, Jason. I know the best way to a woman's heart. I will send her gifts as a peace-offering, such as no other woman on earth can match, a robe of gold spun from the rays of the sun, and a golden chaplet like a band of fire for her head. These gifts will please her.

(To the NURSE)

You—go and fetch the gifts to me! She shall be most envied of all women, wedded to my Jason, and wearing the robes which came down to me from the Sun-god himself.

(The NURSE *returns with the gifts)*

Here, my sons, take these offerings of mine and carry them to the palace. They are such gifts as not even a princess can look at without wanting.

JASON: What are you doing? Why do you foolishly give away your only treasure? Do you think Creon's daughter needs robes and chaplets? Keep your gifts. They may come in useful in your exile. If the princess loves me at all, she will not need presents to make her grant my request.

MEDEA: Please, Jason, don't refuse me this. Do we not tempt even the high gods with offers of gold and blood? The sight of these shining gifts may turn the scale in our favor. She is fortunate. So young, and a queen! And you love her!
But I must think of my sons and the exile that stares them in the face. I would buy their happiness with my life's last drop of blood. Go on, my children. Go to the palace. Bow low and speak sweetly to the princess, and beg her to let you stay in Corinth. And see to it that you give these gifts to the princess only. Mind you, no other hand must receive them but hers. Then come quickly back bringing me the news I long to hear!

(JASON *and the* CHILDREN *go)*

CHORUS: *(Sing)*

> WEEP FOR THE LITTLE LAMBS THAT DIE,
> WEEP FOR THE EARLY-SLAIN,
> WEEP FOR THE BRIDE SO SOON TO LIE
> IN GOLDEN ROBES OF PAIN,

WEEP FOR MEDEA; WEEP FOR HER
  WHO WIELDS THE FLASHING KNIFE;
WEEP THAT A MOTHER'S HAND SHOULD STIR
  TO TAKE HER BABY'S LIFE.

(The TUTOR *and the* CHILDREN *return)*

TUTOR: Good news, my mistress, I have good news! Your worries are all over now. All has happened just as you wished. Your little sons with their fine gifts have won the princess. They are to stay in Corinth!

MEDEA: To stay in Corinth!

TUTOR: Why do you cry out as if in pain? This isn't the way I thought you would receive such good news.

MEDEA: Good news! Good news! Indeed!

TUTOR: Have I stupidly said something I should not have said? Have I not brought you good news as I hoped to do?

MEDEA: You have only said what you had to say. I do not blame you.

TUTOR: Then why do you look so sad, mistress, and why do you cry?

MEDEA: I cry because I must. The gods and I have not done well.

TUTOR: Have courage, mistress. Now you can return to your own country. You will be happy there.

MEDEA: Before I go to mine I must send others to a further one.

(She cries again)

TUTOR: But you are not the only mother to be parted from her children. Some suffering is a part of every life, and should be borne patiently, as being the will of the gods.

MEDEA: I will be patient. I promise you I will. But go in now; get to your work. The children must still be cared for.

(She turns to the children)

O my sons, my sons, you have a place to live in and a home, but your unhappy mother may not live there with you.

They are sending her away before she can have a mother's full joy in you, before she sees you tall and strong, and married. I shall not be there to bless you on your wedding day. I have cared for you in vain, and toiled and worried, eating my heart out for you, bringing you into the world with shrieks of agony, and all in vain.

Always I soothed my anguish with the thought of how one day you would tend me when old and past tending you, and how when I was dead, you would fold my shriveled hands across my breast and bury me with honor. But that will never be. What can I hope for, parted from you, but a life lived out in misery and bitterness? When you no longer see your mother with your dear eyes, you will soon forget her! Why do you look at me like that? How can you smile, my little babies? What shall I do? Where shall I turn? My heart sinks as I look at you. When I see them like this, I grow weak as water clean through. My will is broken. I cannot do this thing!

(Pause)

Then I stand ridiculed; my foes are still unpunished. I must brace myself. To be tender now is to be a coward. Go, my children, go in; and let him who cannot bear to see the coming horror hide his face. My hand shall never shrink. But oh, my soul, how can you do this thing? Spare your sons, your own flesh, your very blood. In some friendly foreign land they may yet bring you peace and comfort. No, no—I will not leave them here to the mercy of their foes. They must die. There is no other way out. And since it must be so, let me who gave them their life take it from them. They were born to die today. I cannot change their destiny. . . .

By now the burning chaplet blazes on my rival's head. By now she writhes, fast in the poisoned robe I wove for her. Dark is the path I tread but my foes shall tread a darker!

(She turns to the children)

And now, as your mother, I have a mother's last words for you, my children. Give me your little hands to kiss again, little hands so innocent of harm, dear little lips that I have often kissed and shall not kiss again forever. Oh, straight, slender bodies, frank open faces that I love! Do not fear! Your mother's blessings shall follow you to lighten up the land to which she sends you. Your father has made this world an evil place for you to stay. Farewell, small clinging hands! Soft, downy cheeks against my own, farewell! Go now. I cannot bear to look on you. It hurts me so! Ah, I know what a monstrous thing I have to do, but rage has mastered me through and through, and routed reason in me.

FIRST WOMAN: Sometimes I think the happiest women are those who never had a child.

SECOND WOMAN: But the glad young voices ringing through the house!

FIRST WOMAN: Yes and the constant worries and all the little aches and pains!

SECOND WOMAN: But the joy of watching them, the little hands to hold, the little feet to guide.

FIRST WOMAN: The bitter we must eat that they may have the sweet!

SECOND WOMAN: But how the heart is proud to see them grown at last. The tender blossom comes to bloom. Fine men that we have bred. Sweet gentle girls in whom we live again.

FIRST WOMAN: But death that covets all bright things will take them too. In the flush of morning he gathers them, and we are left to sorrow and to tears.

*(Pause—*MEDEA *stands motionless, waiting, with her eyes on the palace)*

MEDEA: At last! At last it comes!

(A MESSENGER *appears)*

MESSENGER: Woman, what have you done? Flee from the wrath to come! Put every land and ocean between you and Corinth!

MEDEA: Why should I flee from Corinth?

MESSENGER: The princess is dead. And Creon, the king. . . .

MEDEA: And Creon, the king? Tell me of him! I thirst for news of him. What of Creon, the king?

MESSENGER: He too lies dead, of your deadly gifts.

MEDEA: So young and yet so golden-tongued!

MESSENGER: Are you mad, for sure? Did you hear me aright? The king is dead, I tell you, and by your hand! And do you still rejoice, you who should tremble and fear?

MEDEA: You think me mad? Then think me mad, my friend, but mad with joy! Only tell me how they died. Feast my waiting ears on each groan and shriek. And if in their dying they cursed Medea's name, tell me, for it will be sweet to my ear.

MESSENGER: When we who served you in your happier days, and who have always felt your sorrows as our own, saw our master go into the palace, holding your little sons by the hand, we were happy. We passed the glad word along that you two had patched up your quarrel at last. We crowded around the children to welcome them, kissing their hands, patting their pretty heads. And for very joy, forgetful of everything, I followed them straight into the princess' room.

There she whom we now call mistress in your place sat waiting for Jason to come to her. Angrily, at first, she put her white fingers across her eyes, and turned her face away to keep from looking at your sons. Then our master went quickly to her side, and begged her not to receive them so. "Do not be bitter still," he said, "against those who would be your friends. For my sake, smile on these little ones who are dear to me. Receive the gifts they bring you from their mother. Look on them with favor, and ask your father not to banish them, but to let them remain here with me. Do this, if you love me."

So he pled with her. And when she turned and saw the glittering garments which the children held out to her, she could no longer stifle the joy that rose within her, but promised to do as he asked her. And hardly had the palace gate closed on Jason and the children, before she took out the 'broidered garments to try them on. Smiling at the silent image that smiled back at her from the mirror, she bound the golden chaplet on her head, twining her own shining curls around it to make it fast. Then rising from her seat, she paced to and fro, turning this way and that, now putting out a tiny foot, now kicking back the heavy folds of the golden dress. To think she was so happy in your gifts! Like a bright bird she smoothed the ruffled silk and preened herself.

Then came such a horror as I hope these eyes may never see again. Her cheeks turned white as snow, as if drained of every drop of blood. She grew so weak she reeled from side to side, and to keep from falling where she stood, blindly she groped her way back to her chair. An old servant who stood nearby, thinking some spirit or demon had seized upon her, raised a great hue and cry to drive the evil demon from her body. But when she saw the mad spit drooling from the princess' mouth, and her eyeballs whirling in her head, and all her body pale and bloodless, the old woman changed her cry to one of sheerest horror, knowing now what mortal sickness ailed our mistress. One man ran to find her father. One ran to look for Jason. The whole place was plunged in madness and terror. For a while she lay there speechless, her eyes fast shut as if never to open again. Then suddenly they flew open, and looked about wildly. With a loud shriek she tried to rise, to free herself from the double death that crept upon her. O a thousand times over she must have died! For on her head the golden chaplet rained down hot streams of fire terrible to look on, and the pretty dress your children gave her rippled and crackled along her body like a great golden serpent devouring the living flesh. Up like a running flame she jumped and tossed her burning head this way and that trying to shake off that fiery crown. But as if moulded to her head, it held there, and at every agonized toss it blazed the fiercer.

Undone at last the wretched girl sank down upon the ground, a sight from which only a father would not turn away in sickness

and horror. For in nothing that was left, eyes, face, nor hair
could you recognize Creon's daughter. From her burnt head
there still dripped a mingled flow of blood and fire. The flesh
hung in shreds from her blackened bones, as the hard gum
hangs down from a bruised pine tree. So had the poison ravaged
her. In all the house there was not one of us that dared to touch
her. Creon, her wretched father, not knowing yet her awful fate,
came into her room. Only to find her lying dead.

With a great sob he knelt down and picked her up in his arms,
crying out, "O unhappy child, what cruel god has killed you?
Who has bereaved me of you? Oh, let them lay me too dead
here at your feet!" Oh, mistress, never say again that men do
not weep! But later when his grief had spent itself, and when he
would have risen from beside her, he could not. As the deadly
ivy lays hold upon young laurel boughs and strangles them, so
his daughter's robe now held him fast. Wildly he lashed out and
tried to free himself, but the more he fought against the thing,
trying to rise upon his creaking knee, the more it pinned him
down. Once he jerked himself half free, but shrieked out in pain
as part of his living flesh still clung to his daughter's dead breast.
At length he could bear the pain of it no more, and lay down to
gasp his life away cheek to cheek with the reeking thing that
once was princess of Corinth. And there they lie, the old king
and his daughter, a sight to look upon with tears. Ah, mistress,
if you saw them now even you might weep. . . .

As for you who have done this thing, surely there is a weight upon
your soul, and you must throw it off in your own way. But now
I know for certain what I have often thought, that man is but a
shadow here, and those the envious hold wise and happy are
the thinnest shadows of us all. There never was a happy man.
One man sees brighter days than another, but never yet was
there one happy man.

(The MESSENGER *leaves)*

CHORUS: *(Sing)*
> GO DOWN, O SUN, IN BLOOD, AND HIDE FROM US THE CLOUD OF WOES
> THAT BREAKS ON JASON'S HEAD! FOR CREON'S DAUGHTER LET FALL
> OUR TEARS, FOR ONE SO YOUNG AND BEAUTIFUL AND DEAD.

MEDEA: My mind is made up now, to kill my sons, and then to put Corinth out of sight forever. Be hard as steel, my heart. I will not leave my children here to die by other hands than mine. O wretched hand, oh wretched mother's hand, take up the knife; twine about it, bloody fingers, as if you twined about false Jason's neck! Lock up your heart against pity, Medea; let mercy beat at the door, but do not hear. These are not my children. I never kissed them, nor held them to my heart. They were never dear to me. I never bore them! Believe these lies, today, my heart. Tomorrow you may break.

No, though I must murder them, I still know that they are my own, my very own, and dearer than all the world to me, and that I must forever live alone and unhappy without them.

(She goes into the house)

CHORUS: *(Sing)*
> BEHOLD, O EARTH, AND THOU BRIGHT SUN, TURN NOT AWAY!
>> PHOEBUS APOLLO, HEED
> THY CHILDREN'S CRY. BEHOLD WHOSE HAND WOULD SLAY!
>> ALMIGHTY FLAME, THEY BLEED
>> WHO CALL THEE SIRE.
>> RAIN DOWN THY FIRE
> BEFORE THIS DEED BE DONE.
>> NO MORTAL ARM
>> SHOULD DARE TO HARM
> THE CHILDREN OF THE SUN.
> THESE ARE THINE OWN, MATERNAL ONE, THINE OWN
>> HEART'S BREATH, THY BLOOD, THY SEED.
> SHALL ALL THY LOVE, THAT HARVEST SOWN

IN BLOOD AND TEARS, GO FEED
THIS WILD DESIRE?
BEWARE THE FIRE
OF THEM THAT RULE ON HIGH.
FORBEAR! FORBEAR!
THE GODS GIVE EAR
TO INNOCENTS THAT DIE.

FIRST CHILD: *(From inside the house)* Mother, mother, it hurts me so, your hand about my neck.

SECOND CHILD: *(Laughing)* What are you such a baby for? Mother won't hurt us. Ah!

(A CHILD'S *loud cry is heard. Then a long silence)*

CHORUS: *(Spoken)* WHAT HORROR CLOUDS THE AIR? WHAT GHASTLY CRY? IT IS THE MOANING OF THE CHILDREN WHO DIE!

FIRST WOMAN: *(At* MEDEA'S *door)* Do you call yourself a woman, Medea? Are you a mother?

SECOND WOMAN: You are neither a woman nor a mother, but some obscene fury in woman's form, some new disease cut out of stone.

FIRST WOMAN: You are a sword of retribution, doomed to turn back upon yourself.

*(*JASON *comes in)*

Where is she? Where has she taken refuge? Is she locked in the house or has she gone to some altar for sanctuary to defile it with her bloody hands? Does she think this day's deed will go without vengeance?

If she's gone, let her go. God knows she has enemies enough to hound her and sniff her out of her hiding place. All my thoughts now must be for my sons. I must live for them only. I must save them from the vengeance of Creon's house—innocent instruments in their foul mother's hands!

A WOMAN: Jason! Jason! If you knew what new grief lies waiting for you here, you would have passed by this place forever.

JASON: What! Are her hands not bloody enough yet! Would she murder me too?

A WOMAN: Weep for your sons, Jason.

JASON: You do not mean that! She would not dare! Not her own children!

A WOMAN: They will never live and laugh for you again.

JASON: Where? Tell me where! Where did she do it?

A WOMAN: Open up the doors. Then hold back your tears, if you can.

JASON: What are you waiting for? Batter them in! Tear them down! Smash them open!

(As he batters at the doors, MEDEA appears on the roof, standing in a golden winged chariot. Before her on the chariot floor lie the bodies of the dead children)

MEDEA: Who are you that shout and batter at my door? You cannot awaken the dead so, nor take me who killed them. Now if you have some last, parting curse for me, Jason, say it quickly. You will never lay hands on me again. Not for nothing am I a daughter of the sun! From his own fiery home he has sent this chariot for me, to save me from my enemies.

JASON: You living temple of horror! A stench in the nostrils of gods and men alike! Murderer of your own children! Gloat on the walking death you've made of me! How can the sun still shine on you? Why doesn't the earth yawn at the sight of you and suck you down into its blackest pit? By all the gods, I curse you, Medea! Would that your mother's milk had been poison in your mouth and killed you at her breast! A curse on the evil day I brought you here to be a scourge to Greece! You charnel house of evil! Walking pestilence! What foul thing have you left undone? Traitress to your father! Murderess! Call up your brother's ghost! Call Pelias back from the dead! Go rouse old Creon and my murdered bride! Look at my sons!

Yet the gods must have willed this. They have sat in judgment on me. They have punished me for standing by while you murdered your brother and threw his limbs out on the sea to keep your father from catching us when I took you from his house that evil day. You gave me a sample then of what you were and what you were to be.

And now because you panted in the night for me and could not have me, you have killed my sons. Show me another woman in all Greece who would have done this thing? And yet I passed them by to marry you! It was no woman I married but a beast of the plains, a she-wolf dripping blood from her mouth, and thirsting still for mine. . . .

Oh you are beyond repentance as you were ever beyond mercy. No word of mine can pierce your heart, no damnation touch you! Out of my sight, vile barbarian bitch stinking with the blood of my children! Leave me alone to weep the end of all I had; for I shall never kiss my bride again or speak to my little sons.

MEDEA: Why should I stoop to answer you, Jason? I have paid off an old debt. We are quits now. You owe me nothing. Did you think to put me aside as an old garment no longer useful to you? You reckoned without me, then, you and your princess and old Creon, who hoped to drive me from Corinth. Call me whatever names you will, if it comforts you! I can bear with your curses. For I have done the thing my heart was set on doing. Jason, I have made you suffer!

JASON: Not me alone. This horror that bows me down can bring no happiness to you.

MEDEA: I walk with grief too, but mine is less hard to bear than before; for you cannot mock me now.

JASON: My sons, from what a devil's womb you came!

MEDEA: Oh my babies, you know it was your father's fault that you are dead.

JASON: Not mine! I am free of their blood. I never touched them!

MEDEA: Not with your hands, but with insults to me, and with your new marriage bed.

JASON: The truth at last! Because you still hankered after me they had to die.

MEDEA: I loved you, Jason.

JASON: You lusted for me!

MEDEA: Look at your sons, Jason, your little dead sons. Why do you turn away? Does it hurt you so?

JASON: Not dead, not dead! I cannot believe you have done this thing. The gods will reward you well for this, Medea.

MEDEA: The gods know in whose treachery this deed took root.

JASON: Grant me one last request, Medea, let me bury these, my sons, and shed over them in quiet a father's tears.

MEDEA: Not while I have breath to tell you no! I will bury them myself where no hostile hand can dig them up to defile their little bones. But you, Jason, the cause of all this blood and pain, shall live lonely and apart, and lonely and apart you shall die. Mark what I tell you. I raise my eyes and see you lying dead, your head crushed in by a beam of your own accursed ship. And as you die, may your last breath be sharp and bitter with the thought of me.

(The chariot slowly vanishes from sight)

JASON: The avenging furies damn you!

MEDEA: The gods cannot hear you, Jason. And why do you linger so long from your bride? You used not to linger so!

JASON: Yes, let me go now, to weep my last few days away.

MEDEA: Not few, but many. Long may you weep! Long may you live to weep!

JASON: My sons, my little dead sons!

MEDEA: You had no part in them. They were my own, flesh and bone and blood.

JASON: And for this you murdered them!

MEDEA: It was my way to murder you.

JASON: Let me kiss their lips just once, just once in my grief hold them in my arms.

MEDEA: Are they so dear to you now? They were not once so dear.

JASON: Just once to touch them, once to run my hands across their brows and through their hair!

MEDEA: Not even once. The wind may heed your cries. I cannot hear you.

JASON: I call upon you, all-seeing gods of the earth and sky, to witness how she will not pity me. Behold what I suffer at the hands of this murderess. Yet with what little strength I have, I weep for my dead, and call down the vengeance of the gods on you, Medea, the slayer of my children, who will not even so much as let me touch them or bury them. I curse the day that ever I thrust into your vile body the seed from which they came!

(Only MEDEA'S *mocking laughter answers him)*

CHORUS: *(Sing)*
IMMORTAL ZEUS CONTROLS THE FATE OF MAN, DECREES HIM LOVE OR GRIEF; OUR DAYS THE ECHO OF HIS WILL, RESOUND IN FURY OR PASS IN NOTHINGNESS AWAY.

CURTAIN

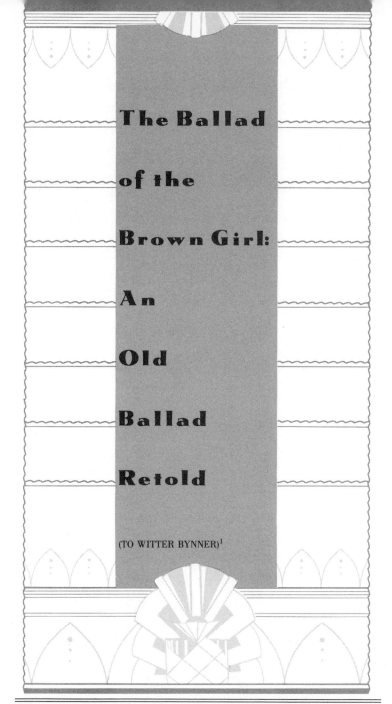

The Ballad of the Brown Girl: An Old Ballad Retold

(TO WITTER BYNNER)[1]

---

[1]Witter Bynner was born in Brooklyn on August 10, 1881, and died in Santa Fe, New Mexico, on June 1, 1968. He was a noted poet in his own right as well as a promoter of poetry. He was an important figure in the early publishing career of Cullen.

THE BALLAD OF THE BROWN GIRL

Oh, this is the tale the grandmas tell
In the land where the grass is blue,
And some there are who say 'tis false,
And some that hold it true.

     .   .   .   .   •   •

Lord Thomas on a summer's day
Came to his mother's door;
His eyes were ringed for want of sleep;
His heart was troubled sore.

He knelt him at his mother's side;
She stroked his curly head.
"I've come to be advised of you;
Advise me well," he said.

"For there are two who love me well—
I wot it from each mouth—
And one's Fair London, lily maid,
And pride of all the south.

She is full shy and sweet as still
Delight when nothing stirs;
My soul can thrive on love of her,
And all my heart is hers."

His mother's slender fingers ploughed
Dark furrows through his hair,
"The other one who loves you well,
Is she as sweet and fair?"

"She is the dark Brown Girl who knows
No more-defining name,
And bitter tongues have worn their tips
In sneering at her shame."

"But there are lands to go with her,
And gold and silver stores."
His mother whispered in his ear,
"And all her heart is yours."

His mother loved the clink of gold,
The odor and the shine
Of larders bowed with venison
And crystal globes of wine.

"Oh, love is good," the lady quoth,
"When berries ripe and sweet,
From every bush and weighted vine
Are crying, 'Take and eat.' "

"But what is best when winter comes
Is gold and silver bright;
Go bring me home the nut-brown maid
And leave the lily-white."

He sent his criers through the land
To cry his wedding day,
But bade them at Fair London's road
To turn the other way.

His bridal day dawned white and fair,
His heart held night within;
He heard its anguished beats above
The jocund wedding din.

The Brown Girl came to him as might
A queen to take her crown;

With gems her fingers flamed and flared;
Her robe was weighted down.

Her hair was black as sin is black
And ringed about with fire;
Her eyes were black as night is black
When moon and stars conspire;
Her mouth was one red cherry clipt
In twain, her voice a lyre.

Lord Thomas took her jewelled hand,
The holy words were said,
And they have made the holy vow
To share one board and bed.

But suddenly the furious feast
Is shattered with a shout;
Lord Thomas trembles at the word,
"Fair London is without."

All pale and proud she stands without,
And will not venture in;
He leaves the side of his nut-brown bride
To bid her enter in.

Her skin was white as almond milk
Slow trickling from the flower;
Her frost-blue eyes were darkening
Like clouds before a shower;

Her thin pink lips were twin rosebuds
That had not come to flower,
And crowning all, her golden hair
Was loosened out in shower.

He has taken her by her slim white hand,
(Oh, light was her hand in his)

But the touch ran wild and fierce and hot,
And burned like a brand in his.

"Lord Thomas," she said; her voice was low,
"I come unbidden here,
But I have come to see your bride
And taste your bridal cheer."

He has taken her by her slim white hand
And led her to his bride,
And brown and white have bent them low,
And sat them side by side.

He has brimmed a cup with the wedding wine,
He has placed it in her hand,
She has raised it high and smiled on him
Like love in a distant land.

"I came to see your bonny bride,
I came to wish you well,"
Her voice was clear as song is clear;
Clear as a silver bell.

"But, Thomas, Lord, is this your bride?
I think she's mighty brown;
Why didn't you marry a fair, bright girl
As ever the sun shone on?

For only the rose and the rose should mate,
Oh, never the hare and the hound,"
And the wine he poured for her crimson mouth
She poured upon the ground.

The flow of wine and jest has ceased,
The groom has flushed and paled,
The Brown Girl's lips are moist and red
Where her sharp white teeth assailed.

Dark wrath has climbed her nut-brown throat,
And wrath in her wild blood sings,
But she tramples her passions underfoot
Because she comes of kings.

She has taken her stand by her rival's side,
"Lord Thomas, you have heard,
As I am yours and you are mine
By ring and plighted word,
Avenge me here on our bridal day."—
Lord Thomas spoke no word.[1]

The Brown Girl's locks were held in place
By a dagger serpentine;
Thin it was and long and sharp,
And tempered well and fine.

And legend claimed that a dusky queen,
In a dusky dream-lit land,
Had loved in vain, and died of it,
By her own slim twilight hand.

The Brown Girl's hair has kissed her waist,
Her hand has closed on steel;
Fair London's blood has joined the wine
She sullied with her heel.

Lord Thomas caught her as she fell,
And cried, "My sweet, my fair,
Dark night has hid the golden sun,
And blood has thicked the air.

The little hand that should have worn
A golden band for me,

---

[1]As in "The Black Christ" and "Incident," spoken insults are as sharp as physical abuse for Cullen. In "The Ballad of the Brown Girl," the action hinges on the insulting words of Fair London and the absence of defending words from Lord Thomas.

The little hand that fluttered so
Is still as death can be."

He bent and kissed the weeping wound
Fresh in her heart's young core,
And then he kissed her sleeping mouth
That would not waken more.

He seized the Brown Girl's rippling hair
That swung in eddies loose,
And with one circle of his arm
He made a hairy noose.

He pulled it till she swooned for pain,
And spat a crimson lake;
He pulled it till a something snapped
That was not made to break.

And her he loved he brought and placed
By her who was his bride,
And brown and white like broken buds
Kept vigil side by side.

And one was like a white, white rose
Whose inmost heart has bled,
And one was like a red, red rose
Whose roots have witherèd.

Lord Thomas took a golden harp
That hung above his head;
He picked its strings and played a tune
And sang it to the dead.

"O lovers never barter love
For gold or fertile lands,
For love is meat and love is drink,
And love heeds love's commands."

"And love is shelter from the rain,
And scowling stormy skies;
Who casts off love must break his heart,
And rue it till he dies."

And then he hugged himself and grinned,
And laughed, "Ha, ha," for glee;
But those who watched knew he was mad,
And shudderèd to see.

And some made shift to go to him,
But there was in his eye
What made each man to turn aside
To let his neighbor by.

His mother in a satin gown
Was fain to go to him,
But his lips curled back like a gray wolf's fang,
When the huntsmen blow to him.

"No mother of mine, for gold's the god
Before whose feet you fall;
Here be two dead who will be three,
And you have slain us all.

Go dig one grave to hold us all
And make it deep and wide;
And lay the Brown Girl at my feet,
Fair London by my side."

And as he spoke his hand went up,
And singing steel swept down,
And as its kiss betrayed his heart,
Death wore a triple crown.

And in the land where the grass is blue,
In a grave dug deep and wide,
The Brown Girl sleeps at her true lord's feet,
Fair London by his side.

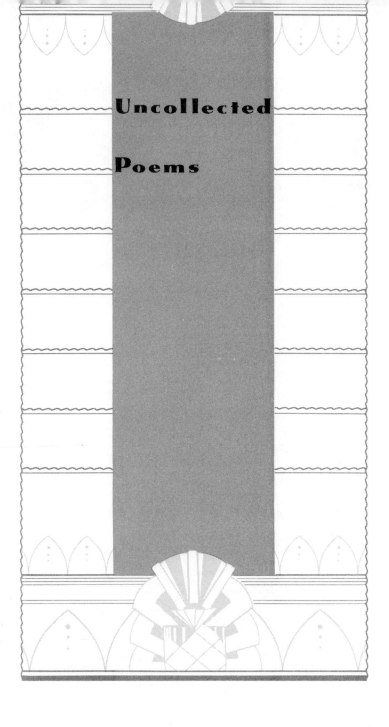

Uncollected

Poems

DEAR FRIENDS AND GENTLE HEARTS[1]

We open infant eyes
Of wonder and surprise
Upon a world all strange and new,
Too vast to please our childish view,
Yet love bends down and trust imparts;
We gaze around
And know we've found
Dear friends and gentle hearts;
Good-day, we smile, dear friends and gentle hearts;
Good-day dear friends and gentle hearts.

When on the western rim
Of time the sun grows dim,
And dimly on the closing eye
Fadeth the earth, the sea, the sky,
How blessedly this breath departs
If it pass out
While watch about
Dear friends and gentle hearts;
Good-night, we smile, dear friends and gentle hearts;
Good-night, dear friends, and gentle hearts.

April 1943

---

[1]Published in *On These I Stand*, New York: Harper & Brothers, 1947.

KARENGE YA MARENGE*

Wherein are words sublime or noble? What
Invests one speech with haloed eminence,
Makes it the sesame for all doors shut,
Yet in its like sees but impertinence?
Is it the hue? Is it the cast of eye,
The curve of lip or Asiatic breath,
Which mark a lesser place for Gandhi's cry
Than "Give me liberty or give me death!"

Is Indian speech so quaint, so weak, so rude,
So like its land enslaved, denied, and crude,
That men who claim they fight for liberty
Can hear this battle-shout impassively,
Yet to their arms with high resolve have sprung
At those same words cried in the English tongue?

August 19, 1942

---

*Do or die . . . —Gandhi [Footnote was part of original text, published in *On These I Stand*, New York: Harper & Brothers, 1947.]

CHRISTUS NATUS EST[1]

In Bethlehem
On Christmas morn,
The lowly gem
Of love was born.
Hosannah! *Christus natus est.*

Bright in her crown
Of fiery star,
Judea's town
Shone from afar:
Hosannah! *Christus natus est.*

While beasts in stall,
On bended knee,
Did carol all
Most joyously:
Hosannah! *Christus natus est.*

For bird and beast
He did not come,
But for the least
Of mortal scum.
Hosannah! *Christus natus est.*

Who lies in ditch?
Who begs his bread?
Who has no stitch
For back or head?
Hosannah! *Christus natus est.*

---

[1]Published in *On These I Stand*, New York: Harper & Brothers, 1947.

Who wakes to weep,
Lies down to mourn?
Who in his sleep
Withdraws from scorn?
Hosannah! *Christus natus est.*

Ye outraged dust,
On field and plain,
To feed the lust
Of madmen slain:
Hosannah! *Christus natus est.*

The manger still
Outshines the throne;
Christ must and will
Come to his own.
Hosannah! *Christus natus est.*

Christmas 1943

APOSTROPHE TO THE LAND[1]

O land of mine, O land I love,
  A Worm gnaws at your root;
Unless that Worm you scotch, remove,
  Peace will not be the fruit.

Let Hirohito be dethroned,
  With Hitler gibbet-high,
Let Mussolini, bloody, stoned,
  Be spaded deep in lye;

Destroy these three by rope or pyre,
  By poison, rack, or blade,
By every destruction dire
  The Christian mind has made;

Yet while the Worm remains to gorge
  Upon the nation's tree,
There is no armor we may forge
  To fit Peace perfectly.

Rend, rend the Swastika in twain,
  The Rising Sun deform;
But our own flag, shall it remain
  The garment of the Worm?

Is there no hand to lift it free
  Of that miasmic kiss;

[1]From *Phylon*, 4th Quarter, 1942, pp. 396–97.

The kiss of hate and bigotry,
  The seal of prejudice?

Is there no knight of burning zeal,
  No gifted Galahad,
In accents of redemptive steel
  To cry, "Rejoice! Be glad!"?

Goliath's David long is dust;
  From what heroic sperm
Shall come the deep and valiant thrust
  To slay the loathely Worm?

The little men with slanting eyes,
  They know our pedigree,
They know the length of the Worm that lies
  Under the lynching tree.

The men with strides that ape the geese,
  They know the nation's thorn:
How one man will his brother fleece,
  And hold his hue in scorn.

From Berlin, Rome, and Tokyo,
  The gibing flashes run:
"That land's good picking for the crow,
  Whose people are not one."

Not till the poll tax perishes
  With peons of the South,
And all that hatred cherishes
  With blatant, twisted mouth;

Not till the cheated cropper thrive
  And draw his first free breath
(Though court and custom still contrive
  His legalistic death);

Not till the hedges fall, the moats
   Be mirrors for the stars,
And fair hands drop from darker throats
   Shall we extinguish Mars.

O land of mine, O land I love,
   The Worm gnaws at your root;
Unless that Worm you scotch, remove,
   Peace will not be the fruit.

TO THE SWIMMER[1]

Now as I watch you, strong of arm and endurance,
  battling and struggling
With the waves that rush against you, ever with invincible
  strength returning
Into my heart, grown each day more tranquil and peaceful,
  comes a fierce longing
Of mind and soul that will not be appeased until, like you,
  I breast yon deep and boundless expanse of blue.

With an outward stroke of power intense your mighty
  arm goes forth,
Cleaving its way through waters that rise and roll, ever
  a ceaseless vigil keeping
Over the treasures beneath.

My heart goes out to you of dauntless courage and spirit
  indomitable,
And though my lips would speak, my spirit forbids me
  to ask,
"Is your heart as true as your arm?"

[1]From *The Modern School*, V (May 1918), p. 142.

LIFE'S RENDEZVOUS

(I Have a rendezvous with death . . .
—Alan Seeger)[1]

I have a rendezvous with Life
    And all travailling lovely things,
    Like groping seeds and beating
        wings,
And cracked lips warring with a fife.
I am betrothed to Beauty, scarred
    With suffering though she may be;
    In that she bears pain splendidly,
Her comeliness may not be marred.
The long, thin sword of dreams I wield
    Is light enough for dark and doubt;
    With "Life and Youth" my battle
        shout,
There is no blow can dent my shield.
I keep my tryst, come dawn or dusk,
    With Life, and find her always fair,
    With cool, soft touch, sleep-scented hair
Perfumed with poppy leaves and musk.
I draw in pride with each warm
        breath—
    Such rainbow seed has youth to sow,

---

[1]Alan Seeger was an American poet born in New York City on June 22, 1888. He went to France to write and study after graduating from Harvard and in 1914 enlisted in the French Foreign Legion. He rebelled against literary conventions, yet he used traditional verse forms. He was killed in action on July 4, 1916. *The Poems of Alan Seeger* (1916) is his only book of poems.

Such long, white roads young feet
                must know,
I have no time to think of death.
I put no faith in any day
        When this impassioned flesh of mine
        Shall less desire its bread and wine
All longing lost in primal clay.
The day God blew a silver horn
        To herald light and fire in birth,
        The day I knew my body's worth.
I was not made for dying scorn.
When I leave earth, a slim, dark boy
        (Whom men misname) will take my
                hand,
        Nor find my wings less eager-fanned
To waft me to Life's clearer joy.

I HAVE A RENDEZVOUS WITH LIFE[1]

I have a rendezvous with Life
In days I hope will come
Ere youth has sped and strength of mind,
Ere voices sweet grow dumb;
I have a rendezvous with Life
When Spring's first heralds hum.
It may be I shall greet her soon;
Shall riot at her behest.
It may be I shall seek in vain
The place of her downy breast.
Yet I would keep this rendezvous
And deem all hardships sweet,
If at the end of the long white way,
There Life and I should meet.
Sure some would cry it better far
To crown their days with sleep,
Than face the road, the wind and rain
To heed the calling deep.
Tho' wet nor blow nor space I fear,
Yet fear I deeply too,
Lest Death should greet and claim me ere
I keep Life's rendezvous.

[1]From *Current Opinion*, May 1924, p. 708.

LA BELLE, LA DOUCE, LA GRANDE[1]

France! How shall we call her belle again?
Does loveliness reside
In sunken cheeks, in bellies barren and denied?
What twisted inconsistent pen
Can ever call her belle again?
Or douce? Can gentleness invade
The frozen heart, the mind betrayed,
Or search for refuge in the viper's den?
How shall we call her douce again?
Or grande? Did greatness ever season
The broth of shame, repudiation, treason?
Or shine upon the lips of little lying men?
How shall we call her grande again?

Has history no memory, nor reason?
What land inhabited of men
Has never known that dark hour when
First it felt the sting of treason?
Petain?[2] Laval?[3] Can they outweigh

---

[1]Published in *On These I Stand*, New York: Harper & Brothers, 1947.

[2]Henri Phillippe Pétain (1856–1951)—French general and national hero of World War I who was discredited as chief of state of the French government in Vichy in World War II and died in prison. Although he was more reluctant than Pierre Laval to collaborate with the Nazis, he imposed discriminatory laws against both the Jews and the Masons during the time he headed the government. He also publicly opposed the Allied invasion of North Africa in 1942.

[3]Pierre Laval (1883–1945)—French politician who led the Vichy government and collaborated with the Nazis. He was executed as a traitor to France in October 1945.

By an eyelash or a stone
The softest word she had to say,
That sainted soul of France called Joan?[4]

Nay even now, look up, see fall
As on Elisha Elijah's shawl,[5]
Joan's mantle on the gaunt De Gaulle:[6]
New Knight of France, great paladin,
Behold him sally forth to win
Her place anew at freedom's hand,
A place for France: la belle, la douce, la grande.

July 10, 1944

[4]Joan of Arc, the Maid of Orleans (1412–31), was the daughter of a shepherd who, while tending the flock, heard the voice of an angel who told her to lead the French Army against the English invaders. Her successes led to the crowning of Charles VII. Joan was captured and burned at the stake.

[5]Elisha (ninth century B.C.)—Old Testament prophet, pupil and successor of Elijah. He was given the prophetic mantle (I Kings 19:19–21 and II Kings 2:8–18) by Elijah as a sign of his authority. Elijah was a major Hebrew Old Testament prophet who saved Judaism from corruption.

[6]Charles André Joseph Marie De Gaulle (1890–1970)—French army officer, statesman, and writer. He was the leader of the Free French resistance during World War II and was elected President of the Fifth Republic on December 21, 1958.

A NEGRO MOTHER'S LULLABY[1]

(After visiting John Brown's grave)[2]

Hushaby, hushaby, dark one at my knee;
Slumber you softly, nor pucker, nor frown;
Though some may be bonded, you shall be free,
Thanks to a man . . . Osawatamie Brown.
　　His sons are high fellows,
　　An Archangel is he,
　　And they doff their bright haloes
　　To none but the Three.

Hushaby, hushaby, sweet darkness at rest,
Two there have been who their lives laid down
That you might be beautiful here at my breast:
Our Jesus and . . . Osawatamie Brown.
　　His sons are high fellows,
　　An Archangel is he,
　　And they doff their bright haloes
　　To none but the Three.

Hushaby, hushaby, when a man, not a slave,
　　With freedom for wings you go through the town,
Let your love be dew on his evergreen grave;
Sleep, in the name of Osawatamie Brown.
　　Rich counsel he's giving
　　Close by the throne,
　　Tall he was living

---

[1]Published in *On These I Stand*, New York: Harper & Brothers, 1947.

[2]John Brown was a famous white abolitionist who, with a small band that included his sons and some blacks, tried unsuccessfully to raid the federal arsenal at Harpers Ferry in Virginia (now West Virginia) in October 1859 in order to foment a slave insurrection.

But now taller grown.
His sons are high fellows,
An Archangel is he,
And they doff their bright haloes
To none but the Three.

Lake Placid, N.Y.
August 1941

LINES FOR A HOSPITAL[1]

Ye blind, ye deaf, ye mute! Ho, here's healing!
    Here's light to brim
    The eyeball dim;
    Here's sound to cheer
    The muted ear;
    Ways to oppose
    The wayward nose,
    And make sweet notes
    From locked throats
Like chimes cascading come, all pealing:
    Ho, here's healing.

November 1943

[1]Published in *On These I Stand*, New York: Harper & Brothers, 1947.

JUDAS ISCARIOT (FIRST VERSION)[1]

Let's talk of Judas for a while,
    Try to picture him—
Not painted black with guilt and guile,
    Not red with crime, and grim;
Not crafty-eyed and insincere,
    Following flesh and gold;[2]
Perhaps we'd shed a fervent tear
    For him if all were told.

I think when Judas' mother heard
    His first faint cry the night
That he was born, that worship stirred
    Her at the sound and sight.
She thought his was as fair a frame
    As flesh and blood had worn.
I think she made this lovely name
    For him—"Star of my morn."

And in Judea's dusty streets
    He romped with other boys,
He felt youth's victories and defeats,
    And made his share of noise.
I think he knew the growing Christ,
    And played with Mary's son,

---

[1] From *Southwestern Christian Advocate*, March 1923, p. 1.

[2] Cullen's references in the preceding lines are to the curse of race among the three major outcast groups of the United States: the black, the Indian, and the Jew. The underlying theme here is to see Judas as metaphysically cursed in much the same way as if he had been cursed for his skin color or ethnicity.

And where mere mortal craft sufficed,
    There Judas may have won.

As any mother's son he grew
    From spring to crimson spring;
I think his eyes were black—or blue—
    His hair curled like a ring.
I think his voice was soft and low—
    This little Jewish lad
Of Christ's own time, of long ago,
    Not wholly good, nor bad.

And then one day young Christ,
    Prophetic eyes agleam,
Told Judas of a far off tryst
    Between him and a dream.
And Judas listened wonder-eyed
    Until the Christ was through,
Then said, "And I, though good betide
    Or ill, will go with you."

And so he followed, heard Christ preach,
    Saw how by miracle
The blind man looked, the dumb got speech,
    The leper found him well.
And Judas in those holy hours
    Loved Christ, and loved him much,
And in his heart he sensed dead flowers
    Bloom at the Master's touch.

And when Christ felt the death hour creep
    With sullen drunken lurch,
He said to Peter, "Feed my sheep,
    And build my holy church."
He gave to each the special task
    Which should be his to do,

But reaching one I hear him ask,
  "What shall I give to you?"

Then Judas in his young desire
  Said, "Give me what you will."
Christ spoke to him with words of fire,
  "Then Judas you must kill
One whom you love, one who loves you
  As only God's son can;
This is the work for you to do
  To save the creature man."

"And men to come will curse your name,
  And hold you up to scorn;
In all the world will be no shame
  Like yours—This is love's thorn;
It takes a strong will of heart and soul,
  But Man is under ban—
Think, Judas, can you play this role
  In Heaven's holy plan?"

So Judas took the sorry part,
  Went out and spoke the word,
And gave the kiss that broke his heart,
  But no one knew or heard.
At last a tree was kind to him
  And took away his breath,
And judging man assigned to him;
  "The wage of sin is death."

I do not think he sweats in hell
  Or raises tearless eyes
To where his favored comrades dwell
  In beatific skies;
I do not think through rain and frost
  His soul fares on and on,

Forever damned, forever lost
    Like old times dead and gone.

I think there is a table round,
    And Christ Himself is head;
And round it all the twelve are found
    Who followed where he led
And Judas sits down with the rest,
    And none shrinks from his hand,
For there the worst is as the best,
    And there they understand.

Ah you may think of Judas, friend,
    As one who broke his word,
Whose neck came to a bitter end
    For giving up his Lord.
But I would rather think of him
    As the little Jewish lad
Who gave young Christ heart, soul, and limb,
    Not wholly good, nor bad.

FROM LIFE TO LOVE[1]

Four winds and seven seas have called me friend,
And countless roads have known my restless feet;
Deep crystal springs and pollened buds were sweet
For sustenance their princely fare to lend,
While nameless birds from grove and blossomed bend
Deluged my soul with song; if it were meet
To love Life so, then Love will but complete
My joy, for Life with Love can never end.
Love, I have heard the sweet of your voice, have seen
You pass the dawn-flushed singing hills between;
Now suppliant I kneel and pray you show
The mercied sceptre favored Esther saw;[2]
The dawn in me has broke, and well I know
That Love is king and creed and Persian law.

---

[1]From *Opportunity*, January 1925, p. 15.

[2]Esther, principal figure of the Old Testament book of the same name. She was the beautiful Jewish wife of the Persian king Ahasuerus (Xerxes I) who persuaded her husband to retract a general order to annihilate the Jews.

NIGHT RAIN[1]

I wake to the sound of a soft, low patter
  That comes like sudden news,
Or like the slow, uncadenced clatter
  Of well-filled wooden shoes.

I know I have not waked for long,
  That I shall dream again,
That God has sent a slumber song
  Of dew and drowsy rain.

I hear it rush the willows through,
  And strike the garden gate;
Far off a love bird's plaintive coo
  Is answered of its mate.

The night rain works a subtle charm
  Day showers never know;
It makes me burrow deep and warm
  Beneath my sheets of snow.

It brims the pansy's eager cup,
  It dives to the oak's dank roots,
Inquisitive, meanders up,
  And climbs to the newest shoots.

It drips a melancholy tune
  As plunging fierce and deep,
It scurries wild across the moon
  To steep my eyes in sleep.

---

[1]From *Crisis*, February 1925, p. 165.

SINGING IN THE RAIN[1]

The grass bends low, the pregnant trees
Bend down like men too full in years;
The rain with dull monotonies
Beats time, and gives the willows tears.
The night goes tense as a padded thief
Whose feet in haunted ways are led,
Or as bereaved who dam their grief
For fear their woe will reach the dead.

With rhymless drip the sloping eaves
Intone a lay, a subtle mock
Whose cadence weird no whit relieves
The tuneless measure of the clock.
But in some glade faun-tenanted,
A lone bird sings of love and pain.
(Oh heart in sorrow garmented,
There's hope while song can hush the rain.)

Ethereal and clear it soars,
A cherub burst of harmony
That floods the night's gloom-mantled pores,
With mellow waves of melody;
Now high, now low, cascades of trills
That climb the stars in a grand finale,
And, loving earth, caress the hills,
And echo long in the windy valley.

---

[1]From *Southwestern Christian Advocate*, May 1923, p. 8.

On heaven's milky balustrade
Leans wistful, longing Israfel
Whose heart-stringed lyre has never played
Celestial tunes so sweet and well.
And I am somewhere worlds away
In God's rich autumn tinted lanes,
Where, heart at ease from life's dismay,
My soul's high song beats back the rains.

THE POET[1]

Poet, poet, what is your task,
Here mid earth's grief and pain?
"To bid them go to distant realms,
Nor enter here again."

Poet, poet, what want you here
Where all is toil and care?
To sing sweet strength into your limbs
That each his cross may bear.

Poet, poet, what do you ask
As pay for each glad song?
"Full guerdon mine if you but love
My tunes, and love them long."

Poet, poet, what old refrain
Is it that rings so sweet?
"A simple line—Life after Death—
And time has eager feet."

Poet, poet, where will you go
At last, fire crowned and shod?
"Upward at length, a sapphire star,
I'll send forth rays for God."

---

[1]From *Southwestern Christian Advocate*, November 1923, p. 1.

One

Way

to

Heaven

This is a satirical novel of the Harlem Renaissance published in the same year as Wallace Thurman's Harlem Renaissance satire, *Infants of the Spring* and just a year after George Schuyler's satirical Harlem novel, *Black No More*. Critics have found Cullen's novel to be structurally flawed, and consider the low-life story of the conversion and marriage of Mattie and Sam to be not convincingly related to the socialite life of Constantia Brandon, Mattie's employer. Yet it seems this division between rich and poor, secular and sacred, servants and masters is precisely the sort of disjunctive breach that Cullen wanted. While there are many figures in *One Way to Heaven* who suggest real life (Cullen warns the reader that only "some of the characters in this book are fictitious," and one can readily see the outlines of such people as white novelist and Renaissance promoter Carl Van Vechten, black minstrel Sam Lucas, race theorist Lothrop Stoddard, black nationalist Marcus Garvey, partygiver A'Lelia Walker, poet Langston Hughes, among others), the novel is only partly of interest as a *roman à clef*. I have not provided notes suggesting who the characters might be, so that the novel might be read on other, more rewarding levels.

For Harold Jackman[1]

---

[1]See earlier note on Harold Jackman, p. 104.

PART ONE

NOTE

*Some of the characters
in this book are
fictitious*

CHAPTER
ONE

Sam Lucas, striding through the raw, mordant December night felt that he had chosen an ill moment in which to come to Harlem. New York was bright and gay, and these colored people looked happy, as he had been told he would find them; but they also seemed too intent upon their own affairs to promise much attention to an ill-starred stranger. Their faces did not radiate that hospitality which he had left behind in the southland. He had been years getting here, dallying on the way, making love and turning tricks, settling here and there for a month or two, or a year, but with his eyes and his heart set more lover-like on New York than they had ever been set on a woman. Time and time again he had unloosed himself from the tightening knots of an embrace and had set his feet on the one way he felt he had to go. He had begged rides in wagons and trucks from town to town (it was a long way up from Texas); he had swung on to freighters and would bear their mark upon him till he died. It was over six years now since he had lost his left arm when, clambering down to escape detection, he had missed his footing and had fallen, with his arm stretched out like an enticement for the sharp rear wheel that had kissed him into unconsciousness. Ever after he had had a feeling of having been buried before his time.

He drew his frayed overcoat more closely about his lean, raw-boned body, and tucked his armless left sleeve into his pocket where it would not flap in the wind. Shivering, he quickened the speed of his gaunt, limber legs, and buried his face down into the confines of his coat collar, letting his own breath rise steaming up to warm his neck and ears. He had a fine, intelligent-looking face which he could never justify with his mind; a slightly elongated head with high-mounting cheek-bones, and sinking jaws, which gave him a hungry, somewhat acidulous look though his stomach might be full and satisfied; he often wondered why his mouth should be so wide and his lips so thin; he sometimes pursed his mouth up when he laughed, ashamed of its reckless expanse whenever he happened to let himself go; but he was proud of his strong, even white teeth, wedged like unpunctured dice in their firm red sockets. He had a woman's conceit for his eyes and his skin. The former were a deep electric brown, and nothing could be blacker or smoother than his skin, marred only where a long knife-wound in healing had left a sweeping streak of tan on one cheek, like a filament of brown hair imbedded in jet.

Suddenly he stopped before a mammoth pile of brown stone which by means of a gilt-and-black signboard proclaimed itself the Mount Hebron African Methodist Episcopal Church. Sam whistled long and loudly as he gazed at it, thinking, "My people sure are rising." Various placards tacked to the ecclesiastical doors or tied to the iron railing which ran along outside the church announced that watch-night services were being held, and that the Reverend Clarence Johnson, a famed singing evangelist from Texas, would preach the last sermon of the old year.

He joined the deepening stream of people entering the church, and as he stood on the threshold, letting his eyes roam for a moment over the vast auditorium, he sensed an involuntary thrill of satisfaction and self-commendation course through him, as though he were contemplating a thing of his own creating. Here he was in the largest Negro church in New York City on watch night. He could not escape the wonder of it. Shaped like a half-moon, the huge auditorium groaned beneath its mingled weight of the righteous and the unregenerate. Every bit of space into which a body could be squeezed with any degree of discomfort, had been utilized. In happy Christian violation of the laws of health and fire-prevention, small, collapsible camp chairs had been placed in the aisles. There would be no such crowd as this again until Easter Sunday morning; the seasons between the celebration of the birth and death of Christ were always slack; only on watch night and at Easter time was the real power of the church flashed forth beyond the range of doubt; only then like some granite octopus did its many doors reach out and suck in to utter satiation. For throughout the year good luck follows him who is found in the house of the Lord when New Year's chimes are sounded; and on Easter Sunday, if it is bright and sunny, church attendance is as happy a prelude to Harlem's fashion parade as to that of lower Fifth Avenue.

Sam managed to squeeze into one of the forward pews, where, after divesting himself of his overcoat, he sat cramped and uncomfortable between a meek-looking brown man and an obese saffron-hued woman who, despite the energy with which she was helping to sing "You must be a lover of the Lord," frankly resented his intrusion, showing her displeasure by singing more loudly and more off key. He flashed the hot electric current of his eyes upon her and let his smile go, not caring into how wide a grin his thin lips might stretch; that smile, he knew, at its best was irresistible. His neighbor capitulated, and withdrew some of her bulk into herself in order to give him a bit more room.

He settled himself, and sat back in a reverie, his heavy black lids drooping down and stemming the bright dynamic flow of his eyes. He let his right hand glide slowly and gently into the pocket of his jacket with a movement at once both searching and caressing, as if he sought to assure himself that something cherished and serviceable was in its accustomed place. An easy, satisfied smile grew and spread over his countenance as his hand encountered the desired object. The smile vanished as suddenly as it had appeared while his hand stroked something in his pocket with the gentle back-and-forth motion with which one might stroke a small and frightened kitten, hoping to ease it of its fear.

He was biding his time. Inside he felt interchangeably hot and cold, and his stomach seemed to recede from him, hollow and sunken, making him feel as though he were falling from a great height. It was always like that when he entered a church intent on giving a performance. Tonight's setting filled him with pride; the immensity of the place, the number of the people, appalled and fascinated him. On this evening's program he felt that he was to play a particular and enviable part, a rôle not to be exceeded even by that of the Reverend Clarence Johnson, whose importation from Texas was there on the outside in large black letters for all to see. *He* had not been sent for, but he too was a powerful instrument in the hands of the Lord. His rôle called for no particular cue; he was his own cue-master. Over a period of eight years he had played this part in twelve states, and hoped before he died to play them all.

It was testimonial time. All around him people were rising, singing, talking, testifying, telling what the Lord had done for them throughout the year, some saying that times had been bad, that adversity and sickness and death had tracked them down, but that when they lay pinned to the earth and gasping for breath, the Lord God Jehovah had reached down and raised them up. Their faces, for the most part, were animated with a sincere fervor that seemed to run from one to another, although here and there were persons who spoke in voices listlessly unintonated, as if they were speaking pieces the import of which was totally lost to them. Many prefaced their testimonials with hymns, some in gayly syncopated time that made their hands and the listeners' rush together impulsively, measures that careened through the body, setting their feet tapping and stretching their mouths wide with loud hosannas and amens;

while others sang tunes that were sorrowful and heart-disturbing, as if the singers bore the weight of the world upon their shoulders, as if the cross were a very near and personal thing of which they could not rid themselves, nor cared to; as if their very happiness depended upon this very sorrow.

Their testimonials were repetitious and rich in homely similes.

"I've put my hand to the gospel-plow, and I can't let go till my harvest comes." The speaker, a tall Indian-looking woman with a beaked nose advancing from a proud, stern face, lifted her hand as she spoke, as if calling upon the elements to witness the un-shakableness of her decision.

"I'm clinging to the old rugged cross." This time it was a man, short, squat, thick-set, his yellow face marked strongly with Asiatic crossings, his short hair curled and rebellious. "I'm climbing the rough side of the mountain," he continued, plaintively, "but Jesus holds me by the hand."

As if the picture were more than he could bear, a young boy seated behind the testifier sniggered outright, and then stuffed his handkerchief into his mouth in a vain attempt to marshal himself into proper church behavior.

Midway of the church a small child stood up and quoted, "Jesus wept." A faint wave of laughter, like a soft wind touching grass, rippled across the church, and died, caught up and lost in the sober realization that God's house was not a place for levity.

There were those who declared with conviction, "I know that my Redeemer liveth," and then sat down with proud, radiant faces. Others simply importuned, "Pray for me," and took their seats shyly, as if confused, like neophytes who were embarrassed in the presence of those whose church membership was longer, whose religious experience was wider. And many combined both prayer and promise, saying, "Pray for me, and on the judgment morning I'll be there to help crown Him Lord of all."

At length when, in their anxiety to testify, dozens of people rose simultaneously from their seats, each endeavoring to be heard above his neighbor's equally futile but valiant attempts, the local preacher, a small, dark man who was conducting this phase of the service, raised his hand, interposing silence.

"This has been beautiful," he said, stretching his hands forth as if he would draw the entire church to him, and bless them. "The Lord has been here and walked among us. We have felt the wind from His garments blow upon us as He passed by. But some of us haven't been able to speak for Him, and it's now time for our preaching. It's eleven o'clock. One more hour and the old year will be gone. I am going to ask all those who haven't testified and who do love the Lord, and you're trying to walk in the way you feel He'd want you to go, just to rise silently and so express your desire to press onward to the higher mark which is in Christ Jesus."

Half the congregation rose and stood silent with bowed heads for a few moments, and then sat down. Of those who had remained seated, not all had testified; some were brazen, unrepentant, untouched. Sam Lucas had not testified, nor did he stand.

A door which gave off from the rostrum opened; two men came out and mounted into the pulpit. The first, the Reverend Mr. Drummond, pastor of Mount Hebron Church, was a thick-set tannish man with exaggerated eyebrows and a copious mustache. His walk was deliberate; his eyes were hazy and gentle. He wasted no time, but walked directly to the lectern, where he proclaimed in a voice so deep that his words issued from his cavernous mouth like growls, "We are glad to have with us tonight our brother in the gospel, Reverend Clarence Johnson, who has come to us all the way from Texas, to break to us the bread of life. All you who know the worth of prayer, pray with him, that what he says may be to the good of our souls and to the glory of God."

Bible in hand, Reverend Johnson advanced, singing. He was slight of build, yet with a slenderness that suggested a dormant vitality; his eyes were bright and hard; they betokened temper and a zealousness unwedded to an equivalent patience. When he moved, he gave the impression that somewhere behind him, or above him, were invisible strings held by steady hands which compelled his movements. His voice was a surprise; for seeing him enter one felt that he was vocally unequipped to send a message into the recesses of that vast tabernacle. But as he sang, his voice went out in rich, clearly-accentuated waves of melody, as if he somehow had managed to reach down and press upward into his throat all the blood and vigor which coursed through his body.

> "I've opened my mouth to the Lord,
> And I won't turn back;
> I will go, I shall go
> To see what the end will be."

It was a good tune, well chosen; it was warm, irresistible to throat and hands and feet, the sort of song which those who didn't know the words hummed, to which bodies swayed in spiritual syncopation; a sturdy hymn which, when it ended, would not die away in a gurgle, as if it had suddenly been throttled, but which would carry in its wake a ripple of amens and hallelujahs. It was elemental Negro religion expressing itself in song.

"I am the Resurrection and the Life."

He had chosen his text and was preaching. Here was no treatise for the learned, no hairs to split for quibblers; if there were doctors and lawyers and school-teachers here tonight, if smart young college girls and boys had sauntered in, with horns and cowbells hidden beneath their coats in readiness for the New Year's frenzy, there were also simple, more naïve, unlettered people here who were hungry for something which he could give them. They wanted the five loaves and the two fish. He had tried to lift his followers up to him when he first started to preach, years ago, a raw, young recruit, with advanced ideas and a fine scorn for simplicity and unquestioning belief. But long ago he had discovered that he must go down to them. If he did not believe all he preached, if sometimes he doubted the virgin birth of Christ and the infinite wisdom of God, after having sent mourners away shining with belief and satisfaction, he scourged himself with penitence, he fasted and prayed, endeavoring to appease he knew not what dreadful Who.

"I have given you these," he would cry; "help my unbelief"; and he would go forth to preach again.

"I am the Resurrection and the Life." . . . The soaring, vibrant voice spoke on. He was no common preacher; he was an artist. There was fire enough in him to commit that truth to the most ignorant hearts before him. He need not make use of the four letters which with utter propriety might be strung behind his name, no more than he needed the two honor keys which he never wore, of which he never spoke, the exact location of which, were he asked, he could not tell. Such insignia he had discarded when he went down to the people, throwing them aside as weights which might too easily beset him. Those who came to him wanted poetry (though they might not have called it that) and song, and all the beaded, miraculous wine of the Bible. They came from the wash-tub, they came with hands calloused from mop and pail and skillet. They had no hunger for the hard bread of reason, but for the soft, easily digested manna of magic.

Slowly and graphically he depicted the betrayal and the cruci-fixion of Christ. He made each feel upon his own cheek the flame of the dastardly kiss, speaking with an intensity that caused many to look at their own hands, half fearing to find them red and raw with the marks of nails; for never had the blows of those far-off hammers been so dinned into their ears. When he spoke of the glory of the resurrection, they saw the three women wonder-stricken before the open tomb, at its side the great and ponderous stone rolled away; he recreated for them the angel standing with his sword of petrified fire; in the fervor of his narration, he gave the angel a name, numbered his wings to the count of six, and told what his specific duties were in heaven. He plied the wings of his imagination and floated away as if on a magic carpet.

And yet the fire did not fall. He had spoken half an hour and the fire had not burned. Here and there someone from time to time said, "Amen," or, "How true!" but for the most part his audience sat before him silent, attentive, but undemonstrative, a half-moon of faces, a rainbow of impassivity. He understood his people well enough to know that where there was no demonstration there was small success. He had hoped he would not be forced to resort to some things tonight. There were means of which he was weary. His most dependable tricks were frayed with use, dusty with time, yet powerful he knew through repetition. He had wanted to end on a note of joy and hope. But he must have the fire.

Now his walk became more spasmodic as he strode the length of the pulpit; his voice grew menacing; his gestures snapped threats as though he were cracking an invisible whip at them. "I am the Resurrection and the Life," he cried. "True, Christ *is* the resurrection and the life, but He is also death and everlasting damnation. To such as believe on Him He will give eternal life, rest in the bosom of Abraham, not only hereafter, but here. He will bind up your wounds, heal your broken hearts, pay your rent, supply food and clothing. But for such as reject Him He has prepared an horrible pit, a place of fire and brimstone, an everlasting hell. You liars, cheaters, whoremongers, where will you spend eternity? In peace with the sons of God, or thirsting in hell with Dives?"

Somewhere far back in the church a woman wailed. His face lighted up as an actor's at applause. With his open palm he smote the Bible before him; a sweeping gesture from his arm sent the lectern lamp to the floor, where the frosted bulb shattered into a small heap of snow-like glass. He was unaware of this calamity. The poet's frenzy and the prophet's power were upon him, and his meager frame trembled out of all control of brain or any restrictive muscle. At this moment he was pure emotion made man.

"Some of us," he reminded them, "have mothers on the other side, and fathers, sisters and brothers and husbands and wives. We promised to meet them on the other side. Have we kept faith with them or have we lied to our dead? If any man sin, he has an Advocate in heaven. Who will place his case in Christ's hands? Earthly lawyers may fail you, but Christ has power before a tribunal greater than any on earth. He is the Captain who has never lost a battle, the Great Physician who has never lost a patient. His names are many and mighty. Some have called Him a little white stone cut out of the mountain, forever rolling and gathering strength. Some have said He was the Lily of the Valley, the Rose of Sharon, the Bright and Morning Star, the fairest among ten thousand. But I think the sweetest name He bears is Saviour. Who will come up before the old year goes out and the new year comes in, and let Him save you? Who will come, just as you are?"

His face was shining, anxious, glowing with sweat. He began to sing:

> "Just as I am without one plea,
> But that Thy blood was shed for me,
> And that Thou bidst me come to Thee,
> O Lamb of God, I come, I come."

The church stirred clumsily like some mammoth shifting in slumber; as the tension relaxed into curiosity, heads were turned to see who would come forward; people looked at their neighbors accusingly, wondering why they did not go up and be saved. The hymn droned on, slow, sluggish, literary. A young girl circled the entire church, groped along the walls, and finally reached the pulpit, where she knelt down and hid her face in her hands. A man shuffled down the mid-aisle and knelt beside her.

But that fire which consumes did not fall. Fifteen minutes to the new year. The hymn slid forward into silence, lost on a pathetic note of defeat.

"Who will come? Who will change his way of living?

> "If I were you I'd make a change,
> If I were you I'd make a change,
> If I were you I'd make a change,
> Oh, my friend, can't you hear God calling,
> Won't you make a change?"

He had come down from the rostrum, and now he stood within the little railing that encircled the lower pulpit. As he sang he held his hands extended toward them, pleading. This new song was something of his own, an invitation which he had created for their need. They understood it, caught it up, swayed to it, paid it lusty tribute with hands and feet. The tempo was lively; with different words and sung a bit more slowly it would have answered admirably as a blues. There was native sorrow in it, and native wit:

"O dancing girl, won't you make a change?"

In the gallery a woman screamed, threw back her head, and beat the air about her, until two women ushers, ample parcels of womanhood that might have been selected for just this purpose, rushed up and held her; they stationed themselves at her sides, pinioned her arms firmly, and let her leap up and down between them as if she were jumping a rope. From time to time as she jumped she cried, "Sweet Jesus." A spare man with aqueous blue eyes set in a sullen, fair face walked up to the altar with a defiant stride, and knelt down, while the thin little brown woman who had been sitting with him ran down the aisle behind him, caught him to her breast, and cried out for all the church to hear, "I thank you, Jesus, I thank you," and then went back to her seat.

The fire was burning now; like a natural man the Holy Ghost was walking among them. Reverend Johnson's eyes were kindled with the zeal of the proselyter. He strode back and forth within the altar rail, letting his hand rest for a moment on each of the heads bowed down before him, whispering to each penitent some word of comfort or some promise:

"If you make one step, my brother, Christ will make two.

"Though your sins be as scarlet, my sister, believe on Him, and they shall be whiter than snow.

"Come without money, sister; come buy and eat; come eat of the tree of life, and drink from the fountain that never shall run dry."

Seven more minutes to the new year, and he had but three mourners there before him. He looked over his audience and saw, not far from him, a withered yellow woman pleading vigorously with a young girl seated at her side. From where he stood he could see that the girl was pretty; the string of flashy red beads that circled her throat lighted up her black face like sunshine on black satin. Her black hat was edged with red, and her lips, pressed tightly and sullenly together, glowed more brightly than he felt they should. He had no reason to, but he thought of Mary Magdelene, and he felt that this woman would be a welcome sacrifice on the altar of the Lord, a tribute which would be taken up in smoke and flames like the venison of Abel. He would go down to her.

The faded yellow woman at her side saw him coming and settled back in her seat to leave the matter in more persuasive hands. He bent over the girl and whispered:

"Are you a Christian, my child?"

She turned dark, resentful eyes on him, and he felt suddenly that even for the Lord's sake he should not have intruded upon her.

"No, I'm not," she said.

"Then why don't you become one tonight? Why don't you change now and become one of God's children? Come, let us pray for you."

She would not answer him, but stared straight ahead of her, and sheer through her smooth even-coated blackness he could see the flush of embarrassment rise up and flood her face.

"Won't you come, my sister?"

A stubborn man himself, he recognized intractability when he encountered it, and so turned away from her at last, ashamed and beaten.

His heart was hot within him; he felt undone and cheated as he walked back to the altar rail; not even the three mourners abjectly curved there could lighten him; he could have passed them all by for that vital arrow-slim figure in red and black which had rejected all the blandishments of the Lord. He felt personally humiliated.

Though there were ninety and nine safely penned into the fold, he keenly coveted this one stray sheep. As he sensed a familiar warmth inundate his cheeks, he cooled them with a brutal, angry stroke from the back of his hand.

And then Sam Lucas and the devil stepped in.

"O mother's son, won't you make a change.
O mother's son, won't you make a change,
O mother's son, won't you make a change,
O mother's son, don't you hear God calling,
Won't you make a change?"

While the church rocked gently back and forth to this verse, Sam rose from his seat and squeezed past the three persons between him and the aisle. His stout neighbor encouraged him with, "Lord help you, son." Tears welled in his eyes, overflowed them, and trickled down his cheeks. He had half the church to traverse in order to reach the mourner's bench. As he walked his left sleeve flapped. People became aware of this physical deficiency, and he could feel their pity flow out and engulf him. Reverend Johnson saw him coming, and his heart gladdened until his face shone.

As Sam reached the rail, he delved into his right-hand coat pocket, threw down something, then knelt down and sobbed.

The evangelist had started toward him, his hand pulsing with a benediction, his tongue a quiver brimming with arrows of consolation. But as he looked down and saw what lay at Sam's feet his hand recoiled as if controlled by a spring; his eyes congealed into pin-points of anger. There at his feet, spread out like a various-colored fan, was a pack of cards, and beside the cards, open and flashing with a sinister defiance, a bright razor.

"This man," the Reverend Johnson commenced in a voice so loud and troubled that Sam looked up in amazement which verged into a half-fearful recognition—"This man—" but his words were lost in the tide of emotion which surged from the altar rail into lower pews and gallery; women wept and clapped their hands, men stomped and shouted. Here was magic which not even the preacher had been able to deal out to them: fifty-two playing-cards, a sharp bright razor, and a sinner's heart all displayed on the altar of the Lord. The very devil had been laid low before them.

"This man—" the Reverend Johnson cried again, and was heard as much as one raindrop among thousands. He looked out over his audience and saw, with wonder tinged with resentment, the dark girl gazing with fascinated eyes on Sam's betrayed instruments of sin. She watched them for a moment, then rose slowly from her seat, wringing her hands. She took her head in her hands and rocked it back and forth, moaning, making soft unintelligible sounds like a hunted animal, wounded and too terror-stricken to cry out lest it reveal its hiding-place. Reverend Johnson forgot what he had to say. He held out his hands to her, and she rushed sobbing up to the rail, where she knelt down beside Sam. Sam looked at her through the slits between his fingers and saw that she was pretty. In her wake eight other persons came to the altar.

Like a man swaying on the edge of a dream, Reverend Johnson knelt to pray. His voice mounted over the congregation and quieted them: "Lord, we thank thee for these many souls who have come into Thy fold tonight. We pray Thy guidance upon them throughout this coming year. We ask that Thou wouldst strengthen their weakness, and make good Christians of them."

And then, as if something outside himself compelled him, he cried, "Thou movest in a mysterious way, Thy wonders to perform. Help us to understand Thee. Amen."

CHAPTER TWO

"What a happy New Year! What a happy New Year!"

The congregation was standing now, singing over and over again, with loud happy voices the familiar words with which they annually greeted the incoming year, although its predecessor, welcomed in with the same sanguine spirit, might have done nothing so to confirm their renewed hopefulness. They were like chronic bargainers, people who buy diamonds and gold watches from strangers accosting them in the street, only to find that the diamonds are bits of stone, and the gold watches good, durable, odorous brass, and yet they continue to buy, hoping to encounter a real bargain in the end. Last year might have been lean, with little flour in the barrel, scant of clothing, an almost constant need of the doctor and his bitter doses, but this year, coming in with its hard, frosty weather, with sinners ready to mend the raveled fabric of their ways, with sinners and Christians both blowing horns and sounding bells in the street, this year would surely be fat and prosperous. And so they sang "What a happy New Year." They shook hands all around. People who had never set eyes on one another crossed aisles, leaned across benches, threaded their way through other happy, grinning groups, touched hands across other hands crossed for a fitful second, and wished each other a Happy New Year. Many wept and let the tears fall in unabashed contentment.

Even after Reverend Johnson had dismissed them they seemed loth to go. They wanted to shake the hands of the new converts and wish them a long and faithful service in the house of the Lord. They especially wanted to speak to Sam and congratulate him; for his had been the most singular victory. Their lively imaginations had already seized upon him and were fashioning legends about him. Here was something they could display when friends scoffed at religion. This man, with his cards and his razor, had probably sauntered into the church filled with derision, or moved by some memory of his childhood which had said it was good to be in the church when the new year came. And he had been struck in the forehead, straight between the eyes, with the words that the preacher had flung against him, just as David, balancing himself on one foot, had let go his smooth little pebble straight into the mocking height of "Golia." That velvety streak which a knife-wound had left on Sam's face, and the imperfection of his empty sleeve, made them think of dark and sinful doings, gambling and drinking and fighting. He was mystery and miracle and the confirmation of faith to them. They wondered how he had felt when the Spirit struck him, whether he had heard voices or seen resplendent shapes guiding him toward the altar. They were grateful to him, and as always there were some who showed their gratitude in the way on which Sam always counted. He hadn't lost his arm for nothing. Many, as they came up to shake hands with him, left a bill or a silver coin in his hand as they withdrew their own. Sam looked hurt as they did this, but grateful; he was too kind to offend them by a refusal.

The cards and the razors still lay on the floor. He bent to pick them up, but the Reverend Johnson stooped down before him, gathered up the trampled pack and the shining blade, saying: "Son, let me have these. I should like to keep them to remember this evening by."

Sam grinned. "Sure, preacher," but he had a growing feeling

that perhaps the Reverend Johnson had said these same words to him somewhere else at some other time. And he thought, "I'll have to buy another deck and a new razor."

The church had thinned out now; only Sam, the Reverend Johnson, the Reverend Drummond, the dark girl in the red-and-black hat, and the faded yellow woman who had come with her, remained at the altar. The sextons, anxious to get home, began flashing the lights on and off in order to convey their readiness to these stragglers. Sam's pocket was heavy with silver, and he too wanted to leave, but something held him back. He was waiting for some move from the Reverend Johnson.

The dark girl came over to him and held out her hand. He took it and found that it was small, and not too rough in the palm. The back of the hand was smooth and cool.

"I want to thank you for what you did for me tonight," she said. "Oh, I'd like to talk to you and tell you what I feel. Which way are you going? Couldn't we walk along together?"

Next to getting religion and making it pay, Sam hankered after women; he aimed to impress them, he liked to feel that he had a way with them. He had never joined church yet but it had led to an affair. As lightly as he had taken his religion he had taken his women, and as often.

He looked at her, seeing her well and fully for the first time. She was black, not dull like pitch, but bright like jet. Her mouth was red and inviting. It was half-open now, and her teeth looked sound and clean. Her hair was straightened, no doubt, but he didn't mind that; he liked black women best. He would put her age at about twenty, no more than twenty-two. Her breasts made a hard, firm outline under her frock.

He smiled at her and said, "We can go any way you say, lady."

Reverend Johnson interposed here.

"I want to speak to this brother alone for a few minutes," he said, and his voice was like a vise. Sam felt it might be embarrassing to refuse.

"Sure thing," he growled.

The Reverend Drummond said: "You can take him into my study, and then leave by the back way. I'm tired, so I think I'll leave you." Looking at Sam, he warned, "I'll look to see you Sunday, brother, so that you can be taken in as a regular and full member with us." And to the girl, "You too, miss."

The girl said: "I'll wait here while you two talk, and when you're ready to go, you can call me. Then we can talk, Mr.—Mr.—"

"Lucas, lady. Sam Lucas."

"Mr. Lucas, then."

Turning to the yellow woman with her, she patted her and drew her coat up about her, saying: "You'd best not wait for me, Aunt Mandy. You just go along, and I'll catch up with you later."

Her aunt squeezed her. "All right, honey. I'm so glad you done joined church at last, I could plumb shout all over again." She went up to Sam and took his hand. "Son, I ought to thank you, too, 'cause my Mattie here joined church when she saw you standing there with them cards and that razor laying at your feet. Let me go 'long now, or I'll sure be shouting again."

Sam followed the evangelist into Reverend Drummond's study. The preacher switched on a light, closed the door behind him, and motioned Sam to a seat. Sam slumped down into a chair at the end of a long table around which the church council probably held its monthly meetings. The evangelist took a seat at the other end. For a moment his hard, lively eyes beat sardonically into Sam's own, downing their effrontery. Sam let his eyes fall, knowing contention was useless. If this had been a woman facing him, he could have let the pure current of his own seeing flow out and conquer her.

Reverend Johnson beat a nervous staccato tattoo on the table; on his forehead and on the backs of his hands the veins stood out, faint blue streaks almost imperceptible beneath their tan covering.

At last he spoke, his voice wavering on the border line of contempt and reverence: "I am not sure that you are not the most despicable man I've ever come across; I'm not sure that you aren't a genius in your way, and I'm far from being certain that you aren't an unwitting instrument in the hands of Heaven."

Sam was confused by so much uncertainty; the word despicable was new to him; yet he had felt its thrust and had bristled instinctively, but he felt the compliment behind the evangelist's misgivings.

Indeed, he was so relieved that he permitted himself a smile, letting his mouth widen until the lips were stretched taut.

"Meaning what, preacher?" he queried.

The evangelist reached down into his pocket and brought out the deck of cards and the razor. He spread the cards out before him, scanning intently their red and black characters as if hoping to discover there the answer to his problem.

"Some people profess to read these things," he said. "I wish I could. I wish I had some way of knowing how I ought to feel about you, and about tonight's happenings." He eyed Sam narrowly. "How long do you expect this sort of thing to continue?" he asked.

"What sort of thing, preacher?" Sam was admitting nothing.

"Four years ago I led a revival in Memphis, Tennessee. You came there one night, the best night I ever had, as far as converts go. You came there with other cards and another razor, and twenty-three converts were taken in."

Sam could not conceal the light of admission that leaped up in his eyes. He remembered vividly, as a singer remembers a night of triumph, that evening in the tightly-packed church house in Memphis. There had been such an excess of religious fervor then that benches and chairs had been splintered as men and women, their hands tightly clenched at their sides, braced their feet against the benches in front of them and beat their backs against their own seats with quick frenzied motions like the blows of hammers. He remembered Reverend Johnson now. Seeing him now and letting his mind slip back four years, he recognized the evangelist fully, and understood now his strange outcry at the altar. The preacher had wanted to denounce him.

But the preacher was not looking at Sam now. His fingers were brushing lightly across the cards and he was talking more to himself than to the dejected, shame-stricken man in front of him.

"I remember that I asked you for the cards and the razor that night. They were sacred things for me then, with as much virtue in them as there would be in Veronica's handkerchief or in bits of the true cross. I took your story and made a fine legend out of it. It never failed to move people. It was a more wonderful thing for some of them than any story I could tell them out of the Bible. And then I learned, through some other preachers who had met up with you, what you had really been doing."

His voice now was like a piece of steel sharpened to a point and driven into the ribs. Sam wished he might grow smaller, might become something too indistinct and vaporous to be cauterized by that voice.

"I burned your cards and shattered your razor to bits," the voice mused on, the small nervous hands still dallying with the cards, "just as I ought to burn these and shatter this razor. I made a special trip back to Memphis, looked at the records of the church, and visited the people who had been converted under me. I found them good churchgoers, strong in their faith. They talked to me about you, and most of them spoke of having joined church after they saw you come up to the altar. They spoke of being moved by you. I couldn't tell them that their fine steady lives, their strong religious faith, were all grounded in a lie."

Sam groaned in spirit and in truth. He wound and unwound his long legs in abject and confused misery.

"Do you know anything about Paul of Tarsus?"

"No." Sam's voice was thin and remote.

"Well," the preacher went on, "he said he was willing to be all things to convert men to Christ. Perhaps I should be willing to accept all means which contribute to their conversion. I suppose I should be willing even to accept you, without really understanding why. There are some things which we cannot understand. You and these cards, this razor, that blood money in your pocket, that fine-

looking young girl waiting out there to talk to you. I cannot altogether understand why she and those eight other persons should
have rejected my pleas, only to be moved by an action at whose
root was the worm of deception. I should have cried out to them
at the altar that they were being moved by something false, but"—
he looked at Sam fiercely—"I wanted that girl up there before me
down at the altar, and when I saw her coming"—his voice sank
down almost to a whisper—"I forgot you and what you stood for.
I only thought of my job, converting people."

He stood up as if to dismiss Sam.

"Well," he said, wearily, "I can't denounce you now, and I'm
too worn out to preach to you. If I were you I'd try to mend my
ways."

Sam started to the door, and then turned back.

"Are you going to tell her?"

"No. I know her kind. Fervent, intense. If I told her, she'd hate
the church and me and you. Anyway, she'll probably not see you
after tonight."

Sam had a vision of her animated jet face and her straight,
unyielding carriage. He turned to the evangelist.

"And if I should see a lot of her?" he asked. "I have a feeling
that I'm goin' to."

"Then you must work out your own souls' salvation," the
preacher said. "I wish you would go now. I'm tired; I feel defeated."

Sam suddenly felt a vast pity for this worn-out saver of souls.
He wished he could do something for him. But he only walked to
the door and let himself out as noiselessly as he could.

The church was soft with darkness and having shut the door
behind him, he stood for a moment braced against its panels, his
hands shading his eyes. At first he thought the girl might have
gone, but as his sight fought through the mellowing gloom he saw
her seated in one of the front pews, her face caught up in her
cupped hands as if she were communing with some spirit buried
deep in the inner recesses of herself.

Walking softly, he reached and touched her before she was aware of him. She started up with a quickly extinguished gasp as his fingers lay lightly on her shoulder. And then she laughed as one does when relieved of the poignancy of a needless fear.

"We could go now, miss," he said.

She rose to follow him, and it came to him that they must disturb the preacher again in order to get out, now that the front part of the church was locked and barred.

He tapped at the study door, and then opened it without waiting for a response. The minister was still seated at the table, his erratic fingers continuing their dance, his hard bright eyes burning like bits of coal. He rose as they entered, and his face assumed a petulant cast, as if they represented a recurring annoyance.

"Sorry to have to bother you again, preacher, but we can't get out no other way. All the other doors is locked."

The preacher forced himself to be polite, looking beyond Sam to the girl who stood just behind him, her face edged like a black cameo beneath the scarlet trimming of her hat.

"That's all right," he said. "This door leads right into the street. Good night and Happy New Year to you both."

"Good night, preacher, and Happy New Year." Sam turned to go, fearful lest these two have something more to say to one another than the mere good-will wishes of the New Year. "Good night, preacher. Happy New Year." The girl turned to follow Sam, but paused and caught his hand at the threshold.

"Wait for me outside, Mr. Lucas," she besought him. "I won't be long. There's something I've got to ask the preacher."

"All right, lady." He smiled at her, but he felt the pit of his stomach giving way inside him and he had a quick desire to walk away into the cold darkness and not be there when she came forth. But he turned to meet the preacher's eyes, and what he saw there reassured him.

"All right," he repeated. "I'll wait outside."

As the door swung to behind Sam, the girl went up and caught the minister's hand. Looking at her, he thought surely she was an acceptable offer on the sacrificial altar and he wished he could assume all the credit unto himself.

She was pressing his hand now and unburdening herself of a turmoil of gratitude. He heard her through the mist with which her loveliness obscured his sight.

"I never knew getting religion could be like this," she was saying. "It makes me feel like something brand new all over. I want to thank you for it. I feel like I'm going to have a good year all through, starting out this way."

He could not answer her, but he was looking at her kindly, his usually gimlet-like eyes clouded into a gentleness by her youth and ardor.

She looked down, and her gaze resting on the table seized upon the cards lying there. They seemed the symbol of her whole life hidden there, held there, beyond any power to change, in those red and black dots. Close by, the razor was a straight edge of fire.

"If I could have those," she looked up at him impulsively, as if letting loose something she had held in check, wanting to say and yet ashamed to utter—"if I could have these to take away with me, to keep, to remember tonight by, and you, and him out there. For that's what saved me. I'd never come forward if it hadn't of been for them." She pointed to the instruments of her salvation, and she could not have hurt him more if she had taken the blade and buried it in his face. That would have been physical; this made him wince in the spirit.

He pressed her hand, and shook his head as one might at a spoiled child. "Those things are better off with me," he said, trying to laugh, but the chuckle was dry and forced. "They are the devil's own tools."

"Not now," she denied him, the light of her conviction streaming out and gathering up the light from the razor. "They are God's now. They couldn't do anybody any harm now. I want them to put away, like something holy, that I can go to and get strength from, just by looking at. Won't you give them to me?"

He thought of the pack of cards he had asked for in Memphis

and of that other razor; he remembered with what reverence he had wrapped them in his handkerchief and laid them away next to his Bible, relics as vital and powerful to him then as Veronica's veil might have been or bits of the true cross. He remembered with what horror and disgust he had burned the cards afterwards and shattered the razor to bits. He could as easily tell her all that as he could take his bony fist and strike her between her two sparkling, pleading eyes.

He walked to the table, gathered up her talismans with shaking hands, unfolded his clean extra handkerchief, placed them in it, and handed the small bundle to her.

"But your handkerchief," she objected.

"Take it, please, like that," he said. "Let the handkerchief be my share in it." The bitterness in his tone was lost upon her.

She placed the small white bundle in her pocketbook.

"Good night, preacher. Happy New Year."

"Good night, sister. Happy New Year."

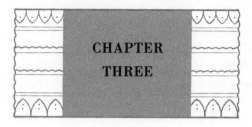

CHAPTER
THREE

Outside on the church steps Sam waited doggedly and defiantly. His own code of ethics never having been of a nature to induce in him an overwhelming faith in that of another, he feared, despite the promise in the minister's eyes, what might transpire back there in the study. It must be well after one o'clock, he thought, but time seemed forgotten by the happy New Year revelers who surged back and forth along the street, blowing horns, throwing colored tape, wishing one another well with happy indiscrimination. He had half a mind to join them, to let them sweep him along like a leaf caught up with other leaves in a mighty wind. What reason, what good reason, he asked himself, had he for staying here? He had done all the good he could, and if he left now he would have placed himself out of reach of doing any further harm.

"Happy New Year, Mr. Lucas. I forgot to tell you that before." He turned and saw her standing there at his side, her teeth gleaming like lights in the ebony framework of her face.

"Happy New Year, Miss Mattie," and he let his own smile go out to her without bridle or stay. He explained readily as he saw amazement and question on her face when she heard him utter her name.

375

"I heard the old lady call you Mattie," he said, adding, "and I remembered it 'cause I wanted to know it. And I wouldn't mind hearin' the other part, too."

"Johnson—Mattie Johnson."

"Happy New Year, again, then, Miss Mattie Johnson." He seemed to have been made gay by her very presence, and knowing her full name became the quintessence of knowledge.

"Happy New Year, Mr. Sam Lucas," she rejoined, matching her memory against his with the pride of a child showing off a new toy.

"Which a way we goin'?" he asked.

"I live up and over, on Fifth Avenue."

They turned in the direction toward which she had pointed, and she made as if to take his arm. But she grasped only the empty sleeve of his coat. He was aware of a tremor of uneasiness running through her as she dropped the sleeve, afraid, it seemed, to anchor herself to anything of such instability. He flicked away both her embarrassment and her fears with a laugh.

"Better try the other side, ef you ain't supatitious."

"What do they say?" she queried.

"That a woman walkin' on the outside is for sale." He hoped he wasn't too forward.

"Well," she said, "I needn't mind that. I'm free, single, disengaged, and twenty-one."

"But not white." He bit his lips, wishing he might recapture these words, thinking she might be sensitive about her color.

But she only flashed her gaze on to his own dark countenance and confirmed his raillery.

"A long ways from white, but still not for sale."

Yet she crossed over and grasped his right arm, snuggled up against him, and tried to match her own mincing steps with his long, uneven strides.

They walked in silence for a few moments, as if to accustom themselves to the reality of one another, as if each were musing on the evening's happenings, and wondering for just what purposes they had been caught up and whirled about in so much space, to be set down suddenly facing one another, breathless with inquiry.

Suddenly she turned to him, her face luminous with a strange fire that smote him and made him uneasy. He had seen this same light shining on the preacher's face, but on hers it glowed with a strength that he felt might burn sheer through his masquerade and reveal him for the arrant trickster he was.

"Tell me how it felt," she said.

He wanted to ask, "What?" but he knew only too well what she meant. "You tell me," he fenced, sending up a petition to the deity of dissemblers to sustain him in this hour of imaginative need.

"Oh, it was like nothing I ever felt before," she was saying. "Like fire burning first, and then like ice, or like a knife cutting. Like fingers running up and down my back, fingers of fire and ice. It was like something pulling me out of myself, up from that bench, although my hands gripped the seat, and I told myself I wouldn't rise and go up there and bow down."

"That's how it was with me," he lied. "Like fire and ice."

He was hardly aware of what he was saying, or of her words, so avidly was he drinking in the clear beauty which seemed to drench her, spumed up and over her as she relived her new religious birth.

"I never wanted to do it that way," she went on. "I used to laugh at Aunt Mandy going to church, and shouting, clapping her hands, and running up and down the aisles, making me ashamed of her. And I only went to church with her to please her, because she wanted me to, not that I felt I needed it."

Her tone grew plaintive, as if she were chastising herself and feeling the pain of the punishment at the same time. "And now, just to think that I started out like that, making a show of myself to the people. But I couldn't help myself. When the preacher came to me, he made me mad, picking me out like that in front of all the church, as if I'd been a bad woman; and I grew stubborn, honery inside, hard like a stone, and I wouldn't go up for him or Aunt Mandy. But when you stepped up, so firm-like and decided, and threw down those cards and that razor, I felt something like fire run from the cards and the razor straight into me and burn my sins away."

He looked at her, so young and well molded, with the marks of her childhood still lingering on her face, as if loath to be erased totally by her womanhood; and it seemed so ridiculous that she should be concerned about her sins, that he asked her, half in earnest, half in mockery:

"And did you have many sins to burn away?"

She was too far lost in her ecstasy to catch anything but the earnestness of his question. "I can't say what they were," she answered. "I suppose, whatever they were, they were all little sins. But Aunt Mattie says we all have a certain amount of sin in us, and the only way to get rid of it is by getting religion. I must have had some sin in me, else why would I have been struck like that tonight?"

"I s'pose so," he acquiesced. "But how does it make you feel now, losin' your sins?"

She looked off into space, away from him, as if she could see her sins in tangible form fading away on the horizon, distorted, impure shapes bidding her farewell forever.

"Peaceful-like," she said, "as if I could walk on air and never drop; powerful-like, as if I could walk through fire and never burn; contented-like, as if I loved everybody in the world."

"You got good religion, miss, better'n mine," he said, adroitly paving the way for future relapses. "I don't feel so sure of myself. I feel like I might stumble ag'in sometime, like I might gamble, or drink ag'in, or love too many women."

She eyed him sorrowfully, as if she had grown wise between the intaking and the releasing of a breath, and she cautioned him firmly in words she had heard at many a meeting with Aunt Mandy, and which she had unwittingly buried deep in herself for this moment's harvesting:

"You must lean hard on the Lord." And she felt as if she had uttered some pearl of wisdom which she alone had discovered and released to a weary, despondent world.

"Look," she said, suddenly, as she delved down into her pocketbook, to draw forth the preacher's handkerchief. "I'd give you these if you hadn't said what you did just then, about not being so sure of yourself. I asked the preacher for them, so I could keep them by me, to look at, to remember tonight by, and you, and him, and to get strength from when I'm weak. But they might tempt *you* away from God."

She unfolded the handkerchief, letting him gaze down on the cards and razor. In spite of his manhood, a soft film crept over his eyes and he felt as if he were seeing earth thrown upon the coffin of a dear friend. But it was not an altogether bitter potion that he was drinking; for its gall was tempered with the honey of her sentiment in wanting these things to keep; and while this liquid made him grimace, it also made him smile.

"I shall keep these always," she was saying, "in a little box, maybe in a little silver box; maybe"—this last was said defiantly, as if she set extravagance at naught where such a keepsake was concerned—"in a little golden box."

She looked at him, while the currents of their eyes mixed and ran hot and dynamic from one to the other, hers filling him with a half-regretful pride that such store should be set by his ancient, fraudulent possessions, his flowing out full and undeterred, stripped of their religious travesty, bright and heady with sensuousness, flowing over her and filling her with a vague, partly disquieting, half-happy uncertainty.

During their talking he had not noticed where she was leading him, but had turned obediently whenever the pressure on his arm had indicated a change in their course. Now she stopped suddenly before a brown-stone apartment house, an unpretentious dwelling-place for simple colored people.

"This is where I live," she said. "Thanks for seeing me home."

"Thanks for lettin' me." He stood there with nothing more to say, yet not wishing to leave.

Impulsiveness was part of her nature, as he could see by now;

so he was not altogether surprised when she put her hand in his and said:

"Tomorrow is New Year's. We're having black-eyed peas and rice. Aunt Mandy has an idea it brings good luck. Won't you come and have dinner with us?"

He could have sung for happiness; instead, he was mute for joy.

"We're having turkey, too," she added, fearful lest the simple fare mentioned at first might not appeal to him.

"It wasn't that," he reassured her. "Your asking me was just so good I lost my tongue. Black-eyed peas and rice is good enough for me. What time you want me to come?"

"About eight," she said. "My name is in the bell, and you'd best take down the number of the house. You might forget it."

"I couldn't forget this house in a million years."

She gave him a smile for this extravagant speech, and went inside. He stood watching the spot where she had been for a moment, then thrust his hand into his pocket where the money, forgotten until now, made a pleasant sound. He walked over to a lamp-post where he might count the profits of his most recent conversion.

CHAPTER
FOUR

A hasty survey of his gains showed that he had over twenty
dollars, enough to board and lodge him for a week at least. The
minister had called it blood money, and while he had sat there in
the study, cowed by the preacher's eyes and distressed by his
sharp biting voice, the money had seemed tainted even to him.
But now, viewed in the clearer light of his immediate needs, as the
wind whipped his legs and fanged his neck and ears, this money
was purified for him, as all preceding amounts similarly gained
had been, by the knowledge of the good it could render his body.
Though he shivered as he walked along, he was inwardly warmed
by the thought of a bed at the colored Y.M.C.A., a new shirt
and tie for tomorrow, and New Year's dinner with Mattie.

He slept far into the afternoon, his whole being drowned and
lost in an unaccustomed sense of security. When he arose he ate
frugally at the Y Cafeteria, guarding his rampant appetite in order
to show a proper appreciation for Mattie's cooking. He bought a
shirt colored blue like an unclouded sky, and to go with it a
magenta-hued tie profusely sprinkled with yellow stars. He sat shivering behind a screen in a stuffy little tailor shop while the tailor
occupied himself with his lone suit of clothes, snipping raveled

ends here and there, drawing up a hole or so, fortifying buttons, and finally sponging and pressing the whole garment. Sam had never felt so beauish before, as he strutted out, his trousers still warm and damp but fronting the wind with edges sharp as razors.

She had said eight o'clock, but he was ardent and unfashionable enough to be beforehand. At seven he was standing in the vestibule of her home, grievously and painstakingly trying with the aid of a sputtering match to spell out her name in the bell. The long corridor of the ground floor, leading to the stairs, was dark and musty, and pervaded with the seeping and mingling odors of many competing New Year's dinners. Other noses more delicately nurtured might have wrinkled in rebellion; Sam's distended in joyous anticipation.

The halls were ill-lighted and labyrinthine, and he was despairing of finding the apartment when Aunt Mandy's voice shrilled down at him:

"Up this way, son."

She stood at the door of her apartment, bright and spirited, in a gay checkered dress which transformed her from the faded-looking yellow woman of the night previous into a creature sprightly and bird-like. It was as if she had worn her religious garments then, and was now attired in festive robes. There were hoops in her ears, and on her fingers glittering circles of dubious value.

"Come right on in, son," she greeted him, as if their acquaintance was founded on ages and not on hours. "I'm powerful glad you could come. The dinner'll be better with a man here instead of just us two women."

He could not answer her for a moment, searching the room for Mattie, piqued that she had not come forth to meet him instead of sending her aunt. Aunt Mandy perceived his alarm, and eased him by saying, as she led him into the small combination parlor and dining-room: "Mattie ain't got home from work yet. She'll be in about seven-thirty."

He sat down drinking in the warmth and homeyness of the place, sinking comfortably into one of the huge chairs of their three-piece

Michigan set, admiring the pictures in their worn, gilt frames hung at irrelevant random around the room, scenes of flowers and foods; liking in particular one study showing a fish and a rabbit stretched on a platter, the eyes of each set like glass, and their necks dripping blood. He admired the handmade flowers stuck in ludicrous vases distributed around the room in a profusion that seemed to him the sum total of all opulence. These people made their own heat, and the small stove perched on its zinc pad gave to the room just that warmth and spirit which he felt a home should have. Here was a likable spot on which to raise his Ebenezer.

In the center of the room a table, shining with the Sunday table-cover and napery, bright like an army with banners as its much-scrubbed and polished cutlery sent forth streams of light, was set for three. The preliminary tidbits lent color and enticement to the setting; at each place was a small crêpe-paper basket filled with peanuts and white mint candy; in one dish a mass of olives with red mouths glistened; in others were radishes and celery; and through the keyhole and under the threshold slit of a door which must lead into the kitchen came the succulent odors of their dinner.

At one end of the table the cloth had been thrown back, and there, until Sam came, Aunt Mandy had been sitting, endeavoring to read her fortune with a much-used deck of cards. It seemed to Sam that the old lady was endowed with a versatile sincerity. Like Peter she was a rock, and no sturdier base could have been unearthed on which to lay the foundations of faith. She was a pillar of the church, giving of her earthly substance to a degree that was truly sacrificial, and of her time to an extent which had made her ignorant of nearly all else save church ritual. There was no concert or benefit given at Mount Hebron at which she was not present. Nothing short of being bedridden could keep her from her Thursday-night class and her Friday-evening prayer-meeting. Headaches, chills, and fevers were excuses for children, backsliders, and sinners; a true Christian must be prepared to lap water like a dog.

Yet, though she was a rock, steadfast and immovable, credulous of all biblical magic, she maintained a decent and sane respect for the things of the world, and a proper fear of the powers of darkness. She was like one caught and twined about by two rival serpents, her religious faith straining her in one direction, her worldly fear and inquisitiveness striving to draw her into an opposing channel. Though she could shout with the best in a way that was beautiful to behold, her light, dry body bounding like a small playful animal endeavoring to free itself from a cage; though she could sit perfectly still in her pew and let the Spirit gradually steal upon her in mesmeric power until she shuddered and twitched and wrung her hands ineffectually, while she uttered strange unintelligible bird-like sounds which she was pleased to call the gift of tongues; though she never tired of telling at Thursday-night class and at Friday-night prayer-meeting "how one Monday night far in the Southland my dungeon was shook and all my chains broke, and my feet was taken out of the mire and the clay and put upon the path that leads to Christ and everlasting peace"—she was not wholly removed from the world. There was much that was pagan and occult in her. Her religion was a somber coat sumptuously lined with superstition. Every nerve-center in her being tingled and responded to signs and omens. Though she was not averse to trusting serenely to the ways of Providence, she often attempted, by reading tea leaves and coffee dregs, and by consulting her cards, to speed the blessings of Heaven or to ward off, if possible, some celestial chastisement. Both sides of her nature had been touched by Mattie's conversion; she was proud to have her niece in the church; she was eager to know how her faith would stand the test, what trials might beset her, what vine-strewn pits might be dug. Last night she had knelt fervently and prayed for light and guidance in these questions; now she was endeavoring to probe Heaven's mind with her cards.

In her checkered dress, with her gold hoops swinging in her ears and her lean sulphuric fingers gleaming with their spurious jewels, she was like a gypsy who had insinuated herself in from the road with promises of revealing all futurity. Sam's fingers itched for the cards, but not for fortune-telling.

There was a romantic segment in Aunt Mandy's mind, into which she was bent to entrap and immure this long dark man. Like Pilate's wife, she was troubled in mind with vague misgivings.

Shuffling her cards, she wreathed her parchment-yellow face into a smile: "I've been tryin' to find out what the new year will bring us, son. I'd just got to this card"—she pointed to the jack of spades—"when the bell rang and up you come." She cackled with mirth at the coincidence.

Sam laughed with her, but would not leave her with her victory.

"But you knew I was comin'," he expostulated.

"No. I knew you was expected, but I didn't know you was comin' for certain. That was different."

They both laughed together at her ability to defend herself. Then he pretended to be offended at the card she had chosen to represent him.

"Don't you think this might 'a' been somebody else?" he queried, picking up the card. "Most in general I thinks of myself as the jack of *clubs*."

She scanned his ebony face carefully; then shook her head ruefully.

"Sorry, son, but the jack of spades is the best I can do for you. Want me to tell your fortune now?"

"What would she say?" he asked, thinking of the earnestness of her voice last night and of the unstinted fervor with which Mattie had entered upon her new life.

"What she don't know won't hurt her." Aunt Mandy riffled the cards vigorously, and set herself to scan the future and to endeavor, if possible, to shape some of its happenings to her own liking.

She plumped them down before him.

"Cut," she commanded. "Three times toward yourself."

He drew his chair up to the table and did as she bade. She turned the three stacks over, and the sight of the well-loved black and red dots set him tingling with desire and regret.

The old lady's fingers caught on to one of the stacks like greedy talons, and Sam, watching her, knew that in her way and for her purposes she was as devoted to these painted oblong bits of cardboard as he.

She spread the first stack out fan-shaped in her hand, and then laid it down. Then she took up the second pack, which she considered more carefully, for it held the jack of spades.

"That's you," she said, showing it to him again as if he had never seen it before. She studied the cards intently, then looked up at him, her eyes charged with mystery and malice.

"You've been a rounder in your time," she accused him—"a rounder and a bad man. There ain't much that's bad that you haven't done; you've drunk, and you've cussed, and you've took the Lord's name in vain. And you've fit. Look at that scar on your cheek!"

So sudden was this accusation, and so naïve, that he was totally disconcerted. He raised his hand to his cheek and felt the smooth ashen line as if it were something unfamiliar.

"But all that's over now," she went on, her claws spreading and tapping the cards. "All that's over; now you've got God in your heart and you're going to settle down and be a different man. A woman's coming into your life."

"A woman?" Sam was eager now. "What she look like?"

"She's thin and dark and good. And she likes you."

Thin and dark and good, he thought; and sometimes she wears a red-and-black hat, he hoped.

"How you know she likes me?"

She looked up at him, all the malice gone now, only the mystery prevailing.

"Cards don't lie," she said.

"But don't you think cards is evil?" Sam wanted to know, finding it strange that such a good churchwoman could fondle them so lovingly.

"It all depends on the kind of cards you have and what you do with them." Aunt Mandy leaned across the table in a philosophic and instructive attitude, seriously ready to produce extenuations for one side of her nature, and to demonstrate that it in no wise interfered with the other. "Them cards you had last night was evil, before you threw them down there at the mo'ner's bench, but when you threw them down, all the sin went out of them, just like Christ sent the evil spirits out of some man or other, and drove them into the pigs. You remember?"

"No, I disremember that story," he answered, truthfully, repressing a desire to simulate wisdom, for fear the avowal of so much information might lead to technical questioning.

"Well, anyhow, the devils left the man, just like the evil left them cards, and now they ain't nothing but goodness in them. As for my cards, they ain't evil, 'cause I uses them for good. If I gambled with them, then that would be sin. I only use them to find out how to keep out of the devil's way. And they've hoped me out a heap of times."

There was the click of a key, and from where he sat looking down the small hall, Sam saw Mattie enter. Aunt Mandy whisked the cards from the table and out of sight.

Mattie was dressed as she had been the preceding evening; with her eyes lively with expectation and apology, she seemed to have grown more attractive with the passing of a day. The severe cold had nipped her face until her cheeks, dark as they were, were centered with a soft struggling purple. She made no attempt to conceal the genuine pleasure which she felt in seeing him again; and he rose up, long and awkward, and thrilled at the simple sight of her.

"I'm so glad you could come," she said. "And I'm sorry to be late, but Mrs. Brandon had people in to dinner today, and I always have to serve when she gives a high-toned dinner. But she's awfully nice, just the same. I guess you've heard of her."

"No, I don't know no white folks here," Sam answered, rejecting the honor.

"But she's not white. She's colored. Dr. Brandon's wife. They're very rich." She was ashamed of his ignorance.

"Oh, you work for colored people." He said it as if he were simply acknowledging a bit of information, but she felt that she had lost caste with him.

While they were talking, Aunt Mandy had been busy carrying in platter after platter of steaming, odorous food. Mattie and her aunt managed to strike the middle way between two extremes of colored people. They neither pampered the belly while the back went bare, nor perished in fine clothes.

Today Aunt Mandy had attempted hopefully to prepare a meal which would be prophetic of the year's abundance. There were black-eyed peas and rice; these were for luck. But for the special glory of New Year's day there were turkey and peas, potatoes of both kinds, one dish of them mashed, rising up white and frothy, the other dish heaped with large yams that had burst their covering and were now bleeding sweetness through their wounds. There were collard greens, verdantly rich like spinach, but infinitely better tasting; biscuits; and pies of sweet potatoes and mincemeat.

They ate for the most part in silence, finding the business of eating too heavenly to be defiled by many words. Only with their eyes meeting and holding above their plates, with their fingers brushing as a platter was passed, and through that infinite understanding which man has with woman and which surpasses all other brands of wisdom, did Mattie and Sam speak to one another and respond.

Sam had hoped there might be something to drink, some homemade wine at least, perhaps something more potent. But there was only coffee, served along with the meal. Aunt Mandy couldn't abide the smell of liquor, and Mattie didn't like it.

After dinner Aunt Mandy pleaded fatigue and a headache, feeling free to pamper herself since there was no church meeting scheduled for that evening, and went into her room to lie down.

"I'll do the dishes," Mattie called after her.

"I wish I could help you," Sam said, looking ruefully at his left sleeve, "but I can't do anything along that line."

"Well, you can come out in the kitchen and sit with me while I wash them."

He helped her clear the table, making trip after trip from the dining-room into the kitchen, carrying a single dish or a fistful of knives and forks in his one strong hand. Once or twice they collided, and turned to laugh at one another. She thought he was decidedly handsome; he thought she was pretty, but different from the usual run of women he had known.

He drew a chair up to the kitchen sink, close beside her, where he could watch the movements of her dark hands, darting in and out of the hot, soapy water like small black fish. She chattered as she worked, telling him all about herself. He sat there with greased insides, a little heavy and a trifle sleepy, but happy to hear her voice beating on his ears. Between the washing and the drying of the dishes she told him all there was to tell. She was twenty-two. She had been born in Alabama. There had been no brothers or sisters. When she was seven her mother had died, and her father had sent her up to New York to live with his brother and Aunt Mandy, because they had no children and wanted her, and because her father had been frightened at finding himself left alone with a seven-year-old girl. Uncle Benjamin and Aunt Mandy had sent her to school and life had been rosy. At first her father had sent small sums of money from time to time to pay for her keep. But after a while these ceased, and even his letters. Though they had written to friends back in her home town, all they could learn was that her father had left, bound no one knew where. They had never heard from him since. But Aunt Mandy and Uncle Ben hadn't minded, because they loved her. They had kept her in school and had even placed her in high school, where she had begun to study French and a terrible kind of arithmetic called algebra.

Sam's eyes were shining with admiration.

"Say somethin' in French," he begged.

"Oh, I didn't take much," she excused herself, "and I've forgotten that." And then she went on. While she was in her second year in high school Uncle Ben had died.

"And colored people don't leave any money, you know," she wound up. "So I had to quit school and go to work to help Aunt Mandy; and I've been working ever since."

"Tell me where to put these." He held a stack of dishes in his hand, balancing them nicely.

"Just over there in the closet, any place. I can put them in order later on. I've been working for Mrs. Brandon for five years now."

"You say she's colored?" Again she felt the displeasure in his voice and it riled her.

"Yes. I like working for my own. You don't like working for them?"

" 'Tain't that I don't like workin' for them, 'cause I never did work for them, but I hear they ain't so easy to get along with; too uppity."

"That's not so." She was wringing the dish towel more vigorously than was her wont. "Black folks know better how to treat black folks every time."

"Well, let's don't fuss." He turned his eyes on her, and she thought they were the finest she had ever seen.

The dishes were all clean now and had been put away. Back in the parlor they sat facing one another, between them the small glowing stove. Outside they could hear the horns and sirens and all the strange confused noises of people walking the streets in search of pleasure.

"You're like all the women," he accused her. "You've left out the part I wanted to hear."

"What part?"

"About your fellers."

"Oh, them? I used to have fellers when I was in high school, and even before; every girl had a beau, but since I started working I been too busy to think about fellers."

"Every woman needs a man." He made her drop her eyes before him.

"Tell me about you," she asked.

A braggart at heart and a weaver of fanciful tales, he wanted nothing better.

"Let's start at the jumping-off place." He stretched his legs and arched his head back to make himself comfortable. "I was born in Texas in a little town so small I don't need to tell its name, 'cause nobody would know it. 'Tain't on the map. Ma had a child every year, and paw was crazy tryin' to get enough to feed them, but they kept on comin'. I didn't have no schoolin'. I can read my name if it's writ big enough, but if you writ it small I wouldn't know it. There was ten of us when I left home over ten years ago, when I was eighteen. God knows how many there is now. Since then I've seen a heap of towns and places. I always liked travelin'. I'm what they call a travelin' man. I had my arm cut off by a train when I was stealin' a ride. Now I'm here in New York and I think it's so fine, and I think you're so nice, I wish my travelin' days was over. That's all about me."

But it wasn't all; it was simply all he willed to tell her. He could have told her of his meeting over eight years ago with the huge blue-gummed man who had taught him the material value of religion. He had forgotten the man's name but he would always be grateful to him.

"My people will do anything when they're happy," the man had said, providing conversation for a group of street-corner stragglers. "I bet if someone went in and threw down a pack of cards and said he had religion the whole church would board and lodge him."

Sam had listened silently, but at the next town he came to he had tried it, as a novice, without even searching out a revival meeting; he had tried it at a simple prayer-meeting service and had been feasted and fattened for days before he shook the dust of his first conversion from the soles of his feet and went on his heathen way. At first he had used the cards alone; later the idea of the razor had come to him; a heavenly vision he called it; and the maneuver had proved a tremendous and ever-mounting success. After he lost his arm, his conversions came upon him more often.

And they were far more profitable; for the sight of his armless sleeve always tinged the religious fervor of his victims with pity, making them give him money. These things he could not tell her.

"How did you get that scar?" she asked him.

"I got that a long time ago. A man was beatin' his wife and I hit him. He cut me."

He could have added that the quarrel between his adversary and his wife had pivoted around himself, but he did not care to tell her this.

He was beginning to like her and to desire her. Had she been another woman, he would have had her in his arms by now, or would have been on his way, rebuffed but merry. He had had few rebuffs, in most cases far more encouragement than he was receiving now.

"I've bought a new dress for Sunday," she was saying, rousing him up out of his thoughts, which had begun to be lecherous. "Couldn't we go together?"

"Where?" The finer edges of his mind hadn't been given enough warning, and they failed to function at this abrupt invitation.

"Why, to church! The minister is going to take all the new converts in together." There was genuine chagrin on her face that he should have forgotten something so important.

"Sure," he promised. "I'll come by for you." He hadn't intended to go back. He had hoped to lose himself in the life of the city until he should feel an itching in his feet to be gone to a new habitat and new spiritual conquests. But to sit beside her in her new dress, himself wearing his new shirt and tie, here was a pleasure worth any heresy he might commit.

CHAPTER
FIVE

When Sam and Mattie and Aunt Mandy entered the church on Sunday morning, their appearance was greeted with a low murmur of excited recognition, more for Aunt Mandy who was one of the veteran worshipers, and for Sam, whose dramatic conversion from sin had already become a story to swear by, than for Mattie. Aunt Mandy was subdued in both mind and body, accoutered physically and spiritually in a manner best befitting the Lord's day. The most celebrated teller of fortunes in the world could not have caught her ear this morning, nor could the glossiest, newest deck of cards have intrigued her hands. She was dressed entirely in black; her diminutive foreign-yellow face was serene beneath her small black hat and totally unreflective of the world's wrongs. Gone were the gold hoops from her ears, and the flashy mendacious jewels from her fingers. This being the first Sunday in the month, it was also Communion day, and she was not one to reach out for the sacred wafer and wine with hands polluted by jewelry. Mattie, too, was soberly dressed, a bit of her dark-blue dress showing beneath her black coat. But Sam was colorful in his blue shirt and his radiant tie sprinkled with yellow stars.

This was the evangelist's last day; the evening sermon would be his last before he should be on to another city, carrying in his slight dynamic body his thunderbolts of wrath against all that was carnal and sinful. He seemed tired this morning, and to spare himself, as if he felt that no wild rallying at this last moment could save those who had not heeded his entreaties throughout the week. As his Scripture lesson he read from the twenty-first chapter of Revelations, from the twenty-first through the twenty-fifth verse:

"And the twelve gates were twelve pearls: every several gate was of one pearl: and the street of the city was pure gold, as it were transparent glass.

"And I saw no temple therein: for the Lord God Almighty and the Lamb are the temple of it.

"And the city had no need of the sun, neither of the moon, to shine in it: for the glory of God did lighten it, and the lamb is the light thereof.

"And the nations of them which are saved shall walk in the light of it: and the kings of the earth do bring their glory and honor into it.

"And the gates of it shall not be shut at all by day: for there shall be no night there.

. . . "For there shall be no night there."

Such was his text. Quietly and reverently he developed it, laying aside his abundant store of vitriol and denunciation. He wished to leave with them a feeling of security and promise. He was curiously tranquil as he talked to them, seeming by some colossal willfulness to check the usual excited gestures of his hands and feet. He was telling them of heaven, and the vast audience was like putty in his hands as they listened to him. Whatever doubts and fears they might have later, when they should file out into the cold of a real world where all was surely not as they would have fashioned it, nor as a God of infinite compassion would have done, they were wandering now in the golden streets of illusion. Their many-colored hands were caressing smooth walls of jasper, and wherever they

turned rich streams of milk and honey flowed. There were four
and twenty elders bowing down in shining robes and glittering
crowns before an indefinable being of unfathomable benignity who
was God. And close beside, shining like the sun, and healed forever of the nailprints in his hands and feet, and with his flowing
side forever stanched, was Christ, their brother.

Reverend Johnson's voice was so quiet and unpretentious that
no one shouted. There was no active demonstration beyond the
voicing of a few low-breathed hallelujahs and amens, and the soft
dabbing here and there at eyes that could not remain dry envi-
sioning so much peace. Sam felt mean and ashamed, but it was
all a well-told fairy tale for him, and he could not, no matter how
desperately he tried, feel conviction. Beside him Mattie sat tense
and beautiful, her face erased of every doubt that might have lingered there, her whole being given over in unrestrained credulity
to the glories of the heavenly landscape. She wished the preacher
might go on and on describing these scenes of a life in which she
now felt that she had a part, for was she not now a co-heir with
Christ and all the saved of the world?

"And there shall be no night there," the minister was closing;
his voice floated soft and low with enticement and promise, "no
night, but every day shall shine brighter than the brightest sun this
world has ever seen. And all that light shall come from God's own
face, and light up the whole heavens, and we that have been purified and washed in Jesus' blood shall walk forever and forever
in that light."

Amen. He sat down as if thoroughly outworn, less from physical
exertion than from spiritual exhaustion. The church, awakened from
its transport, droned like one large fly.

But only for a moment. Reverend Drummond, the pastor of the
church, arose to extend the invitation. He spoke in deep, guttural
tones, which seemed to come from the farthest abyss of the stomach:

"We have listened to and enjoyed Reverend Johnson's beautiful
sermon, and we know what joys are laid up for us in the kingdom

of God. Now we want to welcome into our midst those brothers and sisters who gave themselves to Christ during the week. We want them to become full members of the church now, before Reverend Johnson leaves us, so he can see what good work he has done for the Master. While the choir sings, I want our new members to come forward and stand here in front of the altar. And any, even now, who want to come with them, may do so. There are no set times with Christ. He is always ready to receive."

The organ groaned softly, while the choir, a mingling of light and dark faces in white robes, began to sing:

"I'm so glad I got my religion in time,
I'm so glad I got my religion in time,
O my Lord, O my Lord, what shall I do?"

For a moment it seemed as if the new converts had reconsidered; no one stirred. The minister stood waiting; the evangelist had risen and stood beside him, ready to welcome in the fruits of his own endeavors. Finally a man came forward, and seemed to give the signal which less valiant converts had awaited. People began to come forward from all parts of the church. Mattie nudged Sam.

"Shall we go up now?" she asked.

"Yes," he said so low that she divined his response by the nod of his head rather than by the sound of his voice. It was all right for him to go up and sham by himself, but he felt like a criminal going up with her, trailing his insincerity in the wake of her pure, exalted faith.

He followed her up the aisle, and they stood there together, two such delightful specimens of handsome blackness that the kindly feelings of the audience went out to them in great waves of sympathy and pride.

They stood there, warm and self-conscious, two out of thirty-eight others turning their backs on the things of the world and starting on the path called straight and narrow. They found that joining church was more than the mere giving of their names. The officers and leading members of the church, somber men and women, filed by, shaking their hands and wishing them well. The two ministers came down and welcomed them into the church. The evangelist had reached Sam and had extended his hand without recognizing him. As he looked into Sam's face he seemed to stiffen, but only for a moment. He wrung his hand heartily and spoke to him.

"May you be a good soldier in the army of the Lord, my brother."

And to Mattie, "May the blood of Christ keep you forever in His way."

The church clerk came forward to take their names and addresses.

Reverend Drummond had been keeping pace with the clerk as he went from convert to convert, stopping to speak softly and earnestly to each of them for a few moments, after which he would call forth a name, in answer to which some member of the church would come forward to shake the convert's hand. Sam's spiritual trafficking had been large enough and frequent enough for him to realize what these actions portended. The converts were being assigned to their week-night classes. He wondered what night Mattie would choose; whatever her choice, it would also be his. This would not be his first enrollment which had not terminated in attendance.

Before the minister reached them, Aunt Mandy, happy and proud of the occasion, floated down the aisle like a large-sized doll. She kissed Mattie as she had seen so many other women do, while she envied them, when their daughters or friends joined church; she even gave Sam a swift embarrassing peck on the cheek. And then she whispered to Mattie:

"You must join the Thursday-night class. That's my class, and our leader, Brother Green, is the best of them all. He's got more grace than all the rest put together. And he can pray like—" Words failed her and she simply spread her hands out as if unable to describe the colossal powers of petition resident in her leader.

The minister stood beside them. Sam heard him say, as if he were declaiming by rote something ingrained into him and like food become part of him through much repetition: "The Methodist Church offers its members weekly spiritual sustenance through its class-meetings and Friday-night prayer-meetings. Which class will you join, sister, Monday, Tuesday, Wednesday, or Thursday night?"

Mattie chose Thursday night. She looked anxiously at Sam when the question was put to him; pleasure mounted her eyes when he chose the same night.

"Brother Green," called Reverend Drummond, turning from them to summon a short black man with small red eyes and a large mouth topped and flanked by a bristly mustache.

"I give these new converts over to you, Brother Green," he said. "Look after them the way you do the rest of your members, and don't let the devil lay hold on them again."

Back in his seat again, squeezed tightly and pleasantly against Mattie, his flesh throbbing warmly beneath this remote and artificial contact, Sam felt that he had gone through his ordeal like a man, and that no more would be demanded of him now. But he reckoned without Mattie and the ways of the African Methodist Episcopal Church. For a while he sat in peace, narrowing his gaze into a sidelong slit that shut out all else from his sight and only revealed to him, clean and undisturbed, like a small black cameo cut out of space, Mattie's serene black features. Truly, he told himself, she was lovely and to be desired, so lovely and straight, with the spirit of contemplation and religious zeal easing her face of all else save of thinking on God, her beauty able to shine out beyond the darkness of her costume. He trembled to think how glorious she would look in a dress of flaming red, with bright beads around her throat, rings upon her fingers, metal bands dangling and jingling from her wrists, and she herself caught and whirled about in the mazes of a dance. The picture was rapturous and he closed his eyes, shutting out the real Mattie, filling the dark behind his lids with the gayer Mattie of his imagination. And whirling and twirling her was a jaunty black fellow whose eyes were deep electric currents and whose one arm was as good as two.

Then into his dream of music and fleshly joy there beat the consciousness of that flesh which the church has made her own, and which she sacrifices month after month in prayer and consecration. The white cloth on the table in front of the pulpit had been removed; and there cut in minute cubes in small silver dishes was the bread symbolizing the body of Christ, and in small liqueur glasses was the wine which was His blood.

The evangelist was speaking, and Sam writhed like a rat caught in a trap as he realized what was being said: "Our Lord says the last shall be first and the first last in His kingdom; therefore I have asked Reverend Drummond to let the converts commune at the first table, even before the officers of the church, that we may do our share in fulfilling what has been written. Will the converts come and kneel here before me to eat of that food which is not of the world?"

Sam tasted the gorge of horror and remorse rising in his throat to sicken him. He had no faith; that he was a cheat and a beat he had already acknowledged to himself many times over, but more in praise of his cleverness than in disparagement of his morals. But this he could not, would not do, partake of Communion. The white altar, the cubes of bread, the wine, these were all church magic, powerful ritual with which his scorn and unbelief might not cope. He would not go up, not even for Mattie. But already she had touched him, and quicker than they had spurted up in him had sent his rebellious thoughts draining out of him. He followed her to the altar and knelt down beside her, straining himself against her as if to melt his own unworthiness into her perfect faith.

"Wherefore ye that do truly and earnestly repent of your sins, and are in love and charity with your neighbors, and intend to lead a new life, following the commandments of God, and walking from henceforth in his holy ways, draw near with faith, and take this holy Sacrament to your comfort; and, devoutly kneeling, make your humble confession to Almighty God."

Sam leaned across the rail, trying hard to reconcile himself to his surroundings. He *was* in love and charity with his neighbors; for he didn't care enough about other people to wish them ill, and he *was* in love. But not with God. With Mattie. It was not for God's bread and wine that he was here. It was for the bread and wine that she could give him.

"Almighty God, unto whom all hearts are open, all desires known, and from whom no secrets are hid, cleanse the thoughts of our hearts by the inspiration of Thy Holy Spirit, that we may perfectly love Thee, and worthily magnify Thy holy name, through Jesus Christ our Lord. Amen."

The minister's voice was a denunciation in his ears. Perhaps it was true, that all his desires and thoughts and meannesses were known to God, that some great eye was shining down angry and baleful, its unseen rays probing the very depths of his thoughts, ferreting out the deep unclean recesses of his heart. What awful hurt lay hid for him in those pellets of bread? Would they strangle him as he swallowed them in his unbelief and deceit? Would the beaded red wine, so beneficial to these that believed and drank it in faith, burn like viper's venom for him, and leave him lying there at the altar, writhing in agony as a testament of the wrath of Heaven? He wanted to rise and flee. But he could not before so many people, and in her sight. He closed his eyes and yearned desperately toward belief and faith; but his heart was cold and responseless.

"The body of our Lord Jesus Christ, which was given for thee, preserve thy soul unto everlasting life. Take and eat this in remembrance that Christ died for thee; and feed on Him in thy heart by faith, with thanksgiving."

He looked up and saw the Reverend Drummond standing before him offering him the cubes of bread; behind him was the evangelist, bearing the wine. Sam's hand lay rigid at his side as his dark frightened face mirrored plainly the great struggle transpiring there. The evangelist leaned over and spoke to him, a direct message from one man to another, "Take and eat it, my brother; it was given for such as you."

Sam reached out, took one of the pellets and swallowed it. It went down easily; it tasted the same as any other bread. Assurance flooded him.

"The blood of our Lord Jesus Christ, which was shed for thee, preserve thy soul and body unto everlasting life. Drink this in remembrance that Christ's blood was shed for thee, and be thankful."

"Drink, brother; this is the blood of Christ that washes us white as snow."

The evangelist was smiling at him as if he understood his doubts and distress. The penetrating brown eyes were soft and gentle, filmed over by the beauty of the service. Sam took and drank, and as the tiny sip of liquid slid harmlessly down his throat all his fears vanished and his former arrogance and scorn sprouted up with renewed vigor. Far from being poison, it was not even wine that they served, but a mild grape-juice. He raised his head and looked down the long line of communicants. Their hands were spread out across the white altar-covering like so many flags of supplication and truce; their heads were submissive, their faces, of all colors, were tense and strained; all their being seemed surrendered to some divine force. At the far end of the altar a woman had suddenly gone limp; she lay stretched across the rail, her hands hanging motionless before her, short cries that might have been of pleasure or of pain issuing from her sagging mouth. At Sam's side Mattie knelt with her face hid in her hands.

"The love of God be with you all. Arise and go in peace." The evangelist was sending them away with his blessing. Sam and Mattie rose together, and he saw that her face was glowing and that down her cheeks tears flowed free and unrestrained.

When the services were over Aunt Mandy informed them that, as was her custom, she gave the Lord's day entirely over to His praise and service; therefore she was not going home for dinner, but would have her dinner in the church dining-room, and then would stay for the adult Bible class, for the young people's meeting in the afternoon, and so be ready and on hand for the evening service. Mattie said she would not remain, but would go home, and return for the evening service. Sam offered to see her home.

They walked along in a silence which was mainly fear of themselves, fear of the fierce desires at the roots of their beings that were drawing them nearer and nearer to one another. Sam had forgotten the services of the church as soon and as lightly as he had stepped across its threshold out into the sharp January sun. All that he was concerned with now was the woman at his side, an unquestionably attractive woman into whose life he had come without thought or warning. She was pressed close against him, and it seemed to him that, despite the cold, her hand on his sleeve had scorched through the fabric and was burning the naked blackness of his skin. He wished he knew how to tackle her; for he felt that she was like some new and strange being, unlike the other women he had known. Those others had been like himself, creatures of action and not of speech. They had been bold and rampant, and the few words they uttered had always found in him a masterly interpreter. He knew when a flippant word meant "Take me," and when it meant "Leave me be." But this girl with the small red mouth that he would like to lean over and invade, with the slight hard body that he yearned to crush, expending on it all the concentrated vigor of his lone arm, was strange and mysterious. She seemed near at hand, as close as if they were linked together by a strip of flesh, yet inaccessible, as if getting religion and joining church had suddenly grown walls about her and shut her away from the world. Her eyes smiled at him, but their message was neither "Take me" nor "Leave me be," but rather their unspoken word was "Speak to me" and "Tell me things." The palm of his hand was moist with panic.

As for Mattie, her suffering and doubts were as acute as his. Her mind was as alive as a beehive with questions for which she could find no ready answer. Into the clear stream of her newly-found happiness in her religion, this man's long, lean body was striding, rippling the calm surface of the water, churning up widening whirlpools of passion. She knew that he and the church were now ineradicable parts of her, and she clutched his arm fiercely for fear that he might fade out of her life as quickly and as unexpectedly as he had come. Why had they met? Why had she hardened her heart against the evangelist, and leashed her tongue to silence in scorn of him and his entreaties, only to run like water to the altar at the sight of this man and his cards and his razor? Why at his side did she feel peace and ease and comfort, a security deep and plentiful like falling into a downy bed and sleeping care and thought away? She had pity for him; she could feel the pity welling up in her at the thought of his arm long ago rotted away and gone to earth while he still walked; she felt pity and love surge through her as she looked up at the ashen scar on his cheek; she wanted to brush it with her lips and hair. She thought of the cards and the razor hid away at home in the evangelist's handkerchief; her mind slipped back to her first Communion, so short a while ago, with Sam there at her side, pressed against her, giving her greater peace and imbuing the bread and the wine with a larger significance. She would like to keep this man at her side always. Suddenly she shuddered at the thought that he might leave, and the palm of her hand oozed desperate sweat, moistening his coat.

They were near her home now and she must find some way to keep him with her. She chose the simplest.

"You must come in and have dinner with me. I'll be lonely with Aunt Mandy not here, and I hate eating alone."

She felt silly as she asked him, but the stratagem was welcome to him and saved him from taking the initiative.

Upstairs, after she had changed her dress for a stiff white kitchen frock, she let him follow her into the kitchen and take his place beside her at the sink. He stalked the quick movements of her fingers as she pared the potatoes or opened a can. He was humiliated that he could not do this last for her. She laughed at him, and told him to try his lone hand at making coffee.

After dinner, as they sat before the fire, so brooding a trouble lay on his face that she was troubled too, and wondered if he were slipping away in his thoughts, though there beside her.

"A penny for your thoughts," she bantered him.

"They's worth more'n a penny, 'cause I was thinkin' of you." He turned to her with such whole-hearted admiration shining in his eyes that she blessed her dark skin which hid from him the hot flush of embarrassment and pleasure which leaped to her cheeks.

"What were you thinking?"

"I was thinkin' how a woman needs a man." His voice broke in a frightened quaver. He had never had to talk to women before and he was finding it worse than physical hurt.

"A man needs a woman as well as a woman needs him." She wanted to lead him on to say what she yearned for, and yet she did not care to seem the aggressor.

"I think you're mighty pretty; I ain't never seen a woman prettier." He leaned over and took her hand. She let him have it easily, and he hid it in his own.

"It's mighty little," he said.

"Yes," she assented.

"If I was well and good and had a job, I could be bold and ask you to tie up with me, and even be hopin' you'd do it." His voice was distant and renunciatory, and she felt he might be slipping away.

"But you *are* good," she gainsaid him, hoping he might read in her contradiction her desire that he also be brave. "Christ's blood has washed you free of sin. And you are well and strong."

He passed over her ignorance of his spiritual health; this was one point on which he would never openly enlighten her. But he thought of his arm and feared that she was being charitable and pitying to spare him hurt.

"Oh, I'm well enough," he confessed, "but a one-armed man can't find much to do."

"Where there's a will there's a way." Her whole-souled love and affection took up this poor platitude and arrayed it in golden threads of wisdom. "Mrs. Brandon could find you something to do, maybe something there at her house with me. If not, something some place else; she knows everybody in Harlem. She would help you if I asked her."

She had spoken breathlessly, as if to ward off an interruption.

"And you would ask her for me?"

"Gladly." He caught the love in her voice, as if it had been a ball that she had tossed to him.

He thought of the women he had known before, dark and fair, small and large; they had come to him easily like water thrown upon a hill that has no other way to run but down; and like water he had run from them when he had tired. But these women had been different; they had been his kind, and when he had told them of his professional religion, they had laughed hard, throwing their heads back and showing their teeth, and they had called him damned tricky, and had said that the joke was all on God and that it was a good one. But Mattie had taken his cards and his razor and wrapped them up in a handkerchief, and had put them away, as something to keep her strong. She was not one to be taken and left; she would want a preacher, witnesses, a license to be framed, and a true husband.

He could read his doom in her face: no conquest for a fitful expenditure of passion, but love that was deep and severe like a halter around his neck. He sat with half-closed eyes weighing the good and evil of it. The evil of it: no more wandering off at will, begging a ride, coming into a strange town, letting his eyes burn into and melt some strange attractive woman's resistance; no more striding down a church aisle clutching in his hand a greasy deck of cards and a sharp polished razor, feeling in himself a power deeper than the preacher's. The good of it: this woman whose very existence now had for its cornerstone his own untrustworthy self; an entrance into the comfort and peace of this home, deep chairs, and a fire in a shining stove; a job; children, perhaps.

Her hand lay limp upon her lap where she had let it fall when he had released it. He leaned over and took it again, decision in his pressure.

"Then, Miss Mattie, could you marry me?"

"I couldn't marry no other man."

So simple a statement, so baldly said, in a low, hushed voice that was ashamed of its avowal, but it was more important to them than the rising and falling of kingdoms, than revolutions in China and Russia, than lynchings in Alabama, than a fire in the house might have been, or a murder in the next apartment.

He was no longer shy of her now; all his manhood and assertiveness returned. He rose and took her by the hand and led her to the sofa, where they might sit together. They sat there, taut and strained, his arm hard around her, as if the sinews and bone of it realized that they were doing a double duty.

CHAPTER
SIX

Constancia Brandon, for whom Mattie worked, was the mirror in which most of social Harlem delighted to gaze and see itself. She was beautiful, possessed money enough to be willful, capricious, and rude whenever she desired to deviate from her usual suave kindness; and she was not totally deficient in brains. Tall and willowy, with a fine ivory face whose emaciation spelled weakness and weariness, she quickly dispelled such false first impressions when she began to talk, with either her eyes or her tongue, in the use of both of which she was uncommonly gifted. Her gray eyes had strange contractile powers, narrowing into the minutest slits of disbelief and boredom, or widening into incredibly lovely globes of interest and amazement. They were not the windows of her soul, but they were the barometers by which one might gauge her interest in what one was saying.

Synthesis seemed to have had no part in her making. She had been born in Boston, and baptized Constance in the Baptist Church; but at sixteen she had informed her astounded parents and her equally astounded and amused friends that thenceforth her name was to be Constancia; that she found the religious ecstasies of the Baptist and Methodist faiths too harrowing for her nerves; and that she would attempt to scale the heavenly ramparts by way of the less rugged paths of the Episcopalian persuasion. From the beginning her manner was grand, and she gave one the impression that the great triumvirate, composed of God, the Cabots, and the Lodges, had with her advent into the world let down the color bar and been reorganized, to include hereafter on an equal footing Constancia Brown. She had never experienced any racial disturbances or misgivings, attributing her equanimity on this score to one English grandfather, one grandfather black as soot, one grandmother the color of coffee and cream in their most felicitous combination, one creole grandmother, and two sane parents. She was interested in her genealogy only because she wanted to ascertain if there really were somewhere in the medley a gypsy woman or man whose slowly diminishing blood was responsible for her incessant and overwhelming love of jewelry. From the moment her ears had been pierced they had never been devoid of ornaments; sleeping or waking, she gave evidence of wise and charming investments in bracelets, rings, and pendants.

But her tongue was her chief attraction, ornament, and deterrent. Her linguistic powers, aided by an uncanny mnemonic ability, had brought her high honors at Radcliffe and the headlong devotion of George Brandon. Her schoolmates called her Lady Macbeth, not that she was tragic, but that she never spoke in a monosyllable where she could use a longer word; she never said "buy" when she might use "purchase," and purchased nothing to which she might "subscribe." The first night he met her at an Alpha Phi Alpha fraternity ball George Brandon had pleased her mightily by dubbing her Mrs. Shakespeare.

George Brandon, short, thick-set, light brown, and methodical, was an Oklahoma Brandon whose very finger tips were supposed to smell of oil and money. Constancia, whose lawyer father enjoyed a comfortable if not opulent living, had really lacked for no good thing, and so had been able to meet George Brandon with a disinterestedness and reserve that other young girls of colored Boston had not been able to simulate. She had been amused at his enervated, drawling speech and his dog-like devotion to her, but from that first meeting she had harbored kindly feelings for him because he had recognized her verbal literary ability by the sobriquet of Mrs. Shakespeare. It was inevitable, then, that after six months of frantic courting she should have accepted him when he pleaded that if she failed to do so he would be in no fit condition to be graduated from the Harvard Medical College.

"Not for your money, my dear," she had assured him, "nor for any inherent and invisible pulchritude in yourself, but in order to spare to the world an accomplished physician, will I enter the enchanted realms of wedlock with you."

George had been happy to have her, even on the basis of so stilted and unromantic an acceptance. But the small-sized Oklahoma town to which he had taken her had not been able to reconcile itself to Mrs. Shakespeare. The small group of the Negro *élite* found her insufferable; they never knew what she was talking about. When she was hostess her guests generally left feeling that they had been insulted by her grandiose manners and complicated words; when she was guest her hostess never knew whether her comments on the party were commendable or derogatory. Matters fared no better at the monthly interracial meetings where the races met to exchange ideas and mutual good-will pledges, but not to touch hands. Constancia was elected secretary of the association, and thereafter the minutes were totally unintelligible save to herself, and when read made the bewildered workers for racial adjustment feel guilty of dark and immoral intentions. Mrs. Marshall, the wife of the white Baptist minister, and Mrs. Connelly, the wife of the leading white merchant, resented beyond concealment Constancia's chic vestments, blazing rings, and pendants; nor did they like the composed tone in which she would rise to say, "I unequivocally disagree with Mrs. Marshall," or, "I feel that Mrs. Connelly is in grievous error on this question."

In Oklahoma the Brandons could keep no servants; for Constancia had a strong democratic leaning which would not permit her to speak down to her menials. "I shall speak as I always do," she would say to the vainly expostulating George, "and they must learn to understand me. I do not want to embarrass them by making them self-conscious, by causing them to think that I do not believe that they have as much intelligence as I." And she continued to exhort her unintelligent help to "Come hither," to "Convey this communication to the doctor," or to "Dispatch this missive," until in utter self-defense they rebelled, and in true native fashion quit without giving notice.

Finally, at the repeated prayers of their respective ladies, the Reverend Mr. Marshall and Mr. Connelly, along with several colored members of the interracial committee, intimated to George that for the sake of racial amity it would be better if Constancia no longer kept the minutes of the meetings. And it was in order to placate Constancia for this loss of power and prestige that George brought her to Harlem.

In Harlem, Constancia had found her paradise. The oil-wells of Oklahoma were the open-sesame for which the portals of that extensive domain which goes by the name of Harlem society had swung wide to her. Wherever she went she conquered, and her weapons were various and well selected. Her interest in social activities won over the doctors' and lawyers' wives with whom, as Dr. Brandon's wife, she must naturally spend a part of her time; her democratic treatment of actors, writers, and singers made them her devoted slaves, while the very first week she was in New York her astounding vivacity and bewildering language completely floored Mrs. Vanderbilt-Jones of Brooklyn, who sent her an invitation to the Cosmos ball, and who even consented in all her rippling glory of black silk spangled with jet to attend Constancia's first Sunday night at home. For six days Harlem buzzed with the astonishing sight of Mrs. Vanderbilt-Jones in an animated and gracious conversation with Lottie Smith, singer of blues. Constancia had indeed been more than conqueror.

The Brandons purchased a fourteen-room house in what was called by less-moneyed, and perhaps slightly envious, Harlemites, Striver's Row. George, who, despite the unceasing emissions from

the Oklahoma wells, came of industrious stock and willed to be a
capable practicing physician, was relegated to the ground floor,
while Constancia ruled supremely over the rest of the house.

She was endowed with taste of a diffusive sort, which commu-
nicated itself to the furnishings of her home as well as to her guests.
What money could secure she bought, but indiscriminately. A survey of her home found ages and periods and fadistic moments
juxtaposed in the most comradely and unhistoric manner, while
the contributions of countries were wedded with the strictest disregard for geography.

Constancia never moved an eyelash to corral, but every author
who came to her home either brought or sent an autographed copy
of his books. Constancia dutifully and painstakingly read them all,
after which she would give George an intricate *résumé* (which he
promptly forgot) in order that, should he ever emerge into society,
he might converse with intelligence, and while talking to Bradley
Norris not compliment him on the beauty of a poem which had
been written by Lawrence Harper. No artist or singer was permitted to plead fatigue or temperament at Constancia's *soirées*. He
might offend once, but Constancia would remark within ample
hearing distance that temperament was the earmark of vulgarity
and incapacity. If the erring virtuoso sinned a second time, she
blue-penciled him, and remembered him with an elephant's re-
lentlessness. For this reason her innumerable parties never lacked
excitement and verve, and there was seldom a week in which the
New York Era or the *Colonial News* did not carry a portrait of
"Harlem's most charming hostess."

Lest it be thought that Constancia was built along strictly frivo-
lous lines, let it be noted in all fairness and in her defense that
she found time to belong to sixteen lodges which she never attended, but in which she was never unfinancial, and at whose
yearly women's meetings she was always called upon to speak. She
was a teacher in the Episcopalian Sunday school, because it con-
vened in the morning and so left her free for her afternoon visits
and her Sunday-evening at-homes. She was a member of the Board

of the National Negro Uplift Society and a director of the Diminutive Harlem Theatre Group; and she yearly donated fifty dollars for the best poem "by any poet," (never would consent to stipulate "by any colored poet," although a colored poet had always won the award) published during the year in the *Clarion*, the Negro monthly magazine. Added to this, she belonged to two bridge clubs, one sorority, a circulating library, and she gave one hour a week in demonstrating household duties at the Harlem Home for Fallen Girls.

The freemasonry existing between the races in New York neither pleased nor disturbed her. She was equally gracious to an eccentric dancer from the Lafayette Variety Theater and to a slumming matron from Park Avenue, out with fear and trembling to discover just how the other color lived. When at one of her parties it was suggested to her in fiery language by a spirited young Negro, who could neither forget nor forgive, that a celebrated white writer present was out to exploit and ridicule her, she had replied:

"Ridicule me? If he contrives to depict me as I am, he shall have achieved his first artistic creation. If he does less, he shall have ridiculed himself. And besides, don't be so damnably self-conscious or you will be miserable all your life. Now vouchsafe me your attendance and let me introduce you to the ogre who has come to devour us all."

She had then taken the protesting youngster by the hand, piloted him through her groups of chattering guests, and brought him to a standstill before Walter Derwent.

"My dear Mr. Derwent, I want you to do me a kindness. Here is a young man who is laboring under the apprehension that your frequent visits to Harlem have an ulterior motive, that you look upon us as some strange concoction which you are out to analyse and betray. I wish you would either disabuse him of, or confirm him in, his fears."

And she had left them together, both equally frightened.

After leaving them, she had paused to shout into Mrs. Vanderbilt-Jones's deaf and sparkling ear:

"I have just coupled a diminutive god with a sprouting devil."
She had passed on before Mrs. Vanderbilt-Jones could summon
courage enough to demand an explanation of the riddle.

Mattie had been Constancia's maid for over six years, six days
out of seven. Being maid meant making herself generally useful,
and giving orders to Porter, *l'homme à tout faire*, who was disin-
clined to see work which was not pointed out to him. Mattie adored
Constancia, although she disapproved of her parties and thought
her guests exceedingly strange and curiously mannered. Constancia spoke of Mattie as the perfect maid, a jewel of the first water.
She had reached this conclusion when, coming home one afternoon, she had interrupted Mattie in the midst of her dusting, to
inform her:

"Mattie, I have just been psychoanalyzed."

Mattie had said nothing for a moment, but had ceased dusting,
and had then delved down into her apron pocket, whence she
extracted a small pocket dictionary. After turning its pages and
scanning the word carefully, she had turned to the fascinated Constancia and, without a ripple stirring her smooth black face, had
said:

"Yes, ma'am. I hope you liked it."

Constancia had flown to her, had kissed her, and called her a
rara avis, which had disturbed Mattie throughout the day because
she could not find that in her dictionary.

CHAPTER SEVEN

When, the morning after her decision to marry Sam, Mattie, who had been hovering around Constancia as she presided over the percolator, suddenly blurted out, "I should like to get the day off, Mrs. Brandon, after I do the dishes, for something very important," Constancia, whose wide eyes could express the utmost astonishment, while in reality nothing ever astounded her, exclaimed, "Whatever for?"

"To get married, ma'am."

Porter, who had been piling wood in the open fireplace, but who had been listening at the same time, stopped with open mouth. Constancia was unpleasantly alarmed.

"Whomever to?" she cried, and then, without giving Mattie a chance to reply: "Not to Porter, I hope. Tell me, child, have I been unwittingly fostering a romance under my roof which is going to cost me two good servants? For I could never have you both here. The house would go to rack and ruin while you osculated and doved all day long. Why don't you answer me? *Is* it Porter? Porter married would be a calamity; he is slow enough now."

She turned to George, who was evincing a mild interest in the proceedings.

"Do you hear, George? Mattie wants to marry Porter." Mattie finally interrupted.

"No, ma'am, it isn't Porter. His name is Sam."

Constancia sank back relieved.

"You need not bring the smelling-salts, Mattie, so long as it isn't Porter. Sam, at least, is a respectable Ethiopian cognomen. But you must tell me about him. Where did you meet him?"

"At the revival."

"At the revival? *Was* there a revival? What a place to meet a husband! This is bizarre!"

George, who after many years of married life had not yet become accustomed to Constancia's freedom of speech and inquiry, motioned her to cease bantering Mattie.

"I will not desist, George." Constancia drew a chair up for Mattie. "Sit down, dear, and tell me everything. *Tout, tout, tout!* Why, George, suppose I had been introduced to you at a revival instead of at the Alpha Phi Alpha dance, do you think I would have married you? Not for all the petroleum in Oklahoma."

George, confused and hurt, arose and kissed Constancia, then lumbered out of the room.

She followed him lovingly with her eyes, and while he was still within hearing distance confessed to Mattie, "Child, I would have espoused him had I encountered him at the Kitchen Mechanics' ball. Now let's revert to Sam. What's he like?"

Mattie, dreamy with the memory of the previous evening, of Sam's heavy proposal hastened by her will to have him, feeling still the hard strength of his arm about her, tasting still the cruel sweetness of his kiss, told how she had met him, how his conversion had conquered her hardness and brought her from sin to grace.

Constancia listened with eyes that were wide with a specious incredulity.

"But one arm, Mattie," she argued. "However will you manage with a husband lacking an appendage?"

"That doesn't matter, ma'am. I love him all the more for it; it will make him lean on me all the harder. And besides, that one arm is as strong as two."

"What you say may be perfectly true," Constancia agreed. "And really," she added, reflectively, "his deficiency might have been even more calamitous."

Constancia toyed with her coffee-cup and mused. Mattie was such a good girl and had been such a jewel of a maid. She would like to do something for her. Here was an opportunity to help her in a munificent way.

"What plans have you made for the wedding?" she asked Mattie.

"Oh, we haven't made any plans. Sam is waiting for me at the house. I told him I'd be there as soon as I could get away from here, and then we'd go and get the license together, and come back uptown and have Reverend Drummond marry us."

"Mattie"—Constancia leaned across the table, her gray eyes kindled with largesse—"you must let me marry you from here. You must let me supervise your wedding."

Mattie demurred, "I don't know how Sam would like it."

"He is only incidental, my dear. This is your wedding. You must let me handle it for you."

As if it were settled, Constancia went on, carried away by the prospect, "Is there anybody you would like to come, any special body?"

"No one but Aunt Mandy."

"Well, I'll send George along with you in the car. He can take you down to get the license, and then bring you and Sam and your Aunt Mandy to the house. I'll arrange with Reverend Drummond and invite the guests, just a few friends of mine, to liven up the proceedings. Tell me, Mattie, how do you feel about miscegenation?"

Mattie, who had been taken unawares, without her dictionary, could only gasp in complete ignorance, "About what, ma'am?"

Constancia was so completely enamored of what the day promised, that she condescended to an explanation.

"I mean, my dear, do you mind if I invite some white people to witness the ceremony?"

"Oh, I don't think I'd like that. I don't care much for white people."

"Well, that's very wrong of you. I had no idea you were prejudiced. Nevertheless, it shall be as you like. You are missing a splendid material opportunity, for Walter Derwent has coined enough money on his articles about us to afford a handsome donation to the gift-table. Now I'll call George and you can go see about the license. We'll set the wedding for five o'clock. But you return as soon as you secure the license, for I want to dress you here. Bring Sam and your aunt along with you, so there will be no danger of his changing his mind. I'll have the minister here. . . . George!"

In answer to Constancia's shrill summons, George lumbered upstairs. "Darling, you will have to divest yourself of that badge of servitude," she said, pointing to the white coat he wore in his office, "and people who can't do any better will just have to die. You are having a holiday today. I am going to give Mattie away; that is I am going to have her married from here. I want you to take her and her husband-to-be down to the license bureau, and then bring them back here. Now run along. No, no, no. (Her negatives were like a dove's cooing, and each one was followed by a peck on George's lips.) No protestations. Run along."

As Mattie and George were leaving, Constancia suddenly remembered something. She ran to the door and poked her head out into the cold January air. Her earrings swung gayly.

"Mattie," she cried, "have we any rice?"

Mattie turned in bewilderment.

"Any rice, child, rice? You can't get married without rice. Oh, it's your wedding. How stupid of me to expect you to know what is needed! George, bring back some rice, about two pounds, superior quality."

Inside again, and seated at her desk, with a small golden pen poised over a white tablet, the telephone at her elbow, Constancia was so filled with plans that even she was at a loss where to begin. She thought it might be best to make certain that the minister was unengaged for the hour agreed upon. She dialed.

"Is this the Mount Hebron Methodist Episcopal Church? ... Give me Reverend Drummond, please. ... This *is* Reverend Drummond? How stupid of me! I should have recognized your voice. This is Mrs. Brandon—Mrs. George Brandon. I want to tell you how sorry I was to miss your exquisite revival. I hear it was disconcertingly successful and that sinners were taken in by the hundreds. ... What? there were only thirty-odd? Well, even that is encouraging. Small commencements sometimes make frightfully large endings. Do let me know when you are having another revival. I have so many friends who might profit by attendance. Now to the point at issue. Can you perform a wedding at my home this afternoon at five? I know you will be interested to learn that the contending parties are two of your converts—my maid Mattie and the one-armed man who discarded his cards and his razor. ... You will come? ... How sweet of you. At five, then. Good-by."

She dialed again.

"Mrs. Vanderbilt-Jones? ... Dear, this is Constancia. I want you to drop everything you are doing and be at my house at five o'clock. Mattie is being married. ... Who is Mattie? Why, my maid, the one who makes those delicious anchovy sandwiches that you like so well. Yes, you recollect her now? Well, there won't be any anchovy sandwiches today because I can't make them and Mattie is being married. But you will come, won't you? And bring a present, my dear."

She leaned back almost exhausted, but her Spartan courage could not be vanquished. When she had completed her calls she had exacted promises of attendance, with presents, from Lottie Smith, the blues singer; from Lawrence Harper, the poet; from Stanley Bickford, the architect; and from several less-prominent but socially important personalities. For a moment she toyed with the phone as if undecided about something which she very much wanted to do. Finally she yielded to the impulse and dialed.

"Mr. Derwent please. . . . Oh, Walter, this is Constancia. Listen, dear. My maid Mattie is being married today from my house, and I am calling on my friends to donate something to the gift-table. . . . Yes, the lovely little dark thing who serves so nicely, and who slapped your friend's face last time you were here when he attempted to kiss her. Served him right, too. Well, Walter, I want you to send something, something lovely as you always do; you know your taste is so irreproachable. Unfortunately, the child is prejudiced. . . . Yes, that's it, she has race prejudice and simply refuses to have a black-and-tan wedding. So I can't invite you. . . . No, you *couldn't* pass for colored. Don't be pretentious; she has seen you too often. But you will send a present, won't you. . . . That's lovely. And, Walter, if you think it will console you any, you can read all about it in next week's *Tattler.*"

When George and Mattie returned, about two hours later, with Aunt Mandy and Sam, Constancia was knee-deep in roses and ferns; six canaries in beribboned cages were doing their infinitesimal best to add to the general derangement, while two extra women, hastily summoned, were busy in the kitchen. Constancia paused long enough to give Sam an appraising and appreciative glance.

"He *is* good-looking," she whispered to Mattie. "Now all of you run up to the top of the house and sleep, play cards, bathe, or do whatever you like, while I finish these nuptial trimmings."

The bell rang. Although it was only one o'clock, Lawrence Harper, who adored Constancia and who had been greatly intrigued by the invitation, had come to see what assistance he might offer. In his hand he held a package tied with blue-and-red ribbon.

"For the bride and groom," he explained, handing the package to Constancia. "May they read and adore them."

"What is it?" asked Constancia.

"My poems, of course! I got them at the author's reduction rate."

"The poet's mite. How sweet of you! Well, just sit down somewhere and write another poem."

A messenger came in holding gingerly a large box which, when Constancia took it, was much lighter than it looked. Inside were twelve fragile gold-rimmed champagne glasses and Walter Derwent's card, inscribed, "To Mattie with lilacs and geraniums." Constancia held the glasses up to the light, where they sparkled anticipatingly. "Walter must have thought *I* was being married," she commented. "Next time I see him I'll make him supply that for which these glasses were intended."

At three Mrs. Vanderbilt-Jones drove up in suburban dignity, and in a taxi. She had bought a new ear-trumpet which she was clutching violently in one hand while in another she held a fair-sized package.

"Constancia," she complained, "I wouldn't have come for anybody but you. You have no idea how expensive it is to take a taxi from Brooklyn to New York. It's sheer banditry on the part of these taximen. The Subway is cheaper, of course, but so tedious and smelly."

"Have you ever tried the Paris metro, second class?" Constancia inquired.

"I have never tried anything second class—that is, to my knowledge. Here, take this present. I hope you like it."

Constancia undid the package and discovered a beautiful porcelain vase. It was so lovely with its blue water and willow trees that she half envied Mattie for it.

"Ravishing," she said. "Is it Sèvres?"

"Certainly not," protested Mrs. Vanderbilt-Jones, petulantly detaching her veil. "It is Ovington's latest.

"Constancia," the old lady continued, settling herself comfortably where she would be most in the way, "come here and sit beside me for a moment. There, that's a dear. I have something of social importance to tell you. I am moving to Harlem. Brooklyn bores me. There is so much life here, and such smart people, and you. I am moving into a very select apartment in that new district known as Sugar Hill. I can't say that I think the name is at all dignified, nothing like *Brooklyn*, you know. But the houses are so lovely. All the white people are moving out, bless them, and only the best colored people are moving in—doctors and lawyers and teachers."

Constancia groaned audibly.

"I have the loveliest apartment," the dowager went on; "seven rooms completely overlooking the city. What a view! And just think, dear, *two bathrooms!*"

Constancia slid to the floor, to busy herself anew twining roses and ferns. Mrs. Vanderbilt-Jones waggled a dropsical finger at Lawrence Harper, but the bard refused to budge. The old lady closed her eyes and fell asleep thinking what temperamental people poets were.

Lottie Smith and Stanley Bickford came together at four. Stanley, tall, indolent, and so Nordic that he spent the major part of his time patiently explaining that he could look as he did and according to American standards be colored at the same time, brought a small parcel which gurgled when Constancia shook it.

"This I shall confiscate, Stanley," she admonished him. "I want these people to enjoy their honeymoon."

Lottie, whose boast was that she could put all the other Smiths to shame with her moaning, was slight, brown, and indescribably chic. She drew fabulous sums and spent them all on clothes; she always looked as if she had come directly from the rue de la Paix. She had burdened herself with two packages; both were circular, but one, wrapped in plain brown paper, was about five times the thickness of the other, which was encased in silver tissue, bound with ribbons of many colors.

Lottie was the only one who made Constancia gasp and stutter. She was so unlike what she ought to be; more like a successful business man's or a doctor's wife in appearance than like a blues singer.

"How Louise Boulanger you look today, Lottie, and how prodigal you are, and how like you to bring two presents!" Constancia complimented her.

"Well," boomed Lottie in that deep contralto voice worshiped from coast to coast, "they are all records—records of the St. Louis blues. These five (pointing to the somber package) are by my rivals. And this (holding up the festively decked disc admiringly) is by me. I want your maid to try these others first, and then I want her to play mine, and see how lousy the others are in comparison."

At this juncture Mrs. Vanderbilt-Jones, having sufficiently refreshed herself, descended upon Lottie to enchant her with the tale of the two bathrooms.

Constancia twined the last rose among the ferns with which she had draped the stairway down which Mattie was to come. She cocked her ear for a moment to see if above the profundity of Lottie's voice pouring into Mrs. Vanderbilt-Jones' trumpet, and over the clatter of a cocktail-shaker which Stanley was manipulating with affectionate and consummate artistry, while Lawrence stood near by, reading *"à haute voix,"* his latest poem, she might not discover some coördinated melody in the abandoned rapture of the canaries.

She beamed upon them all, and excused herself.

"Enjoy yourselves in your several ways. I am going up to dress the bride."

Upstairs, she found Sam stretched out stomach down upon a sofa. His face was buried in his arm, while low staccato noises emanating from his direction demonstrated that he was sleeping the sleep of the weary and perhaps of the frightened, if not of the just. Aunt Mandy, arrayed in blue silk, was perched doll-like in a rocker, her small hands spread out on the arms of the chair, her little bird eyes contentedly contemplating her jewelry. The gold hoops were back in her ears. Mattie had drawn a chair up to the sofa, where she sat demure and brooding, keeping happy and guardian watch over Sam.

"Let him sleep," whispered Constancia. "He'll merely have to lave his face afterwards, but you must hurry and get accoutered. You and your aunt come into my room while I transform you into a bride."

"I had planned to be married just as I am, ma'am." Mattie regarded her soberly-cut blue dress as if she found in it all the sartorial excellence necessary.

Constancia merely took her by the arm and drew her along, motioning to Aunt Mandy to follow. "My dear," she said, "this is the one occasion on which you must look your supremest, no matter how dowdy you may become afterwards. One's marriage is not a quotidian affair. I want Sam to be overcome by your loveliness when he sees you, asphixiated, as it were. I want him to think you are a butterfly which has broken its chrysalis and flown straight to him. Men like finery and pretty things on a woman—our men, especially. There's nothing to retain them like a splash of color, or a gold tooth, or some beads around the neck. I have set my heart on having you wear these things. Look!"

She held up the dress; it was cherry-colored; to Mattie's touch it was softer than the stuff of a spider's web. On the floor were a pair of slippers, a darker crimson, with tiny black-velvet bows.

"They're lovely!" Mattie exclaimed. "But I couldn't wear them; they wouldn't go with my color. It's much too red, and I'm too dark."

"Nonsense!" Constancia reassured her. "There's not a lovelier combination than black and red. Just try them on for me."

Mattie allowed herself to be persuaded, and when, after a bit of tucking and pinning to make the dress fit her, she stood before the mirror and looked at herself, and then gazed down to where her little feet peeped out as if half afraid to issue forth in their finery, she was incredulous of her loveliness. Aunt Mandy could only stand off, and then circle her, her hands clasped in admiration, her tongue clucking excitedly as if she were a bantam hen calling her brood.

"Now sit down and compose yourself," Constancia urged Mattie, "while I get dressed."

After Constancia had arrayed herself in a clinging gray dress relieved by a large green brooch, and had changed her swinging gold earrings for others which were longer and which sparkled with small green stones, she descended to see what other arrivals had come while she had been occupied with Mattie.

She found Reverend Drummond in animated conversation with Stanley. "But the church is necessary even to an architect," the minister was saying, while Stanley's childish blue eyes were staring with polite attention but with scant conviction.

Dr. and Mrs. Wilbur Roach had arrived; and Counselor and Mrs. Geoffrey O'Connell, while aloof and to themselves, as if hatching a plot, were the society editors of the *New York Era*, the *Colonial News*, and the *Tattler*. There were two new gifts on the table—a samovar from the Roaches and an envelope from the O'Connells, probably a check, for the slight, monocled lawyer was sure to donate something practical.

"I'm so glad to see you, Reverend." Constancia tendered the pastor a heavily-ringed hand. "We'll be ready in just a moment."

She looked across at Stanley and saw the pleading in his eyes; she had compassion for him. She remembered that he had wanted to be a concert artist before veering off to architecture, and that in his long drink-nervous fingers there still resided a magnetism that could draw harmony from a piano as the magnet draws the nail. "Stanley," she said, in her most improvising tone, "I wish you would play for us, Mendelssohn or Wagner, when Mattie starts down the stairway. You might go over to the piano now and limber your fingers up."

Darting her beams of affectionate gratitude, he scuttled to the piano, where his fingers arabesqued across the keys in the sheerest ecstasy of deliverance.

Reverend Drummond gazed fondly after him.

"A fine young man, a splendid architect, I've been told, a real credit to the race," he growled, "but terribly misguided. He has no religious affiliations. I should like to talk to him sometime and put him on the right track."

"I'll bring him to your next revival," promised Constancia. Then

424

raising her voice and addressing them all, "I shall send the groom down now."

She floated upstairs. Sam had washed the sleep from his eyes, and was pacing the room nervously when she entered. George sat moodily in a corner, silently anathematizing Constancia and her mad whims, but letting his devotion for her show all too plainly in his eyes as she rustled into the room.

"It'll soon be over," she consoled Sam. "Take him downstairs, George. They are waiting."

"But where's Mattie?" Sam was not accustomed to pre-marital etiquette, and he had been apprehensive since he woke up to find Mattie gone.

"Oh, she's about," Constancia assured him; "she'll just be fashionably tardy."

As he encountered the unfamiliar faces in the drawing-room, Sam let all the boldness of his gaze go out and affront them. They were not of his world. They had what he hadn't and didn't want— money and schooling; they were society. He eyed them insolently, not bending his head when they bowed to him, raging inwardly as he saw them gaze in astonishment at his lonely arm. What a fool he had been to let this girl drag him here into this marriage.

Lottie Smith, to whom social status was unimportant, in view of the number of Harlem ladies to whom she was *persona non grata*, save when on the stage or when they were seeking a benefit performance for some one of their numerous charity enterprises, went over to Sam. "Let me congratulate you," she said. "Mattie is such a pretty girl."

Mrs. Vanderbilt-Jones, who often disconcerted people by hearing what she was supposed to miss, jerked the blues-singer by the sleeve. "I think you are a bit premature, Lottie," she warned. "Congratulations are due after the ceremony."

Just then Constancia's ivory face appeared at the head of the stairs, thus terminating what might have been a warm argument endangering the friendship of the dowager and the cantatrice. A gem-studded finger was crooked into a signal for Stanley who launched forth into the "Lohengrin Wedding March," while Sam looked up to behold a rapturous vision.

His heart spurted like a fountain within him, sending strong currents beating for release in the palm of his hand, in his ears, and in the somber veins of his temples. Here was the vision which he had seen at the Communion table, but a reality far more ravishing than the dream. Mattie in a bright-red dress, her small dark feet encased in crimson slippers with black-satin bows! Her hair was curled and glossy. A sheaf of roses was in one arm. Her arms made music as she descended the stairs, for as she walked, the thin silver bracelets which Constancia had loaned her jangled and exulted. Her face, enkindled with happiness, rose up above the bouquet like a larger flower for which these others were only a setting, like an animated black tulip, rich and smooth and velvety.

Oh, I will love her and be kind to her and never leave her, Sam promised himself as he thought of his vision and of the black young fellow whose one arm boasted the strength of two. Behind her came Aunt Mandy and Constancia.

Reverend Drummond stood before them with open ritual. George stood at Sam's side, Aunt Mandy at Mattie's, and just in back, jubilant and serene, was Constancia.

"Have you a ring?" the minister asked Sam.

"No." Sam's great shame was in his voice.

"I have a ring," said Mattie. She turned to Sam and gave him her flowers to hold. "It was my mother's." She untied her handkerchief and extracted a plain gold band.

"With this ring I thee wed, and with my worldly goods I thee endow." Sam repeated the words after the minister, feeling small and cheap within himself as he realized their hollow unimportance. He was bringing her nothing but himself, a liar, cheater, professional religionist. But he would make amends. He would be good to her. He would find work and slave, and save, and keep her as the minister had said, "for better, for worse; for richer, for poorer; in sickness and in health," till death should part them.

"I now pronounce you husband and wife. Those whom our God has joined together let no man put asunder."

Forgetful and scornful of his surroundings, Sam encircled Mattie with his arm. Kissing her, he murmured, "Baby, baby!" while she leaned against him with closed eyes, time and space, guests and surroundings, outdistanced by her happiness.

"Let me congratulate you, Mrs. Lucas." The minister was holding out his hand, stiffly and with ceremony. But Constancia would not have it so. She was gay and happy; the wedding had been a ripping success; she could see the long columns in the *New York Era* and the *Colonial News;* she already saw by faith her picture in the next issue of the *Tattler,* and the caption: "Harlem's most charming and original hostess has magnificent" (the word would certainly be *magnificent*) "wedding for her maid." She was supremely blissful.

"Everybody osculate!" she cried, clapping her hands.

And lest she might not be understood, she leaned over and kissed Sam full on the lips. He stood stiff with rage and resentment, which was not lessened when the minister, after much cajoling by Constancia, pecked Mattie lightly. The women all kissed Sam, with much laughter and coyness, to his infinite disgust and helplessness. Mattie graciously entered into the sport, although it was of no import to her that she was being kissed by one of the famous poets of her race. What mattered was that she would be kissed by Sam over and over again. When Stanley Bickford approached with his blond hair rising in military precision, his fair face flushed, and his blue eyes anticipating the reward of his playing, Mattie drew back from him and looked appealingly at Constancia.

"My dear," said Constancia, with a trace of hurt in her voice, "do you think I would betray you? He's *colored.*"

Mattie suffered herself to be kissed.

Reverend Drummond could not be persuaded to remain for the supper. He was wary of these people. He was sure there would be dancing and he felt there were liquors on the table. He had seen Stanley cache the cocktail-shaker as he entered, although it had been too late to conceal the glasses. He drew up the marriage certificate for Mattie. It was a large shiny paper somewhat resembling a diploma, but less severe. On it were roses, and a huge silver bell to ring in all the joys of their matrimonial life. At the bottom there was the picture of a book, open and lined; this was for the signatures of the witnesses. Everybody wanted to sign, and as there weren't lines enough, the names were allowed to spread riotously outside the book.

"It reads like the Social Register of Harlem," commented Constancia as she signed with a flourish.

After he had given Mattie her certificate and had pocketed his fee, the minister left, firmly refusing Constancia's entreaties to "stay for a bit of collation." As the door closed behind him, Stanley rushed to the piano, where he began to play the slow, sorrowful, almost religious strains of a blues. The music invaded Sam until he forgot his alien dislike for these people. He seized Mattie and swung her off into a dance. For a moment it was so blissful to feel his arm about her, and to sense his hot and desirous breath upon her cheeks, while his fine dark eyes unleashed their full power on her, that she allowed herself to float away in his arm. But suddenly she remembered certain mystic symbols tied up in a white handkerchief and hid away; her mind slid back to the white altar with the bowed repentant heads circling it; she thought of the dark, sinful hands faltering out for bread and wine. She stiffened in his arm.

"Sam, Sam," she whispered, "we're church members now. This isn't right. These things don't belong to us any more."

Her protest filled him with doubts and suspicions; small currents of remorse, ever widening and gathering strength, ran through him and shocked him. Had he, after all, chosen the better part? Was his own trickery to come back upon him like a boomerang, separating him from that felicity toward which he had dreamed in taking this woman? Was her religion, rooted and grounded in him, to be a barrier between them?

"Let's don't think of that now," he entreated. "Let's only think of bein' glad and happy; let's only think of lovin' each other." He held her more tightly, laughing at her half-hearted struggles, melting his will and his love into her, striving against the Holy Ghost, and conquering. Her taut body relaxed; she flung her head back until he had to brace his arm to hold her.

"All right," she assented, "let's only think of love tonight and of being happy. Play something fast," she cried to Stanley.

As the music quickened its pace the crimson slippers flashed in and out joyfully, the web-soft, cherry-colored dress whirled and flashed, its folds flaring out like the dress of a ballet-dancer. God! but she was a dancer, Sam thought. Elation filled his breast, and his mind romped ahead to other dances to come. Aunt Mandy, who could find good in cards and fortune-telling, hated dancing and drinking. She sat back in a chair and shut her eyes to blot out the abomination. The other guests formed a cordon around them, urging them on, with clapping hands, time-tapping feet, and those short, spontaneous cries which are the Negro's especially copyrighted expressions of delight. Sam and Mattie broke away from one another; they improvised; they strutted and glided, approached one another and backed away, did as much of the cakewalk as they could remember, and cast in for good measure all the dead-gone and buried steps of Negro dancing which came to mind: they shuffled, balled the jack, eagle-rocked, walked the dog, shimmied and charlestoned, till, breathless and riotously happy, they could only lean panting against each other, in blissful exhaustion.

"Bravissimo!" approved Constancia. "Now on to the viands." She threw out her hands and herded them into the dining-room as if she had been a farmer shooing chickens. Constancia was known as a bountiful hostess; the table, loaded with chicken salad, cold ham and tongue, olives, celery, pickles, and hot, buttered rolls, evidenced her decision not to imperil her reputation. Eggnog frothed in a bowl in the center of the table. Mattie caught Aunt Mandy's scandalized eye, and refused to drink, despite Sam's tender entreaties. But when Porter ambled in with iced bottles at

the sight of which Mrs. Vanderbilt-Jones forgot her dignity to the
extent of exclaiming, incredulously, "Champagne!" Mattie refused
to look at her aunt. The pop of the bottles fascinated her, and the
sparkling liquid became one final irresistible sin which she would
commit on this night of love. She lifted her glass with the rest.

"*Skoal!*" cried Constancia.

"*Buvons!*" exhorted Stanley.

"To Mattie and Sam!" said Lawrence. The liquor had made
him prosaic; he had wanted to say something in rhyme, but it
wouldn't come.

Mattie tasted her drink and made a wry face; she didn't like it.
She set the glass down, but Sam picked it up, kissed the rim where
her mouth had been, and drained it.

"How romantic! How perfectly like a lover!" Mrs. Vanderbilt-
Jones said, with glistening eyes. "It all takes me back to my marriage with Mr. Vanderbilt-Jones. If he were only living to be here
with me now! My dear," she said, turning to Mattie, "you will
remember this day when you are like me." Her voice trailed off
in revery, her thought sank back into her slightly reeling brain.

But Stanley finished it for her, *sotto voce*, to Lottie, "Yes," he
mocked, "with an ear trumpet, and two bathrooms on Sugar Hill.
May Heaven forbid!"

Suddenly Constancia remembered something. She rushed up to
Mattie in agitated inquiry. "Where are you honeymooning?"

Mattie laughed. "I hadn't thought of that."

Sam fidgeted uneasily, and cursed Constancia for a meddling
fool.

"We're not going away," explained Mattie. "I've got to keep
my work, and Sam has to find a job."

"But there must be a honeymoon," insisted Constancia, "of
some sort. No wedding is complete without one. Why not go to a
theater?"

Sam liked the idea; shows always pleased him.

"Where?" he asked.

"Some place downtown," said Constancia, "to one of the smart revues." She flicked back her sleeve and looked at her watch. "No, time has overruled that suggestion. It's already eight-thirty."

"Well, we could go to a colored show," said Sam. "I'd like it much better, anyhow." He hated to relinquish the idea, and he was anxious to get Mattie away to himself. "The Sable Steppers are at the Lafayette."

"Just the thing, the physician's very prescription," agreed Constancia. "I'll phone for a box for you; you just have time to make the nine o'clock show. Porter can drive you over and then I'll see that your aunt gets home safely."

As Sam and Mattie were leaving, George came in with a huge pan of rice into which the guests delved; they threw the rice after the departing pair with spirited but inaccurate aim, and with small concern for the cracks and crevices in Constancia's house.

From her doorway Harlem's most ingenious hostess watched her car round the corner. The wedding had been most successful. She stooped and gathered up a few grains of the rice which lay on her brownstone steps like hard snow.

"Hail to Hymen!" she sighed as she sallied back to her guests.

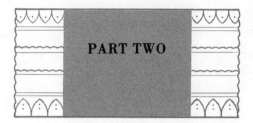

PART TWO

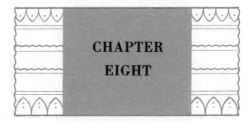

CHAPTER
EIGHT

Life for the moment seemed more fine-favored and worth living to Sam than ever before. He took his awakening the next morning as a prelude to what the whole of his days to come would be. He had not felt Mattie shift her head from the crook of his arm, and it was with a somnolent surprise that, answering a tug at his sleeve, he looked up with puckered brow to find her bending over him. The ripples in his forehead receded into the smoothness of understanding as remembrance of last night began slowly to flood his brain. Although he closed his eyes sharply to give the dream, if it were a dream, time to abandon him, when he opened them again Mattie was still there. He turned and sat up, taking in anew the four close walls, the bedroom so tiny that two abreast could scarcely pass between the bed and the wall. He leaned over and sent the window shade swirling up so that the faint apology for sunlight which trickled in from the airshaft might bathe the room in its grayness, more like the light of early evening than of broad day. He wondered what time it was, and whatever time it might be, he hoped Mattie wouldn't want him to get up so early; he hated early rising. He yawned and stretched his hand up, vigorously shaking the sleep out of it.

Mattie sat down on the side of the bed and leaned over against him.

"Lazy?" she accused him.

"No, tired."

"Tired?" Mattie shunted back with lifted eyebrows and arms akimbo in an attitude of mock incredulity. "Tired of what?"

He eased down into the sheets again, from where he looked up at her with squint-eyed playfulness. "You ought to know, Mrs. Lucas," he said. "You know," he went on, avoiding the light tap she aimed at him, "I was 'fraid to open my eyes at first; thought last night and the days before might 'a' been nothin' but a dream. But here's you and here's me." He sat up again and surveyed his kingdom, "And here's home."

He noticed for the first time that she was fully clothed, dressed in a tailored suit the somber cut and dark hue of which contrasted sharply with the cherry-colored dress in which he had last seen her.

"Why'd you get up so early and dress?" he protested.

"It isn't early. It's eight o'clock. Time working-people were up and about. You know, Sam, there's no rest for the weary. I've got to get Mrs. Brandon's breakfast this morning same as every other one."

"But the honeymoon ain't over yet, honey. We ain't used up even a quarter of it." He pulled her down to him and kissed her. "A quarter did I say?" He smacked his lips. "We ain't even started to nibble on that moon."

Mattie ran her fingers through his hair; it wasn't easy going, for the pomade with which he had plastered it for his wedding, until it glistened like black satin, had dried, and the hard knotty curls had reverted to type until they were now a mass of little tight balls, like a patch of dwarfed and withered black grapes.

"No," Mattie mused. "You're right, honey boy, we haven't even started to nibble. We haven't even bit down hard into it; we've only drawn our tongues across it, scraped it with our teeth and tasted the sugar to make sure it was there. And now that we know

it's there, if we just nibble a bit day by day, we'll have that honeymoon for mighty nigh forever. Ain't that better than just swal-
lowing the whole cake today and snuffing ashes tomorrow? At any
rate, thinking about it that way makes it easier for me to leave you
and go off to work."

She stood up, smoothing her dress, as she continued, "But I
thought you ought to have your breakfast before I go, and I've got
it all fixed."

He made to get up, but she pushed him back gently. "No, this
morning you're going to eat in style, served in bed with brown-
skin service, or near-brown, anyway. I made up my mind long ago
that I'd bring my husband his first breakfast to bed, that is, unless
I happened to marry a man with money. Then, of course, we'd
both have breakfast in bed."

"Well," Sam laughed, "that's one fine dream all shot to pieces."

She brought him water in a basin and washed his face in spite
of his protestations; and then on a tray orange-juice, coffee, scram-
bled eggs, bacon, and toast. "I'm giving you just what Dr. and
Mrs. Brandon will have this morning," she told him, pridefully,
"unless it's a bit of brandy which they take in their coffee sometimes. And of course"—she waved her hands airily in summary
dismissal of the thought—"you wouldn't want that, anyhow."

"No, I wouldn't want that, anyhow," Sam echoed, so slowly that
she laughed in spite of her disapproval that he should really have
wanted brandy.

She sat and watched him eat, saying that she would snatch a
bite for herself at Mrs. Brandon's. He took it as his due that she
should so serve him, the circumstances being what they were. He
told himself that after she had gone, and after he had caught up a
bit on his sleep, he would get up and go out and try to find a job.
He was genuinely excited at the prospect of a steady job, something to which he had not allied himself for many years.

After Mattie had gone, he lay gazing up at the ceiling and smiling, thinking how strange and fine it would be for him to be coming
home on Saturday nights with money in his pockets and a little

present for Mattie. Not that he would bring her his envelope un-opened; he wasn't that kind of a man. A man should always be the boss in his home, he felt, and should open and pull the purse strings as he willed. The man ought to be head of the house. Well, he *would* be as soon as he had a job.

He turned over on his side and drew the covers more closely about him. Blazes! but it was cold; too cold to think about getting up for a while. Maybe Aunt Mandy would have a good hot fire burning when he did get up. He hoped she would. If there was one thing which he hated worse than getting up early, it was getting up in a cold room.

When he awoke again it was well after noon and the January sun had waxed so strong that a sliver of cold sunlight had come down the shaft and now adorned his bed with a spot of imitation warmth. He could hear a rustling and to-do in the kitchen. The power of strong black coffee invaded his nostrils, seeped down into his abdominal regions, and made him aware of a new hunger. Must be Aunt Mandy getting lunch, he told himself; well, it couldn't be ready any too soon for him.

Aunt Mandy was frying chops when he came into the kitchen. Fork poised lightly in hand, she welcomed him with an enthusiastic grin. She was a bit put out that she had been asleep when Mattie left and so hadn't been able to banter her; but she thought to take it out on Sam. She curtsied to him in mock reverence, and set her small, black, tantalizing eyes full on him.

"Good mornin', son. Sleep well?" The intonation of her query gave every indication that a negative response was expected.

But Sam was feeling shy and reserved. "Like a top," he said.

The little old lady was highly amused. She shook the long glis-tening fork, with which she had been probing the chops, at him, and wagged her head. "You tellin' me that and expectin' me to believe it? Lord! boy, see any green in my eyes? Think you can buy me for a fool?" She pulled the skin down from her eye and rolled her eyeball back until only the clear white shone out at him.

"Like a top, indeed!" she snorted, and Sam burst out laughing in spite of his embarrassment.

"Ben's been gone a long time," she said, looking past the chops and past Sam and past time into the past. "But I still know there's nothin' like bein' married and lovin' one another." She brushed the moisture away from her eyes and attacked the chops with renewed vigor. "Now ain't I becoming the sentimental old fool, with Ben dead and gone all these years and me gettin' moony about him now!"

"You was plumb sweet on him, wasn't you, a'nty?" Sam was leaning indolently against the kitchen door like some sleek two-legged animal. His gaze took in the kitchen and Aunt Mandy; if he turned his head he could see from where he stood the snug living-room, and leading from it the pitifully small hall, their foyer. It all seemed very natural to him, as if he had been holding on to some slender string all his days, winding it carefully around his hand, holding his breath lest it might break and the severed skein be swept away in the wind. Life was a silken thread which he had succeeded in holding on to until it had brought him here. Now he could throw it away; let the wind take it; let it go. His traveling days were done.

"I was gone on him for twenty years." He had forgotten Aunt Mandy for the moment, and her high-pitched voice brought him back with a jerk from his dreaming. "Son, you'll never know what real livin' is until you've lived out rain and shine, good times and bad, sickness that's just around the corner from dyin', and everything that makes up life with one person, like I did with Ben for twenty years. Even now I can't think of him without this crazy feelin' here; and when I go to meetin' and they start talkin' about heaven, sometimes I don't know which one I want to see first when I get over there, Jesus or Ben."

"He must 'a' been awful good to you, a'nty."

"Well, he was just a man, son, no better than most of you. Any woman what gets one of you ought to know before she takes you

that mostly she's takin' a bundle of trouble—sweet, sweet trouble."
Her eyes frolicked at the memory of the pain and worry Ben had
caused her, and her flat withered bosom heaved a sigh of regret
that it was not all to be borne again.

"You know, a'nty"—they were seated at the table, where Sam
was enjoying his lunch as much as if breakfast had never been—
"I feel about Mattie the way you did about Ben, only more. I'm
so sweet on her that all the fine times I had before I met her, all
the times that seemed so swell then, don't seem like nothin' now.
I feel like I know what the preachers means when they says you
must be born agin. You watch and see how little trouble I'm goin'
to give her. I'm goin' to be so good to her she's goin' to have to
beg me to stop."

"You is, son?" She was all unconcealed merriment and disbelief. "I hopes so. But that's honeymoon talk you doin' now. I hope
to God it don't run out. My Mattie's the stickin' kind, and whenever
she goes into anything she goes in for keeps."

She leaned over to pour him another cup of coffee; her wee
inquisitive face peered up almost beneath his nose as she asked
him, so abruptly that he drew back in dismay, "When you thinkin'
about findin' a job?"

The question was distasteful to him at the moment. He was
feeling so prime and well-nourished, slightly sleepy again. He
thought a nap now might do him good. But, no, he had to go to
work; he wasn't a rounder any more. He was a married man. His
wife was pretty. How pretty he knew, as he remembered how people had looked at her at the theater the night before. As they had
taken their seats, one coffee-colored rowdy, overcome by the cherry
dress and Mattie's piquant black face, had exclaimed, "Must be
recess up in heaven; they's let an angel out." And Sam had not
been offended, but had grown cocky like a rooster, proud of the
envious eyes upon him.

After the theater he had had to beg long and ardently before
Mattie would consent to go to the Savoy for a little dancing. She
had said it wasn't right for church members; but he had argued

that church members weren't held accountable for a little sinning on their wedding night. Finally she had gone with him, and how she had danced! How washed out and faded the yellow and light-brown hostesses had appeared in comparison with her. He had seen more than one man, taking his ten-cent dance with one of these girls, pause and lose his step looking at Mattie. And what a tremendous joy it had been for them to scorn a taxi and to walk home after the dance, his arm supporting her, infused with the strength of two arms now by the full tide of possession. Yes, he must find something to do.

"I'm aimin' on goin' out huntin' for somethin' this afternoon, a'nty. What you think a man like me can find to do? What kind of a job you think they got for one-armed people?"

"What sort of a job did you have last?"

"The last steady job I had was helpin' paw on the farm."

"Well, they ain't no farms up here." He could sense her disapproval of his period of idleness. "We got to think of somethin' else. You couldn't be no policeman. It would be nice if you could be a policeman."

"We better rule that out, a'nty; that's the one thing I couldn't be."

"And you couldn't be a fireman, could you?"

"No, a'nty, I ain't never heard of no one-armed fireman; they ain't that hard up. We better think about somethin' simpler than that."

"You know I'm sorry about that, Sam"—she was very wistful and regretful. "I'd like so much for you to get a job where you had to wear a uniform. I think you'd look grand, you're so nice and tall."

"How about an elevator job in one of these dicty apartment-houses? I might get somethin' like that. That would mean a uniform all right. I'll go out in a little while and see what I can find."

But when he crossed over to the window and looked out through the frosty pane, the sight of the few people outside scurrying past with their coats tightly drawn about them and their coat collars turned up transmitted to him a feeling of how cold it must be out there, and reassured him how good it was to be inside where there was a fire. He shook his head, and went and sat down before the stove, where his full stomach and the heat sent him off into a quick doze. When he awoke, blinking his eyes against the light which the early darkness had caused Aunt Mandy to switch on, he could see heavy flakes of snow hurtling past on the outside. He couldn't find a job in weather like this. He could smell the supper simmering in the kitchen. At the table, with her back toward him, Aunt Mandy was busy telling her cards. He got up and went over to her.

"What they sayin' today, a'nty?"

"They ain't sayin' much today. Can't seem to make any sense out of them; they get like that some time, get just honery and cussèd, like people."

"See any job in them for me?" He wanted her to know that he really meant to work and that a job lay very heavily on his mind.

"I wasn't tryin' to find that out." There was a faintly disapproving note in her tone. "But I guess there's a job for any man what gets up and looks for one."

"Don't worry, a'nty," he placated her, patting her on the back. "I'll find something to do. It just takes time."

He leaned over and took up the cards which she relinquished. "Do you know any games to play with these? Somethin' you and me could play to make the time go quicker? I wish to God Mattie was here."

She was mollified now, but reluctant. "I ain't accustomed to playin' card games, but I did used to play casino with Ben sometimes. You know that one?"

"Yes, I know that one, but it ain't very excitin'. Can you play coon can?"

"What on earth is that?"

"It's a game where you make 'leven cards out of ten."

"Now, son, you know they ain't no truth in that. How you goin' to make 'leven cards out of ten?"

"Well," he laughed at her, drawing his chair up more closely, "that's the secret. Some coons can and some can't. Here's one what can."

"Can what, boy?" She was immensely flattered that he was willing to take up his time with her, and she had already forgiven him for not having gone in search of work. She was even ready now to say a good word for him should Mattie censure him.

"Play coon can," he answered, and they both fell to laughing with that heartiness with which Negroes laugh at anything which they feel worth being merry over.

She was an apt pupil, and before the afternoon was ended he had let her win several games so as to keep her feeling kindly toward him. He even succeeded in teaching her to play black-jack, although he experienced a bit of a problem here, for she found it difficult to count and seemed bent on forgetting that face cards valued ten. He persuaded her into adding to the excitement of the game by dividing a box of matches between them; they used these for chips, and when the game was ended, after two hours of playing, he had let her win every match. His difficulty in holding his cards, because of his one arm, amused and charmed her. She laughed that he should place his cards on a chair drawn up beside him, and pushed under the table out of her sight, leaning down to fish one out whenever it became his turn to play. She was delighted with him. And he felt warm toward her and knew that he would always have an ally in her.

When they had finished playing, he set the table for her. It was awkward for him, but he felt that in doing it he was diminishing any criticism which might be directed to him on the score of idleness. Then he sat down before the fire again and thought of Mattie. She would soon be in. She generally came in about six, Aunt Mandy told him.

How he hated this weather. He surely would be glad when it began to get warm and a man could go out and enjoy himself instead of moping around the house. If it hadn't been for the snow, he might have had a job by now, for it had been his absolute intention to look for a job after his nap this afternoon. He hoped Mattie would understand. Tomorrow the snow would be over, no doubt, and he could go out and look for something. He dozed off again.

CHAPTER NINE

It is very strange that in the home of an American Negress (if I used this designation in the presence of any of my colored friends any place except in Constancia Brandon's drawing-room, I should be drawn and quartered immediately, although I cannot see why) I should find the one bit of atmosphere which reminds me of England. Her salon is every bit like a patch of Hyde Park dug up and transplanted to America; it is the one place in which the vaunted Yankee freedom of speech and thought are really given full leeway. Here one says what he thinks, and whether it be boresome, brilliant, or brutal, his right to say it is seldom challenged.

Whether this extract from a letter written by Donald Hewitt to his mother was fully comprehensible or merely scandalous to that Victorian lady is beyond the point. What is true is that what this tall, finger-snapping, yodeling Englishman avowed in writing, all Harlem that mattered, and much of colored Baltimore, Washington, and Philadelphia, admitted tacitly. Constancia's monthly *soirées*, held the first and third Mondays in each month (June, July, and August excluded), were as analogous to a gala grand-opera performance as the Lord's prayer done on the head of a pin is similar to the same petition prepared for the naked and unembellished eye—that is, her *soirées* were far more interesting than the opera galas.

The joy and verve of these gatherings were cloaked under the uninviting and prosaic auspices of the Booklovers' Society, but it was known at large, and admitted by more than half the group itself, that they never read books, although now and then they might, under pressure, purchase the latest opus of some Negro novelist or poet. This was especially true in the case of the Negro members (the group was uncompromisingly interracial), who discovered, much to their chagrin, that the white members of the society were inclined to take Negro literature far more seriously than they. A case in point was Samuel Weinstein, the Columbia University student who was assembling a thesis on Negro writers; he not only bought and read books by Negroes, but had the embarrassing habit of remembering plots, authors' names, and isolated lines of poetry. He was a thorn in the flesh of most of the darker members of the society, for whom the chief *raison d' être* of Constancia's *soirées* was the impromptu program, the buffet collation, and the inevitable dancing which brought the evening to a close.

To give the devil his due, the Booklovers' Society at its inception had not belied its name. It had really been organized in the interest of books by and about Negroes, and in the fatuous conviction that the members of the society would live up to the obligations laid down for them in their constitution and by-laws, to wit: to buy and to read books by Negroes; to read (purchase optional) books about Negroes; *and to be a small but loyal body on which the Negro writer can depend for sympathy, understanding, and support.* Intelligent discussion of one book a month was inscribed as a basic tenet of the society.

When Constancia had first come to Harlem she had been aroused to the need of just such a society by repeated attendance at the monthly book discussion held at the local public library. She had found the meetings amiable, and a pure waste of time. There were seldom over twenty people present, and never more than five or six had read the book under discussion, although no one seemed to feel that the absence of even bowing acquaintance with the work should render him ineligible to criticize it. Constancia had finally wearied of the oft-repeated excuse, generally the prelude to an unintelligent tirade against the book, of, "I haven't read the book yet, but in view of what I have heard, I do feel that it should never have been published."

"What these people need," she thought, "is a real locale, a stimulus of lights and warmth; a cocktail before and after; and, when all the broadsides have been fired and friendships blasted, a bit of collation to lay the troubled waters."

Therefore quietly—though some in later embittered moments said slyly—so as to avoid the rabble, she made overtures to several of the more animate frequenters of the library symposium, with whom as a nucleus she formed her own Booklovers' Society. From the first the venture, small and select, was highly successful. The points of view represented were diverse and fractious. Miss Sarah Desverney, one of the local librarians, had risen to heretical heights and had forsaken the monastic coldness of the library meetings to warm her toes at Constancia's fire and the cockles of her throat with Constancia's wine; but she eschewed the heart of the fire. For her no Negro had written anything of import since Dunbar and Chesnutt.

Bradley Norris, to whom everything not strictly New Negro was anathema, was the bane and bait of poor Miss Desverney, to whom he took an unholy delight in reciting bits of *vers libre* and unconventional quatrains in which the Negro was depicted as being drunk with jazz and void of pudency. The antics of these two were a constant delight to the conniving Constancia.

Then there was Samuel Weinstein, bushy-haired and bespectacled, serious in his native way, sincerely attracted to his Negro friends, yet never able to understand their lack of serious design. Because he could not reconcile a deficit of intent with Jewish consanguinity he had finally abandoned as untenable a long-cherished hope that the Negroes might be the strayed descendants of the lost tribe of Israel. As he never allowed his sincerity to be sullied with sentimentality, his caustic comments on Negro life, authors, and books were generally received in deferential and silent awareness of their truth, by all except Mrs. Harold De Peyster Johnson.

Mrs. Johnson was a teacher in the New York public-school system, and *ipso facto* a person of more than ordinary importance in Harlem Society. Her race consciousness dated back some seven or eight years. She had, as it were, midwifed at the New Negro's birth, and had groaned in spirit with the travail and suffering of Ethiopia in delivering herself of this black *enfant terrible*, born capped and gowned, singing "The Negro National Anthem" and clutching in one hand a pen, in the other a paint-brush. In the eyes of Mrs. De Peyster Johnson this youngster could do no wrong, nor had his ancestors ever been guilty of a moral lapse, or of an intellectual *faux pas.* Of misalliance, yes. This she sadly acknowledged as row after row of multi-colored faces, ranging from blackest jet to palest blond, and all representative of the young Hercules at whose shrine she worshiped, met her own dark countenance each morning. It was Mrs. De Peyster Johnson's boast that she was probably the one American Negro who could trace her ancestry back through an unbroken and unsullied line of Negroes straight to the first slaves landed in America.

"I find more to be proud of in that," she said, "than if they had come over on the *Mayflower;* for I don't believe the *Mayflower* had princes on it, while my ancestors were the blue-bloods of Africa. I am really one of the F.F.V.'s."

Mrs. De Peyster Johnson was certain that the Black Prince had been a Negro.

She carried in a worn and outmoded pocketbook, for the conversion of any disbeliever, a long strip of parchment on which her genealogy was traced in veracious black and white. Although she had not bothered to trace it farther than the Jamestown slaves, she was confident that if she cared to go to the trouble and expense, she could claim direct descent from the Queen of Sheba.

From among her suitors she had deliberately rejected Thomas Asquith, who was sandy-haired, anemic, and scholarly, and toward whom she yearned in spite of herself; and had, with a true martyr's resignation and hope in the ultimate reward, married De Peyster Johnson, soot-colored, amiable, and totally lacking in interest and sympathy for the New Negro.

"There is something basically wrong and foreboding," she thought, "in a Negro who is light-complexioned, sandy-haired, and named Thomas Asquith. It is evident at once that someone's brush-heap has been invaded. There might even be reason for questioning the racial purity of one named De Peyster Johnson; but one look at De Peyster is enough to convince any skeptic that his name is merely a matter of circumstance, instead of evidence of a skeleton on the family tree."

Fifteen years of slowly diminishing hopefulness with De Peyster had finally convinced Mrs. Johnson that unbroken lines sometimes ended abruptly. In spite of prayers, candles to the Virgin and sundry saints; in spite of a visit to Rome, where she had kissed the toe of St. Peter's statue; in spite even of a bit of red flannel snipped from De Peyster's undershirt, dipped in asafetida and worn with cumulative courage around her neck, there was no junior De Peyster. Often at evening, sitting with stacks of papers before her, inspired essays sweated from forty-five youthful New Negroes, she would look up from her toil to cast a withering and malevolent gaze on De Peyster, who, with mouth open and fast-shut eyes, offered her his evening serenade from the parlor sofa. Her eyes would mist for a moment as her thoughts reverted to Thomas Asquith, by this time probably the sire of divers little sandy-haired New Negroes. She sometimes felt as if she could bear no more; but she always ended by putting the fox back into her bosom; she would cross the room, slap De Peyster's mouth shut, and return to her papers. The blue pencil would descend in tender correction upon some gross orthographical error, while the pale face and sandy hair of Thomas Asquith faded into limbo.

Mrs. De Peyster Johnson had emerged victorious from numerous clashes with her immediate superiors because of her set ideas as to just how and what the New Negro should be taught. Each morning she opened class with the singing of the Negro national anthem, while the afternoon dismissal was always preceded by a spiritual. Her young charges humored her and sang beautifully, but whispered among themselves that she was more unbalanced than inspired. She was once brought up on charges of evading the school curriculum, it being pointed out that while her pupils could recite like small bronze Ciceros, "I Too Sing America," and "Brother, What Will You Say?" they never had heard of "Old Ironsides," "The Blue and the Gray," or "The Wreck of the *Hesperus.*" They could identify lines from Hughes, Dunbar, Cotter, and the multitudinous Johnsons, but were unaware of the contributions of Longfellow, Whittier, and Holmes to American literature. Their race-minded mentor finally bowed to the syllabus; but twice a week, with the aid of ice-cream and cake, and with the promise of Olympian leniency at the end of the semester, she cajoled her charges to her home, where she sang spirituals to them and taught them Negro literature. So strongly did she emphasize racial purity that the darker children were on the verge of becoming little prigs and openly snubbing their lighter-complexioned comrades.

With these, then, as the core,—Miss Desverney, Bradley Norris, Samuel Weinstein, Mrs. De Peyster Johnson, and a few kindred spirits, each acting as a foil or as a stick of dynamite to the other, as the case might be, the Booklovers had actually read and discussed books for at least six months. But the very ideals of bodily comfort on which Constancia had founded the organization effected its change from a small select society, with but a single aim, into a large polyglot group whose aims were legion. Gradually the little birds told, or the winds wafted rumors, of the cocktails with which the Booklovers' meetings were always opened, and of the irreproachable buffet suppers with which they ended. Close friends, pleading the privilege of their amity more than any literary proclivities, induced Constancia, whose warm heart could never resist an appeal that was insistent enough, to invite them "just this once." And like the worms in the ballad, they brought their friends, and their friends' friends, too, until Constancia was finally forced to make admittance to her *soirées* "by invitation only." By this time books had been relegated to that sphere in which most of the society thought they belonged—the lowest sphere of importance. Instead of literature, life written in major letters was dissected from all angles and with the utmost shamelessness. The cocktails were magical in loosening the most tightly nailed tongues, and Constancia's guests were soon discussing birth control, race suicide, the rise and fall of the French Cabinet, and whatever one word or another might lead to. Happy indeed was the foreign writer or the emancipated Southerner who came to Harlem looking for copy and who was fortunate enough to light on one of Constancia's evenings, and to be admitted. If he had his wits about him he could always leave with a story. Sometimes, in their more sober moments, the protagonists in these chronicles deplored their wholesale distribution to the world, but more often they were proud to have figured in them.

Donald Hewitt's letter of praise to his mother had been occasioned by a happening which could of a truth have taken place in but one of two places—in Hyde Park or in Constancia's drawing-room. It was an unwritten rule of Constancia's that thoughts were sacred, though they might often be stupid, and that language, though it might not always be the king's, was the proper conveyance for thought. Therefore, in her drawing-room one might say, as he felt so disposed to say it, whatever he thought, and whoever was shocked or resentful immediately stamped himself as having wandered outside his intellectual milieu.

Donald was a young Englishman with charming manners, no prejudice, a great deal of money, and a misdirected desire to write. Since Donald was very anxious to do a book on America, and especially on Harlem, Walter Derwent, who piloted everybody who was not an out and out Negro-phobe to Constancia's home, guided him to one of the meetings of the Booklovers.

"I am sure I shall love you people," Donald drawled, kissing his hostess' hand, and thereby causing her to doubt his nationality.

"You have so much life and color about you, and you seem to enjoy yourselves so completely."

"Yes," assented Constancia, her ivory skin still tingling to the brush of Donald's lips. *"Carpe diem* is our motto."

"I am writing a book," Donald went on. "I have been writing one for years, but this one I shall surely finish. I am going to write about your people and dedicate it to you." (Had they been elsewhere in Harlem than in Constancia's home, Walter might have whispered to this novice in race relations that "your people" coming from white persons sets a Negro's teeth on edge. He was glad that at Constancia's race relations existed in theory only.)

"Walter chose a most opportune evening for your *début*," Constancia informed Donald, with a smile. "You will probably learn a great deal about Negroes from one who has made a life study of them and who professes to know them better than they know themselves."

"Indeed!" the slightly nonplused son of Albion voiced his elation. "What did she mean?" he queried, as Constancia wandered off without having given any more detailed information, as was her dramatic custom.

"I don't know," said Walter, "but it will probably be a trump card when she plays it. Constancia rarely plays anything else."

But not even Walter Derwent, accustomed as he was to Constancia's boldness, had the remotest suspicion of the surprise which that eventful evening held in store. Indeed, the night at first gave every indication of petering out as nothing more than a social gathering at which a pleasant and boring time was enjoyed to the full. The attendance, to be sure, was record-breaking with people milling through the house in small gossipy groups as if they were on the scent of perfumed Easter eggs which had been carefully hidden away from them. Donald had drunk more than a score of cocktails which Mattie and Porter, both retained for these monthly gatherings, were dispensing with a prodigality shocking in a country addicted to prohibition. He was now a silent third in a conversation between Constancia and Miss McGoffin, an Irish-American missionary lady of abolitionist descent, whose aim it now was, since the American Negro had demonstrated the possibilities, to Christianize all Africa.

"Just see what Christianity has done for you people." Miss McGoffin let her eyes wander in approval over the appointments of Constancia's home. Her approbation suffered a slight curtailment as her gaze rested on the bare sepia-colored back of Lottie Smith, whose robes were always cut to show off to advantage what was to the unprejudiced eye a real adornment. "As I was saying"—Miss McGoffin simply would not back water—"see what Christianity has done for you people. I want very much, when I return to Africa next month, to take with me some message from their brethren on this side of the water."

"You must give them our love," said Constancia.

"They will be so pleased," murmured Miss McGoffin.

"And you must meet the duchess later on in the evening, and Lady Hyacinth Brown," Constancia added. "They will be sure to send even longer and warmer messages."

"Duchess? Duchess?" Miss McGoffin was undeniably thrilled at the prospect.

"Yes," said Constancia, "the Duchess of Uganda, *née* Mary Johnson. You'll love her."

"I'm sure I will," admitted Miss McGoffin. "What people you do have, Mrs. Brandon! Tell me now, coming back to my African charges—I am trying to teach them spirituals. Of course they have never had the proper incentive for them over there, but you have no idea how they do rally to the mood and tempo. Sometimes as I shut my eyes over there in the African wilds and listen to them sing your songs that I have taught them in my poor way, I can fancy myself back in Georgia or Alabama or, or . . ."

"Or on Broadway?" suggested her hostess.

"Why, yes, to be sure," Miss McGoffin was more than agreeable. "What I want to know is, are you people writing any more spirituals? I should like so much to carry back a brand-new batch with me to show that civilization has not destroyed your creative instinct."

"Indeed!" said Constancia with apparent emotion on the subject. "Indeed we *are;* we almost had run out of them for a while, but plans are under way for a fresh supply at any moment."

"I am so glad," sighed the relieved Miss McGoffin. "I never tire of hearing them."

Just when Donald, damning first impressions, had sadly concluded that his hostess was as demented as her missionary guest, he was rewarded with what was without doubt a wink from Constancia's beautiful left eye. He sauntered off, eased of his fears, to join a rather largish group to which Bradley Norris was reading a poem. Miss McGoffin followed him and took a seat beside Stanley Bickford.

Bradley's poem was doomed, by the very nature of its perverseness, to be a failure. The poet felt like a renegade as he read it. Here was he, who had never stooped to rhyme before in all his youthful literary career, one both by sympathy and talent unmeet for the rigors of a sonnet, reading, with evident pride in his achievement, a sonnet, rhymed, metered, and allegorical. Let his comrades turn their heads in shame and cry, *"Et tu, Brute!"* They would learn in the fullness of time that he had merely done this to show the facility with which that sort of thing could be done, while a patternless poem made one sweat his very blood. It meant nothing to Bradley, and there was no one present sufficiently enlightened to tell him, that his rhymes were atrocious, that his meter limped, and that six of his lines were lacking in the proper number of feet which custom and decency have made indispensable to the sonnet. The message in itself was innocuous enough. Bradley had just discovered what every poet learns sooner or later, and the sooner the better, that the joys of the flesh are no less lovely than those of the spirit, and that the time allotted man for their enjoyment is infinitely more abridged. He looked like stout Cortes as he stood holding his bit of paper before him, declaiming in dulcet tones, if in poorer language, Herrick's advice to young men and maidens.

"Leave nothing for tomorrow; live today!" he fairly shouted the closing line in a frenzy of rapture and abandon.

"O tempora, O mores!" lamented the scandalized Miss Desverney. "The poets of today are not those of yesterday. Dunbar would never have written anything as hedonistic and heathenish as that. You young poets are very glib in giving advice, but I wager you wouldn't want your sister to follow it."

"But I haven't got a sister," protested Bradley.

"That's just it," sniffed Miss Desverney, in triumphant rebuttal. "But if you had one . . ."

"I shouldn't bat an eyelash even if she married *white*," retorted Bradley.

Miss McGoffin touched Stanley Bickford on the arm. "That was a very lovely poem," she offered by way of commencing conversation, "but I didn't follow it altogether. What did it *really* mean?"

Stanley, who never followed any poem, was more than a little annoyed that Miss McGoffin should have interrupted him at this moment when his mind was full of plans for the new swimming-pool which he had contracted to build. Without turning to scrutinize her, and thinking her Nordic silhouette as false as his own, he attempted to interpret the poem to which he had not been listening.

"Taken in a nutshell, it means that niggers have a hell of a time in this God-damned country. That's all Negro poets write about."

"Oh!" There was so much abject and unsimulated consternation in Miss McGoffin's cry that Stanley was instantly aware of his mistake.

"I beg your pardon, madam," he pleaded, "but if you will analyze that sentence, you will see that I was neither swearing nor blaspheming, but merely stating a fact."

But the outraged missionary lady had already swept away in what is commonly known as high dudgeon.

"That's a very rude young man over there," she complained to Constancia.

"Which one?" Constancia was prepared to see any one of her guests pointed out to her.

"That *white* one, I blush to say," deplored Miss McGoffin, pointing to Stanley, who was drowning his chagrin in another cocktail.

"Oh," laughed Constancia; and she was just about to explain to Miss McGoffin that Stanley was not as Nordic as he appeared, when Lottie Smith, who adored Stanley, pulled her away.

"Don't enlighten her," Lottie implored. "So long as she thinks Stanley belongs on *her* side of the fence, let her. She might have him lynched!"

It was at this juncture that Constancia, hearing herself asked for in tones which indicated that the quester still had her acquaintance to make, turned to greet a tall, tin-lipped man whose extreme pallor gave him a funereal and apocryphal look. He was somberly attired in a suit of thick black material the ancient cut of which imparted to the onlookers that thrill which some natives always experience in anything which can be labeled foreign, whether it be a lack of good manners, or the apparent resolution to dress as unlike one's fellowmen as possible.

"Professor Calhoun, I opine?" asked Constancia, coming up to him and extending a brilliant-covered, ivory-pale hand which the professor chose to ignore as he bowed in a formally stiff and embarrassed manner.

"I am afraid there has been some mistake." He drawled the words in a tone with which phonetics can never cope, but there was in it all the laziness and languor which evoke a panorama of cotton-fields, red-clay earth, bandanna handkerchiefs, and Negro women suckling at their breasts white infants whose claim to distinction and aristocracy when they are older will be the fact that they milked those somber breasts.

"If there has been an error, it has been one of omission rather than of commission," confessed Constancia. "In engaging you through your lecture bureau, I did not deem it necessary to indicate my racial handicap. I feared you might be shy about lecturing before people on whom, from what I have read of your discourses, you have such valuable and esoteric information. I am prepared to pay the honorarium exacted by your bureau; I hope you are prepared to fill your part of the contract."

She spoke and looked as if she felt that there could be no doubt that the professor would fulfill his part of the mysterious bargain; nevertheless, in both her speech and her regard there was a trace of mockery and a challenge, which the professor chose to accept.

"I am prepared to fulfill my part of the contract, madam, but not to deviate from the usual tone and procedure of my lectures," he replied, pursing his lips dryly.

"That is more than satisfactory to me," said Constancia, with a smile. "In my home you are in a veritable temple whose reigning deity is free speech; if I stooped to facetiousness I might even say of unbridled loquacity. I should feel that I had been cheated should I have the impression, after your lecture, that you had altered or suppressed one thought out of deference for or courtesy to your audience. And as your hostess, I am willing to answer for your safety."

As she led her gangling guest across the room she smiled to herself, as the gods must smile just when they are about to let loose upon the earth some plague, or some divine prank like a cyclone or a tornado, which mortals must submit to, good grace or bad. She felt as if she were making history, as indeed she was.

It is said that in some rural districts where calendars are not as prevalent as sun and rain and death, and where the days glide by without any very definite way existing of marking them, the denizens of those regions have quaint but adequate means of referring to the past. "That happened," they will tell you, "the year John's heifer had her brindled calf," or "Sue was born the year lightning struck her mother's apple tree." And quaint as these temporal devices may appear to those who are calendar born, they probably evoke more intensive responses in the listeners than the recital of a mere number might do. Even so, there are still persons in Harlem who designate the happenings of a certain year as having taken place "the year the Southern professor lectured at Constancia

Brandon's." A Harlem journal recapitulating in its column of "to-day's events, one, five, or ten years ago," will never omit, when the anniversary rolls around, to remind its readers that "today this many years ago, Professor Seth Calhoun of Alabama lectured at the home of Mrs. Constancia Brandon."

A genius for the unusual, coupled with a desire to maintain at any cost the high standard of amusement and instruction which she had set for herself as being indispensable to the success of her *soirées*, had caused Constancia to engage Professor Calhoun to lecture before the Booklovers' Society. The decision called for a temerity bordering on both the cruel and the ridiculous at the same time; but those questions of propriety and suitability which another hostess might have been obliged to ponder long and seriously were airily dismissed by Constancia. The idea intrigued her; it would be the acid test to which she would submit the hordes of guests who drank her wine, danced away the shining surface of her floors, and kept her house in that continual state of happy disorder which was really dear to her heart. This would be a means of separating the sheep from the goats, and of discovering if the Negro really had the sense of humor which some people attributed to him.

"An irrefutable evidence of a sense of humor," she thought, "is the ability to laugh at oneself, as well as at one's tormentors and defamers. If we haven't learned that in these three hundred years, we have made sorry progress."

And she had invited her professor.

Professor Calhoun until that winter had been an obscure teacher of sociology in an even more obscure Southern college. But during all his lean and undistinguished years he had been writing a book, which had finally appeared under the title of *The Menace of the Negro to Our American Civilization*. The tract had been composed with a bitterness and a fierceness that had aroused the country to the dark peril which confronted it. Lynchings doubled, the professor's own state leading in gracious compliment to its scribe; mothers kept their children in after dark, while many a gay and debonair young blood was informed in no uncertain terms that he would

immediately be cut off without a penny were it discovered that he
had been philandering with a maiden not strictly Anglo-Saxon. The
women's clubs and the Rotary associations of all the larger American cities invited the professor to come, for magnificent fees, to
explain further the growth of this horrible cancer which had at first
been but a negligible scratch on the national anatomy. The lectures, to be sure, were but a repetition of the contents of the book,
but there was the added attraction of beholding the crusader in his
glory. Constancia had paid three dollars and eighty-five cents to
hear him lecture at one of the city auditoriums. Unless one scru-
tinized her closely, her cream-colored face gave little indication
that she belonged to the American pariahs; and she had sat serenely through the professor's lecture, fascinated and amused,
hearing herself and those of her ilk called in language which was
at once musical, courtly, and vituperative, everything except a child
of God.

Now as she led the famished-seeming lecturer to a corner of the
room where she had already provided a pitcher of water and a
glass set on a table on which he might lean should he become
nervous, she had her first feeling of apprehension. She wondered
if her guests were as intelligent as she hoped they would be, if
they would crown her effrontery with success or let her down in
ignominious defeat. She was not reassured by hearing Bradley Norris whisper to Stanley Bickford, just as she and Professor Calhoun
passed by, "It must be Ichabod Crane." But she shook her head
just a trifle more gayly and stepped just a bit more jauntily as she
walked past them. She motioned the professor to a chair, and then
braced herself firmly against the side of the table in preparation
for a speech on which more depended than on any speech which
she had ever made.

"Friends and members of the Booklovers' Society"—her voice
was tinged with the slightest tremolo, her gray eyes were wide in
a way which was evidence of the seriousness of what she was about
to say—"it has been many a day since we have had the I hope not
dubious distinction of being addressed by a personage as sought-

after, and as much in the public eye and on the tip of the public tongue, as our guest of the evening. I think it was the mellow bard of Scotland who importuned Heaven for the insight into himself that he might scrutinize his ego as others beheld it. We are going to be granted a poet's prayer this evening; we are to see ourselves as by one who has studied us long and ardently, with a microscopic seriousness that has revealed some things to him which our simple mirrors have been reticent about revealing to us. As your hostess and his, I have pledged him your discreet and impartial attention. You have no idea what *sort* of pleasure it affords me to introduce to you Professor Seth Calhoun, who will address us on "The Menace of the Negro to Our American Civilization."

Like a bit of willow waving in the wind she turned to the professor, and clapped her fine and tapering hands together. For a moment that seemed an eternity to her there was silence in the room, and then her guests showed their mettle. Their applause invaded and gladdened the heart of their hostess; the professor rose to speak before an audience whose acclamation eclipsed that of any before which he had ever spoken. Since there was not a person there who had not heard of him and who was not aware of his thoughts on his particular subject, the applause was more for Constancia's boldness than for any pleasure which they hoped to experience from what they were about to hear. There were, however, three renegades in the room who could not bring themselves to see the humor of the situation, three who sat with hands tightly clasped in a futile spiritual agony. Miss McGoffin had not forgiven Stanley Bickford's interpretation of Bradley Norris's poem; now hearing the professor's name called, she was forced to clutch the rounds of her chair and to bite down savagely on a bloodless lip lest she make herself ridiculous and add to the further confusion of this strange evening by fainting. She heartily wished she were anywhere at all at the moment save in Constancia's drawing-room. Every delicate fiber in her frail, missionary-abolitionist frame tingled with horror. Surely, she felt, the world was topsy-turvy and everybody in it madder than Alice's hatter, when a person like

Professor Seth Calhoun could accept an invitation to speak at the home of a Mrs. Constancia Brandon. As for Donald Hewitt, his gentle English spirit was aroused to battle. He was all for rising and booting the professor into outer darkness, and might have utterly ruined himself in Constancia's eyes had Walter Derwent not held him back.

"But she can't know the man," Donald protested. "She can't have an idea of what he is apt to say, or she would never have invited him."

"Oh yes, she has," said Walter, still firmly holding on to Donald's coat. "No one is going to enjoy this half as much as Constancia, not even the professor."

Donald sank back with a sigh of resignation and distress.

Mrs. De Peyster Johnson, feeling that the columns of the temple which she had erected to the New Negro were about to tumble about her ears, rose to leave, intent on taking her lares and penates with her while they were yet intact. Unfortunately, she had to pass by Constancia, who grasped her firmly by the arm, pulled her down to a chair beside her and directly facing the professor, whispering at the same time, "If you desert me in this my hour of need, there can be no subsequent parley on reparations."

Whatever else the professor may have been, and however much he may have deserved the application of certain uncomplimentary epithets masquerading behind the serene brows of his auditors, it can in no wise be said of him that he was cowardly. The Douglas in his hall frightened him not a bit. Some have said that his hands shook slightly as he held his typewritten manuscript before him, and that under cover of the thick walnut table his knees had a tendency to meet; but Constancia, who was nearest him, avowed that he was the soul of precision and coolness.

"Frigider than a cucumber," she always said whenever she related the incident.

For well beyond an hour he stood before them, and in a warm Southern tone, which was none the less decided, told them about themselves; while Miss McGoffin with each successive point prayed that the floor might open up and engulf her; while Donald Hewitt sat miserably holding a hand tightly over his eyes, as was his childish way when spiritually disturbed; while Walter Derwent sat in a corner and took notes, already shaping in his mind some clever sentence which he would employ in his recital of the affair; while Mrs. De Peyster Johnson became more and more the picture of race-consciousness outraged and trampled upon; while Constancia sat at the professor's side and fanned herself placidly with a green ostrich feather; while the rest of the audience, for the most part, sat in respectful silence. The professor's voice gained in strength and conviction as he mounted toward his peroration. From time to time, Stanley Bickford would applaud at some particularly telling denunciation of Negro morals and manners. These were the moments when Miss McGoffin most wished that she were not present; for while it was intensely unpleasant that one white man should stand before these poor people, and thus injure them, it was even more disturbing that another representative of her race (as she imagined Stanley to be) should add insult to injury by such gratuitous approval.

"It cannot be denied by a person of refined sensibilities that the Negro generally exudes a most unpleasant and disagreeable odor." It is to be noted that the professor had some difficulty with the word Negro; his acquaintance with the term seemed to be of recent date, for it cannot be said that his pronunciation of it was of the clearest; he pronounced it somewhat as a cross between *negro* and *nigra,* as if making a concession to both a momentary courtesy and to custom.

"Hear! Hear!" cried Stanley Bickford as the professor demonstrated the ineffectuality of soaps, unguents, and perfumes against the native odor of the Negro.

"How very discouraging," complained Lottie Smith to Stanley Bickford. "Here I am sprinkled down with *quelques fleurs,* and what's the use?"

Bradley Norris had a nasty and mischievous thought running through his head. He wondered if the potency of the racial odor was in direct proportion to the lack of Caucasian admixture. If so, he marveled how the professor could remain in the same room with Mrs. De Peyster Johnson. And if the Duchess of Uganda should arrive, they would all be obliged to clear out!

The professor's summary was a gem. The many-colored coat of all the fanatics and zealots of all time seemed to descend upon and envelop him, as with shining eyes he declared in senatorial tones, "It is the duty of white America to look to itself, to protect its sons and daughters from the insidious and growing infiltration of black blood into the arteries of this glorious Republic. There can be no quarter between the white man and a race which can truthfully be stigmatized as indolent, untrustworthy, unintelligent, unclean, immoral, and cursed of heaven. Their only salvation and ours lies in a congressional enactment returning them to Africa, the land of their fathers."

The Duchess of Uganda and Lady Hyacinth Brown, who had been attending a meeting of the Back-to-Africa movement earlier in the evening, and who had arrived in time to hear just the closing portion of the professor's lecture, led the applause which shook the house as the professor sat down. Whatever else he may have said, his ideas about Africa were in accord with those of the duchess and of Lady Hyacinth. The professor sat flushed and uncomfortable, now that his speech was over, while the applause augmented instead of subsiding. Constancia, turning toward Mrs. De Peyster Johnson, was shocked to find that race-conscious lady sitting with her hands tightly pressed, lest they indulge in approbation against her will.

"Why, Mrs. De Peyster Johnson," protested Constancia, "have you no sense of appreciation? Do applaud, if you don't want to mortify me completely."

"Is it *compulsory*, Constancia?" The racial indignation in Mrs. De Peyster Johnson's voice would have melted a heart of stone, but not Constancia's.

"It's the very framework of the temple," she said, so firmly that Mrs. De Peyster Johnson was prevailed upon to bring her hands together in two quick pats which were as loud as the brushing of two feathers against one another. However, the gesture was enough to placate Constancia.

Lecturers and speakers were never submitted to the grueling of a questioning period at Constancia's. It was her conviction that if they had not been able to impart their ideas to their audience during the hour allotted them, they were probably undecided themselves as to just what their thoughts were. In the case of Professor Calhoun there could be no doubt as to what his thoughts were on the Negro.

The Duchess of Uganda, with her beautiful soot-black face, like that of a Botticelli cherub, in shocking contrast with her huge shapeless body, had hemmed the professor in.

"I cannot say that I had the pleasure of hearing the whole of your discourse, which, if it was on a par with the ending, must have been very inspiring," the duchess was saying in a voice which was really beautiful and which Constancia always spoke of as being "so divinely contrastful to the duchess' body," "but I am in hearty agreement with your ideas on the rehabilitation of Africa by the American Negro. Oh, the green forests of Africa, the amber water of the Nile, the undiscovered oases of the Sahara, what foundations to build upon!"

"The duchess is an elocutionist by *métier*," explained Constancia to the slightly alarmed professor. "Won't you let me offer you something after your strenuous discourse, something by way of refreshment, a glass of punch perhaps?"

Reaching forward to take from a tray which Porter was carrying a thin glass of scarlet iced liquid, she smiled as she noticed the professor's hesitation and embarrassment.

"Maybe you are thinking of running for political office somewhere in your part of the country, Professor, or of lecturing in some of the larger Southern cities, and it would not be distinctly to your advantage if the news of this evening's condescension reached those sections. I promise you that the papers will carry nothing of it, and that your constituents will be left in blissful ignorance of your courtesy." She held the glass out temptingly toward him.

The professor smiled in spite of himself. "This will be my first time, madam," he explained, as he took the glass, "to eat or drink with Negroes."

"Really, Professor?" asked Constancia as she clinked glasses with him. "Do you mean to tell me that this is your first time to have social intercourse with Negroes?"

"My first, madam," reiterated the professor, gravely.

"Ah"—Constancia waggled her finger at him—"you are indeed tardy in arriving at what your section of the country has been doing for years."

The professor had drained his glass. He stood awkwardly, turning it in his hand.

"Allow me," said Constancia as she extended her hand to relieve him of the toy. Then, as he passed the glass to her, and just as it appeared to be safely within her grasp, she allowed it, inadvertently—ah, certainly inadvertently—to fall to the floor, where it splintered on the hearth. Her sparkling eyes met the professor's unflinchingly. *"Mea culpa*, Professor," she sighed, adding, "I am sure you must be fatigued by now and longing to get away." She reached down into a bosom fragrant with powder and perfume, and perhaps with those odors which the professor had so deplored. Her eyes twinkled as she handed him an envelope. "Here is your fee, Professor, and thank you for a pleasant and instructive evening."

"A bull's-eye!" whispered Walter Derwent to Donald as he wildly scribbled the scene on the back of an envelope.

In spite of the enthusiastic reception accorded it, the professor's lecture seemed to have dampened the usual high spirits which prevailed at these meetings. Constancia's guests left early, apparently in need of repose after having seen themselves through the professor's lens. Donald Hewitt was the last to depart. He loitered around until only he, George, and Constancia remained. Then it was that he took his hostess' hand and kissed it fervently, too young and naïve to veil his ardor because of George's presence.

"Madam," said the young Englishman, "you are lovely, you are marvelous! I adore you!"

Constancia had an intuitive feeling that this was one of the most genuine speeches Donald had ever made.

She let her fingers stray lightly over the blond head still bent above her hand. "How old are you?" she asked, gently.

"Twenty-two." Donald proclaimed it proudly as if it were the year of wisdom and of love.

"And I am on the other side of thirty-five," said Constancia. "There is just enough similarity in our ages for us to be very good friends. Good night. And come whenever you want to again. I give you *carte blanche.*"

"George," she cajoled, as with her husband's arm around her waist she slowly climbed the stairs to their bedroom, "you must learn to kiss my hand like that young Englishman. It means so much to a woman on the other side of thirty-five."

CHAPTER
TEN

When Constancia had hit upon the kind and generous impulse of marrying Mattie from her home, she had had no ulterior motive in view, had envisaged no future date when Sam would add to her popularity and prestige by contributing to the success of one of her evenings, even though at the expense of the Duchess of Uganda. But Constancia had been born under a lucky star and belonged to that fortunate group to whom, having much, the heavens with inexplicable and illogical generosity promise more.

That a wedding may be a matter of great momentary importance, yet not magical enough to change the ingrained thoughts and actions of a lifetime in the twinkling of an eye, Mattie was to learn slowly and sorrowfully in her fitful experience with Sam. When he asked her to marry him, he had done so only after what to him was due deliberation, and with the wavering intention that surely he would find work to do the next day or the next week after his marriage. It was, however, fully two months after, and then only due to Constancia's intervention, that he drew in his long legs from in front of the parlor stove and set out to earn his share of his and Mattie's living.

Mattie had been too deep in love and too lost in religion to scold, or to show by word or look that she was hurt or disappointed. With her religion had come a fatalism, and she was leaving all to the Lord. Daily Aunt Mandy nagged her for keeping a good-for-nothing man lying around the house and in her way, although daily the old lady took out her cards, read Sam's fortune, and then became his partner in one of the many card games he had taught her. Daily Mattie was forced to answer in the negative when Constancia asked if Sam had started to work. Finally, Constancia had taken the matter in hand herself, and with Mattie at her side had routed Sam away from the fire one March morning, and had taken him to a job. It was a job with a uniform, much to Aunt Mandy's joy, and with great prestige and privilege attached, although the nature of it was not entirely to Mattie's liking. It savored too much of the world, the flesh, and the devil. Constancia had been able to do nothing better than to secure Sam the rôle of ticket-chopper in one of the small variety and movie houses of the neighborhood. It was work which could be manipulated with one hand, and which at the same time, with the attendant uniform, afforded Sam a real opportunity to show off his fine height and slim, swaggering figure.

It was a gorgeous uniform of smooth bright green material, with square padded shoulders, gold epaulettes, and with black braid fronting the sleeves and surrounding the buttonholes through which large brass buttons shot their fire. Sam felt like a general or drum-major, and thought that working might not be so distasteful as long as he could be attired in such a manner.

The evening on which he first donned his glory happened to be one on which Mattie had been retained at Constancia's, where a party was being given for Herbert Newell, a young Negro who had just published a novel. As the doors of the theater swung open to liberate its audience from the land of fancy and at the same time to liberate Sam from his toil, he thought it might be a pleasant idea if he passed by Constancia's in order to wait for Mattie and to walk home with her, and incidentally to let her feast her eyes upon his new-spun raiment. Unfortunately, he liked himself so well in his new finery that he thought it worthy of a stimulant, with the result that by the time he reached Constancia's home it was only by the bright lights which illumined the house from roof to cellar, and by that second sense which some drunken men seem to acquire, that he was able to locate his destination.

The party was for Herbert Newell, but the evening became that of the duchess and of Sam. Not many people had read Herbert's novel, although it had been out for several months and had been commented upon in the Negro and white press (denounced by the former as an outrage against Negro sensibilities, and lauded by the latter as being typically Negro), yet almost everyone present came up to the author, shook his hand, and congratulated him. Poor outspoken Lottie Smith naïvely made herself an enemy for life by admitting that she was waiting to borrow Constancia's copy of the new book. Herbert, a very dark, belligerent young Negro, was brutally frank, and shocked several of the more sentimentally minded guests by informing them that art as such didn't mean anything to him, and that he had not written his book for the sake of anything so nebulous, but merely to make some money.

"Not," he added, "that I expect to make it from Negroes."

"I suppose I shall buy it," sighed Mrs. Vanderbilt-Jones in a tone of deep resignation. "I'll buy it out of pride of race, although from what I hear, I shall hardly like it, I fear. I don't see why our writers don't write about *nice* people sometimes." She gazed grandiloquently around the room to show Herbert the fine material at hand.

"Yes, Herbert," interposed Constancia, who had just come up at this point. "I understand that the heroine of your book is a prostitute, and that the hero is a stevedore. How can anything good come out of Nazareth, or anything to which we as a race can point to with pride come out of a combination like that? I quite agree with Mrs. Vanderbilt-Jones. You should have written about people like Counselor Spivens, who has just been incarcerated for a year for converting to his own use money awarded one of his clients in an equal-rights case; or like Dr. Strong, whose new limousine is the reward of Heavens knows how many abortions; or you might have woven a highly colorful tale around Mrs. Vanderbilt-Jones's own niece, Betty, who just . . ."

"Constancia," interrupted the old lady as she flounced off, "if I didn't love you so much I should positively hate you."

Constancia smiled and laid her hand on Herbert's arm. "Write whatever you want, Herbert, and don't give a continental about them. It will take them centuries, anyway, to distinguish between good and bad, and what is nice and what is really smeared over with a coating which they call nice. I just heard poor Mrs. De Peyster Johnson, to whose credit it can at least be said that she has read your book, declare, simply because you are a New Negro and therefore dear to her heart, that your novel was as good as anything that Wells or Bennett had written. And when I added that it was much better than anything written by any of the Russians, she agreed heartily. That's race pride with a vengeance for you, and self-criticism that isn't worth a penny."

"I wish they were all like you, Constancia," Herbert assured her. "I'd know then that they had some intelligence, and that when they condemned my book they had something to back up their dislike, and that when they said they liked it they were really doing something more sincere than making conversation with me. Half a dozen of them tonight have already asked me what the white people will think about the race when they read my book. Good God! I wasn't writing a history about the Negro. I was trying to write a novel."

"Yes," agreed Constancia as she waved to the duchess and to Lady Hyacinth Brown, who had just come in, "I suppose there are any number of us who pass perfectly wretched nights sleeping on our backs instead of on our stomachs, which we would find more comfortable, because we fear what the white world might say about the Negro race."

"Sometimes it makes me feel like I should like to chuck it and pass for something else," said Herbert, seriously, although a near-by glass which gave back his countenance showed one which was far too sable to pass as anything Caucasian, not even excepting the Italian and the Spanish.

"I never feel like that," said Constancia. "God knows there is nothing chauvinistic about me. I often think the Negro is God Almighty's one mistake, but as I look about me at white people, I am forced to say so are we all. It isn't being colored that annoys me. I could go white if I wanted to, but I am too much of a hedonist; I enjoy life too much, and enjoyment isn't across the line. Money is there, and privilege, and the sort of power which comes with numbers; but as for enjoyment, they don't know what it is. When I go to so-called white parties sometimes and look around me, I have a feeling that the host has been very wise in breaking down color conventions, and that is most cases his reason is selfish instead of being due to an interracial complex. I have seen two Negroes turn more than one dull party, where I was longing for home and Harlem, into a revel which Puck himself would find it hard to duplicate. As for variety, I think I should die if I were obliged to look into the mirror daily and to see nothing but my own parchment-colored skin, or to turn and behold nothing but George's brown visage shining back at me all day long, no matter how much adoration it reflected. When I get tired of George and myself I have simply to phone for Stanley Bickford—and Greenland's icy mountains couldn't send me anything more Nordic, with a nose more aquiline, with more cerulean eyes, or with hair one bit more prickly and blond. Let me dial another number and I have the Duchess of Uganda, black as the ace of spaces and more beautiful than Lucifer, or Lottie Smith, brown as a berry and with more real vivacity than a twirling dervish. No, thanks, I wouldn't change. So long as I have my happiness to consider, I'll not go to the mountain. If the mountain wants me, let it come to me. It knows where I am."

"I am going to write a book about you some day, Constancia," threatened Herbert.

"If you call it *Nice People*, it will be a terrible misnomer," said

Constancia, turning to greet the duchess and Lady Hyacinth Brown, who were rushing over to their hostess in concerted excitement, if the floating undulation of Lady Hyacinth, a mode of ambulance which she never abandoned even in her most tense moments, and the waddling propulsion of the duchess may be termed rushing. Behind them like a lost shadow stalked Donald Hewitt.

Some day Lady Hyacinth and the duchess, the latter more deservedly, will find a chronicler worthy of recounting their adventures and of properly fixing their status in Harlem society. They were an excellent foil to one another; yet each was so much the other's complement that since the inception of the Back-to-Africa movement, and since the laying of the accolade upon them, they had been inseparable companions, both working for the same cause, each respecting the power of the other, and neither in the least jealous of her sister's attainments.

By way of explaining the duchess and Lady Hyacinth, it may be noted that the Back-to-Africa movement was the heart and entrails of a society whose aim it was to oppose to the American slogan of "The United States for the White Man" the equally non-inclusive shibboleth of "Africa for the Black Man," in this case, the favored descendant of Ham being the American branch. The society held its meetings in a large barn-like building which had once been a church, and certainly one not dedicated to the gods of Africa. Credit must be given the society for realizing the importance of something which most organizations for civic or racial betterment are inclined to ignore, namely an appeal to the pleasurable instincts of man. With the Back-to-Africa movement went costumes that rivaled those of the private guard of the king of England; parades up and down the broad avenues of Harlem every Sunday and once or twice during the week; thunderous orations at the seat of the cabal; and wild, heady music blared forth by a specially trained, constantly practicing brass band. Added to this was the beautifully naïve and romantic way in which the society marched forward to meet the future. Its members were not doomed, like the Israelites, to sweat and toil and perish many in the wilderness before tasting any of the joys of their Canaan. The Back-to-Africa movement realized that it was simply a matter of constantly lessening time before Africa should be back in the hands of its rightful sons and daughters; therefore, in order to speed the zeal of the members, the officers began to parcel out what they already considered as properly, even if only remotely, theirs. Out of deference to the existing powers they did not proclaim an Emperor of Africa, but they did elect a President for the Nonce. With his election their deference to lesser dignitaries ceased, and the far-off, unsuspecting African territories were parceled out left and right, as dukes, counts, and marquises of Africa were created without stint and without thought of the complications which might arise should the Negroes, once returned to their ancestral home, decide upon a republican form of government.

It had been a bright day indeed for her who had been born simple Mary Johnson (as she was often reminded by Constancia when the spirit of the malicious was upon her) when the President for the Nonce of the African Empire, in recognition of fifteen thousand dollars which her argumentative talents had garnered for the general coffers of the society, had bidden her kneel, had laid his accolade upon her, and then had bidden her rise, Mary Johnson no longer, but Mary, Duchess of Uganda, first of her line, and spiritual and temporal head of the house of Uganda.

It had been a day no less luminous and no less marked of Heaven when she whose husband was a mere government employee, too stubbornly intrenched in the monthly assurance of a government check to see rising into the future the glorious edifices of the New Africa, had also knelt to rise, in recognition of ten thousand dollars raised for the general coffers, Mrs. Hyacinth Brown no longer, but Lady Hyacinth Brown, undisturbed by the social complications of a mulish husband who must continue to be introduced as plain Mr. Brown.

With their advent into the nobility there came a rise in social importance if not in actual social status. Few Harlem hostesses could forbear the pleasurable thrill of including on their guest lists the names of the duchess and of Lady Hyacinth. To be sure, as the wife of a railway mail clerk, Lady Hyacinth had already possessed a not unenviable niche in Harlem society; whereas the duchess, as a once-talented, if now slightly declining elocutionist, had also been greatly in demand; but the glories of governmental patronage and of elocution were shabby indeed in comparison with those of nobility.

Lady Hyacinth, being the less complicated personage, is the more quickly disposed of. She was a special type from which a well-known and disturbing generality has been drawn for almost every play or novel written to combat miscegenation. Any young Englishman, colonial expatriate, or Southern aristocrat left unprotected with her for five minutes was certain to develop an incurable case of *mammy palaver.* Her elongated languorous body, deepsunken eyes shaded with heavy velvet lashes, the perfect blending of colors in her skin, and her evident consciousness of her seductive powers, would have arrested any author in search of the perfect half-caste siren. The only drawback was that one soon tired of Lady Hyacinth; she was neither witty, amusing, nor intelligent; she was merely disturbingly beautiful. She was clever enough, however, to ally herself with the duchess and, when the moment presented itself, to shine by silent comparison.

But the duchess was a character, a creation, a personage in whose presence one felt the stir of wings and heavenly vibrations. Constancia declared the duchess was as beautiful as Satan; but she erred; there was nothing Satanic or diabolic about the duchess, not even when she was descanting upon the beauties of that Africa which she had never seen. Indeed, looking at her, one was apt to feel, if he could forget the body to which it was attached, that some divine sculptor had taken a block of the purest black marble and from it had chiseled that classic head. She reminded one of beautiful Queen Nefertiti. In her youth, when her figure, trim and lissom, was a perfect adjunct to the beauty of her face, the duchess had been the toast of half of Negrodom, including many who until they gazed upon her had never felt that beauty could reside in blackness unadulterated. Now in her fortieth year, only in the shapelessness of that bulk with which the years had weighted her down, did she give evidence of the cruelty of time; her face still retained the imperishable beauty of black marble.

The duchess had come along in a day and time when the searing flare for the dramatic which gnawed at her entrails had had no dignified outlet. There was little which a black girl, however beautiful, might do on the stage; and because Mary Johnson, even as a girl, had been the soul of dignity, she had put the stage out of her mind as something unattainable, and had decided to be an elocutionist. Even so, the way had been hard and thorny. The duchess was not one to truckle; she certainly had not forsworn the stage in order to lend herself as a diseuse to anything less than dignified, and to little less than might be labeled classic. Therefore to Negro audiences which might have rallied to her support, had she regaled them with the warm dialect of "When Malindy Sings" and "The Party," she chose to interpret scenes from "Macbeth," "Hamlet," and "The Merchant of Venice." To audiences and intelligences to whom it was utterly unimportant whether the quality of mercy was strained or not, she portrayed in a beautiful and haunting voice the aspirations of a dark Lady Macbeth, the rich subtleties of a sable Portia, and the piteous fate of a black Desdemona.

And success had not been hers.

Finally, as many another artist has turned from the dream of his youth to something baser but more remunerative, the duchess, in the face of want, had turned from elocution to dressmaking. Her nimble fingers and inventive mind had done for her what her voice had failed to accomplish; money had rolled in until she had finally been able to open two shops and to do nothing herself save supervise.

But the worm of an unfulfilled ambition lay tightly curled at the root of material success; and at the dropping of a handkerchief the duchess would willingly recite for any club, charity benefit, or simple social gathering.

With the passing of the years she had developed a decided predilection for martial pieces and had added to her standard Shakespearian repertoire such hardly perennials as "I am dying, Egypt, dying," "The Charge of the Light Brigade," and "The Black Regiment." The recital of the gallant doings at Balaclava had once thrown her into a state of embarrassment from which only Constancia's quick wit had saved her. The members of the United Daughters of African Descent still chuckle at the memory of it.

It happened at the annual meeting of the Daughters, a conclave at which Constancia, in the guise of mistress of ceremonies, had finally heeded the duchess' importunings, and had called upon her for a recitation. The duchess was charmed, and she looked to Tennyson's poem to help her to eclipse totally all other participants on the program. She began beautifully, her "Half a league, half a league, half a league onward" soaring over the benches into the gallery of the auditorium and completely terminating every whisper. Never before had the Daughters given such gracious attention. But midway of the glorious account, at what would seem the crucial moment, something went blank in the duchess' mind, or, to be more exact, her memory failed her absolutely. Her right arm was raised, her right foot extended and pointed, as she proclaimed "Cannon to right of them." Twice she repeated the designation of that particular section of cannon. Her memory still in abeyance, she was so discountenanced and flustered at the fourth repetition that even her usual beautiful diction suffered, with the result that she uttered unmistakably, *"Cannern* to right of them." It was then that Constancia, who was seated behind her, pulled the duchess' sleeve, at the same time importuning her in a whisper which escaped no one, "For God's sake, Duchess, genuflex and sit down."

A singular comradeship had sprung up between the duchess and Donald Hewitt, and Harlem soon became accustomed to the sight of the tall, fair-haired, imbibing Englishman, more often tottering than maintaining that dignity which is held synonymous with his nationality, accompanied by the short, hard-breathing, elocutionist.

They complemented one another's educations admirably. Into dens and retreats of which she had never dreamed the duchess followed Donald, squeezed her gargantuan form into diminutive chairs, and bravely sipped at strange, fiery beverages while Donald gulped down others by the score. Impervious to the imprecations hurled at them by those with whom they collided, they would often dance everyone else from the floor until they alone were left, free to dip and glide and pirouette from one end of the dance space to the other. Then back at their seats, just as his head began to sag and his eyes to glaze, Donald would lean across the table, plant the blond refractory head firmly on his crossed elbows, and beseech the duchess to recite. It is to be doubted that the melancholy soliloquy of Denmark's prince or the gentle pleadings of Portia have ever been uttered under stranger auspices. Over the savage blare of brass and the shrill screeching of strings, cutting into the thick, sickening closeness of cabaret smoke, drowning the obscene hilarity of amorous women, reprimanding the superimposed braggadoccio of inebriated males, the beautiful voice of the duchess would rise, clear and harmonious, winging across the table to Donald. *"To be or not to be. . . ."* The pure sweet voice of African nobility would go on soothing one of England's disillusioned children with the divine musings of England's best. *"Nymph, in the orisons, Be all my sins remembered."* Often as not when the last soft syllable fell from the duchess' lips, England's son would be peacefully sleeping; for always when the duchess began a Shakespearian recitation, Donald was forced to veil his eyes. With the most charming frankness he had explained his reason for this seeming discourtesy to Constancia one evening when she came upon him with covered eyes while the duchess, as Ophelia, was declaiming, *"O heat, dry up my brains! tears seven times salt, Burn out the sense and virtue of mine eye!"*

"I adore the duchess," Donald had apologized, "but I simply cannot look at her when she does Shakespeare. Her voice is as divine as any I have ever heard, but her color and form collide with all my remembered Ophelias and Portias. I cannot get those tall, flaxen-haired women of my race out of my mind; they linger there so obstinately that the duchess, so physically dissimilar, for all the ebony loveliness of her face, looms like a moving blasphemy on the horizon of my memory. But you won't tell her, Constancia, will you?"

Constancia had promised to keep his secret; so Donald continued, whenever it was a question of the duchess' Shakespearian repertoire, for which he himself often asked, to shade his eyes, thereby gaining for himself the reputation of being her most sincere and enamored admirer.

It was never a question of anything more between them than open and candid comradeship; they amused one another, and life seemed more pleasant to them because of the acquaintance. Such a mild state of affairs irked Lady Hyacinth, who looked upon Donald with a favorably prejudiced eye which, alas! found no answering gleam in those blue orbs so childishly centered upon the duchess.

It was give and take between Donald and the duchess. If he dragged her off nightly to mushroom-growth cabarets, or insisted upon taking her to Park Avenue teas where she was lorgnetted and avoided by all except her constant companion and a few daring males, she also had her hour. Docilely Donald followed her to Back-to-Africa meetings, where he sat, hot and uncomfortable, beneath the hostile gaze of thousands for whom he was but another inquisitive and undesired representative of all that was bleached and base; and it was only the duchess' extended scepter that secured him grace and safety. The duchess piloted him in and out of dark, mysterious hallways, made him climb innumerable flights of creaking stairs as she went her rounds soliciting funds for the movement. Never did he balk, for always he envisioned the evening's close—music, dancing, the slow fumes from forbidden beverages insinuating their wily passage into his brain, and across the table from him a beautiful black, middle-aged sybil ready to lull him to sleep with the opium of the world's dramatic wisdom.

Constancia, although ordinarily charity itself, had no sympathy with the duchess' nostalgia for Africa, and had never opened her purse to the duchess' insistent and plaintive pleadings for a donation to the cause. "I am in favor of back-to-nature movements," she excused herself, "for everybody except George and myself. George knows nothing about African diseases, and I can't abide tsetse flies, tarantulas, and dresses made out of grass. No, thank you, I wouldn't change Seventh Avenue for the broadest boulevard along the Congo."

"You are totally devoid of race pride, Constancia," the duchess had complained, bitterly, an indictment against which Constancia knew it was useless to defend herself.

Donald, equally unsympathetic to the Back-to-Africa movement, and marveling how any inhabitant of Harlem could look forward with relish to life in Africa, had been less impervious to his comrade's entreaties. He had capitulated by giving the duchess a princely check, accompanied by the ungentlemanly and unphilanthropic wish that it might do the movement no good whatever, and that, should it ever be used toward the purchase of a ship, that unholy conveyance might get no further than New York Harbor.

The reason for the duchess' and Lady Hyacinth's excitement the night of the party for Herbert Newell was soon made apparent. Both the noble ladies were panting with an unsimulated eagerness to be the first to break the important news, but Donald, who was ironically calm, if a bit unsteady, stole their thunder.

"The duchess has just discovered a marvelous record concerning the aviatic exploits of one Lieutenant Julian," he explained. "A marvelous poem, set to entrancing, barbaric music. The noble sentiments expressed in the verses make the duchess and Lady Hyacinth certain that the record can be a mighty weapon in awakening the American Negro to a sense of his duty. In order to aid the duchess in a work with which I have not the slightest sympathy, I have just donated one hundred of these records to the cause. The duchess contemplates sending them to all the centers where there are branches of the Back-to-Africa movement. I've brought along one for you to listen to."

They had to crowd close to the victrola in order to hear; for near by Mrs. Vanderbilt-Jones and Agatha Winston, a sleek, *café-au-lait* soubrette, who had just returned from eighteen months of European triumphs, were having a shouting bout. Agatha had gone to London over three years past with a sepia-colored musical comedy which had not caused a conflagration on the Thames. The sponsor of the engagement had paid the actors a tithe of the wages promised them, and then had left them to scuttle for themselves. And they had scuttled in dreary, dejected bands of three and four, some back to America, others across Europe as far as Russia, improvising as they went. An egotistic streak had caused Agatha to shun all offers of partnership, and to shift for herself. She had worked her way to Paris, where a slight ability to sing and dance, the knack of crossing her eyes, and of twisting her limbs out of joint, while attired in the minimum amount of clothes permitted by the French penal code, had soon made her the darling of France. She was now back in America for a brief visit to Harlem, intent on dazzling a world too immersed in having a good time to be more than faintly amused by a French maid, the display of divers gifts from infatuated European royalty, and the consciousness that it all emanated from a talent which could be duplicated and eclipsed in any Harlem pleasure cave.

"An Earl with a coat of mail and everything, and I turned him down." Agatha's voice soared in strident self-approval over the soft preparatory grating of the needle.

"And to think you could have been an earless, the first colored earless in the world, a stepping-stone for the race," Mrs. Vanderbilt-Jones shouted back her disapproval, and clucked her tongue.

Clustered around the victrola, Constancia, the duchess, Lady Hyacinth, and Donald formed a trembling and excited group which was soon augmented by Lottie Smith, who, never having been to Europe, couldn't abide Agatha's airs. As the first bars of the rich mongrel music, in which notes of Africa, Harlem, and the Orient could be traced, flooded the room, Lottie rolled her eyes upward in an ecstatic convulsion, and snapped her fingers rhythmically, while the duchess stood with bowed and pensive head, as if the strains of a Negro "Marseillaise" were causing her ample bosom to seethe and stir with patriotism. In gusty Jamaican pride the voice of the singer heralded the exploits of Lieutenant Julian:

> "At last, at last, it has come to pass,
> *Hélas, hélas!* Lieutenant Julian will fly at last,
> Lindbergh flew over the sea,
> Chamberlin flew to Germany,
> Julian said Paris or eternity."

The chorus with which this melodic eulogy opened set the keynote of racial pride and hope which was to run through the amazing verses:

> "Negroes everywhere,
> Negroes in this hemisphere,
> Come, come in a crowd,
> Come let us all be proud,
> When he conquers the wave and air,
> In his glory we are going to share.
> He said Paris or eternity.

> "White men have no fear,
> White men have conquered the air,
> Julian with him will compare,
> About his life he has no fear,
> Why should we not do what we can
> To help this brave colored man.
> He said Paris or eternity."

"They simply *cannot* love like *colored* men," Agatha's indecent and compromising avowal shocked in midair with the termination of the panegyric on Lieutenant Julian.

The duchess heaved a mammoth sigh, and wiped away a pearly tear as the last heroic strains died off.

"What do you think of it?" she asked Constancia, who had not yet recovered.

"Very soulful, Duchess," Constancia assured her.

"And its possibilities?" persisted the duchess.

"Limitless," conceded Constancia.

"I love the change from alas to *hélas* in the chorus," said Lady Hyacinth, dreamily. "I don't know why, but it gives me a catch in my throat, probably because it's so foreign and unexpected."

"I don't think it's so hot as sense," confessed Lottie, bluntly, "but the music would make a grand stomp; it's so aboriginal."

"I am going to use it on the lecture platform," said the duchess, "as I go from city to city addressing our branches. It will inspire thousands to a sense of the possibilities inherent in the simplest black man. I do wish, however, that he had said *Africa* or eternity instead of *Paris.* That would be so much more effective for my purpose."

"Lottie," urged Constancia, anxious to sidetrack the duchess from her favorite topic of African redemption, "won't you sing something for us, the 'St. Louis Blues,' perhaps?"

"There's nobody to play for me," demurred Lottie, "or I would. Stanley's not here yet."

"You might sing *a capela,*" suggested Constancia.

"I'm sorry, Constancia," said Lottie. "You know you never have to beg me, but I don't know '*A Capella*'; and there's nobody to play it, if I did. Maybe the duchess will recite. I love to hear her do that piece where she goes mad and talks so crazy."

"I suppose she means Ophelia," said the duchess, haughtily, ignoring Lottie and addressing herself to Constancia.

"Yes," confessed Lottie, unabashed, "that's the one. I think it's *simply* a scream."

"I assure you that it wasn't written as a scream, Miss Smith"— the duchess' dark eyes were charged with enough indignation and disgust to annihilate a less imperturbable soul than Lottie.

"Have it your own way, Duchess," Lottie retorted, "but it's a scream to me."

The duchess did not stoop to further argument, fearful lest an extended discussion rob her of this opportunity to shine.

"I don't feel very Shakespearian tonight," she confided to Constancia. "I feel martial. I feel the urge to recount the heroic doings of my people. I could do either 'Black Samson of Brandywine' or 'The Black Regiment.' Which shall it be?"

"Why not do both, Duchess?" asked Donald, gallantly.

"You dear greedy boy, I will," the duchess conceded as she tousled his hair and inwardly thanked him from the bottom of her heart for affording her an excuse to render both recitations. "I shall start with 'The Black Regiment.' But I must have silence."

She stepped to the center of the floor, where, after bowing profoundly, she stood in meditative and dignified reproval until all the diminutive whispers, sudden coughs, and epileptic squirmings had ceased.

O black heroic regiment whose bravery has been recounted so nobly by the poet Boker, your immortality is assured so long as there remains a Negro elocutionist to chant your glory! From your dust may flowers rise as garlands for the head of the duchess and all her kind! Well might Ethiopia's estranged children, captives in a hostile land, let roll down their gay painted cheeks, a few furtive tears, as the duchess, trembling with pride and devotion, unleashed that divine voice:

> "Dark as the clouds of even,
>   Banked in the western heaven,
>   Waiting the breath that lifts
>   All the dread mass, and drifts
>   Tempest and falling brand,
>   Over a ruined land—
>   So still and orderly
>   Arm to arm, and knee to knee

MY SOUL'S HIGH SONG

Waiting the great event,
Stands the Black Regiment.

"Down the long dusky line
  Teeth gleam and eyeballs shine;
And the bright bayonet,
Bristling and firmly set,
Flashed with a purpose grand
Long ere the sharp command
Of the fierce rolling drum
Told them their time had come—
Told them what work was sent
For the Black Regiment."

There was no need for Donald to veil his eyes now. The duchess
was in her element. As if the ghostly regiment stood behind her
listening in serried ranks of impalpability to the recital of their
bravery, her voice now soft and tender, now rich with frenzy, now
high and courageous as if in the midst of battle, swept everything
before her. Listening to her, her auditors felt that there was nothing
in heaven and hell which their race might not surmount, and even
Constancia felt a hard unfamiliar tightening of the throat. And then
that opulent petition to which the lords of the land would never
open their ears brought the poem to its close:

"Hundreds on hundreds fell;
  But they are resting well;
Scourges and shackles strong
Never shall do them wrong.
Oh! to the living few,
Soldiers, be just and true!
Hail them as comrades tried;
Fight with them side by side;
Never in field or tent
Scorn the Black Regiment!"

By all that is fine and touching there should have been no applause, there should have been nothing but dark bowed heads, their obeisance hiding proud, glistening eyes. And for a full minute the duchess should have stood there, Ethiopia eloquent, stretching forth her hands for justice and equity in exchange for courage and proven fidelity.

And then while the rumor of great and mighty actions was still with them, while the ghosts of the Black Regiment were yet there, suffused with the memory of their mortal greatness, the duchess should have evoked the towering majesty of "Black Samson of Brandywine," that fierce black scythe of destruction whom a black poet has sung and whom black declaimers kept alive.

But, alas for the serene and somber Spirit which hopes to reign supreme and tranquil at a Negro gathering. Shut laughter and raillery out; with cotton in every crevice and keyhole bid them begone, yet will they filter their way back through the shaft of light that steals in under the lowered window-shade!

Even as the duchess, sensing the dramatic opportunities of the moment, made the transition from regiment to lone soldier, cleared her throat, and introduced, "Black Samson of Brandywine"—at that moment even, he who in a bright-green uniform with gold epaulettes had made his dizzy way from glass to glass through a maze of streets to Constancia's home, stood beautifully balancing himself in the doorway. The gold buttons flashed their radiance into the room, and mingled their fire with the amber, unclouded enchantment in Constancia's eyes. Like a lioness defending her young, the duchess turned with open mouth and outraged countenance to confront the intruder, while Lottie Smith rose from her chair, shrieking, "It must be Black Samson himself!"

"No," disagreed the enchanted Constancia, as with one hand she supported the tottering duchess, while with the other she beckoned Sam to abandon his perilous perch on the threshold, for a place among the company, "it's only the Emperor Jones!"

Later, as they walked home through the fine Harlem twilight, Mattie rebuked Sam for having endangered her position by his precipitate and unsolicited entrance into her mistress' home; but in her purse was a crisp new bill of generous denomination and in her ears still echoed the laughter with which Constancia had said: "The duchess and Sam made my *soirée*. As I refuse to donate to the Back-to-Africa movement, I am giving this to Sam. And don't scold him."

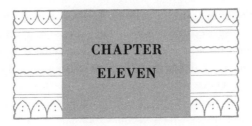

CHAPTER
ELEVEN

April, changeable and undecided, blew now warm and now chill
on Harlem. And like children playing a game, Harlem ran in and
out, sloughing overcoats today, loitering on street corners, sowing
in laughter and rich talk the rumors of spring; tomorrow shivering
back into yesterday's discarded mantles, grumbling at the indecent
insistence of winter. But gradually the cold subsided, day by day
lost ground, as Harlem, in Harlem's way, rushed out to meet the
spring. For to others spring may come, may be allowed to come
slowly and painfully as if in travail, but Negroes go out to meet the
spring, and rip it brutally from the too slowly yielding womb of the
earth. The thinnest sliver of sunlight, the most tepid harbinger of
a zephyr, the first insolent blade of grass feeling its way through
pavement crevices, are heralded with drums and banners, as if all
the batteries of August's sun were beating down in burning gold
and bronze, as if indeed the year had played a trick on spring,
and without transition had gone straight to summer.

In Constancia's neighborhood the procedure is more orderly.
They too go out to meet the spring, but, being people of circumstance, doctors, lawyers, teachers, owners of houses, payers of
direct taxes, their method is genteel and studied. Constancia, to

be sure, if it suited her capricious fancy, might thrust her lovely head out into the air, sniff at it like a happy cur, and cry, "Glory!" if she felt so disposed; but not her neighbors. Their ways were not raucous; they who bear the yoke of gentility must bear it as to the manner born. They dance a minuet with spring, and take no step out of season. There is a studied time for the taking down of the winter curtains; there is the precise moment when measures are taken for flower-boxes which in their appointed time will fringe the windows and line the entrance steps; now one does not put the car into the garage so soon, but allows it to remain just outside in the street, in case after supper it might not be deemed too chilly for a drive through the Park. There is a decent time too for bringing one's chair out on the stoop and sitting there awhile. In Constancia's neighborhood one does not change one's winter clothes precipitately for the habiliments of spring, but one goes slowly through all the nuances of diminishing warmth. One's skin is tender, one's lungs are delicate; April is treacherous, and one safeguards one's health. There is more rapport between Constancia's neighborhood and fashionable Fifth Avenue, than between the latter and that of Sam and Mattie, although Sam and Mattie, too, live on Fifth Avenue.

Where Sam and Mattie live one cannot take time to mince words, one cannot be exact about when winter curtains go up and when they come down. Suddenly you discover that Christmas is within hailing distance; this morning the lady for whom you do day's work had you put up her curtains; and so tonight, though tired, you hang your own. Suddenly it is warm again; you feel spring on your cheek; Mrs. Cohen will not have her curtains down until the 15th of April, but yours go down today. Order and precision are part and parcel of means; they get mislaid in the struggle for existence, as do many other of the niceties which obtain in Constancia's neighborhood. Spring is in the air. Your windows go up with a bang that is everything but studied and proper; you shout across the airshaft to your neighbor; you don't know her very well, but you ask her why she doesn't come over sometime; she promises to do so; you bring a pillow and place it on the window ledge; you lean there happy, drinking in the sun, telling your neighbor all your business, learning all hers. It is good to gossip; it is fine to feel the spring. If it keeps up like this you are going to take off that heavy underwear tomorrow. If tonight is as warm as last night you will take your pillows down and sit on the stoop. What a summer it will be if spring is like this! You don't think you will go to Mrs. Cohen's today. There is something independent in your blood. You have your own work, your own spring cleaning to do. Let Mrs. Cohen get somebody else for a day, or do without. At least she will do without *you*. Spring has declared a holiday. Not only for you, but for many others. The street below is suddenly warm and dark with life, where yesterday it was cold and deserted. It takes but a breath of spring to bring these dark bees out of their hives to sip at the warm, pestiferous flowers of the city. The drones are happy. In loud boisterous groups they collect on the street corners; they swap yarns, and invent lies, embroidering them with solemn faces masked with every semblance of verisimilitude. You would think them the happiest people under the sun, and for the moment they are, as their laughter, unrestrained and strident, mounts up through the slits in the fire-escape. Out in the back yards some are singing, the only sort of work they will ever do, able-bodied men and women hiding underneath dark glasses eyes which can probe the night, masking the strength of their legs in a painful halt which a veteran actor would envy, raising their deceitful voices in rich harmony for the few pennies which you throw them grudgingly, because at heart you know there is no truth in their blindness, only miming in their lameness.

Spring takes some slowly, easing into them and accepting from them the slow consciousness of warmth with which a snake, frozen all winter long, begins slowly to change from harmless rigidity to a final deadly quickness. But others are taken suddenly, like Sam; besieged by restlessness, the world becomes a prison for them, and they begin to look around for any hidden means of escape. Anything that savors of duty and routine becomes torture. A traveling man more than any other resents the daily come and go, the similarity of each succeeding day, the paucity of unchanging nights. And there is no worse goad than memory, to show him how bare today's existence is in comparison with yesterday's.

What most you loved you begin most to hate, to find fault with, to search a reason for abandoning. And there is no torture worse than endeavoring to hate when at heart you know there is cause only for love; nothing as contemptible as trying to pick a quarrel when there is reason for nothing but peace; nothing more cowardly than leaving when every reason you advance bids you stick to your guns.

And if in spite of all you remain, like Sam, it is at the cost of too much in the end. Living becomes an endless array of petty quarrels, tears, recriminations, pleas for forgiveness, torrential moments of fierce physical attempts at atonement, which leave one happy and exhausted, but no happier on the morrow.

With a growing uneasiness in which he could scent a presentiment of evil Sam watched the divergent ways of his path and of Mattie's widen; the farther he looked into the distance the more apart they were. And try as he could, there was no way of denying that the way of both was of his own choosing. Mattie's whole life lay wrapped in a white handkerchief and laid carefully away in a drawer. She had made a shrine of his cards and his razor. The magic would never depart from them for her. She had erected a temple to them; they were as much to her as leaves from the burning bush might have been. It sent a chill through Sam as he watched her from time to time with the cards spread out before her, the razor laid alongside them, and her dark lovely head bent above them, in silent inexplicable communion, her lips moving in prayer and petition. Whenever they quarreled she went to her talismans; and though Sam hated them, and scorned them, and knew better than anyone alive that there was no virtue in them, he had neither the heart nor the courage to destroy them.

He knew how much they meant to Mattie. He never would forget the first time he had realized how much they meant. It was during the cold period when he just could not get his will together enough to face the wind in search of work; when despite the silent protest on Mattie's face, despite the half-serious recriminations of Aunt Mandy, he had spent his days beside the fire, playing cards with Aunt Mandy. One day two of the cards had been swept from the table in a sudden gust of high merriment by Aunt Mandy, as she laughed at some outlandish witticism with which Sam was currying her favor; the cards had fallen into the fire and been burned. The deck was useless without the missing members; and Sam suddenly thought of Mattie's cards hidden away in their room in the dresser drawer.

"Suppose we use Mattie's cards?" he queried.

Aunt Mandy had hesitated for a moment, for she knew the store Mattie set by those cards. But in her sight Mattie's cards were more of an abomination than her own. She did not like the way Mattie pored over them, "making a brazen image out of them, like the golden calf," as Aunt Mandy expressed it. It was wrong; it was sinful. And so she had said nothing to deter Sam from getting them.

The game went on amid that laughter and raillery which bound Sam and Aunt Mandy together. They were so engrossed in their battle that they did not hear Mattie enter; and it was only when they looked up, to find her staring at them in anger and sorrow, that they looked down guiltily at the cards in their hands. Sam would never forget Mattie's look as she silently gathered up the pack, nor her voice as she turned on the threshold to tell them, "I'd be ashamed to do a thing like that, and afraid God would strike me dead."

And that night she held him close as if she were afraid some evil spirit would enter the room and bear him off; while in his heart had died forever the thought of revealing to her how little blessed those cards were, how deeply cursed that razor. She would be able to understand that a converted man could backslide, but never that one could play with God as he had done. He remembered the minister's words, "She'd hate the church and me and you."

There is no telling to what depths of despair and everlasting unbelief Mattie might have been hurled had she discovered how small a part the hand of heaven had played in her conversion, how devoid of heat, how lacking in chill, how absolutely neutral had been the fingers of fire and ice which she had felt playing along her spine the morning she came through. Those who are born to their religion, accepting it passively because their fathers before them bowed to the same god, or those who enter in the full possession of their faculties, after having weighed the good and evil points, are not subject to that exaggerated devotion which comes with a miracle. Though Mattie's life had been simple in the extreme, having in it nothing that might be called sinful, more serious than the absence of her name on the church register, with her conversion came all the horror of little sins and all the sudden holiness which made Sam's life a martyrdom.

She saw in her conversion the white and glistening hand of God; and after the night of her wedding, when for a moment to please Sam she had bowed to love and had danced, she danced no more, save for Christ. Young as she was she entered into the life of Mount Hebron with a piety and an assiduity which put many of the veteran sisters and brothers to shame. She never missed a class-meeting or a prayer-service, and Sunday was one long interminable attendance at church. People began to look forward to hearing her speak at testimonial time; for all the fervent sayings which she had heard year after year while attending church as a sinner now came to mind, and were spoken with downcast eyes, in a voice conscious of the unworthiness of the speaker, yet with a firmness which marked young Sister Lucas as one who would go far in the church.

Sam backslid gently but firmly, and after a month of church attendance ceased to be a practicing Christian, and though Mattie laid him on the altar morning after morning, it was of no avail.

The sort of job Constancia had secured for Sam had made matters worse, and Mattie soon came to feel that it would be better to perish than to gain their living as her husband did his as a doorkeeper in the tents of the wicked. For once, passing by the theater, she had seen one of the women performers resting in the little court which led to the stage door. The woman, fawn-brown in complexion, was gaudy in a harrowing, feline way, with high arched eyebrows, vividly-painted lips, and a sleekness about her that made Mattie tremble for Sam, who stood in the theater door, gayly garnering tickets. Sometimes Sam brought her things which he found in the dressing-rooms of those women after they had gone on to another theater—bits of ribbon, a comb, a rhinestone buckle. She never dared ask him how he came by these things, and though she took them, she never used them.

One night he returned home, happily rousing her out of sleep with a frightening bellow into her ear, holding up for her approval a bright-red kimona which one of the women had left. She could see in his eyes that he admired it, thought it fine, and felt that it was a real gift. But the nature of it, the intimacy of it, a too familiar gesture in Sam's fingers as they fondled it, frightened and hurt her. She took the kimona in her hand, but an odor of stale perfume made her drop the garment as if a scorpion had stung her. "I can't wear that," she said, turning away from him and hiding her face against the wall. "It would make me feel cheap and common."

Sam had not been able to understand, and the rejection of his gift had filled him with slow anger. He had let it lie on the floor, where it lay shining like something malevolent, as he silently undressed and climbed into bed. He had not taken her in his arm nor kissed her, but they had slept back to back in sullen distrust of one another.

Mattie had forgotten the incident the next morning. It happened to be Sam's day off, and Constancia was letting her free a half-day also, in order that she might do something which she had long desired to do. She had wanted to invite Reverend Drummond to have dinner with her and Sam. Sam had consented, even if none too graciously. The crimson kimona caught Mattie's eyes as she leaped out of bed lightly so as not to awaken Sam; she took the offending garment up gingerly and thrust it away in the clothes closet. She bent over and kissed Sam before setting out for her half-day at Constancia's.

She had counted on Sam to help her with the dinner, at least to be near her and to talk to her. But when she came home aglow with the prospect of entertaining her spiritual adviser, Aunt Mandy informed her that Sam had gone out soon after breakfast and had not indicated when he would return. She had thought nothing of it, and had continued gayly with the preparations for her dinner. She had bought the best her money could buy. Reverend Drummond seldom dined with his members, and it was only after much pleading that he had consented to dine with her. Mattie felt decidedly happy.

The afternoon passed; all the preparations had been made; the dinner sang and hissed on the stove; the table was a thing of beauty. Aunt Mandy and Mattie were happy. They only wished Sam would hurry home. He would hardly have time to wash and spruce up a bit before the minister would be there. It was already within half an hour of the time. And then Sam had come in. Mattie turned to meet him, took a few joyous steps toward him, before she stopped transfixed with all her heaven toppling about her. He had embalmed his anger in liquor, and now stood before her evil and unforgiving. She tried to lead him to the bedroom and coax him to sleep; but he was not drunk to the point of being inoffensive. He had merely taken enough to be disagreeable and vengeful. Pushing her aside, he had staggered to the closet, where he had retrieved the unappreciated kimona.

Pleading had been of no avail, nor tears. When Reverend Drummond, kindly and hungry, entered, he found two sorrowing, shame-stricken women making apologies for the head of the house, who sat with his dirty shoes resting on the edge of the white tablecloth, and over his knees a scarlet kimona.

The minister had not wavered; if anything, his eyes had flickered with amusement, as he blessed the table, with Sam's feet still high in the air. He was a man of tact, and his grace was not only that of the church. He had talked kindly to Sam, had assured him that the kimona was pretty, and had even exacted from Mattie a promise to wear it. "That is not too much of a sacrifice in order to keep peace in one's home," he had said. And he had made them kiss, and had thrown back his head and laughed uproariously at them as they did so.

Then gently the minister had leaned over and eased Sam's feet from the table.

As Sam ate, his clouded brain began to freshen up and he soon felt that the minister wasn't so bad a person, after all. He was jolly despite the cut of his cloth, and left them little time to mope as he regaled them with story after story. One in particular had made them laugh until the tears ran down their faces.

"These young preachers have it easy," Reverend Drummond explained. "They should have come along in my time when a man had to be worth his salt and had to have more than the grace of God in him to win and keep a congregation. Now most of them come to churches that are ready to receive them with courtesy at least, if not with open arms. I wonder what they would do if they had to meet a congregation like my first one. They required preaching of the rousing kind, and in order to get it they never kept a preacher longer than two years. Every new preacher was subjected to a real test. When he went to the church to preach his first sermon, no one welcomed him. The entire congregation greeted him seated with their backs turned away from him. They could not see him. The test required that in order to keep the charge he had to preach so vigorously that by the time he ended more than half the congregation had turned around to look him in the face. That called for *preaching!*"

"And how did you come through," Sam asked, with glistening eyes; for there was something in this story that made him think there were more ways to heaven than one, and that his cards and razor might not be as bad as they were painted.

Reverend Drummond leaned back and laughed. "I won them all," he said, "but I ended up with my coat and collar at my feet. And they kept me five years."

After the minister had gone, Mattie took off her company clothes and decked herself in the scarlet kimona. Sam stumbled around unsteadily, helping her to clear the table. They had never been happier.

CHAPTER TWELVE

What will women not do for this man called Jesus? What have they not done for Him? What will they not expend in time and money and love to spread His story, to win Him converts, to build Him houses, to rout all other gods before Him? The women have always been more faithful to Him then the men. Think only on Mary Magdalene and that ointment which might have been sold to feed the poor, as practical, male-thinking Judas wanted to do; think of the three women who went to the tomb for His body while the men were still deep in inactive sorrow. What and whom will a woman not sacrifice, forsake, insult, make a target for shame, for His kingdom's sake? Think on Mattie.

Shame and misery encircled her like a shroud, pressed in upon her and disturbed her waking hours, kept her suffocated and dream-ridden at night. The man through whom she had come to her Saviour was steadily slipping away, slowly and without any effort to save himself, sinking back into the ways of sinners. Mattie felt weak and companionless as she went to church Sunday after Sunday, and to meeting after meeting, alone or with Aunt Mandy, but never at her side that man whose sudden but brief conversion had set the church on fire, had sent tremors of fire and ice coursing along her spine. She could hardly speak for shame when they inquired about him. She felt that she would die beneath the slow Christian smiles that were half sympathy and half derision as they shook their heads and clucked their tongues. With deep loyalty she explained that a man must work, that he cannot always choose his occupation, and that Sam was obliged to toil on Sundays. And then on his one night free he was tired. The thought struck her, "Too tired to serve his Jesus!" And she determined that at all costs she must put her arms under him, whether he willed it or not, and extricate him from the quagmire into which he was sinking.

If only she could get him to church again, she thought, some power in the atmosphere, some breath of divine air, might fan his cheek, might blow into his heart and stir to fire again the dead ashes there. She dared not ask him directly and openly, nor reproach him too earnestly with his apostasy. For something intuitive and part of her womanly equipment told her that his mind and feet were wavering on a line, and that it needed little for him to cross it and to be off and gone forever. Yet she felt that the only way of fastening him securely to his life with her lay in getting him back into the fold.

Delilah pleading to know where Samson's strength lay hidden; Salome dancing for John's head; Mattie determined that Sam should not lose his soul: Three women, one with a glib tongue, one with twinkling feet, and one burning with religion; all three armed with the asp of coquetry.

Sam on his day off lay sprawled upon his bed, watching Mattie as she slipped into her clothes. Sun filtered through the windows and made him throw back the covers. He pitied Mattie that she could not lie abed with him. Peace and contentment and the promise of rest lay on his black handsome face. Something in the day and the season stirred him to a consciousness that Mattie was as lovely as ever. He tugged at her dress. Looking around at him, she felt and knew the love that was keeping him there with her in spite of himself. But first and foremost came her Lord Jesus.

She bent and kissed Sam fervently. Caught and locked in the grip of his arm, she stroked his head, whispering, "Love me?"

He lay with his head on her bosom, lay laughing and smiling up at her, as he answered only with his eyes, but in unspoken words that held no negative.

"Then promise me something," she went on, hurrying lest he interrupt her. "Let us go out together tonight. It's been a long time since you've been out with me. Promise."

To Sam going out meant joy, people, laughter, music; something to which Mattie had not given herself since their wedding night. He smiled happily, and squeezed her as he said: "I promise. Where?"

"Somewhere I want to go," said Mattie, evasively.

"All right." Sam turned over, happy and sleepy again.

That evening Mattie maintained her air of secrecy, dressed herself with a touch of spirit, while Sam chose his tie sprinkled with yellow stars. As they sauntered out into the warm Harlem air, Mattie prayed to Heaven to meet her halfway. Sam was lost in dreams and in the feel of Mattie close to him, the bright lights and the high hearty laughter of his people all around him. He walked as if he were a poet thinking on immortal lines instead of a ticket-chopper out for an evening stroll. It was only when they stood under the great white light of the church that he realized where she had been leading him. He drew back scowling, one reluctant foot already poised on the church step. Mattie braced herself for the combat.

"Not on my evening out. I don't call that a holiday, nor an evening out, going to church," Sam protested. Mattie could feel his arm stiffen beneath her light pressure.

"You promised," she pleaded, meeting his disgusted stare with a look all injury and ill treatment.

Angrily he pushed her ahead of him, and entered the church. Mattie felt that the first skirmish had been won, as they took their seats, while people, remembering Sam, pointed him out and whis-

pered his story. Despite the warm weather, the church was well
filled for the prayer service. Aunt Mandy, to whom Mattie had not
confided her hope of getting Sam to the meeting, was already there,
rocking back and forth and moaning beautifully.

The meeting promised to be one of the best. The music was
good; the hymns chosen were the rollicking kind; the spirits of the
audience seemed to mount higher as if each hymn and testimonial
were the rung of a ladder which was taking them nearer and nearer
to that Beulah land of which they sang. The testimonials were frank
and flagellant; each speaker seemed to find a special joy in open
confession, in announcing to all the world his unworthiness as a
partaker of life and the many joys which Jesus was showering upon
him. In each voice was a fierce knout with which they scourged
themselves. There was not one there who seemed to feel that he
had a right to joy and laughter. They all, according to their own
admission, were steeped in sin. Their only hope was that Christ's
blood might cleanse them.

Sam alone sat sullen and unmoved, brooding through half-closed
eyes, eaten up with anger that Mattie should have tricked him into
coming there. Beside him Mattie sat communing with Heaven as
she had done the day of their first Communion together. Then they
had been, as she had thought, entering upon a new and beautiful
life together. Now her lips were moving in a silent petition that
Christ stoop down and gather up once more into the palm of His
hand this man whom she loved.

Time was passing, and Sam had not joined in on one hymn, nor
spoken one word for his Jesus. To Mattie's timid suggestion that
he testify he had merely mumbled something under his breath
about leading a horse to water but not being able to make him
drink.

At last, silently calling Heaven to her aid, Mattie rose to testify
for them both.

All eyes were turned upon her as she stood there ready to speak,
for that glory which they had wanted to expend on Sam had, after
his defection, been transferred to Mattie; she was now an acquisi-

tion toward whom the church pointed with pride, even if with pity, on account of her backsliding husband.

"Brothers and sisters"—she spoke so low at first as to be almost inaudible—"the Lord has done great things for me, and His praise is forever in my mouth. He has withheld no good thing from me. I have given Him my word, and I can't turn back."

"Amen, child," breathed Aunt Mandy, fervently, from her seat in the amen corner, among the aging handmaidens of the Lord.

"There is only one thing I am asking of the Lord," Mattie went on, her words coming with a rush as if she must get them out quickly or they would not come at all. She turned and bent her eyes full on Sam, and there was such devotion in them as would not be downed by the seething anger with which he looked up at her. "I want Christ to reach down and take my husband back into His fold."

The church held its breath. Here on a plain meeting night was drama that by rights belonged only to revival time.

Sam felt as if all the curious, pitying eyes turned on him were so many stones; he shrank down into his seat as if to ward them off. Still through his misery he could hear his wife's ecstatic, fervent voice: "Reach down, O Lord, and turn him back into the path which leads to glory. Before death's sickle cuts him down, take him back, Heavenly Father, into your fold!" The church loomed up before him as one vast accusing eye, as one great voice pleading for his redemption. He could bear no more. Suddenly he arose, not to seek the altar as once he had done, but to push brutally past Mattie and to make his way toward the door. An usher who made as if to bar his way suddenly stepped aside as he saw the hot shame and the unreasoning bitterness on Sam's face.

Mattie stood defeated as a certain minister had done; and no miracle came to her aid.

CHAPTER
THIRTEEN

To Mattie's surprise, Aunt Mandy, that stanch Christian, had sided wholly with Sam. She always contended that it was Mattie's open prayer which goaded Sam on to Emma May. It wasn't decent, she argued, to air one's family wash in church as Mattie had done. In one's secret closet, yes, with only one's God to hear, one might ask for anything, strip one's life and soul bare, but in open church, that was a different matter. She, for one, felt that Sam had behaved as any outraged and humiliated man would have acted under like circumstances, when he had informed Mattie afterwards at home, "You'll never shame me again; I never hopes to enter church again unless they brings me in feet first." In vain Mattie had thrust a too tardy hand up to his mouth in an endeavor to stem his blasphemy; the words were out. And although she had cried half through the night, Sam, lost and unrepentant, had slept soundly at her side.

There was a bond between Aunt Mandy and Sam which the old lady herself could not explain, but which seemed to tighten with no perceptible effort, and to relegate Mattie to a second place in her aunt's affections. Sam sometimes felt tempted to tell the old lady the real story of his conversion; he was sure that she would have laughed in spite of her disapproval.

With ever-deepening distress, Mattie beheld the forces of evil working against her. Aunt Mandy, who, until Sam had entered on his job as doorman at the Star Movie Palace, had never beheld any cinema performance save stereopticon views of the "Suffering and Death of Christ," became a devotee of this sinful new amusement. Sam was not doorman for nothing, and Aunt Mandy was filled with pride and importance because she was able to come to the theater at will, and to enter gratuitously simply because her tall, elegantly-attired nephew was there to wave her in with a grandeur which might easily have been mistaken for ownership.

Now that her afternoon game of cards had been lost to her by Sam's work, Aunt Mandy hastened feverishly each morning to tidy up the house in order that she might be at the theater almost as early as Sam. It mattered not to her that she must often see the same performance over and over again; in each showing there was always something to laugh at anew, or something which she had missed in the previous representation. Sam contrived to keep a seat in the back row ever available for his crony, and there she would perch, like a little wizened yellow bird, looking with happy eyes on worlds of which she had never dreamed before. From time to time, as business slackened, Sam would leave his post at the door and come over to talk to her, to her infinite delight and belief in her growing importance.

It began to be rumored at Mount Hebron that Aunt Mandy was falling off in her Christian duties; for now, as often as not, although she might leave home in the evening with her mind sternly set on the prayer-meeting at Mount Hebron, she was likely to end up at the Star Palace. Mattie felt as if her aunt and Sam had entered into a conspiracy against her.

Sam was not as loving as he had formerly been. The spontaneity and the fire of his affection seemed to have cooled, and no graciousness or studied attempt on Mattie's part was able to revive it. Mattie remembered the disturbing beauty of the show woman whom she had seen in the theater alley one day, and she shuddered.

But she had cast her net of suspicions too high; she needed to aim lower and nearer than at the fleeting, flashily dressed show girls who were only transient beams in Sam's eyesight. She knew nothing of Emma May's conquest until Aunt Mandy told her.

For some time Aunt Mandy had been watching Sam and Emma May, and pitying Mattie.

Though Aunt Mandy realized that a natural intimacy must exist between the lone usher of a small theater and the doorman, there were certain glances and signs, too frequent whisperings, sudden bursts of laughter with something shameful in them, which she felt did not proceed from business relations. For one thing, Aunt Mandy thought Emma May might have found other means of passing her time when there was no one to usher to a seat, than by chatting with Sam and keeping him away from her; and there was the too frank and too open way in which Emma May would stand with her light-brown hand on Sam's shoulder. A light, indifferent touch, perhaps, but to Aunt Mandy that small brown hand was a talon of possession. There was, moreover, a crude voluptuousness about Emma May which aroused Aunt Mandy's enmity and distrust; she felt as if Emma May could have and ought to have done something to check the sinister flowering of her attractions. The old lady disliked the pagan roundness of the usherette; the massive gold hoops in Emma May's ears were vulgar, not small and decent like her own. That gold tooth in Emma May's mouth was a deliberate decoy, as were the bracelets jangling with her every movement, and the scent of diluted perfume which always heralded her ap-pearance. Emma May always passed the time of day with her, but Aunt Mandy, too distrustful to be polite, would never respond.

And as Mattie wilted, Emma May blossomed and insolently tightened the grasp of her round, brown hand on Sam's shoulder. Aunt Mandy looked on with sorrow, but in silence; for there was nothing concrete on which she could base her suspicions. These unproven suspicions made her querulous and argumentative with Mattie. She tried to arouse her niece out of the lethargy into which her religion was drowning her. "Praying won't stop a man what's slipping away to other women. You have to win him back with something quicker than that," said the old lady, her eyes half hinting a wisdom which she was afraid to broach to her God-fearing niece.

"What's quicker or more powerful than prayer, Aunt Mandy?" Mattie asked, so piteously that her aunt risked the suggestion that had been so long quivering on her tongue.

"Sometimes when the angels is too busy to help you, you have to fight the devil with his own tools," the old lady broadened the hint, but only slightly. She had begun to stand in awe of the righteous, church-going Mattie whose simon-pure religion made the old lady feel that she herself was the sorriest backslider in the world. Aunt Mandy was not going to come out plainly with what was behind the mystic simplicity of her words until Mattie should invite explanation by a show of sympathetic interest.

"There isn't anything more powerful than prayer, and what Heaven won't do, hell can't," said Mattie, despairingly. "Yet," she continued, plaintively, "if I knew some certain way to get Sam back, and loving the way he used to be, I think I'd try it."

There was such misery and hopelessness in the thin black visage which looked up from Mattie's cupped hands that Aunt Mandy let the die fall. "I know a woman," she said, eagerly, "who can tell what's going to happen, and change it. She can mix a powder strong enough to win any man back."

But Mattie had not reached the brink of despair, as her aunt could see, even though there lay between her and that bottomless pit but a few scant steps which she was steadily diminishing with a sure, if with an unconscious, step. She looked up at her aunt with all the fine scorn of which she was capable. "You mean conjuring, don't you, Aunt Mandy?" she inquired. "I haven't come to that yet. I still have Jesus."

Proud and sorrowing, bolstered up only by her faith and by the sudden realization of life growing within her, too proud to speak to Sam of that life which was as much his as hers, she watched him ease down from an ardent lover to the level of a perfunctory husband. He became now merely the man who shared her household, but all the magic and soaring of loving was gone.

And Mattie could not lay her finger on the sore.

There were nights when Sam did not come home at all, nights when Mattie tossed about in sleepless worry until Sam returned just early enough to snatch a few hours' sleep before being off to work. Mattie was too proud to ask an explanation and Sam vouchsafed none.

Aunt Mandy berated Sam whenever she had him alone for a moment; but he treated her with a good-humored condescension that let her angry words fall from him as water from a duck's back. When she upbraided him and threw Emma May's name at him, he only laughed softly and whistled through his teeth at her.

Finally, Aunt Mandy could stand Mattie's pain-racked, pining face no longer. After all, Mattie was her niece and blood *was* thicker than water.

And she told Mattie about Emma May, while Mattie listened in a pathetic silence which went straight to Aunt Mandy's heart.

"I remember her," said Mattie, simply. "She is very pretty."

And that had been all. She had said no more. Aunt Mandy had been so annoyed that she had wanted to slap Mattie. It was all right to be religious and lost in the inner life, she felt, but there were things in this other life which were important. And loving was one. She never could have confirmed another woman's beauty as Mattie had done, if it had been a question of Ben. Though she lost all Paradise for it, she would have done something about it.

Mattie was not the confiding kind, however; and underneath her righteousness the primitive slept a not eternal sleep. All day the lively brown face of Emma May stayed before her, leaped in and out of her path like a dancing demon; the loud, uncouth laughter of Emma May ran out of the kitchen faucet and hissed out of the steam of the kettle. Emma May's gold hoops disturbed her during the night; they became large bands of steel which bound and squeezed her until she awoke, ashy with terror, drenched with fright, to find day streaming in upon her and no Sam at her side.

Man has yet to raise up a stronger god than Eros. The wood of the cross is poisoned by his venomous arrow.

Mattie decided that she would go to Emma May. If Sam were there, too, so much the better. She would confront them together. Even in the midst of her heart-break, custom was strong upon her, and she knelt to pray before leaving the house. She knew that Emma May, besides being usher at the Star Palace, was also obliged to do the early-morning dusting. She wrapped herself in a light spring coat, although it was hot enough to go without an outer wrap. That coat was to serve a purpose; for under it she concealed, clutched close to her bosom, a small sharp hatchet. Taking it was an intuitive, unstudied gesture, an obedience to the hypnotic suggestion of a cold, unreasoning fury.

The doors of the Star Palace were open wide. As Mattie entered, she could hear Emma May's low humming as she went from row to row, dusting the hard wooden chairs. Even in her workday clothes, a plain gingham apron and a dust-cap on her head, Emma May was pretty. The gold hoops made shining arcs on either side of her face, and from underneath the dust-cap a twist of thick black hair had crept, to form a curl on her forehead. Mattie stood in the doorway and watched her for a moment. There was no sign of Sam.

Emma May looked up to find Mattie confronting her.

Emma May had never seen Mattie before, but she knew it was Mattie and she waited.

The jungles produce no thing that hates another with a hate more deadly than that with which Mattie hated Emma May.

"You are Emma May," said Mattie.

Emma May rested a light-brown hand on one of the chairs with that same inoppressiveness which was still like the clutch of possession with which Aunt Mandy had seen her lay her hands on Sam.

Emma May did not answer.

"I am Sam's wife," said Mattie.

Still Emma May did not reply; only her brown eyes meeting Mattie's squarely responded with unspoken and bitter mockery. Suddenly the mockery died in the bright eyes as a slim black hand swept up and closed over the fawn-brown throat; with her other hand Mattie hugged the hatchet close to her bosom.

Gone was the gentle servitor of the gentlest of all the gods. The primitive woman, she whose skin is neither white nor black, she who is older than her Jesus, looked out of Mattie's blazing eyes and spoke with her rasping tongue. "Was he with you last night?"

Emma May was helpless in the furious grip, and, more than that, desperately lost in that fright which fleshy women have in the presence and strength of their leaner, fiercer sisters. She could only nod her head and gurgle an acquiescence, until Mattie released her and sent her stumbling against one of the seats.

They stood eying one another for a moment, while Mattie's anger subsided as quickly as it had risen, until only shame and confusion covered her at the thought of what she, a church-going, God-fearing Christian had done, and of the wilder, more fearful thing she had contemplated, but had not carried through. She opened her coat from the seclusion of which the hatchet fell with a dull thud to lie between her feet and Emma May's. She wanted to ask Emma May's forgiveness. She wanted to get away to herself and weep. She wanted to pray to her Jesus. She wanted Aunt Mandy's arm around her. She wanted Sam. She wanted anything except the thought of what she had meant to do, of how she had intended to scar Emma May's too pretty fawn-brown face. She slowly gathered her coat about her and walked away. As she reached the door she turned, and caught sight of Emma May turning the hatchet about in her hands in fright and perplexity.

Mattie felt as if she were like a wounded cat dragging itself to a caressing hand as she made her way to Constancia's. Constancia did not fail her. She quickly noted the dull, bewildered gaze, the slackness of the usual deft hands, the low-pitched, unintonated responses to her sallies. Constancia, into whose life adoration had dropped like a rich red plum shaken from some celestial tree, still had that ineradicable feminine thought that a man is at the root of every woman's slightest suffering.

"Is it Sam, Mattie?" Constancia asked, all the raillery fled from her cloudless amber eyes, and nothing left there but solicitude for her maid's happiness.

"Somewhat," was Mattie's loyal and non-committal response.

"Too black and handsome," said Constancia as she shook her head in pity. "An evil combination."

When she returned home that evening, Mattie knew that Sam had not been there at all during the day. She had no heart for anything. She held her breath for fear he had gone forever, although she derived some consolation from the thought that his clothes were still there, and that he would have to come to fetch them, should he be leaving. By now he knew of her visit to Emma May. She wondered how he would take it. She didn't care, if only he wouldn't leave.

Seated at the front window, she looked down at the sweating, swarming mass of life strutting and posturing, laughing in the face of the sweltering June heat, and she too laughed inwardly as she thought of the growing, rounding bit of life which she would add to that below, a life of which she had not yet told Sam, lest he think it but a trick to win him back to his sweet ways with her. She closed her eyes in happy contemplation of that blossoming, unborn bit of black humanity.

Hearing the door bang, she started up from her dreaming, fearful and anxious; but it was only Aunt Mandy, who had gone to meeting for a change and who had returned. The old lady was tired. She knew nothing of the day's happenings, but she had plumbed the depths of Mattie's unhappiness at Sam's absence from home. She went over and kissed her niece and patted her sleek black cheek.

"Don't worry, honey," she admonished her. "It will all come out right in the end." And she had dragged her weary limbs into bed.

Mattie sat by the window awhile longer, dreaming of her first meeting with Sam, thinking back to the evangelist and his gentleness, of her refusal to heed his petitions until Sam had shown her the way; surely that evening had not revealed itself as a precursor to the misery of the present moment. She rose and went into their bedroom, where, too tired and anxious to sleep, she sat by the window and gazed out into the dismal airshaft on which the bedroom gave, as if some glimmering fairy landscape lay revealed there. Drowsiness came down and conquered her, and she sat there lost in sleep until she was awakened by the feeling of someone there in the room with her. As her eyes fought back their still sleep-laden lids, she knew it was Sam. He was stumbling about in the room, and his breath invaded the narrow confines of their chamber with a stench of whisky that sickened her. She watched him for a moment, too utterly happy that he had come home to think of upbraiding him. She sat silent and jubilant, immersed in the simple contentment of his presence.

She did not even move when she saw him lurch to the dresser and fling open the drawer in which she kept her talismans.

Only when her sacred cards were flung to the floor, and when she saw in Sam's hand the razor which he had not touched since the night of her conversion, did she catch her breath and clutch her throat to keep from screaming. With horrified eyes she saw him heave toward the bed, saw the open razor flash in his hand, up and down, up and down, like an arc of moonlight; she heard the thin summer sheets crack as the sharp blade slit them through. She heard the rip of the mattress until she could bear no more. It was as if he had slit her heart, as he had meant to do. She knew now what a cruel vengeance he had wanted to exact for her visit to Emma May. In abject pity of herself, she watched him as he swayed above the bed, panting and drunkenly satisfied.

"Sam!" She could scarcely recognize her own voice, it was so low, so lifeless and bare. He reeled around in amazement not comprehending that she was still there and that he had only demolished the bedding instead of her warm, too clinging flesh.

It did not matter now what happened to her. Those strokes had been meant for her. She went over to him. Now that his fury was spent, he was like a small boy who has been caught in mischief. No thought of what he had meant to do lingered with him.

"You meant that for me, Sam, didn't you?" She did not know why she was asking him to confirm what she too plainly knew. Tears welled in her eyes, but did not fall.

Suddenly anger that her love meant so little to him overcame her, as she thought of the child she was carrying. With a quick, hot hand she reached up and ripped open her shirt and undergarment, until her bare black bosom gleamed out at him with its faint, yet already visible, signs of her coming motherhood. She took his hand and placed it on the mound. "You would have killed me and your baby," she told him. "And afterwards you would have swung!"

The next moment he was at her feet, sobbing, and she was bending over him, stroking the hard tight balls on his head. At their feet the cards were scattered across the room like the ribs of a huge fan, bound together by strips of carpet. And close by, forgotten and useless, as harmless now as it had been hateful a moment past, gleamed the razor.

He held her close as if he would keep her against all the world, and she felt a salvation greater than Heaven's pin him to her.

Later she gathered up the scattered strips of their sheets and thrust them with a tremor into the closet. The mattress had been ripped apart so badly that it would have to be sewn together before they slept on it. Sam watched her get the needle and coarse black thread; like a sorry, beaten dog he followed her with his eyes as she made ready to sew up the rents. Lumberingly he stumbled over to the bed, where he knelt down and aided her to stuff the straw back into the cheap mattress; and then he helped her hold the mattress-covering taut so she could sew it. This was his peace offering. She accepted it as she would have taken a rainbow as a sign that only fair days were to follow.

He held her to him that night as he had not done for many nights past. The last thing she remembered before falling to sleep was the thick sound of his voice, saying, "A little baby, a little black baby, like me and you."

CHAPTER
FOURTEEN

Summer had gone, and with it all that summer held.

Mattie lay on the parlor divan, thinking what hopes that high season had held for the chill days that were now upon her, and how cruelly the cold had ransacked her small house of warmth, chilling its lone occupant. All summer long she had held Sam by a thread, a thread so thin that she had trembled to think of its insecurity; but she had laughed to feel it hold more insistently every day. When that thread should break at last it would mean the beginning of a life to which Sam would be forever anchored and stayed, from which Emma May would never be able to entice him. She had known all along that she had not wholly defeated Emma May. There had been intervals when she had felt Emma May tugging away at her fragile happiness, but hope had always revived in her as she had watched Sam's face light up whenever he talked of the son he was sure she was carrying for him. . . . Lying on the divan now, watching the fire curl up in the stove opposite her, she fingered absently the cheap black dress she was wearing, as she thought with bitterness of the dreams she had watched grow in Sam's heart at the thought of his son. It had amused him highly to think how black the child would be, coming from them, the utter distillation of race. It had been fun to see Sam build and demolish his great air castles, to hear him choose and reject the work his son was to do; no rounder like himself—not his boy; he would be a doctor or a lawyer or a teacher, something fine. "And when he's rich and great," Sam had said over and over again with his son's destiny in his eyes, "as black as he'll be, nobody will be able to say it's on account of his white blood, because there ain't a drop between you and me." And Mattie had sat at his side, matching dream with dream, feeling the thread by which she held him grow stronger, seeing in the distance the gold hoops and bright eyes of Emma May pass into nothingness. . . .

All that was passed now. Of it all nothing remained more tangible than this black dress which she was wearing for a dead baby toward whom she had been too weak and pain-racked to turn her eyes. All that was gone, but she would never forget Sam's snarling, disappointed face as she had smiled up at him in her pain, not knowing then that the thread had been too brittle; nor his voice that had crushed her into a deadly coma when he had cried out, "Not able even to born a baby!" And he had gone. Back to Emma May. That had been years ago, hadn't it? No, only a few weeks. He had not come back once. He had not seen the baby buried. Aunt Mandy alone had attended to that. Sam had offered the old lady money when she passed by the theater, to plead with him to return; but he had said that he was through with a house where there was so much religion and so little strength. . . . Mattie had sent the money back proudly. Mrs. Brandon would not let her want. Her strength would soon return. She had never seen the righteous suffering nor their seed begging bread. Her friends at Mount Hebron had been good with gifts of money and food. And Aunt Mandy was still not too old to do a little day's work. Let him keep his money and spend it on Emma May. . . .

Pride wields a bitter tongue, but love eats bitter bread. . . .

Fingering her black dress, she heard the low, suffering voice of affection drowning the strident voice of pride. She knew there was nothing in the world that she regretted losing so much as Sam.

The dead baby was a stranger whom she had never known, no more to her now than a wound that had closed and healed over, of which memory was the only scar; but Sam was the man Heaven had sent her, to whom Heaven had intrusted her salvation, through whom she had gone to Jesus. Tied in a white handkerchief laid away in the dresser drawer of their deserted room were her talismans, still holding their glory.

She must stop this daydreaming. Aunt Mandy would soon be home from her day's work; it would soon be time to eat, and then to sleep another lonely night away. With less effort than she had thought it would take, she lifted herself from the divan. She seemed to feel the glow and warmth of life which had been suspended in her these past three weeks, quicken and begin to flow as if a slow, reviving liquid were being poured into her dusty veins. She would soon be able to go to Mount Hebron again, where she had not been since a few weeks before her confinement. Perhaps prayer in the house of the Lord would prove stronger than in one's own little apartment. She would pray for Sam's return; she would pray for Emma May, not for her hurt in any way, but that she might turn from her sinful living. She paused a moment, to lean against the side of the table, a plate poised in her wasted black hand, while a recurring thought of which she had not been able to rid herself these last days danced impishly before her. Were there really some things which Heaven could not do, that unholy men and women could bring about with a drop of liquid, or a pill dropped into one's coffee? Her dark cheeks burned at the memory of a conversation she had had with Aunt Mandy soon after Sam's departure. The old lady had been sitting beside her, holding her hand, alternately berating and pardoning Sam. Mattie could see even now her aunt's credulous, halfway apologetic look as she had talked to her of a recipe which had never been known to fail. It called for a cake which, when eaten, would turn wayward feet from any wandering road back to the ways of home, which would change any man, however cold, into the sweetest lover born. Mattie remembered how she shuddered when her aunt had leaned close to her, as if she were afraid that the very shadows might hear her, and had whispered into her ears the tally of the obscene ingredients of that charm. She had forbidden her aunt ever to speak to her again of that sinful cake.

Mattie did not know just how she happened to be at Madam Samantha's. She only remembered that she had not been as strong as Christ; she too had reached the point where she had cried out in agony, "My God, my God, why hast Thou forsaken me?" But, unlike her Elder Brother, she had not been able to continue, "Thy will be done." She would not let Aunt Mandy know that she had come here. Aunt Mandy would exult too much if she knew that Mattie had finally succumbed to her insistent plea that all means of redress were not confined to Mount Hebron's altar. Mattie wondered what Mrs. Brandon would have said, had she known. She would laugh, probably, and call her foolish.

As she waited in Madam Samantha's living-room, twirling the madam's card about in her hand, Mattie felt that surely one who promised so much ought to be able to do something for her. Madam Samantha's manifesto assured the identification of lost jewels, the revelation of the past, present, and future, and a happy adjustment in all affairs of the heart. As Mattie gazed about the drably furnished parlor she was relieved to find that the madam was a religious person. There was nothing here to frighten; none of the terrifying things of which she had heard and against which she had had to fortify herself before venturing into the madam's presence. There were no skulls about; nothing sinister. On the wall hung a large picture of the madam arrayed in an ample white robe, as if she were the mother superior of some religious order. There were many crosses and burning hearts and several religious prints, one of which represented the beginning of the world. God sat on a high white cloud, surveying His handiwork. He was a venerable white gentleman, but the two disembodied attendants who flew beside Him, smiling their joy at His new creation, were beautiful, curly-headed colored cherubs. Mattie felt infinitely more at ease after she had seen this picture.

When Madam Samantha entered the parlor a few moments later, Mattie was surprised and a bit disappointed to find her so simple. There was a faint kitchen odor about her, as if she had just been interrupted in the preparation of her evening meal. In the eyes of one who had not read her card and been forewarned, she might have passed as a mere housewife or cook. A plump, middle-aged brown woman, with an imperturbable face, there was no sign of magic upon her, nothing in her visage or manner that might identify her with those who behold with a more than human eye. She did not even wear her white robe.

She did not ask Mattie why she had come to her, but merely drew up a small rocking-chair and sat down, facing her client and rocking. For a moment she sat looking at Mattie as if not seeing her, as if looking beyond her and through her, with a vacuous stare on her placid, unchanging face. Her tranquillity agitated and frightened Mattie, who had been prepared for something more violent. She was not equipped to meet this ease and precision. Suddenly Madam Samantha leaned toward Mattie and took both her hands in her own; the mystic's hands were moist and had a greasy feel, as if she had just taken them out of dish-water. She closed her eyes and leaned back in her chair, still keeping Mattie's hands in hers. Mattie could see now that Madam Samantha's closed eyes were twitching, as if some dormant nerve had suddenly been galvanized into life, and she could feel an appreciable strengthening of the grip by which the two clammy hands entwined her own.

And now madam was speaking: "I see lights, and lights, and lights opening up before you." This dramatic commencement was indispensable to Madam Samantha. Those who came to consult her usually came in darkness, and lights were a good omen, a symbol in which her clients could read their eventual triumph over the evil forces which they usually felt were working against them.

"You are in trouble." With her eyes still closed Madam Samantha hazarded a guess which nine times out of ten brought a bewildered affirmation, and bits of involuntary information which might serve as further clues.

As Mattie inclined her head as a sign that she had divined correctly, the mystic opened her eyes and looked at her fully. What she saw in the drawn black face, almost lost in the surrounding black of her funereal attire must have confirmed her thought that Mattie was a respectable person, one for whom she would hazard a strayed husband as being more likely than a lax lover.

"I see a dark man," said Madam Samantha, and the fierce grip of Mattie's hand in her own confirmed her conjecture. "And a light woman," she continued, employing a rarely failing combination. Mattie's nails sank sharply into Madam Samantha's oily palms.

The mystery-probing eyes were fluttering again. Mattie watched them roll upwardly convulsively, until she could see only a ridge of white being flayed by a frenzied lid.

"All will be well in the end," said Madam Samantha at last. She had regained her composure and seemed to have triumphed in her struggle with the spirits. "The spirits tell me that you will overcome. I see lights and lights about you." She leaned forward and smiled as if the séance were over.

Mattie felt weak and unsatisfied. It was not encouragement that she wanted. She wanted something occult and powerful, some dark, ancestral way of overcoming.

"I want him back," she heard herself saying, sorrowfully. "I want to know some way of getting him back. I hoped you could tell me."

"I know a sure way, but it will cost you an extra dollar," admitted Madam Samantha, cautiously.

"That will be all right," said Mattie.

Madam Samantha arose and left the room for a moment. When she returned she carried a little bottle in which was a colorless liquid like water. "This water is holy," she explained, handing the phial to Mattie. "You must take something he has worn or had about him, something he has loved or cared a lot about. Sprinkle it with this water, then put it under your pillow and sleep on it. Do this for three nights' running and he will come back. I can't say how soon or how late, but he will come back."

It was a matter of rigid belief with Madam Samantha that every wanderer came back sooner or later.

That night Mattie pleaded a headache in order that she might get to her room early. She was glad when Aunt Mandy had finished fussing over her and had gone to her own room. The old lady was happy to get to bed herself; the strain of working again left her tired and spiritless.

Mattie fidgeted about, poking into drawers and into the corners of the bedroom closet, searching for something worthy of bearing the test of bringing Sam back to her. Madam Samantha had said it must be something he had cared a great deal about, something he had loved. She held up a soiled tie which she found in the closet. It was sleazy, and frayed at the ends. She cast it aside as unworthy. A torn handkerchief and a buttonless shirt fell into discard with the tie.

Suddenly as her hand groped about in one of the drawers she stopped transfixed, as if something had nailed it there. Something that he had loved and had had about him, Madam Samantha had said. There was nothing that he had loved at one time more than that on which her hand was resting. These things had been very dear to him. As if she were bringing to light an embalmed memory, she drew forth the handkerchief. The steel ridge of the closed razor smote her as she unloosed the knot by which she had shut her talismans in, while the cards rested there in a compact greasy pack. She laid them on the bed, never taking her eyes from them as she undressed. She found nothing strange in kneeling to pray before she carried out Madam Samantha's instructions. As she dropped the liquid on the cards, she agitated them in order that the fluid might spread impartially along the frayed edges, and in between. With a fierce, imploring finger she smeared the razor handle and the back of the blade with the liquid. The handkerchief had not been his; it could not aid in the charm. She folded it carefully and put it back in the drawer. She placed the razor and cards under her pillow, and climbed into bed.

CHAPTER
FIFTEEN

"Wake up, honey, and know that God do answer prayer!"

With Aunt Mandy's admonition in her ears, Mattie sat up with a start, rubbing her eyes to keep their sleep-weighted lids from falling back upon them. In the frosty twilight, outlined like a tiny harmless ghost, Aunt Mandy beamed down upon her niece, her small bright eyes snapping with excitement. Before her aunt could explain, Mattie knew. Sam had come back! And she had not slept three whole nights through on the cards and razor baptized with Madam Samantha's holy water! This would have been the third night. The charm was still underneath her pillow. And Sam had returned! As she jumped out of bed to grab up the scarlet kimona, thankful that she could welcome him back attired in this peace-offering, she wondered which had drawn him home, her prayers or Madam Samantha's charm. Now that she felt that no aid other than Heaven's was needed, she hoped that Jesus had done it all.

But it was not Sam who turned to meet her as she rushed past Aunt Mandy into the cold parlor. She stopped short with disappointment striving with fear on her face as she saw Emma May standing there, but a different Emma May from the one whom she had gone seeking with a hatchet clutched against her bosom. That woman had been lovely with a loveliness which Mattie had resented more than her insolence, and she had been gay and defiant, with her derisive eyes mocking Mattie's pain and discomfiture. She had been strong enough to win Sam back after the baby had been born dead. But the Emma May who stood there now had been stripped of that happy animation; the round predatory hands hung listlessly at her sides; the brown eyes, heavily penciled with the deep dark rings of sleeplessness, were filmed over with nothing more challenging than worry and fear.

Emma May did not give Mattie time to speak.

"Sam's sick," she said. "He needs you."

"Did he send you for me?" Mattie steadied herself against the door, knowing it did not matter whether he had sent or not. She was his wife; for that alone her place was at his side. And more than that, wild horses couldn't have kept her away now. But it would be sweet to know that in his time of need he had turned to her, that this other woman had not been all-sufficient.

"Yes, he sent me for you," said Emma May. She seemed totally oblivious of the circumstances under which they had had their previous encounter.

All Mattie's resentment of Emma May blew over and away like smoke.

"How long has he been sick?" she called from her room, where she was dressing feverishly.

"Four days," Emma May called back. "We had a fuss at the house one night after the show was over. He couldn't forget the baby. He was always talkin' about it. That's what we was fussin' about. He got mad and ran out. When he came back in the mornin' he didn't have his coat, and couldn't tell how he'd lost it, 'cause he was stinkin' drunk, and cold right to the bone. He was shaking like a leaf. I put him to bed, and he's been there burning like a furnace ever since."

"Did you have a doctor?" Mattie already had her hat and coat on. She felt almost comradely toward Emma May as she opened the door to let her by.

"He wouldn't let me get a doctor. Said all he needed to do was to stay in bed, and that it would pass. But I don't think it will pass; he's been hackin' and spittin' blood."

They were out in the street now, and walking rapidly, close to each other, almost as if their arms were intertwined. The early-morning air stung them fiercely; it was little past one o'clock and there were few people on the street. The winter had killed all the dazzling drones.

Emma May didn't have a whole apartment. She had rented a large room and a small alcove in a private house not far from the Star Palace. The alcove served her for kitchen, while the one large room made up the deficit.

For a moment Mattie could hardly make out anything in the room after Emma May had opened the door softly and let her in. Emma May had left one light burning in the hope that Sam would feel better, and not be so lonely if there were light about him; but to keep it from being a glaring and disturbing cheerfulness she had wrapped a dark-blue handkerchief around the bulb, so that the light that was sifted through was mellow and misty.

Sam was sleeping, but battling for his breath, almost as if he had to wrench it from his disobliging body. Mattie tiptoed up to the bed, and as she looked down at him she felt like crying out aloud. It was cruel that just four days of sickness should wreak such havoc with him. These four days had wasted him more than the bearing of her baby had done her. He had been lean, to be sure, but in a hard, straight way, like a nail or a column of ebony; but he was whittled down now to a soft pliant travesty that mocked the withdrawal of all his strength. He was no more than a caricature of himself as he lay there, his cheeks so sunken that she felt that they must be touching inside his mouth; and his lips, which had never been full, were now so slack and loose, and so fallen away from his teeth as to be grotesque.

She leaned down and touched him, but almost drew her hand back in fright as it burned beneath the scaly dry heat of his forehead. She was so close to him that she could see how the fever had routed away all the jet-black sleekness of his skin, leaving it dry and ashy. She wanted to weep. He opened his eyes and looked at her, and they were the only beauty about him which had not been violated. They were still brilliant and dynamic, the finest eyes she had ever seen. He looked at her for a moment as if she were a stranger. And then in his weakness and sleepy sickness he struck her by calling her "Emma May."

"It isn't Emma, Sam. It's Mattie." She corrected him gently and without reproof.

"How'd you know I was sick, Mattie?" His eyes fluttered up in painful surprise, and his low striving voice was devoid of any expectation. Mattie looked up quickly at Emma May, who was standing near by, still wearing her hat and coat as if she were lost in her own room, or a stranger who had just chanced in. Emma May threw out her hands in a half-weary, half-defiant gesture, and turned away.

So Sam had not sent for her at all; not even in his sickness had he felt a need of her. Emma May had simply come to her as a last resource, because Emma May was tired and worn out and of no use to him while he was sick. But even for this half a loaf Mattie was grateful, glad to be near him even in another woman's house, even at another woman's behest.

"Emma May came for me," she said, stroking his head.

"It was good of you to come, Mattie."

"It was my duty," she said, simply, but he knew it was more.

"Hadn't we better get you a doctor, Sam?" Mattie was anxious now, and filled with a deep fear of the time lost, during which he had been allowed to lie there undoctored, as if his malady would eat itself away and so cure him. She made as if to get up, but his pitifully wasted black hand reached out to deny her.

" 'Tain't no need to hurry now," he said. "How's A'nt Mandy?"

"Well, Sam, and missing you."

"Good old A'nt Mandy." He coughed his admiration out with a sudden spasm that frightened her.

Seated on a trunk near the window, Emma May seemed to have

forgotten them. Her eyes were closed, and her head was leaning against the wall as if she were too exhausted to move an inch farther. Mattie was sorry for her, and grateful, too, that she had stayed by Sam and had ministered to him so long. But the righteous flame that burned in her bosom, the flame which Sam himself had enkindled, would give her no peace.

"Don't you think I'd better send for Reverend Drummond, Sam?" She hoped he wouldn't be angry at the suggestion, but she had her duty to do. She had his soul to think of.

"What good can he do me, Mattie?" She could sense a soft irony in the low-pitched question.

"He could pray for you, Sam."

"Can't you do that, Mattie, if you think it will do any good?"

Kneeling down at the bed, she kept his hand in hers while she unbosomed herself to that God whom he had taught her to know, not knowing Him himself. She poured out in all the confidence and assurance of the simple the weight of her overburdened heart. Her voice overcame Emma May's strong snoring, and fell on Sam's ears like a far-away and pleasant music. He heard nothing of what she was saying, but her hand in his was like a sedative seeping through his skin. When she had finished and rose up, slipping her hand away, he stirred and looked at her sheepishly. "I'm afraid I went to sleep," he apologized.

"That doesn't matter, Sam. It's good if you can sleep." She drew a chair up softly beside the bed. "Try to sleep again, I'll sit here beside you and watch."

She sat there quietly for a while half frightened by the queerness of the situation in which she found herself ministering to her husband in another woman's home. Emma May had abandoned them entirely in the blessedness of repose. Sam lay with his eyes contrarily open now, watching Mattie with a strange childish happiness in his eyes. Suddenly he beckoned her to lean close to him, as if he wanted to tell her something secretly, something he had just thought of.

"Mattie, you're a grand woman," was what she heard as she

leaned over him, praise enough to set all the bells of heaven ringing for her, and to charge her eyes with tears. She could only pat his hand. The tribute had cost him a spasm of pain.

"I'd like to go home," he continued. Mattie's heart leaped at the thought that she would not have to sleep on her charm again. But she tried to persuade him to wait until morning. It was too late, she told him, to disturb himself now. She would sit there beside him until morning came; then she would take him home. But he became querulous and insistent, hacking and spitting blood, until she had to wake Emma May to tell her that she was taking him home, and to ask for his clothes. Emma May accepted the news with the lassitude of complete defeat, and even with an alacrity which Mattie thought unkind and disproportionate with Sam's worth. Emma May brought the clothes and laid them on the bed. Then, as if some sudden inner delicacy whispered to her, she stepped into the alcove that formed her kitchen, drawing the curtain after her and shutting herself off from Mattie and Sam.

Sam, his whole body in a tumult of fever, was pitifully weak, unable to stand alone, and Mattie had to dress him in bed. When she had finished dressing him she had to ask Emma May to help her get him downstairs. They found a taxi with an amiable young fellow glad of a fare and willing to aid her in getting him home.

"I'll send for his other clothes," said Mattie as she got into the taxi, and she wondered if she ought to ask Emma May to come to the house. But she thought better of it. If Emma May came she would not deny her, but she could not bring herself to invite Sam's woman to her home. She felt sad for Emma May going back to her empty room.

Aunt Mandy welcomed the wanderer back with a loud, raucous geniality that seemed strange coming from her elfin throat, and he tried to laugh back at her in the old happy way, but the pain throttled the laughter in him and made him clutch his side with a short, low whistle. Mattie undressed him and put him into their bed again, and neither knowing nor caring whether the results might be dangerous, she climbed in with him, to fall asleep with his scorching body locked in her arms.

Dr. Brandon said it was pneumonia the next morning, double, and with pleurisy. In a brisk professional tone he gave her instructions about binding Sam's side to keep the water from rising, and then he told her that there was little cause to hope for Sam's recovering. He could not put up a good fight; he had held nothing back in living, and there was no reserve now on which he could draw. Liquor had torn down every defense. Dr. Brandon said he was sorry for her, and if there was anything he and Mrs. Brandon could do, she had but to call on them.

When the doctor had gone, Sam wanted to know what he had said, and she told him that the doctor had ordered quiet and plenty of air, and had said that he would pull through. But her simulated gaiety could not deceive him, nor override the wisdom of those who are about to die. He looked at her quietly, and lay unstirring, lost in the few thoughts he could wrench away from the sharp, stabbing pains in his side. He asked her to lift his head a little; it hurt so much to breathe.

All day he lay silent and ebbing, coughing bright clots of blood into the handkerchief which Mattie held to his lips. Aunt Mandy, who had stayed home to help Mattie, brought him a bit of chicken broth which Mattie tried to feed him with a spoon, but it pained him to swallow.

He fell into a heavy doze with Mattie's hand cooling his parched forehead. When he awoke it was evening, dark in his room, and he could hear Mattie and Aunt Mandy talking in the room next to his. He lay still, shamming with the sly trickery of the sick who feel that things are being kept from them.

"He's going, Aunt Mandy. Dr. Brandon told me so."

There were several hard, rhythmic beats of a rocking-chair before he heard Aunt Mandy reply, "We all got to go some day."

"I know that, Aunt Mandy, but that don't make it any easier for me. I could stand it a little better if I knew how he was going. He's been out of church so long. But if there was some way of knowing that he was going to be saved, I could go on living and hope to meet him and my baby someday."

In the bedroom the sick man almost laughed aloud. As if there could be any meeting afterwards, any place, between them and that little black baby that hadn't lived an hour!

"Sometimes there is a way of knowing." Aunt Mandy's voice floated in to him like something veiled and insidious, something not of the earth.

"How do you mean, Aunt Mandy?" Sam felt as if he could see Mattie sitting out there, leaning closer to her aunt, her sleek black face shining with a desire to know.

"Sometimes God sends us visions. To the ones what's been good and believing, and what's served Him all their days, He sends a sign. When my mother died we knew for sure where she was going, because she cried out that there was lights shining all around her, and music, singing, and her own mother who'd been dead twenty years came and stood at the bed all dressed in white. But if you're going to be lost—"

"What then, Aunty?"

What then, indeed? What other fairy tale was that old woman out there going to tell Mattie? Sam braced himself to keep from moving. It was funny to be dying like this with these old darky superstitions ringing in his ears.

"If you're going to be lost, you still has visions, but of another kind. It gets dark and you can't see with your eyes wide open, and sometimes the devil himself comes for you like a big black bat or a snake." The old lady was enjoying herself. This was the proper talk for a death-room, and her rocker beat a sweet, complacent cadence as she went on. "There was a family at my home in the South, so bad that every one of them went to the devil, mother, father, and son. They still talk about the Higginses where I come from. They was always drinking and fighting and cussing, and they never darkened the door of the church. The mother died first, and with her last breath she told old man Higgins she would scratch his eyes out in hell. The son Ike died with his boots on. A man caught him with his wife, and ripped his stomach open. Old man Higgins let the county bury the boy and never even went to the funeral. But when *he* died, they say a little coal-black man with one eye in his head danced down from the attic with chains dangling behind him, singing, 'If you're ready, old Higgins, let's go.' And folks say that on the outside of the house his wife and his son Ike stood, three times their natural size, ready to show him the way to hell.''

The old lady paused for breath, and there was silence for a while to be broken finally by Mattie's querulous, anxious voice: "I'd like so much to know. I'd give my life to be sure he was saved. Maybe I'd better send for Reverend Drummond, anyhow."

Sam had a sudden panicky feeling. He didn't want Reverend Drummond. If he were going to die, he wanted to die in peace. Even now, on his dying pallet, he didn't believe any more than he had believed the night he looked through the slits of his fingers at Mattie at Mount Hebron Church, no more than he had believed the first night he had tricked God with his cards and razor. His way had been the best for him, and there was nothing the preacher could add or take away. He had enjoyed living and loving, and what was there to fear in dying? All his life he had played tricks, and when he had been caught the troubled preacher had not denounced him. That evangelist had been swell. Now one more trick was left him, the sweetest, kindest trick of all, to keep Mattie from too much weeping, and to ease her simple, believing soul. For Mattie would go on believing and going to church. She would never get the benefit of her beauty, never sow it wildly and reap a whirlwind of passion. She would never go off with another man as he had done with Emma May. With an infinite pity he thought of his cards and his razor, so rotten a base for such a good woman to build her life on. And she would go on and on believing in them, and he would be dead and buried and she would tell over and over how he had saved her, and never know that it had been a trick. But one more trick now while this steady tightening in his throat was still loose enough to let him speak, a sweet trick to set at ease the mind of this good woman who loved him, and who still in his dying had no thought except for what she called his soul.

The bed creaked as he turned, and before he could call her, Mattie was there at his side. It was so dark that he could only see her eyes and the polished arc of her teeth.

"I was sleeping," he said, "but the music woke me up."

"Music, Sam? What music? There hasn't been any music." Her credulity had not yet snapped at the deceptive hook he was dangling before her.

"Oh yes, there was music, the sweetest kind ever," he insisted. "And why have you got the lights on so soon? They seem brighter than ever; they almost hurt my eyes."

He heard her suck her breath in sharply, and he saw the dark outline of her hand rise and clutch her breast; she was caught, thoroughly ensnared. She turned from him and fled to the door, where she called for Aunt Mandy. The old lady came running.

"Tell Aunt Mandy, Sam, tell her what you told me." Mattie could scarcely get the words out; she leaned above him, breathless and staring, made more comely by her belief in this sign of redemption. Aunt Mandy stood mystified at the foot of the bed.

"Prop me up, Mattie; it's hard breathing." He thought of an old song he used to sing, "Turn me over on my left side, 'cause my right side hurts me so."

Then when her arm had eased him up on the pillow so that the demon in his throat seemed to subside a little, he told Aunt Mandy, "There was such sweet music, singing, and playing like I never heard before. And I asked Mattie to turn the light down a little. It's so bright it hurts my eyes."

He could feel Mattie's hand tremble on his forehead. Aunt Mandy stood transfixed and mute. He knew that for them he was forever saved.

• • •

During the night the demon clogged his windpipe completely. Mattie had slept on a couch in the front room at Dr. Brandon's suggestion. She found him cold, and suddenly handsome again. Remembering that he had heard music and seen lights, she did not weep loudly as she desired to do, but she sorrowed decently, with quiet tears. She would tell Reverend Drummond how he had died that he might know that he could truthfully preach him saved. She would invite Emma May to the funeral.

THE END

Essays
and
Speeches

THE DEVELOPMENT OF CREATIVE EXPRESSION[1]

Countee Cullen
Frederick Douglass Junior High School

ACCENT ON CREATION. Sometime over two years ago when the assignment was given me, it was decidedly not to my liking. It was hoped that the Junior High Schools could tap, or mine, or dig into the rich latent resources in the minds of the Junior High School pupil and which, like the princess in the fable, needed only the appropriate kiss to be galvanized into proper expression. Wouldn't I care to take on a class in creative writing and see what acres of diamonds I could discover, or failing that, what few nuggets of gold? Recognizing behind the soft purr that seemed to leave the choice entirely to me the deeper administrative rumble that told me everything had been decided anyhow, I let my silence be misinterpreted, and the class was mine.

There is this important distinction to be reckoned with in comparing a *club* devoted to creative writing and a *class* bound and laid on the same altar. The pupil chooses his club; his class is thrust upon him. The lamb that looked at me out of every imaginable hue of eye encased in every imaginable color of face (for

---

[1]From *High Points* 25 (September 1943), pp. 26–32.

ours is practically a one hundred percent Negro pupil load) had no idea of the slaughter to which they were being led. I had determined that the ultimate accent was to be on the writing of verse, but how was I to apply that knife where it would hurt the least?

Directness, I reflected, where it is not brutal, is laudable and, like the straight line, lets you know what's what at once. Would the direct approach be brutal in a case like this? Or would a not too reprehensible form of bribery (a weekly season ticket to the neighborhood movie, say, or something slightly monetary) be better! Directness won out, for bribes on no matter what intellectual level are uncricket, and they run into money.

"This class," I announced, "is going to write poetry." I did not say *Verse*, for why aim at all if not high? The groans, so akin to the final bleating of the reproachful lamb, the despair on those bright young faces, the sense of doom that filled the room, made me doubt the wisdom of the direct approach. The die, however, had been cast; the Rubicon might be boiling, but plunge I must. It was as if they had put their utmost trust in me only to meet the rankest sort of betrayal. From all over the room came sibilant expressions of disapproval. "I couldn't possibly write a poem." "I don't like poetry anyhow." "Will it have to rhyme?"

"Will it have to rhyme?" The despair in that question was like a straw that a man, swirled around in the Rubicon might well mistake for a good solid log. I hastened to explain that rhyme, though extremely ornamental and an indication of more than ordinary versatility, was not absolutely necessary to the writing of a good poem. This piece of news was met with nods of approval and a general lessening of tension. When I suggested that what one had to say, and the vigor, or beauty or imaginative qualities of the language went a long way toward making a poem, I won them over—halfway.

I BEGIN. I remember that I began, not by asking them to write a poem but to exercise their imagination. The world was in pretty much of a mess, wasn't it? Even they could see that. Suppose, I said, by some hook or crook each of us woke up one day to find in his hands a magic wand, a real one that he could use just as he pleased. How would he use it? Let each boy bring me in next time a composition entitled "If I Had a Magic Wand." They knew what I was talking about, and it was good to see the blood rush back to their blanched cheeks and the light flood their eyes again, and it was better still to see that some of them were jotting down ideas. What they would have done with those magic wands had they had them was enough to restore my lost faith in human nature! Mountains of ice cream, rivers of soda pop, toys without number (they were an 8B class, remember), all these had their place in the proper functioning of a wand, but they were only secondary to the good use those wands could be put to in serving the owners' families, and humanity in general. Imagination ran riot, and they were firmly launched on a career which was to include more than how to write a friendly letter and the several types of business communications.

I knew I could not teach them how to write a poem. No one could, to my way of thinking, but I hoped I could keep them from being frightened at the sight of a poem; I hoped I could help them like good poetry when they saw it or heard it, and if, in the process, I could discover some more than ordinary spark so much the better. I began by reading to them, chiefly lyrics, pointing out their simplicity and their singableness, and ended by confiding in the class that I felt they could do almost as well.

POINT OF DEPARTURE. *A Child's Garden of Verses* was my point of departure. They liked the straightforwardness of the verses, the easy apparentness of the rhymes, and the themes, almost all of which awoke an interest in themselves. So when I suggested as a topic that they choose some toy they were especially fond of, and identify themselves with it, writing verses in which the toy could speak for itself, they jumped at the idea. They turned themselves into wooden horses, toy submarines, choo-choo trains, tops, marbles, balls, etc. And strange to say every paper handed in, as most of the subsequent have been, was an attempt at rhyme. One boy felt that he could not write a real poem but that he could write about "Making a Poem." He wrote (with what labor and exactitude at rhyming can readily be seen) the following:

> A little boy was sitting at a table;
> He was trying to write a poem, if able.
> He sat there for a time,
> Trying to think of words to rhyme.
> He pushed away the paper in despair
> While the pencil was poised in mid-air,
> And great was his grief
> That his thoughts were so brief
> That flew before he could get them on paper.

MOTIVATION. I could not leave them to their own devices and say simply, "Write a poem." There had to be motivation and enough variety to keep the experiment from palling. It was a class experiment, not simply for a few selected and more than ordinarily interested pupils; and every boy had to be induced to take part. Mother's Day, arriving providentially at the moment, gave us a real reason for writing a poem. What boy would not like to write a poem in honor of his mother? We cast about for a title and decided, not without heated debate, that the simple *To Mother* would be as good as any. The first verse was the same for all the class; we worked it out together choosing a line suggested by this boy, another by that boy and word or structure changes from the rest of the class. For the second verse each pupil was on his own, and I have rarely spent a pleasanter or quieter period than when those boys were putting the finishing touches on their poems to their mothers. I went over the verses in time for them to be rewritten and to be presented to their mothers, without smudge or erasure, at the proper moment. At least one mother wrote me that she enjoyed her son's poem.

The same class was assigned me for three terms, from 8B

through 9B, and after the ice had been broken in 8B, it was practically impossible to get them to do anything in composition without having someone turn in a rhymed version. The progress they made toward becoming genuine poets at some time in their lives I concede to be little, indeed. After they left me, the one I considered my best bet and to whom on graduation I gave a medal for creative talent confessed that he had not written two lines after leaving school. *Sic transit.* However, I do feel that the class as a whole profited by the experiment, that they had fun, and that because they were doing something "special," they worked better as a group than they would have worked if they had been doing the same exercises every other class of their grade happened to be doing.

EXPERIENCES. I dwelt very little on the technical terms of verse. Iambic pentameter would have meant little or nothing to them even in 9B, but they grew of themselves critical of the senseless rhyme and of the unrhythmical line; and when a rhyme was original they did not fail to voice their approval. When they were in 9B and about to graduate, they did two things which pleased me and made me feel that the experiment was worth while. I was ill and out for two weeks during which time they wrote a booklet of verses, made a cover for it, and entitled it *Poems to Our Teacher, From 9B2.* To be sure, some of the verses complained that I was a hard taskmaster, that they were now having a happy respite from verse-writing, and that a prolonged vacation might not do me too much harm. But every one of them had bitten his pencil and written a poem. That was the point. One I especially enjoyed was more than mildly inquisitive. The writer called it *Recovery:*

> I hope you will soon get well,
> That you may answer the school bell;
> I pray thee do tell,
> If your nurse is a pretty damsel.

The second pleasurable thing they did was when they took their final test in composition. They were not my official class and took their test in their home room with their own teacher. I gave them their choice of writing a simple composition (a friendly letter, I believe) or of writing a poem entitled *Autumn*, adhering strictly to the rhyme scheme *aaab*. Their official teacher says she was astounded as she watched more than three quarters of the class fix their gazes on some far corner of the ceiling, wrinkle their brows, and set out to do a poem. The test period was only one hour, and part of that had to be given over to a test in spelling. Under such conditions I do not feel that the following poem about autumn by a 9B boy is to be lightly regarded:

> Leaves are falling to the ground;
> Grass is dying, turning brown;
> Snow will soon be falling 'round;
> It's autumn.
>
> Boys are hurrying off to school;
> Summer's gone; it's getting cool;
> No one's swimming in the pool;
> It's autumn.

I found the limerick and the parody especially helpful in getting the interest of the entire class. Both of these are happy forms, and a class does not mind working if it can laugh a bit as it does do. When we decided to do a parody, I thought it best to tie the work up with the current memory selection which happened to be Henley's *Invictus*. I suggested the title *Evictus*, explained it, and left them to their own devices. The results were good and of a variety: a tenant evicted from his home, a drunkard assisted with a pedal force from a barroom, a boy ejected in disgrace from his classroom, a king dethroned. One of the mildest-mannered boys of the group wrote the following denunciation of himself, relieved only by the sound advice of the last line:

Out of this place that covers me,
Dark as the future from day to day,
I curse whatever fate may be
For my reproachable way.

In the full clutch of circumstance,
I have wandered from place to place;
I have stolen when I got the chance,
And now I'm afraid to show my face.

Beyond this place of my dark years
Looms but the horror of my death;
But when my time to go appears,
I'll fight for life till my last breath.

I cannot stop, although I try;
I'll always be no good;
I'll be a tramp until I die;
But none of you should.

I'm glad to say that the poem as autobiography is purest imagination.

Another boy, early imbued with the socially significant, might have written his parody after reading *The Grapes of Wrath*. At any rate, he translated *"evictus"* into *Put Off the Land* and wrote the following:

Here where once grew the crops of all the land
Is nothing but a heaping hill of dust;
No other crop will grow on this barren strand;
There is nothing around but the earth's crust.

We are driven away from this dreary dust-bowl,
Where once grew the trusted grain;
This sand has neither heart nor soul,
It seems we never shall grow our cress again.

No one lives in this barren place
Where once were beautiful fields;
The winds and sand now run a race
Across the land that grew our meals.

Having known better poets who rhymed worse, I did not quarrel
with *fields* and *meals.*

NEW FIELDS. I am now at work and the same experiment with
another goup which I have had for a year. The mantle of their
predecessors seems to have descended on them with intensity. They
cram my pockets with verse at any time of the day, they have their
own pockets filled with them, and in addition they have, unasked,
turned their club periods into literary field days where original
murder mysteries, poems, radio skits, and plays without end make
them the pleasantest club periods I have ever experienced. One of
the boys seems genuinely gifted, so much so that the class refers
to him as "our poet."

One of the exercises I have found most to their liking we have
called *How Would a Poet Say This?* taking the premise that the
poet says what he has to say in not quite the usual way. Choosing
a group of words (trees, rain, spring, stars, wanderlust, winds, the
sea, snow, winter, night) we have tried not so much to write poems
about them as to show in one line what these words convey to us
pictorially. I do not think that the following examples show a lack
of imagination:

Spring rings the doorbell of the seasons . . .
Rain is the flowers' reservoir . . .
At night the stars make the skies a Broadway of the heavens
When it rains, it is just the angels crying with joy over the good
    things we have done (it doesn't rain much, does it?) . . .
Spring is here, and all the earth has turned Irish . . .
Night is a blue coat God wears every twenty-four hours
Snow is nature's salt . . .

The sea is a footless realm which only dead men tread . . .
Snow is the yarn with which the polar bear spins his coat . . .
Trees in winter remind me of unfurnished houses . . .
Winds are violent songs in motion . . .
Spring is an invitation to summer . . .
Snow is harmless, friendly bombs . . .

Each of the groups given me to work with has been a *one* group;
I do not think I would have had this to write had they not been.

"THE DARK TOWER" COLUMN FROM *OPPORTUNITY* MAGAZINE, APRIL 1928

We journeyed late last month for the first time to the far South, passing with some slight tremors of the heart through Virginia, the Carolinas, Georgia and a bit of Alabama to Talladega, a fair college brimming with eager young Negroes intent on drinking at the Pierian well despite the indifference of their native states. We had our Pullman reservation from New York, and so were not made to change at Washington, although in the wash room next morning a young Georgian returning home from West Point without benefit of sheepskin informed us casually and somewhat proudly that he didn't think we could get a reservation on our way back. We thanked him.

As our train whirled deeper and deeper into what we could not help considering the fastnesses of a benighted country, we felt that the hand of the rioter had dug its nails deep into the soil of this land leaving it red and raw with welts of oppression. We thought of the neat, orderly precision of the New England landscapes we had seen; we were far from these now, not so much in distance counted in miles as in distance of spirit and feeling; we were far from the genial, even if less carefully groomed, atmosphere of New York. We were in an untutored land among a proud folk who would not be taught. Strange incredible stories stirred to remembrance within us, and we shuddered at the sight of a charred bit of stick stretched like a slumbering snake along the road; we knew not of what insane rites it might have been part, what human torches it once might have served to light.

Save in the case of the Negroes, who are protected by their natural coloring, the brick-red Georgia and Alabama clay has a richer look than the faces of the people. The latter are inert, easy with life, listless with living, worn with the ardor of keeping others in their place. The Pullman porter, a man who had lived in Birmingham all his life, confided in us that there was "nothing good here but the climate." But if a man has a climate he loves, and a plot of ground he knows will answer to the caresses of the husbandman, why should that land, though it were a desert, not blossom like the rose? If only the South loved the Negro as he is capable of loving her—there is no end to what might be.

One finds emancipation in strange places, and in stranger forms. Our conductor was a bluff, hearty fellow, given to interspersing his remarks with quaint oaths from another world. While our berth was being made down, he invited us into the drawing room, which was unrented, for a smoke and a chat. We learned that he was a Southerner, a Georgian, a former showman, who knew and had toured with Dudley[1] in his heyday, and had helped manage the career of Sissieretta Jones.[2] He was reminiscent and garrulous. His talk glowed with admiration for the late Henry Lincoln Johnson.[3] "My mother," he said, "is a typical Georgia cracker, but if you

[1]Sherman H. "Mule" Dudley (1864–1940) was a comedian who organized the first black theater circuit which, during the twenties, controlled almost thirty black theaters.

[2]Sissieretta "Black Patti" Jones (1869–1933) was a noted soprano who was often, in her hey-day, compared to the Italian prima donna Adelina Patti.

[3]Henry Lincoln Johnson (1870–1925) was a black lawyer from Georgia. He served as Recorder of Deeds in Washington, D.C., from 1912 to 1916 and was the author of *The Negro Under Wilson*.

want to make her fight, just say something against Henry Lincoln Johnson." We were amazed at this manner of taking us to his bosom, but grateful for the tribute to one of ours.

At Talladega we felt the presence and cordiality of the President's wife and of the students as a grateful benison to a stranger in a far country. These young men and women were eager and wide awake; they were growing culturally; they were not allowing their horizon to be limited by a little man-made power; what could the white pool room straggler in their little town know of them, save what he failed to admit: that their presence in Talladega was its one claim to distinction. We slept well in Talladega, for the abiding things like the moon and the stars shine on all alike without fear or favor.

When leaving next morning, we had to ride a little way in the Jim Crow section, three hours before picking up our reservation in Atlanta. But what could the white man sitting in the coach in which we were not allowed know of the memories we had to keep us company? Three hours of enforced segregation pass all too soon when one can muse upon Tourgee Du Bose playing with infinite care and fondness his own composition *Intermezzo* that he sent us last year from Talladega to win one of the *Opportunity* prizes; when one can hear above the roar of the too intimate wheels the rich baritone of Frank Harrison singing "The Kashmiri Love Song"; when the eye of the mind can see, slender and lovely, the fingers of a slim brown girl as they ripple over black and white keys bringing sheer music out of such an inharmonious association. What could they know, those people to whom we were as pariahs, of all this? And yet we wished they might have known.

THE LEAGUE OF YOUTH ADDRESS

from The Crisis, *August 1923*
(Speech delivered at Town Hall, New York, under auspices of the
"League of Youth")

Youth the world over is undergoing a spiritual and an intellectual awakening, is looking with new eyes at old customs and institutions, and is finding for them interpretations which its parents passed over. Youth everywhere is mapping out a programme for itself, is banding together in groups whose members have a common interest. In some places these various youth movements, such as the German Youth Movement, are assuming proportions of such extent that they are being viewed with trepidation by those who desire to see things continue in the same rut, who do not wish the "old order to change, yielding place to new."

And so it is not to be wondered at that the young American Negro is having his Youth Movement also. We in America have not yet reached the stage where we can speak of an American Youth Movement, else I had not been asked to speak this afternoon. The American Negro's Youth Movement is less ostentatious than others, perhaps, but it is no less intense. And if there is any group which is both a problem for itself and a problem for others, and which needs a movement for the solving of both it is the American Negro. Details and specific instances of what I mean may be met with daily: segregation, discrimination, and just this past week the barring by an American board of a colored girl from entering The Art School at Fontainebleau, France, because her presence *might* be objectionable to certain people who would be along, this supposed objection being based not on character, but on color. Surely where such conditions obtain a movement is needed. I may say that the majority of people, even my own people, do not realize that we are having a Youth Movement at all. It is not crying itself from the house tops. It is a somewhat subsurface affair, like a number of small underground currents, each working its individual way along, yet all bound at length to come together.

In the first place, the young American Negro is going in strong for education: he realizes its potentialities for combating bigotry and blindness. Those colleges which cater exclusively to our own people are filled to capacity, while the number of Negro students enrolled in other colleges in the country is yearly increasing. Basically it may be that this increased respect for education is selfish in the case of each individual without any concern for the group effect, but that is neither here nor there, the main point to be considered is that it is working a powerful group effect.

Then the New Negro is changing somewhat in his attitude toward the Deity. I would not have you misconstrue this statement. I do not mean that he is becoming less reverent, but that he is becoming less dependent. There is a stereotype by which most of you measure all Negroes. You think of a healthy, hearty fellow, easily provoked to laughter, liking nothing better than to be slapped on the back, and to be called a "good fellow"—and to leave all to God. The young Negro of today, while he realizes that religious fervor is a good thing for any people, and while he realizes that it and the Negro are fairly inseparable, also realizes that where it exists in excess it breeds stagnation, and passive acquiescence, where a little active resistance would work better results. The finest of lines divides the phrase "Let God do it," from the phrase "Let George do it." And there are some things which neither George nor God can do. There is such a thing as working out one's own soul's salvation. And that is what the New Negro intends to do.

Finally, if I may consider myself to be fairly representative of the Young American Negro, he feels that the elder generations of both Caucasian and colored Americans have not come to the best mutual understanding. I mean both North and South. For the mis-understanding is not one of sections, but is one of degree. In the South it is more candid and vehement and aboveboard; in the North, where it does obtain, it is sly and crafty and cloaks itself in the guise of kindness and is therefore more cruel. We have not yet reached the stage where we realize that whether we side with Dar-win or with Bryan we all spring from a common progenitor.

There is a story of a little girl of four or five years of age who asked her father, "Daddy, where were you born?" "Why, I was born in San Francisco," said her father. "And where was Mother born?" "Why, in Chicago." "And I, where was I born?" "In New York." The little girl thought this over for a while, then said, "Fa-ther was born in San Francisco, Mother in Chicago, and baby in New York. Isn't it wonderful how we all got together?" Wouldn't it be wonderful if we could all get together? The Young Negro feels that understanding means meeting one another half way. This League has taken a splendid forward step. Will it go further?

In the words of a Negro poet, I bring you a challenge:[1]

How would you have us? As we are?
　Or sinking 'neath the load we bear?
Our eyes fixed forward on a star?
　Or gazing empty at despair?

Rising or falling? Men or things?
　With dragging pace or footsteps fleet?
Strong willing sinews in your wings?
　Or tightening chains about your feet?

---

[1] The poem quoted here is James Weldon Johnson's "To America," which appeared in his 1917 collection *Fifty Years and Other Poems*.

It is a challenge to be weighed mightily. For we must be one thing or the other, an asset or a liability, the sinew in your wing to help you soar, or the chain to bind you to earth. You cannot go forward unless you take us with you, you cannot push back unless you retrograde as much yourself. Mr. President, I hope this League will accept my challenge and will answer it in the new spirit which seems to be animating youth everywhere—the spirit of what is just and fair and honorable.

COUNTEE CULLEN TO HIS FRIENDS[1]

Paris, January 18, 1929

Dear Friends: You to whom I have owed letters so long; certainly it is an inspired editor who suggests a series of open correspondence to you as a means of retaining a friendship that has perhaps begun to wane under ill-treatment. Tactfully the editor adds that what I say may at scattered intervals interest you. . . . I am not psychologist enough to attempt an interpretation of the soul of Europe, nor physician enough to diagnose its maladies for comparison with American ailments; for it is only the scientific mind that is discriminating enough not to measure by its own temperament the mores of a foreign people. Europe with America for its yardstick may be disappointing, but Europe measured in its own terms is like an inspirational tonic. . . . Thinking back with no attempt at an orderly survey, this new life at first assumes the aspect of a kaleidoscopic view of cities: Le Havre, Paris, Marseilles, Algiers, Berlin, Vienna, Étaples, Geneva, and again Paris. The mem-

---

[1]From *The Crisis* 36 (April 1929), p. 119.

ory of each city is illumined by some incident or series of happenings, mostly personal, some trivial, but each a guarded souve-
nir. . . . Le Havre [is] unique because it marked the Seven League
Boot stride from continent to continent; a seaport town, rife with
sailors and scurrying, perspiring tourists, a town with which to pass
the time of day but not to engage in lengthy conversation; a town
to remember for an exhibition of Americanism overseas: the three
ladies were evidently of German extraction, for the two elderly ones
seemed to find it less of an effort to converse in that language than
in a broken English. The youngest, however, a woman about forty,
had been thoroughly Americanized and it pained her terribly to
use her ancestral tongue even when conversing with her mother.
Poor, excited lady; she had misplaced her baggage, or rather an
irresponsible porter had misplaced it for her; and the boat train
was about to leave for Paris. The lady knew no French; it never
occurred to her that perhaps her train companions might be able
to stumble through a sentence or two. Therefore she attempted to
make the train conductor understand English by bawling it into his
ear very loud and very fast. When this novel method of teaching
a foreign language in one lesson failed, she remarked with real
feeling and disgust, "Why I thought everybody over here spoke
two languages." The conductor surely spoke French and it is not
past belief that he may have been well versed in Chinese. But to
the Lords of the Earth two languages mean your own and English. . . . Then Paris en route to Algiers. It was July 13th; tomorrow Paris would celebrate her Independence Day and the Fall of
the Bastille. We must stay over for the parade. We had missed
it two years ago, and we hankered for a sight of the strapping
black French colonial who, we had been told, led the parade with
twirling baton, glistening face, and the gayest of martial strides.
But, alas, though in Paris, we fell asleep as New Yorkers; conse-
quently we arose at eleven to view a parade that had already
passed at nine. . . . Then off to Algiers by way of Marseilles
to rest there for a day or two in the hope of meeting

and exchanging a word with Claude McKay,[1] but he was too deep in the beauties of Seville to get to Marseilles before we sailed for Algiers. . . . Algiers, a deceptive hussy of a town, a sort of whited sepulchre, beautiful with its white, sun-kindled roofs glimpsed from the deck of a slowly incoming steamer, but squalid and sickly under closer inspection. . . . Berlin, an orderly, clean, regimented city, as if on dress parade; the Germans shaped for joviality but in the main serious-miened. Remembered incidents: Crab-soup at Kempinsky's; a chance encounter on the street with the Marcus Garveys;[2] a similar encounter with J. Francis Mores, a former luminary of the old Lafayette Stock Company.[3] He played Valentine when we saw our first opera; it was *Faust* and given by the Lafayette Players, and Abbie Mitchell was a heavenly voiced Marguerite.[4] Drinking coffee in a Berlin cafe and suddenly hearing the strains of "Nobody Knows the Trouble I've Seen" being softly wafted to us from a distant corner of the room; looking up gratefully to see the pianist watching us, his expression conveying the wish to make a stranger welcome with some remembrance from his own people. . . . Vienna, where we were shown about by a group of socialist friends who displayed with pride the city govern-

---

[1]Claude McKay (1889–1948) was an important Jamaican poet, novelist, and polemicist who was a major figure of the Harlem Renaissance, although he was abroad for most of the 1920s. His 1928 novel *Home to Harlem* was the first black bestseller.

[2]Marcus Garvey (1887–1940), Jamaican-born race leader who formed the Universal Negro Improvement Association or the UNIA movement, which was popularly called "Back-to-Africa." A very powerful mass leader with little skill at investing money or using tact, Garvey eventually was jailed and deported on mail fraud charges.

[3]The LaFayette Players Stock Company existed from 1914 to 1932. Since there were virtually no plays written by black writers at the time for black actors (and very few by white ones), this black theater company performed popular white dramas and musicals of the day. Because of mismanagement, the company folded, but between 1916 and 1923 it put on a new play every Monday.

[4]Abbie Mitchell (1884–1960) was an actress and singer. She was the wife of black composer and songwriter Will Marion Cook and appeared in several of his shows. She also sang opera.

ment's efforts to meet the housing needs of a highly impoverished people. Cooperative apartment houses that covered blocks and squares; simple, unpretentious dwellings of little beauty, but built for endurance and service. "We have no money," our friends explained, "for ornamentation. We must expend all for utility." We visited one of the apartments, a one-room, kitchenette and bathroom arrangement for which the occupant pays less than one dollar per week. Vienna and the Socialist watchword: *Freundschaft* . . . Étaples, a southern summer village in France noted for at least one luminous distinction as being the summer home of Henry Ossawa Tanner.[5] "And did you once see Shelley plain?" We have slept in Tanner's house, have watched him cut and mix salad at his table, seasoning it with the meticulousness of the conscientious artist; and we have witnessed in him one more instance that the coming of years and the accumulation of honors need not dull a man's human sympathies and his wit, nor make him unduly vexed at youngsters who stand in his studio and ask him witless questions about his easels and his oils. A drive with Tanner to Paris Plage and to Le Touquet of the famous Casino where evening regalia is required for permission to enter and stake your money on little red and black balls. But gaming tables are not for poor poets; a peep into the halls of chance must suffice. . . . Geneva and a happy week there as the guest of the Quaker Hostel, all arranged through Mabel Byrd, formerly of the Brooklyn and New York Y.W.C.A.'s . . . international gatherings where every conceivable race and country were represented; the air shot through with intense hopes and prophecies for world peace, the brotherhood of the races, the millennium. And always and everywhere a keen interest in the Negro, in many instances a livelier knowledge of what he is doing than is found in his own purlieus. . . . Geneva

---

[5]Henry Ossawa Tanner (1859–1937) was a black American painter who tremendously influenced the younger artists of the Renaissance. One of the earliest black expatriates, he studied under Thomas Eakins, but left for Paris in 1891, to return to America only once.

and a mountain drive on a brisk October morning; the summit reached, and fronting one in the distance the cold, austere majesty of Mount Blanc, a moment to remember as long as the mind can remember beauty. Leaving Geneva with a sort of welcoming farewell ringing in our ears, "Come back to Geneva and read your new poems to us when they are finished. . . ." Then Paris again, and well, Paris needs another letter.

COUNTEE CULLEN ON FRENCH COURTESY[1]

Paris, March 1, 1929

One may reasonably be expected after a six months' sojourn in a strange land to arrive at some definite opinion of the people. All the labels and tags should by this time be sifted and assorted. I recall that it has taken singularly less time for many visitors to America to arrive at the most definite and erroneous conclusions about us, and that many white excursionists on a rapid and casual visit to Negro quarters have satisfactorily, to their thinking, pigeon-holed the entire race, with astonishing celerity, if with dubious acuteness. After all, the tendency to generalize is so innately human that it should be pardoned. Moreover, the truth of any matter is an elusive and many colored thing. Therefore, it is with little faith in my own observations that after my half year's stay among them, walking their streets, talking to them when I could do so without seeming offensively inquisitive, that I find myself thinking of the French as a people of consummate politeness, of a most enlightened tolerance, and of a sad impecunity.

The manners of the French are amazing, and must occasion

---

[1]From *The Crisis* 36 (June 1929), p. 193.

foreigners, especially the younger element of Americans and the
suddenly and vulgarly well-to-do, many moments of acute embarrassment. For it has never seemed to me that politeness has played
a large part in American living. It is true that Southerners, both
black and white, lay strenuous and oft repeated claims to an ex-
clusive lien on hospitality. But that is another matter. A politeness
of the French variety cannot conceivably exist in a section of the
country where one group despises the other and merely grudgingly
tolerates its continued existence. The American pace in general is
too swift to allow the display of social solicitudes that one thinks of
in connection with politeness *à la française.* It is a brand that
cannot thrive on hurry. There, probably, is the reason it has
reached so genteel a growth among the French. Though Negroes
are mythically accredited with the world's most comprehensive understanding of the importance of leisure, I doubt that even we can
even slightly approach the Gallic appreciation of that blissful state.
It seems that, for the French, tomorrow is a far more important
time than either yesterday or today; for tomorrow may be done all
that he put off doing yesterday, all that he will probably delay
doing today. He is very like the schoolboy dallying with the lessons
that he knows must eventually be learned, but only at the last
moment.

"Sir" and "Madam" and "Ma'am" have long since disappeared
from current American speech, unless there be parts of the country
where they are held over as interesting relics of ante-bellum days.
Nowadays one answers questions crisply with a short, curt, hurried
"yes" or "no"; trappings are obsolete; it is not even required that
children be hampered with them in their relations with their parents or with their teachers. Perhaps such expressions would have
a false ring in a democratic country. I recall an incident that occurred not so long ago in New York when, in a mood of singular
amiability and humility, I answered "yes, ma'am" to a question
put to me by a lady. It was so much wasted abasement, for the
lady informed me that in these enlightened times no one said
"ma'am" any more, nor "sir."

Now that I think of it, a possible explanation occurs to me. At the time, the lady, though far on the shady side of life, was still a maiden, technically speaking. Since then she has managed to edge into the marital state and may have changed her mind about those obsolete expressions. After all, "Madam," in her case, was truly inappropriate, and may have smacked of a smirking levity on my part. But in France, it is the mark of the stranger, of the crude man from across the waters, not to employ these ancient impediments of politeness. An excellent thesis, I am sure, one that would warm the hearts of the sovereign board of any of our American universities would be: "How Many Times Per Day Are 'Monsieur,' 'Madame,' and 'Mademoiselle,' Used in French Conversation and What Is the General Effect of Such Extravagance on the Morale of American Visitors?"

What purchaser in an American store has not at some time in his experience had that guiltiest of feelings induced in him by the surliness of a storekeeper suddenly called from his newspaper, his lunch, or a choice bit of gossip, that he, the buyer, was actually being favored far and away above his natural deserts in being allowed to make a purchase at that particular moment? But whatever your purchase in a French store, be it a bit of bread that you must carry through the streets with no more hygienic covering than your naked hand, a bottle of wine, or an automobile, your visit to the Frenchman's shop has all the earmarks of a social call. On entering, you are at once most solicitously bid good day; if it is your second visit to that particular store, your health is a subject of vital importance to the proprietor; and because your wife has not accompanied you this morning (having been with you yesterday) he is breathless in his anxiety lest any fatality may have occurred to her during the night. And when you depart with your badly tied package of little things falling every way but right, your total expenditure having amounted to about twenty-four cents in American currency, it is the sheerest ill breeding for you not only not to wish the proprietor good day, but to hope that you will see him again.

To one accustomed to the manners of passengers riding the Interborough Rapid Transit Lines, the politeness encountered on the Paris subway, or Metropolitan, seems incredible. One does not kick, scratch, shunt, jostle, or tickle the person in front of him out of his path as he nears the station where he desires to exit. But gently, suavely, softly, he begins in time to ask those in front of him if it is their intention to descend at the next station. If such is not the case, they squeeze aside into themselves and allow him to pass, until by a gradual process of elimination, the polite passenger finds himself at the door when the train glides into the station. Of course, this form of social consideration could not as easily be employed in the subways of New York, as the natural temperament of the people would be against it.

In some quarters I have heard French politeness explained away as having a commercial basis. I doubt seriously that this is so, that any commercial consideration could so change and modify an entire people. It seems to me something innate, a natural inherent streak, something fine and delicate, left over perhaps, as a French lady told me, from the days when France had kings and a court through whose vices shone the virtue of impeccable manners. The lady, who is an arch royalist even now, decries what seem to me the most magnificent manners I have ever encountered. To her these are nothing, compared with the manners of those days that are gone forever (for even she has no hopes for the return of a royalist regime). Not having smelled the flower in its dewy days, I can only say that if it be a bit wilted now, it still exhales a rare and charming savor.

COUNTEE CULLEN IN ENGLAND[1]

London, May 18, 1929

All the year I had said, with a boundless faith in Browning, "I shall go to England in April. Surely then the lilacs will be out in Kew; the lark will be soaring; and the thrush will be singing each song twice over." But I had forgotten that London is not all England. April in London was like late September, quite unlike the glorious sun-dappled weather we had left behind in Paris; even now in mid May it is only the intrepid soul who has doffed his top coat in London. And like the weather was the district into which I first moved, the London boarding house environ where all the houses are alike, advertising bed and breakfast at two pounds and a half per week, with no mention of the numerous pennies that must be placed in the little gas slot if one wishes to keep from freezing; dull and sober places, each like the eye of some Argus[2]

---

[1]From *The Crisis* 36 (August 1929), pp. 270, 283.

[2]Argus is the figure in Greek mythology who is described as having a hundred eyes in his head or all over his body. He was slain by Hermes and his eyes were transferred to the tail of the peacock.

of stone reflecting back the frigid gaze of its brother across the way. I began to pine for the rich warmth of Paris, and the budding trees of the Parc Montsouris which I could see every morning from my window and whose leaves I could hear each night sighing and soughing in the wind. . . . Then like salvation out of the sky came a friend with an invitation to come to Surrey and spend a few days seeing the English country side. . . . Those were crowded days, because they had to be few, as the friend was leaving soon to teach in some mountain fastness in Switzerland. Then I saw how blue an English sky can be those rare moments when the grayness has been routed from them, how unbelievably green the grass can be, how golden the crocuses, as if touched and gilded by a Midas' hand. I saw enmeshed in a bit of wiring for one agitated and fear-freighted moment a blackbird, and I had time to note the opulent yellow of its beak before it extricated itself and zithered away. I laughed at the puffy, squire-like breast the robin flaunts; I heard the strange, shrill cry that is made by the chiff-chaff who is the harbinger of spring. I heard the thrush exemplify his reputed wisdom by singing his lay over not twice but many times. And there was a gay, good-humored lark who trilled us a sermon one morning on our way to the little country church that dated back to the thirteenth century; we could not see the songster because he was up in the very face of the sun and our earthy sight could not brazen out that brilliance, but we knew the singer was there by the drops of music which sprayed us like a silver cascade falling from the skies on to the thirsty earth. In three days I think I learned why Englishmen are so proud of their little island in the sea and why the songs of their poets are so vainglorious. I carried a lighter heart back to London town thanks to my friend who rescued me at a crucial moment. He is finding a new sort of loveliness in Switzerland, but none more radiant than that of his own Surrey. . . . Then back to London and out of Russell Square to lodgings on Edgware Road, a noisy boisterous thoroughfare whose one redemptive feature is the legend that once Francis Thompson used to haunt its purlieus, Thompson[2] whose music was as mighty and as intense as Milton's, if less ambitious. As I walk the streets of Edgware Road, it is pleasant to think that here, perhaps on this spot where I place my foot with such unconcern, was probably composed a line or more of "The Hound of Heaven." Poor Thompson, what an ostensible derelict he was, and yet how favored and radiant a spirit, for surely he communed with splendors with whom more respectable people had not even a bowing acquaintance. At the end of Edgware Road stands the famous Marble Arch through whose portals no vehicle is allowed to pass except the king's. And directly in back of the arch is Hyde Park, where I have passed many a jolly evening listening to the political and religious harangues for which this spot is famous. Here the different sects of Christianity, side by side, Catholic and Protestants in their various guises, sell Christ like merchandise across a counter, each trying to outbid his competitor. And here and there scattered throughout the crowd are the buzzing flies in the ointment, pointing out with much raillery and good humor the defects of the various systems. It reminds me of a slave on a block, but this slave has a running side and his hands and feet are mutilated with the rough caress of nails. . . . Then London began to be hospitable to me and I began to meet people, and to learn how charming the English can be, and how effortless that charm can appear. . . . I am still astounded at the assiduity and disinterestedness with which the Quakers, especially Winifred Cramp and John Fletcher, have endeavored to find me readings and hospitality in other English towns, Bristol and Oxford and Sydenham; I shall never cease to marvel at the intense pleasure which Winifred Holtby,[3] an English novelist, took in helping me to place a few poems with English journals and in aiding me

---

[2]Francis Thompson (1859–1907) was a minor British religious poet whose most famous poem is "The Hound of Heaven" (1893).

[3]Winifred Holtby (1898–1935) was an English novelist and essayist who wrote a study of Virginia Woolf and had a considerable interest in the indigenous peoples of Africa.

to get a reading or two, aware as she was of the usual sad state of the bardic purse. . . . One or two personalities stand out in mellow relief for happy remembering: Humbert Wolfe,[4] a gifted poet who is also sane enough to be in the government employ, having me in for tea one afternoon at the Ministry of Labor (for the heavens may fall and the earth be buried thereunder, but the drinking of afternoon tea in England, I ween, will stand forever. It is a custom as ritualistic as going to bed and rising, and far more regular; tea is served in theaters and movie houses during the intermission nearest four o'clock and in every English household); John Galsworthy,[5] veteran wielder of the pen, waving the wand of welcome over us at a dinner of the P.E.N. Club; May Sinclair[6] sitting on one side of us, answering in monosyllables and crisp sentences our timid endeavors to draw her into talk; Henrietta Leslie[7] on the other side of us, gay and delightfully garrulous, treating us to wine in spite of our remonstrances, and pointing out the celebrities. . . . Then etched in our memory more than any of these is the little lady in the gray coat who was waiting in the anteroom at Friends House the same day I was there. We had both come to see John Fletcher. Her interview was first, but it had hardly begun before John Fletcher came out and said, "I want you to come in and meet Ethelreda Lewis."[8] And this frail, mild-mannered lady who I had thought surely was the head of some Ladies' Aid Society had given

---

[4]Humbert Wolfe (1885–1940) was a British poet, lampoonist, playwright, and Deputy Secretary of the Ministry of Labor.

[5]John Galsworthy (1867–1933) was a Nobel Prize-winning English novelist, dramatist, and poet.

[6]May Sinclair (1865–1946) was a British novelist, ardent feminist, and biographer of the Brontë sisters.

[7]Henrietta Leslie (G. H. R. Schütze) was born in 1881 and died in 1946. She was a British novelist and playwright.

[8]Ethelreda Lewis (189?–1946) was a South African novelist who teamed up with an old English adventurer and African trader named Alfred Aloysius "Trader" Horn to produce a book of exploits called *Trader Horn*, which became an international bestseller.

us *Trader Horn* with all its wild and fierce adventurings. "It amuses me," she said, "when they accuse me of being the sole author of *Trader Horn;* for I was forced to give up my schooling when I was thirteen, whereas Aloysius Horn had a splendid education extending through his eighteenth year." I feel sure that the saints on earth today are few and form a most eclectic society; but I am equally sure that Ethelreda Lewis belongs in that number. I have not been able to analyze the reason; I do not care to analyze it; all I know is that she gives one a feeling which is out of and beyond the flesh. I was as conscious of that aura about her as I was aware of the shining circle of white hair coiled about her head, as I was aware of her unconsciousness of her own spirituality. Not a political person at heart, she has come to London from Johannesburg, South Africa (and may go to America) in an endeavor to raise funds for the South African native, funds with which to provide him with the decent recreation of which she says he stands so sadly in need. The state of the South African native seems not far removed from that of the American Negro slave when slavery was at its zenith. I hope Ethelreda Lewis may go to America and carry back for her South African project a considerable sum from American Negroes who, remembering their own not far distant lot, should be imbued with a sympathetic spirit for those in whose behalf Mrs. Lewis contends.

COUNTEE CULLEN ON MISCEGENATION[1]

Paris, April 1, 1929

Madame Claire Goll[2] is slight, blond, and pretty; born of French parents and educated in Germany, she can write her books in either language and translate them herself for publication in the other. She speaks English with a prepositional inaccuracy that is at once charming and amusing, and to me, as I listen to her across the tea table, an index of what similar grammatical mésalliances I must be guilty of in my attempts at French. There can be no doubt that Madame is largely and sincerely interested in the Negro. On her wall hangs a magnificent African mask; on her bookshelf shines in the luster of a new and recent edition her German translations of two of René Maran's[3] books; and Madame admits with a bit of

---

[1] From *The Crisis* 36 (November 1929), p. 373.

[2] Claire Liliane Goll (1891–1977) was the German and French author of a number of novels and collections of poetry.

[3] René Maran (1887–1960)—born in Martinique, Maran became famous for his novel, *Batouala*, which won the Prix Goncourt, the highest literary award for a young writer in France. Maran became good friends with several of the leading Harlem Renaissance writers and *Batouala* (1922) was widely admired in black American literary circles.

real chagrin that for some time she has been compiling an anthology of verse by Negro poets, only to find her work in vain through the recent publication in Vienna of Dr. Anna Nussbaum's anthology, *Afrika Singt*.[4]

Madame's interest in the Negro has further attestation in that her latest novel *Le Nègre Jupiter Enlève Europa* (The Negro Jupiter Ravishes Europa) is a story of miscegenation. The mythical allusion does seem to me altogether well-chosen, for Europa was a young and beautiful maiden whom Jupiter, who never allowed the vast and exacting duties of godhead to interfere with his amatory holidays, bore off and seduced after having first transformed himself into a bull in order that Juno might not recognize her dallying and recreant spouse. But Jupiter was the king of all the gods, more of an autocrat than the former czars of all the Russias, and an *enlèvement* by him was a neat and finished job. On the other hand, irrespective of the inroad that black men in various capacities are making into European life, swallowed up as they are among the white population, they are no more to be feared than a handful of sand added to the millions of grains that make the Sahara, no more than a cup of water thrown into the sea.

The story concerns the meeting, at a reception given at the Swedish Embassy in Paris, of Alma Valery and Jupiter Djibouti— Alma, a lovely blond woman of French and Swedish parentage and of small mental equipment, Jupiter, an African Negro, an executive in the cabinet of the Minister of Foreign Colonies, and in his own land a prince of the blood. They are married, and rapidly the story goes forward to what the formula, even in a foreign country, seems to require of such a novel: the husband's embarrassment and the wife's chagrin at the stares and the remarks, as often overt as sotto voce, that attend their presence together at social affairs and in the

---

[4]Dr. Anna Nussbaum was a German socialist scholar who, according to Countee Cullen's father, the Reverend Frederick Cullen, "was a friend and great admirer of my son, Countee Cullen." The full title of Nussbaum's book is *Afrika Singt: Ein Auslese der Afro-Amerikanischen Lyrik* (1928).

streets; a growing jealousy on the part of Jupiter and an increasing antipathy on Alma's part, dire portents of an end which even the arrival of a baby does not curtail, the infidelity of Alma and her subsequent murder by Jupiter. I have no personal brief for inter-marriage, but I do await eagerly the advent of that pioneer who will in the face of . . . it is true, not millions, but surely several . . . successful interracial marriages forget his formula and write one such story in which the ending will be happy and probable. It is my belief that such marriages when they prove unhappy, have color no more than others as the cause of their disintegration. Traced sedulously to their final causes we should probably find in most cases vanity, cockiness, touchiness, satiety and a hundred and one other abstractions of the human ego that play havoc, un-less firmly taken in hand, with any two people, irrespective of their color; although it is easier, in cases where color differences do appear, to cast all the blame in that direction. Though it is evident that Madame Goll is sympathetic with the Negro, it is equally evi-dent that she has allowed herself to become too readily receptive of some outworn shibboleths. Jupiter, contrary to the depiction of Negroes by many authors, is the soul of cleanliness; in fact he seems rather on the verge of scrubbing his health away. But to offset this, because he is a Negro, he is gifted with olfactory powers that border on the ridiculous. Also there is more imagination, I opine, than accuracy in Jupiter's acute desire to be lighter com-plexioned, a desire so intense in his childhood that having heard that if one stayed in the rain long enough this miracle would be accomplished, he sallied forth and stood naked and shivering for hours in a storm, with the result that he barely escaped death by pneumonia, and finally rose from a sick bed cleaner but no paler. He was even tormented with the idea that in heaven there might be some black angels instead of a fulfillment of the Christian prom-ise that all should be as white as snow. Jupiter would doubtless have changed the wording of that enticement to read not "though your sins be as scarlet," but "though your skins be as pitch" . . . "they shall be white as snow." Fantastic reasoning is stretched to its uttermost in this assertion: "stuffed snails angered him, for he had an instinctive disgust for all things spirally shaped. Perhaps he might have, on reflecting, found the cause of this repulsion: it was because of his hair, of which each one formed one of those accursed spirals." Yet as I drank Madame's tea and talked with her I could forgive her this gigantic heaving of Pelion on Ossa; for when Madame speaks of the Negro's artistic endeavors today, she is well nigh irresistible if one does not hold himself in check against the enormity of her enthusiasm.

Madame is of the opinion that little of artistic merit is now being produced in America except that which is being done by Negroes; the American short story writers and novelists have run out of material; the American poets are monotonous and repetitious; but the Negro alone has life and action and material unplumbed out of which the new literature is to come. In vain I mention some names: Frost and Robinson and Millay; Anderson and Cather and O'Neill; timidly I venture the opinion that these are names before whom it is just to bow the knee, and that their ore does not seem to have run out. Madame makes me feel that I am recreant, disloyal, a literary heretic, a blind man stumbling along in the light of the new day. Just archly enough not to offend me, yet accusingly, she turns to one of my poems, and indicts me for my love of Keats, for concerning myself with names like Endymion and Lancelot and Jupiter. It is on the tip of my tongue to ask why Keats himself should have concerned himself with themes like Endymion and Hyperion, but I am drinking Madame's tea. . . . Later, out in the cool Parisian air, I ponder where all this will lead us. Must we, willy-nilly, be forced into writing of nothing but the old atavistic urges, the more savage and none too beautiful aspects of our lives? May we not chant a hymn to the Sun God if we will, create a bit of phantasy in which not a spiritual or a blues appears, write a tract defending Christianity though its practitioners aid us so little in our argument; in short do, write, create, what we will, our only concern being that we do it well and with all the power in us? Ah, Madame, I have drunk your tea and read your book and thought you a charming hostess, but I have not been converted.

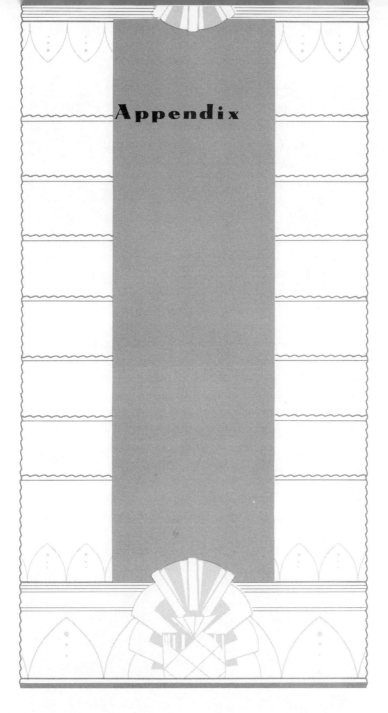

Appendix

The Prologue and Epilogue for The Medea,
which Cullen called "Byword for Evil."

CHARACTERS
(In order of appearance)

JASON
Prince of Iolcus

MEDEA
Princess of Colchis

ABSYRTUS
Medea's Brother

NURSE

TUTOR

THE TWO SONS OF JASON AND MEDEA

CREON
King of Corinth

FIRST MESSENGER

AEGEUS
King of Athens

PANDION
Prince of Athens

SECOND MESSENGER

CHORUS

PROLOGUE

TIME: *A summer evening*

PLACE: *Colchis; a garden near the King's Palace. As the curtain rises,* JASON, *a young man in his middle twenties, is seen walking back and forth in the garden. From time to time he halts at the left and looks into the distance. He appears nervous and impatient. Suddenly he opens his arms wide, and* MEDEA, *a young woman near the same age as Jason, runs breathless to his embrace.*

MEDEA: Jason!

JASON: Medea! You are late tonight. I had begun to fear.

MEDEA: To fear what, Jason?

JASON: That you would not come.

MEDEA: Have I failed you yet? Should I lead you two thirds of the way, then leave you abandoned in the end?

JASON: Forgive me, Medea, but until I hold the Golden Fleece in my hands, until I lay it, glittering and malevolent, at my uncle's feet, and thereby regain the throne he usurped at my father's death, I have no peace, no quiet, no faith, no trust!

MEDEA: No faith, no trust, in me, Jason?

JASON: *(Fiercely)* Help me get the Fleece, Medea!

MEDEA: You shall have it, Jason. The Fleece and your throne, too. I swear it!

JASON: Medea!

(He embraces her)

MEDEA: But it was difficult tonight, Jason. I do not know if my father suspects me of aiding you or not, but I have found his eyes of late less filled with affection than with questions he dreaded to shape into words. Tonight, after the evening meal, he ordered me to my rooms under the strict care of my nurse, and forbade me to leave. A guard was placed outside my brother's door. Only with tears and gifts could I persuade my nurse to let me through at last.

(There is a patter of feet, and Medea's brother, ABSYRTUS, a lad of ten or twelve, runs in)

ABSYRTUS: *(Jumping and laughing)* And what do you think I did, Jason? I made a ladder of the coverings of my bed, and climbed down the wall. Wasn't that a trick to play on the guard, Jason? He'll lose his head you know, if my father finds out.

JASON: He must not lose his head, Absyrtus, for if he does, I fear I shall lose mine, too.

MEDEA: Go back to your post now, brother, and keep good watch. Warn us with the usual signal at the first sign of danger. This is the last time, Absyrtus. Watch well!

ABSYRTUS: *(To Jason)* And after that shall I have my gift, Jason?

JASON: Just as it was promised, Absyrtus.

ABSYRTUS: Oh, how sharply I shall watch, Jason. I shall watch like father's old dragon guarding the Fleece.

(Exit ABSYRTUS*)*

MEDEA: All now depends on me, Jason, and on your faith in me. With my aid you yoked the fiery bulls and sowed the dragon's teeth as my father bade you. But this last test is the most hazardous and cruel, and without my help certain death to any man. Not even my father can go near the dragon that guards the Fleece, for fire from the beast's nostrils burns the ground in a huge circle all around him. I only can approach him, and with songs and incantations taught me by my mother subdue him to the meekness of a lamb. There is no sword can pierce his scaly hide; only cunning may avail against him. Jason, will you trust me with your life?

JASON: Have you not held it in your hand since first I came here and looked at you standing at your father's side with your wide and cloudy eyes? But without the Fleece my life is nothing to me. I trust you then with what, until I hold the Fleece, is but a useless thing.

MEDEA: Then listen well, Jason, for if the wheels of this plot grind not until the end that we have planned, death is the only reward for you and your men, and though I am my father's daughter and heretofore most beloved by him, I may not hope to outlive you. Tomorrow I will mix a sweetmeat for the dragon, a cake made of milk and wild honey, flavored with certain herbs my mother taught me of. This will he take from my hands and no other, and eat. Then for the space of one full day sleep will overcome his mighty coils, and freeze the fire in his throat. At the appointed time, Jason, go forward without fear, and take the Fleece.

JASON: *(In awe and admiration)* Medea, what a woman you are, from whose fragile hands a dragon will take its food! What sons you will beget!

MEDEA: *(Looking at her hands)* My hands are not fragile as other women's hands, Jason. They are terrible and tenacious, they are swift and strong, and sometimes they frighten me. Nor am I, in all my being, as other women are, Jason. I have the wisdom of serpents, but if trodden on, their venom too.

JASON: *(Shuddering a little)* Venom? Not you, my love, but if you have, my love will never give you cause to use it.

MEDEA: Remember, Jason, return not to the palace with the Fleece, for my father would know you had not won it fairly, and he would murder you and all your men before he would let you depart with his treasure. Make straight for your ship at once; see that your men have everything in order for sailing, and I will join you there. And, Jason, the boy goes with us, too.

JASON: *(Protestingly)* Absyrtus? Must we deprive your father of him also? To steal his daughter and his treasure is one thing, but why should I take his son and heir? What possible excuse could I have for that? Let the boy remain as a prop for his old age, and a double comfort for his loss of you. I have eaten your father's bread, Medea, and called him friend.

MEDEA: Bread eaten is but bread, Jason, and friend is but a name. I cannot leave my brother behind. He is the second dearest mortal on earth to me now, and long he was the first. My mother commended him to my care as she died. He goes with us, Jason.

JASON: He goes with us then, Medea.

MEDEA: And my nurse, too?

JASON: There are nurses in Greece, Medea, but if it pleases you, let her go, too. *(Then tenderly)* But my Queen will not lack servants of her own in her new country.

MEDEA: Shall I, in truth then, be a Queen? Long ago that was prophesied but never until now did I credit it. Once when a child, still small enough to cling to her hand, as my mother led me through the town, a beggar woman whined at us for alms. And for the penny my mother gave her, she read a glittering fortune in my palm. "The little girl shall sail across the water and be a Queen in a great country," she said. But even as she smiled and predicted me a crown, her eyes went wide with fear, and shuddering she mumbled a frightened thanks and fled from us. Why do you think she shuddered, Jason, if I am really to be a Queen?

JASON: *(Laughing)* No doubt the night was cold, and so she shuddered.

MEDEA: But no, Jason, it was such a night as this, all hot and starry.

JASON: *(Laughing more)* Then it was the heat that made her shudder, or else the envy inherent in humanity, as she stood there in her rags, clutching your mother's penny, reading that you should be a Queen. For so you shall be, and doubly crowned, Queen of my country and Queen of my heart.

MEDEA: Wine is in your words, Jason, and your tongue is a hive of honey, but weigh well your promises, here on this giddy brink where we stand poised together, and speak me not so fair, nor promise me so rashly, if you mean not what you say.

JASON: *(Protesting)* Medea!

MEDEA: *(Her fingers across his mouth)* Please, oh please, before you answer me, Jason, let me speak what's in my heart. Then answer me fairly. I love you, Jason. Mark with what little effort those burning words are spoken. Are the maids of Greece so frank, or would they deem such an avowal forward and unmaidenly? But we are not overcultured here in Colchis, nor constrained to any niceties of passion or language. I have heard it said that in your country they speak of us as savages and barbarians. So be it; our manners are what they are, our country being what it is. So when I say I love you, it is a truth as simple as saying I eat when hungry or sleep when weary. I love you, Jason, and shall love you till I die. I will change my fierce manners for your gentler ones, my barbaric country and people for the culture of Greece, if you wish me to. Only, if you love me not truly and deeply, tell me now, Jason. I still will love you, will still quiet the dragon that you may seize my father's Fleece, and still will aid you to escape, alone.

JASON: What? Go alone, and leave you to your father's vengeance, Medea?

MEDEA: That was not the answer my heart cried out for, Jason. Love me not for the aid I bring you, nor for the risk I run, but for myself, if at all.

JASON: And so I do, Medea. My answer was but a soldier's whose first thought was for your safety. I can only echo your own words, Medea: "I love you, Medea, and shall love you till I die."

(JASON *embraces her. Suddenly there is a short sharp whistle. The lovers step apart, and stand waiting anxiously.* ABSYRTUS *enters)*

MEDEA: What is it, Absyrtus? Is there some danger?

ABSYRTUS: There is a man walking at the far end of the garden, sister. His head is bent low and his hands are locked behind his back. I think it is our father.

MEDEA: I know what worries torment his mind, Jason. He cannot conceive how you have yoked his fiery bulls and escaped the wrath of the iron men after you planted the dragon's teeth. But even now he is certain that you cannot seize the Fleece from his dragon. Let us part now, beloved. He must not see us together, lest he suspect how his daughter betrays him.

JASON: *(Holding her hand)* Call it by some kinder name, Medea.

MEDEA: No, call it the ugly thing it is, which will but prove the more how much I love you. Treasure up the counsel I have given you, Jason, that nothing may go amiss tomorrow. When next I see you, it will be on your ship where I shall surrender myself your happy and eternal prisoner.

ABSYRTUS: Shall I go, too, to Jason's ship, Medea?

MEDEA: Yes, and on it, Absyrtus. But not a word of this to our father.

(She catches hold of him)

You promise, Absyrtus?

ABSYRTUS: *(Squirming and looking at Jason)* Shall I really, Jason, go on your ship? Shall I sail a little way on it, Jason, just a little way, shall I really?

(JASON *nods)*

MEDEA: Promise, Absyrtus, promise me now, no word of this to father.

ABSYRTUS: Of course, I promise. I am no babbler, sister.

(He turns to JASON)

And now, Jason, have I stood guard well these three nights?

JASON: *(Saluting him)* You have watched like a soldier, Absyrtus.

ABSYRTUS: And shall I have my new sword that you promised me? One such as the Greeks use?

JASON: That you shall, tomorrow when Medea brings you to my ship. I myself will fasten it to your thigh, and you shall show me how a very captain of captains walks before his men. But mind you, do not let it trip you up.

ABSYRTUS: I shall walk like you, Jason.

MEDEA: *(Laughing)* Why will you walk like Jason?

ABSYRTUS: *(Strutting)* Because I want to be a great man like Jason. I want to sail the seas and fight dragons, so and so

(He whirls an imaginary sword)

and . . .

(He hesitates)

JASON: Yes, and what else, Absyrtus?

ABSYRTUS: *(Slyly)* And run away with the beautiful daughters of kings.

(THEY ALL *laugh; the* BOY *joins their hands together, and gently pushes them, still laughing, ahead of him. He follows twirling the sword he will receive tomorrow, and killing dragons at every stroke)*

CURTAIN

EPILOGUE

TIME: *Twenty years later*

PLACE: *Athens, the king's palace. As the curtain rises, the stage is bare of persons.* MEDEA *leading* AEGEUS, *now blind and white-headed, enters. The aged King leans a little on her arm. This is a new Medea, entirely different from the fierce creature we have known hitherto. Time has subdued her to a calm, majestic matron whose mien and manner proclaim the Queen. She wears a flowing robe of white. She leads the King to his seat, arranges his robes about him, then stands back to watch him with an air of approval and affection.*

MEDEA: There! So! For the last time, husband. Tomorrow a new king sits in your stead.

AEGEUS: And happily a better one than I. Our son! Too long has a blind king striven to deal justice to the people.

MEDEA: They have not complained, my lord. There is none in Athens but speaks in your praise, and in all the free cities of Greece no King who does not hold you as his pattern.

AEGEUS: *(Laughing)* Sweet words and pleasant, Madam, but 'tis less the tongue of the people that utters them than the flattery of a devoted wife.

MEDEA: When was I wont to flatter, my lord, or to praise without just cause?

AEGEUS: In truth, never, and I did but jest to tease you! But come, sit beside me, here where your place has ever been these many years. For the last time let us sit quietly upon our thrones together. If good be spoken of me in this kingdom, what but better can be urged of you? We have ruled together since first you became my Queen, and whether for good, let the people say. I know only this, my dear, that without you to counsel me, this darkness that is mine by day and night. . . .

MEDEA: *(Interrupting him quickly)* Was it not agreed long ago, my husband, that what the gods in their inscrutable wisdom have done is better borne in silent resignation?

AEGEUS: *(Sighing deeply)* It was so agreed, my Queen, and I did mention my blindness not in complaint of the gods, but more in praise of you. For let us not deceive ourselves: a blind king is no credit to a throne, nor to a people, and had you not been wisdom itself and all devotion, my rule had ended with my sight! You have been the eyes I lost, and though not to see is a doom scarce less horrible than not to breathe, I have been more fortunate than most, and may never weary of thanking you who are my second sight. But you would dwell on happier things, and indeed I would, too. Come sit beside me, and let us plan, with that same joy the lowliest couple in our kingdom would use, the future of our son.

(MEDEA *sits beside him*)

Tomorrow he sits where you and I now sit. His will be the king's justice, and I have no fear of the righteousness with which he will dispense it.

MEDEA: *(Proudly)* I think you need not fear. There is none but hold him an excellent prince, and what more than that could foretell an excellent king?

AEGEUS: To be well thought of by the people is a good sign indeed. And then, too, his name . . . there's much in a name . . . Pandion, that was my father's name. In truth there never was a better king, and long after he died I was known more as Pandion's son than as Aegeus. Thus did the people seek to impress upon me the sanctity of the mantle I wore, so stainless had my father left it. And now another Pandion shall follow him.

MEDEA: You love him overmuch, my lord.

AEGEUS: And have I no just defense for that? How else should I love him, this son of my latter years, I who feared to go without issue to my grave? How else should I love him, but overmuch? Believe me, Medea, and take no common jealous offense in this avowal, for in loving him I do but love another part of you, but in all my kingdom there is nothing dearer to me than my son. As you have humored me before, I pray you do so again, and tell me what is he like?

MEDEA: Surely you would not have me repeat . . .

AEGEUS: Yes, that I would! Again and yet again! I am his father! Could ever his virtues weary me? His intellect first! Does it not glow as warm as Venus on her couch?

MEDEA: As I have said a thousand times, Aegeus, he does not fall below the intelligence expected of a prince.

AEGEUS: The praise you shower on your son, Madam, is tepid, but no cause for alarm. Now his virtues?

MEDEA: He is generous, and loves truth as he may never love a woman, and quick to feel another's wounds.

AEGEUS: He'll make a king! His vices, Medea?

583

MEDEA: A trifle too disposed to . . .

AEGEUS: What, would you, his mother, admit flaws in our son? Would you catalogue his defects to me, his father? I'll not own him less than perfection's self. His face and form?

MEDEA: Comely.

AEGEUS: Which may be said of any Athenian youth. But what distinguishes *my* son?

MEDEA: *(Slowly, looking into the distance and away from the King)* He carries himself *(She hesitates)* as you did when you were young. No man, though a stranger, who saw him but would say, "There goes a King's son!"

AEGEUS: My bearing when I was young; 'tis little, yet 'tis something. I am afraid you have made him too much your own, Medea. I dote so much upon him that I would hear you say, "Aegeus, he has your face, your hands, your hair, your eyes . . ."

MEDEA: *(Shuddering and turning from him)* No, not your eyes, my lord, not your eyes!

AEGEUS: Forgive me; no, not my eyes. I could not wish my son doomed to these burnt out pits of night.

(Enter a MESSENGER *who bows and stands waiting)*

Who stands before us, Medea?

MEDEA: The Prince's messenger, my lord.

AEGEUS: We give you leave to speak.

MESSENGER: The Prince would know if his parents are disposed to speak with him.

AEGEUS: Assure the Prince of our love and most eager disposition to have him at our side.

(Exit the MESSENGER, *enter the* PRINCE. *The* PRINCE *is straight and comely and about twenty years old)*

Pandion! My son!

PANDION: Father!

(The PRINCE *approaches and kneels before his father, who places his hands upon the Prince's head. The* PRINCE *rises and kisses* MEDEA *on the cheek)*

Mother!

AEGEUS: Touch your ears, Pandion, and tell me if they do not scorch your fingers.

PANDION: What do you mean, father?

AEGEUS: Your mother has been painting your picture for me.

PANDION: *(Bowing to Medea)* I must ask then, sire, that you make allowances for the artist, and if she spread her bright colors too lavishly, remember she is my mother.

MEDEA: *(Protesting lightly)* But Aegeus, who was it who would admit no flaws in his son? Was it I?

AEGEUS: *(Laughing)* The truth is, Pandion, that we both do love you.

PANDION: For which, father and you, dear mother, my own love and thanks are a most feeble and inadequate return. Yet it is relying on that love, father, that I have come to seek a favor.

AEGEUS: Is it so urgent a request, my son, that you must make it today, or do you come simply to give me the joy of granting you some last desire? Yet, were I in your place, I think I should not beg today what I might command as King tomorrow.

PANDION: Tomorrow will be too late, father. Tomorrow I am to become King to please you, for though I have not said so before, the thought brings no pleasure to me. For fear of wounding you I have kept buried my unwillingness to reign, but truly I would not be King, not now nor ever. Father, if you love, tell me I need not be King!

MEDEA: But you are a King's son!

AEGEUS: If I love you, Pandion? Your request is barbed like an arrow. Since when have you doubted my affection?

PANDION: Forgive me, father; not *if* you love me, but *as* you love me, tell me I need not be King!

MEDEA: Who will reign then, Pandion, if you do not?

PANDION: Why father, as he has always done, as long as I can remember, with you there beside him. He is strong and active yet, and the people love him. Why should he give up his throne to me?

AEGEUS: Because I am old, Pandion, and blind, and the people should have a young king with clear, bright eyes, such as your mother says yours are.

PANDION: Then choose one from the Princes of the city, one who aches to wear a crown and wield a sceptre, as I do not.

MEDEA: Pandion, you distress your father!

AEGEUS: No, let the boy speak his mind, Medea. It will give him ease. What would you do, Pandion, since you would not be King?

PANDION: *(Passionately)* I would sail the waters of the world, father.

(MEDEA *puts her hand to her breast and listens in fascination and distress)*

My kingdom should be a ship, and sailors my people. The sky should be the rood of my palace and stars my tapers to read by. I would buy and sell, barter, and learn the ways and languages of strange people.

MEDEA: Pandion! What folly! What mad talk is this?

PANDION: Mother, I have but said what was in my heart from the day that I was born. Can that be madness?

AEGEUS: *(Gently)* And I understand, Pandion, believe me, I do. My son, if I were still your father, but not the King, I should say "Amen" to all you've said, bid you go and bless you as you went. But I *am* the King, Pandion, and you are my son. The sons of kings are not born to sail the waters of the world, but to sit on thrones and, though weary themselves, unfalteringly dispense justice to the peoples committed to their care. You should have chosen a lowlier father, Pandion, but having chosen me will you repudiate the kingly calling of our house? My father whose name you bear was King, and left a name like a legend. I have striven, even in my blindness, to be worthy of that name and reputation, and hoped to see both bettered by you. Few are the fortunate kings who have had sons to whom they were willing to cede their thrones before death lifted them from their seats. Your mother and I are weary, and we had hoped to pass our final days in some quiet corner of this kingdom, confident that we had entrusted our throne and our people to competent and loving hands. Will you still go wandering, Pandion?

PANDION: *(Greatly moved)* Have I your leave to withdraw, father?

MEDEA: *(As if to restrain him)* Pandion!

AEGEUS: Yes, my son, but where will you go?

PANDION: *(Gently)* I go to the shore to watch the waters and the ships for a while, Father. After tomorrow I do not know when I shall find time to watch them again. Kings are such busy men.

(Exit PANDION*)*

AEGEUS: *(Proudly)* My noble boy! I might have known he would not fail me in the end. The blood would not let him.

MEDEA: *(Startled)* The blood, my lord?

AEGEUS: My father's blood and mine. They are voices singing in his veins, and in the end he could not but heed. He will be a worthy king.

MEDEA: He will be restless, Aegeus.

AEGEUS: Time will wear away his restlessness. Time and a woman.

MEDEA: A woman?

AEGEUS: *(Fondly, reaching for her hand)* Yes, even as I have had my Medea to light up my shadowy days, so Pandion must have his Queen to steady him. We must comb the cities of Greece for a wife worthy of our son. We will send envoys into Sparta and Ithaca, into Corinth and all the free cities of Greece.

MEDEA: *(She snatches her hand away fiercely)* Not Corinth, Aegeus, not into Corinth. Would you mingle my blood with blood of that false city? Never will I consent to that. Have you forgotten what that city means to me? What a flood of bitter memory the very name lets loose in me!

AEGEUS: That was thoughtless of me, Medea. The old wound rankles still, I see. I thought it healed. Then we will send no envoys into Corinth, although they say the maids of that city are passing fair.

MEDEA: *(Hotly)* The wound was healed, my lord. Would you open it again?

AEGEUS: Be calm, my Queen, no Corinthian maid shall wed our son.

(Enter the Prince's MESSENGER*)*

But we are not alone.

MEDEA: 'Tis Pandion's messenger. Speak.

MESSENGER: The Prince bade me say that at the palace edge where the sea begins he found an old sailor washed in from a wreck. Nothing remains of his ship but the broad beam to which he clung with gashed and bleeding head.

(MEDEA *shows a dawning suspicion)*

Further the Prince bade me say he wishes a carpet spread in the palace that he may place the old man on it, that aid may be administered him, or at least that his last moments may be less painful.

AEGEUS: Let the Prince's wish be law! Let the carpet be spread then! Let it be spread here!

MEDEA: *(Clutching his arm)* No, Aegeus, my lord, I beg you not here, not in the palace! Not for such a man! Let him be taken to some peasant cottage near by. Why should some strange dying sailor be brought here?

AEGEUS: *(Firmly)* Let the carpet be spread here, in this room! Medea, Pandion has foregone one longing dear to his heart and his peace of mind; shall so simple a request as this be denied him? Does this not augur well for his reign that on the eve of mounting the throne he should show concern for the unfortunate?

MEDEA: Aegeus, hear me; I know not why, but my heart and the unfailing voices of my woman's mind cry out against this sailor. Do not bring him here, Aegeus!

AEGEUS: I will not deny my son again!

MEDEA: *(Rising, coldly)* Give me leave to withdraw, my lord!

AEGEUS: *(Restraining her by the hand)*   No, my Queen. Be not angry with me, nor let us end our happy reign like sparrows disputing over a crumb. I will not give you leave to desert me in this cloudy mood, and I beg you go not without it. Be as you were ever wont to be with me, and though I may not see them, let me sense in your voice the accustomed smiles upon your face.

(MEDEA *sits reluctantly. As she does so,* PANDION *enters supporting
an old sailor with bandaged head. Weak and worn as he is,
we still may recognize* JASON. MEDEA *starts and turns her
head away)*

PANDION: *(Leading* JASON *to the carpet and gently easing him
down)* There! Is that better?

JASON: Much, gracious Prince, thanks to you, better than I ever
hoped to be again.

AEGEUS: I cannot see the face of him who speaks, Pandion, but
his voice is known to me. The sound of it brings back my youth
across the years and the days when the sun was not yet a memory.

JASON: *(Rising weakly on one elbow)* Old friend Aegeus, is it really
you?

AEGEUS: Yes, Jason, it is I, but if your friend or not lies with you
to say.

JASON: *(Gasping)* Can dying men bargain with the living, Aegeus?
How does the wounded dog come but on his belly, and what
does he want but a corner to lie in and lick his wounds? How
does the sailor sucked in by the sea, then spewed forth again,
come but as driftwood for burning?

AEGEUS: Be welcome, Jason, for old times' sake, be welcome,
and speak not of dogs and driftwood in the house of a friend.
Be welcome of us all, of my Queen and me, and of our son.

JASON: I am already beholden to your son for the little life that's left me, and never feared for less than this noble welcome from you. Yet the parting of this breath would be easier if in your gracious lady's voice I found an echo of yours. Nay, start not, Medea, nor hide your face from me. Behold how fallen I am! See how the years have humbled me! Read how little we are in the hands of the gods, how foolish to resist them. I have not sought you out nor come to harm you. Do you remember your dark prophecy of long ago? Even as you said, I die a victim of the ship I loved. But I would not die hated in the sight of one who in time did hold me dear. Why was I wrecked upon this shore if not to die at peace with you? The ill will I harbored in my heart for you the years have blown away. Your son has rescued me that I might die as a Prince should die, surrounded by his friends. Your husband, the noblest King in Greece, still bids me call him friend. *(He stretches his hand toward her)* Medea, be at peace with me!

MEDEA: *(Coldly)* My husband and my son have spoken in word and deed, and who am I to gainsay the will of him who is King of Athens today and of him who will be Athens' King tomorrow? What is a woman ever but an echo of her men? Be welcome, Jason.

JASON: For that I shall be easier in my dying.

PANDION: But we will not let the great Jason die! Live to tell me of the Argo and of the great warriors who sailed in it with you. What medicine and care can do will not be spared. You will live, Jason.

AEGEUS: Our son speaks for us all, Jason. We will not let you die.

JASON: *(Weakly)* No, this is the end for which I came into the world. This is the little moment no man may escape. *(He begins to cough and gag)* Wine, Prince, a sip of wine to rout the sour taste of death that floods my mouth even now! Wine! Wine!

(PANDION *claps his hands and a servant brings him a beaker of wine. As the* PRINCE *starts toward Jason with the wine,* MEDEA *rises from her seat as if to speak; she grips the end of her chair as the* PRINCE *slips an arm under Jason and sets the beaker to his lips)*

(Drinking)

Let the thanks of a dying man sweeten your days, my young lord. Aegeus, the gods have been good to you. No Grecian King has so comely a son. And I have a gift for you, sweet Prince, one worthy of your kindness to me. Take it, and remember Jason!

(He suddenly snatches a dagger from his belt and stabs PANDION)

PANDION: *(Shrilly)* Father! Father!

(The PRINCE *falls back dead;* MEDEA *screams and rushes to him)*

AEGEUS: *(Holding his hands blindly before him)* Pandion, speak to me; oh, Pandion, my son, speak to me!

JASON: *(Fiercely)* Call on him in vain as I once called on sons of mine! But never will he speak again! Never will he answer you again! Now I can die happy, Medea. How well you schooled me! How long I waited! How long I planned! Thanks be to the gods who wait on human misery, who give me vengeance even as they give me death! Son for son, Medea, hope for hope, life for life! And still you triumph in having but one son for me to kill! Why had he no twin, Aegeus, that I might have strangled him with my other hand!

(JASON *sinks back exhausted on the carpet)*

AEGEUS: *(Sobbing)* My son, Pandion, Prince of Athens, my son, my son!

(MEDEA, *dry-eyed, rises from beside her son. She advances slowly toward* JASON *who triumphantly picks up his bloody dagger and extends it toward her)*

MEDEA: *(Shaking her head)* No, Jason, that weapon is not for me; for I've a keener blade than that laid by for you. My son is dead, and you are avenged on me, Jason, but hear at what a price! Never, since the world stood, were there two as accursed as we. *(She points to the dead Prince)* Pluck back the fallen lids from his eyes, Jason, and gaze into your own. Reach out and take his lifeless hand, then tell me if 'tis not your own hand that you hold. Is it the dew of death or the colder sweat of horror that breaks upon your brow, Jason, for fear of what more I have to say? Then let your heart break, too, as you look at what you were when I first knew you. Look at your son!

AEGEUS: No, Medea, no! Are you mad, Medea?

MEDEA: *(To the King)* Be still, my lord, and hear your kingdom crash!

(She turns to Jason)

Blinder, Jason, blinder far than this poor blind king whose very life you've taken without touching him. For there lies his life, Jason, but it was your life, too, yours even more than his. Think how I loved you, Jason! Think how I strove to keep you! Remember how bitter my hate was only because it was a hate still love. Could I have left you ever without some consoling memory of you to hide with me? Could I have promised *him* a son had I not felt your seed stirring to life within me? When since time began have women conceived alone? Could I have done the blackest deed woman yet lifted her hand to without the hope of this boy to brace me? Could I, Jason?

JASON: *(Aghast, and in agony)* You lie, Medea! Pity, Medea, have pity and say you lie!

MEDEA: May my tongue rot, but . . . look at him, and believe your eyes. See if every nerve and fiber in his body, dead though he is, does not cry out "Father" to you.

(JASON crawls to the Prince, touches his face, looks into his eyes)

JASON: *(Aware of the truth)* My son, my son! How shall I face you when I overtake you on the black road you travel? Have pity on me and reproach me not, for I will not let you travel it alone.

(He stabs himself and dies)

MEDEA: *(To Aegeus)* The Prince is dead, my lord.

(Then quietly)

And his father.

AEGEUS: *(As in a dream)* And his father?

MEDEA: *(As to a child)* Yes, my lord, and his father. Jason, too, is dead.

(The KING does not answer, but stands silent and rigid as stone)

Speak! Cry out! Curse me! Rail at me, then! Do you think you are hurt more than I because he was not your son? But he *was* mine, my flesh, my blood, all that I held as hostage against the scorching memory of the past. Pandion! Pandion!

AEGEUS: Softly, Medea; though kingdoms fall and men die, a man must think still. A man must put two things together and make a third; though the earth rock like a drunkard and stagger him, still a man must think. Then the Prince was not my son. That were enough to kill me, Medea, but there is more. There is a thought which like a worm feeds on my brain. It spreads like fire, Medea, nor can all remembrances of past devotion dampen it! Yea, though I urge all your subsequent kindness as a barrier, I cannot stop this blaze! I came of a line of men who were clearsighted, Medea, until the day they died. Why was I stricken blind? Why only me of all my house?

(He muses)

I never yet have looked at Pandion's face. Before the boy was born this darkness came. I said it was from the gods; I said the gods were punishing me for too dearly coveting what their wisdom had denied me, for trying with magic to beget a son. But there was no magic wrought, and the boy was no son of mine, but Jason's from the first. Why am I blind, then, Medea?

(His voice rises to a shout)

Woman, why am I blind?

MEDEA: *(Unmoved)* Why should I lie to you now, Aegeus? Here with my dead before me, to lie would be kinder, but I am too weary now for kindness. Listen, my lord. There is a certain herb which, brewed and drunk, forever draws a veil across the sun. This when I knew the child's time near, I gave you to drink.

(Simply)

Therefore you are blind.

AEGEUS: *(In horror)* There was a viper frozen in the cold and a foolish king who warmed it at his breast.

MEDEA: I knew too well if you but looked upon the child, he should be known for what he was, the very breath and life of Jason. How could it have been otherwise? Then you too should have driven me forth from Athens, with stones, as a strumpet is driven.

AEGEUS: It needs not the casting of stones to proclaim the strumpet.

MEDEA: I have had my share of names, Aegeus, and will have through all the years to come. Yet though I become a byword for evil in worlds not yet conceived, believe me in this . . . by your lost love for Pandion, believe it! . . . in these two things only have I wronged you: in that Pandion was not your son, for this was beyond my power to do, and in that I blinded you to keep this unhappy secret from your heart. In all else, with gratitude to prompt me, I have placed your happiness before my own. I *have* been the eyes you lost, as you yourself so justly said, and had the gods but willed, Pandion were still your son.

AEGEUS: In these two things only! It is as though you said, "I have murdered you, but you shall have a decent burial." For twenty years I walked in darkness, and regretted not that the light of my eyes was dimmed, because there was another light that glowed in its stead. I had a son! Now I have neither sight nor son!

(Bitterly)

In these two things only have you wronged me!

(He reaches for her, but falls to the ground)

Oh, to be so helpless and a king!

MEDEA: Tax not your strength, my lord. Call up your men! Their swords are long and sharp. And I am weary.

AEGEUS: *(Crying out)* No, no, let no man touch her but me!

(He fumbles and crawls, striving after her)

With my own hands would I wipe out this outrage. If only my hands might reach you!

MEDEA: Will that give you peace then, old man? I had thought to go a cleaner way. These latter years the sight of blood has grown strange to me, and the need for it. There had been such peace since the boy was born—until now—yet—will the spilling of more blood bind up your broken heart, light up the darksome caverns of your eyes, or make Pandion more truly yours? Then I will do a good deed while there is still time.

(She crosses swiftly to where JASON lies, picks up the dagger at his side, and returns to AEGEUS)

Here is a dagger bright with the blood of a son and a father. It will not shrink from a mother's. And here is a wound once healed festering anew in a bosom more bruised than all the world's. The King's justice, Aegeus! By the King's hand! Strike hard!

(She taunts him)

As if you had eyes, strike deep!

(She leans down and places the dagger in AEGEUS'S hand, then

bares her bosom to him. The KING *totters to his feet and stands wavering before her. He raises the dagger, then suddenly wheels and plunges it in his own breast)*

AEGEUS: *(As he dies)* She was your mother, Pandion! For that I could not kill her!

MEDEA: *(Bending over him)* Even in your dying courteous, but with a courtesy misplaced and unavailing. You have not spared me, my lord, only delivered me into my own relentless hands. I think yours would have dealt gentler with me.

(She places a covering over the King, then walks slowly toward her throne and sits there. Suddenly her eyes light up, she leans forward speaking as if addressing some form in front of her)

You gods of mockery and laughter, who shaped my heart and destiny, when will you shape another as miserable? Have you not done with me yet? Was it for this you made me a Queen? What deaths and destructions still, what mightier bolts of doom do you think to fashion me? Have you not glutted your fill on what the human heart can bear, and still beat on? Evil gods, what could you engender but evil men? But neither god nor man shall conquer Medea!

(She draws a small vial from her bosom)

A drop only, and this fierce heart beats no more! Here in so small a space is peace beyond the gods to take away.

(She drinks and as she does so, the CHORUS *enters and quietly surrounds her, drawing nearer and nearer as she continues to speak)*

It is fire for a moment, but the ashes will be cold.

(She tosses her head and writhes)

Nay, it does not hurt. By Apollo, could fire hurt *me?*

(She moans in spite of herself; she becomes aware of the CHORUS)

What grisly attendants are these sent to light my way to hell? I'll
not go with you. I need you not! I'll go alone. Is that my little
brother there? How could those limbs, severed and strewn across
the ocean floor, be knit together again? Come, you daughters of
Peleas! Would you have your father young again? Wood, fire,
and a cauldron then!

(She starts up and points at a figure)

No, Princess of Corinth, Royal Harlot though you are, none shall
have sons by Jason except Medea!

(And now she screams and closes her eyes)

No, no, that sight alone I cannot bear; those two murdered infants
there with blood across their throats and cries for mercy strangled on their lips! Your father killed you, I tell you! Jason killed
you! I swear he did! I never touched you! I was your mother!

*(And now as the poison glazes her eyes and stiffens her limbs, she
becomes the Medea we saw at first, the young Medea Jason first
knew. She laughs and seems to thrust back gently an imaginary
form bending over her)*

Nay, Jason, plead no more. Why should my Jason plead? Because
I love you, I will do this thing for you. You shall have my father's
Golden Fleece, Jason, never fear. There, love.

EPILOGUE FOR *THE MEDEA*

(She caresses an imaginary Jason, *unmindful of the dead* Jason
not far from her)

You shall have the Golden Fleece, Jason.

(She smiles and her head sinks on her bosom)

THE CHORUS: *(Intones, as at the end of Act 2)*   Immortal Zeus
controls the fate of man, decrees him love or grief; our days the
echo of his will resound in fury or pass in nothingness away.

CURTAIN

RENDEZVOUS WITH LIFE: AN INTERVIEW WITH COUNTEE CULLEN

by James Baldwin
DeWitt Clinton High School Magpie, *Winter 1942*

> I have a rendezvous with Life
> And all travailing lovely things
> Like groping seeds and beating wings
> And cracked lips warring with a fife.
> I am betrothed to Beauty, scarred
> With suffering though she may be;
> In that she bears pain splendidly,
> Her comeliness may not be marred.

The above lines were written twenty years ago by a Clinton schoolboy who in his senior year became editor-in-chief of the *Clinton News* and of the senior issue of *The Magpie*. He handled both assignments with assurance and ease. Later he was to become one of Clinton's most distinguished alumni. His name is Countee Cullen.

"My first published poem," Mr. Cullen told me in a deserted classroom in the Frederick Douglass Junior High School where he now teaches, "was published without my knowledge in the *Clinton News*. It seems that there was a controversy between a Clinton teacher and an outsider in which the outsider held that high school students were unable to write acceptable verse, and the Clinton teacher held that they were. My poem was published to prove the Clinton's teacher's contention—and it did," said Mr. Cullen, modestly.

That was the beginning of a distinguished career as a writer.

Countee Cullen was born May 30, 1903, the son of a Methodist minister and his devout wife. His father is still pastor of a church at One Hundred Twenty-eighth Street and Seventh Avenue. "My parents," Countee said, "had no objection to my being a poet, as writing poetry cannot be considered a means of making a livelihood."

"Why not?" inquired your startled reporter.

"Poetry," explained Mr. Cullen, "is something which few people enjoy and which fewer people understand. A publishing house publishes poetry only to give the establishment tone. It never expects to make much money on the transaction. And it seldom does."

Yours truly, who had been under the impression that one simply published a book and sat back and watched the shekels roll in, sat aghast. "I never knew that," I said. "I guess a teaching job comes in pretty handy, then."

"Yes," he admitted. "Also, I *like* to teach."

Mr. Cullen then briefly reviewed how he had received his bachelor's degree at New York University, his master of arts at Harvard, and how in 1925 his first book of poetry was published. It established him at once as one of the [most] important of the younger Negro poets and brought him in 1926 the post of assistant editor on the Negro magazine *Opportunity*. In 1928 he received the Guggenheim Fellowship in Paris. The Guggenheim Fellowship, he explained to me, enables an author to live for a year, do nothing but write, and still be alive at the end of the year. It sounds like something out of Shangri-la.

When his twelve-month paradise had ended, Mr. Cullen came

again to grips with earthly practicalities and the exigencies of making a living. Eventually, he became a teacher of French in the aforementioned junior high school.

To date, Mr. Cullen has published six books of poetry, one of them being an anthology of Negro poetry, called *Caroling Dusk.* His latest, *The Lost Zoo,* written by request, he talked of as follows: "Some of the children I was teaching had read of my work and wanted to become better acquainted with it. However, most of it was too far over their heads for them to be able to appreciate it. They asked me to write something that they could understand. *The Lost Zoo* is the result."

Needless to say, I rushed home and investigated the book. I found it a very charming fantasy told in verse except for its prologue and epilogue which are in prose. The title page says it was written by Christopher Cat and Countee P. Cullen. The prologue explains that Chris is Mr. Cullen's pet cat who has been with Mr. Cullen so long that they have even learned to talk to each other. Chris tells him the story of the lost zoo and Mr. Cullen passes it on to us. Chris supplies all the footnotes to the text and a wiser or more charming cat you have never met. However, you probably would not be too anxious to see him in a dark alley. There's something eerie about a cat who not only laughs but can, on occasion, be bitingly sarcastic.

The Lost Zoo tells the story of all the animals who were left behind when Noah built the ark. There was a sleep-a-mite-more (the name describes him), the Squilililigee (the name gives you a clue as well as anything else might), the Wake-Up-World (who had twelve eyes of different colors) and "the Snake that walked upon his tail" (the female couldn't, just the male). All these animals and a great many more were left behind and drowned, and the story of the mass catastrophe is one of the author's most engaging pieces of work. It was written for children but this blasé grown-up enjoyed it more than the home-work he was supposed to have been doing.

Asking Mr. Cullen, as per custom, for some secret of success, I was told: "There is no secret to success except hard work and getting something indefinable which we call the 'breaks.' In order for a writer to succeed, I suggest three things—read and write—and wait."

"Have you found," I asked, "that there is much prejudice against the Negro in the literary world?"

Mr. Cullen shook his head. "No," he said, "in this field one gets pretty much what he deserves. . . . If you're really something, nothing can hold you back. In the artistic field, society recognizes the Negro as an equal and, in some cases, as a superior member. When one considers the social and political plights of the Negro today, that is, indeed, an encouraging sign."

Mr. Cullen expects to have his latest book, *Autobiography of a Cat*, published early in 1942. "It will be in prose," he said, "and one of my few attempts to get at the masses."

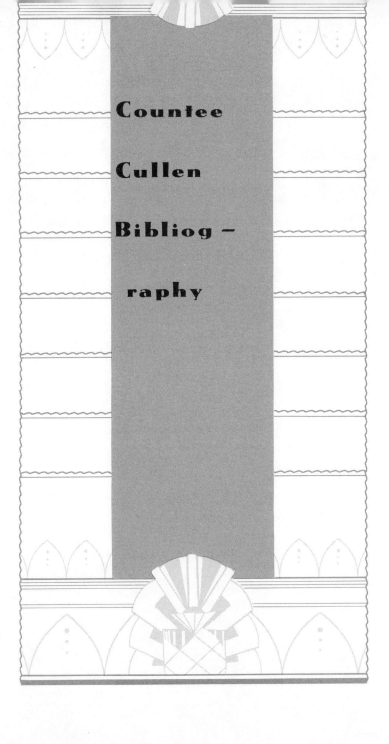

Countee

Cullen

Bibliog –

raphy

I. BOOKS BY COUNTEE CULLEN

Color (New York: Harper & Brothers, 1925).

Copper Sun (New York: Harper & Brothers, 1927).

The Ballad of the Brown Girl: An Old Ballad Retold (New York: Harper
& Brothers, 1927).

The Black Christ and Other Poems (New York: Harper & Brothers, 1929).

One Way to Heaven (New York: Harper & Brothers, 1932).

The Medea and Some Poems (New York: Harper & Brothers, 1935).

The Lost Zoo (A Rhyme for the Young but Not Too Young), published as
by Christopher Cat and Countee Cullen (New York: Harper & Brothers, 1940).

My Lives and How I Lost Them, published as by Christopher Cat and
Countee Cullen (New York: Harper & Brothers, 1942).

On These I Stand: An Anthology of the Best Poems of Countee Cullen,
selected by the author (New York: Harper & Brothers, 1947), published posthumously.

II: ANTHOLOGIES EDITED BY COUNTEE CULLEN

Caroling Dusk (New York: Harper & Brothers, 1927).

III. ARTICLES BY COUNTEE CULLEN

"Tendencies in Modern American Poetry by Amy Lowell," *The Magpie*
20 (January 1921), p. 31.

"The League of Youth Address," *The Crisis* 26 (August 1923), pp. 167–
68.

Review of Mark Van Doren's *Spring Thunder and Other Poems, The Measure* (January 1925), pp. 15–17.

"The Negro Sings His Soul," review of Howard W. Odum and Guy B.
Johnson's *The Negro and His Songs, Survey* 54 (September 1, 1925),
pp. 583–84.

Review of DuBose Heyward's *Porgy, Opportunity* 3 (December 1925), p.
379.

Review of Langston Hughes's *The Weary Blues, Opportunity* 4 (February 1926), pp. 73–74.

"The Negro in Art: How Shall He Be Portrayed: A Symposium," *The Crisis* 28 (August 1926), pp. 193–94.

Review of James Weldon Johnson's *God's Trombones: And the Walls Came Tumblin' Down, The Bookman,* October 1927, pp. 221–22.

Frank Ankenbrand and Isaac Benjamin, *The House of Vanity,* with an introduction by Countee Cullen (Philadelphia: Leibman Press, 1928).

"Countee Cullen to His Friends," *The Crisis* 36 (April 1929), p. 119.

"Countee Cullen on French Courtesy," *The Crisis* 36 (June 1929), p. 193.

"Countee Cullen in England," *The Crisis* 36 (August 1929), pp. 270, 283.

"Countee Cullen on Miscegenation," *The Crisis* 36 (November 1929), p. 373.

"Elizabeth Prophet: Sculptress," *Opportunity* 8 (July 1930), p. 204.

Introduction to James Weldon Johnson's "The Creative Negro" in *America As Americans See It,* ed. Fred J. Ringel (New York: Harcourt, Brace, and Co., 1932), p. 160.

"Development of Creative Expression," *High Points* 25 (September 1943), pp. 26–32.

IV. "THE DARK TOWER" SERIES (COLUMNS) FOR THE MAGAZINE *OPPORTUNITY*

Opportunity 4 (December 1926), pp. 388–90.

Opportunity 5 (February 1927), pp. 53–54.

Opportunity 5 (March 1927), pp. 86–87.

Opportunity 5 (April 1927), pp. 118–19.

Opportunity 5 (May 1927), pp. 149–50.

Opportunity 5 (June 1927), pp. 180–81.

Opportunity 5 (July 1927), pp. 210–11.

Opportunity 5 (August 1927), pp. 240–41.

Opportunity 5 (November 1927) pp. 336–37.

Opportunity 5 (December 1927), pp. 373–74.

Opportunity 6 (January 1928), pp. 20–21.

BIBLIOGRAPHY

Opportunity 6 (February 1928), pp. 52–53.
Opportunity 6 (March 1928), p. 90.
Opportunity 6 (April 1928), p. 120.
Opportunity 6 (May 1928), pp. 146–74.
Opportunity 6 (July 1928), p. 210.
Opportunity 6 (September 1928), pp. 271–73.

"The Dark Tower" columns of January 1927 (pp. 24–25); September 1927 (pp. 272–73); June 1928 (pp. 178–79) were not signed by Cullen and so I assume they were not written by him. All columns listed here as his were signed. "The Dark Tower" column of October 1927 (pp. 306–6) was written by Richard Bruce.

V. TRANSLATIONS FROM THE FRENCH

"Haiti and Haitian Society" by Jenner Bastien, *Opportunity* 6 (June 1928), pp. 176–77.
"Negroisms" by Fernard Gregh, *Opportunity* 8 (April 1930), pp. 124–25.

VI. PLAYS

Countee Cullen, *The Spirit of Peace*, unpublished, no date.
Countee Cullen and Arna Bontemps, *St. Louis Woman*, unpublished, 1946.
Countee Cullen and Owen Dodson, *The Third Fourth of July: A One-Act Play*, *Theatre Arts* 30 (August 1946), pp. 488–93.
Countee Cullen and Larry Hamilton, *Heaven's My Home*, unpublished, 1935.
Countee Cullen and Waters Turpin, *Let the Day Perish*, unpublished, no date.
Countee Cullen, *One Way to Heaven*, unpublished, 1932.

611

VII. BOOK-LENGTH STUDIES OF COUNTEE CULLEN

Blanche E. Ferguson, *Countee Cullen and the Negro Renaissance* (New York: Dodd, Mead, and Co., 1966).
Margaret Perry, *A Bio-Bibliography of Countee P. Cullen, 1903–1946* (Westport, Conn.: Greenwood Publishing Co., 1971).
Alan R. Shucard, *Countee Cullen* (Boston: Twayne Publishers, 1984).

VIII. ARTICLES AND CHAPTERS OR SECTIONS OF BOOKS ON COUNTEE CULLEN'S WORK

Houston A. Baker, Jr., "A Many-Colored Coat of Dreams: The Poetry of Countee Cullen," in his *Afro-American Poetics: Revisions of Harlem and the Black Aesthetic* (Madison: University of Wisconsin Press, 1988), pp. 45–87.
James Baldwin, "Rendezvous with Life: An Interview with Countee Cullen," *The Magpie* 26 (Winter 1942), pp. 19–21.
Bernard W. Bell, *The Afro-American Novel and Its Tradition* (Amherst: University of Massachusetts Press, 1987), pp. 133–36.
Robert A. Bone, *The Negro Novel in America* (New Haven: Yale University Press, 1958), pp. 78–80.
Arna Bontemps, "The Harlem Renaissance," *The Saturday Review of Literature*, (March 22, 1947), pp. 12–13, 44.
Stephen H. Bronz, *Roots of Negro Racial Consciousness, the 1920s: Three Harlem Renaissance Authors* (New York: Libra Publishers, 1964), pp. 47–65.
Nicholas Canaday, Jr., "Major Themes in the Poetry of Countee Cullen," in Arna Bontemps, ed., *The Harlem Renaissance Remembered* (New York: Dodd, Mead, and Co., 1972), pp. 103–25.
Eugenia W. Collier, "I Do Not Marvel, Countee Cullen," in Donald B. Gibson, ed., *Modern Black Poets* (Englewood Cliffs, N.J.: Prentice-Hall, 1973), pp. 69–83.
Ronald Crimeau, "Countee Cullen and Keats's Vale of Soul-Making," in *Papers on Language and Literature* 12 (Winter 1976), pp. 73–86.
Walter C. Daniel, "Countee Cullen as Literary Critic," *CLA Journal* (March 1971), pp. 281–90.
Arthur P. Davis, *From the Dark Tower: Afro-American Writers, 1900 to*

1960, (Washington, D.C.: Howard University Press, 1974), pp. 73–83.

——, "The Alien-and-Exile Theme in Countee Cullen's Racial Poems," *Phylon* (Fourth Quarter, December 1953), pp. 390–400.

Owen Dodson, "Countee Cullen (1903–1946)," *Phylon* (First Quarter, January 1946), pp. 19–20.

James A. Emanuel, "Renaissance Sonneteers: Their Contributions to the Seventies," *Black World* (August 1975), pp. 32–45, 92–97.

Blyden Jackson, "Largo for Adonais," in *The Waiting Years: Essays on American Negro Literature* (Baton Rouge: Louisiana State University Press, 1976), pp. 42–62.

Blyden Jackson and Louis D. Rubin, Jr., *Black Poetry in America: Two Essays in Historical Interpretation* (Baton Rouge: Louisiana State University Press, 1974), pp. 46–51.

David Kirby, "Countee Cullen's Heritage: A Black Waste Land," *South Atlantic Bulletin*, No. 4 (1971), pp. 14–20.

Charles R. Larson, "Three Harlem Novels of the Jazz Age," *Critique: Studies in Modern Fiction*, No. 3 (1969), pp. 66–78.

John S. Lash, "The Anthologist and the Negro Author," *Phylon* (First Quarter, 1947), pp. 68–76.

Michael L. Lomax, "Countee Cullen: A Key to the Puzzle," in Victor A. Kramer, ed., *The Harlem Renaissance Re-examined* (New York: AMS Press, 1987), pp. 213–22.

Shirley Lumpkin, "Countee Cullen" entry in *Dictionary of Literary Biography, Vol. 48: American Poets, 1880–1945, Second Series*, Peter Quartermain, ed. (Detroit: Gale Research Co., 1986), pp. 109–16.

Frank Luther Mott, "The Harlem Poets," *The Midland*, No. 5 (May 1927), pp. 121–28.

Margaret Perry, *Silence to the Drums: A Survey of the Literature of the Harlem Renaissance* (Westport, Conn.: Greenwood Press, 1976), pp. 53–59, 80–84.

J. Saunders Redding, *To Make a Poet Black* (Chapel Hill: University of North Carolina Press, 1939), pp. 108–12.

Eugene B. Redmond, *Drumvoices: The Mission of Afro-American Poetry*, (Garden City, N.Y.: Anchor/Doubleday, 1976), pp. 179–85.

Charles Scruggs, *The Sage in Harlem: H. L. Mencken and the Black Writers of the 1920s* (Baltimore: Johns Hopkins University Press, 1984), pp. 113–15.

Alan R. Shucard, "Countee Cullen" entry in *Dictionary of Literary Biography, Vol. 51: Afro-American Writers from the Harlem Renaissance to 1940*, Trudier Harris, ed. (Detroit: Gale Research Co., 1987), pp. 35–46.

——, "Countee Cullen" entry in *Black Writers: A Selection of Sketches from Contemporary Authors*, Hal May, Deborah A. Straub, Susan M. Trosky, eds. (Detroit: Gale Research, 1989), pp. 124–29.

Alan R. Shucard, Fred Moramarco, William Sullivan, eds., *Modern American Poetry* (Boston: Twayne Publishers, 1989), pp. 60–62.

Amritjit Singh, *The Novels of the Harlem Renaissance: Twelve Black Writers 1923–1933* (University Park: Pennsylvania State University Press, 1976), pp. 80–83.

Robert A. Smith, "The Poetry of Countee Cullen," *Phylon* (Third Quarter, 1950), pp. 216–21.

J. H. Smylie, "Countee Cullen's 'The Black Christ,' " *Theology Today* 38 (July 1981), pp. 160–73.

Darwin T. Turner, "Countee Cullen: The Lost Ariel" in *In a Minor Chord: Three Afro-American Writers and Their Search for Identity* (Carbondale: Southern Illinois University Press, 1971), pp. 60–88.

James W. Tuttleton, "Countee Cullen at 'The Heights,' " in Amrijit Singh, William S. Shiver, Stanley Brodwin, eds., *The Harlem Renaissance: Revaluations* (New York: Garland Publishing, 1989), pp. 101–37.

Jean Wagner, *Black Poets of the United States: From Paul Laurence Dunbar to Langston Hughes*, trans. from French by Kenneth Douglas (Champaign-Urbana: University of Illinois Press, 1973), pp. 283–347.

Bertram L. Woodruff, "The Poetic Philosophy of Countee Cullen," *Phylon* (Third Quarter, 1940), pp. 213–23.

James O. Young, *Black Writers of the Thirties* (Baton Rouge: Louisiana State University Press, 1973), pp. 168–72, 207–9.

IX. DISSERTATIONS

Ruth Taylor Baker, "The Philosophy of the New Negro as Reflected in the Writings of James Weldon Johnson, Claude McKay, Langston Hughes, and Countee Cullen" (M.A. thesis, Virginia State College, 1941).

Isaac William Brumfield, "Race Consciousness in the Poetry and Fiction of Countee Cullen" (Ph.D. thesis, University of Illinois at Champaign-Urbana, 1977).

Barbara Christian, "Spirit Bloom in Harlem: The Search for a Black Aesthetic During the Harlem Renaissance: The Poetry of Claude McKay, Countee Cullen, and Jean Toomer" (Ph.D. thesis, Columbia University, 1970.

Robert E. Fennell, "The Death Figure in Countee Cullen's Poetry" (M.A. thesis, Howard University, 1970).

William Harold Hansell, "Positive Themes in the Poetry of Four Negroes: Claude McKay, Countee Cullen, Langston Hughes, and Gwendolyn Brooks" (Ph.D. thesis, University of Pittsburgh, 1972).

Ruth Marie Mescher, "A Critical Evaluation of the Poetry of Countee Cullen Preceded by an Analysis of the Five Major Poets Who Influenced Him Most" (M.A. thesis, Washington University in St. Louis, 1947).

Beulah Reimherr, "Countee Cullen: A Biographical and Critical Study" (M.A. thesis, University of Maryland, 1960).

Alan Robert Shucard, "The Poetry of Countee P. Cullen" (Ph.D. thesis, University of Arizona, 1971).

X. OTHER BOOKS ABOUT THE HARLEM RENAISSANCE, AFRO-AMERICAN AND AMERICAN LITERATURE, AND CULTURE IN THE 1920S

Chris Albertson, *Bessie* (New York: Stein and Day, 1972).

Jervis Anderson, *This Was Harlem* (New York: Farrar, Straus, and Giroux, 1982).

Houston A. Baker, Jr., *Afro-American Poetics: Revisions of Harlem and the Black Aesthetic* (Madison: University of Wisconsin Press, 1988).

——, *Modernism and the Harlem Renaissance* (Chicago: University of Chicago Press, 1987).

Arna Bontemps, ed., *The Harlem Renaissance Remembered* (New York: Dodd, Mead and Co., 1972).

Stephen H. Bronz, *Roots of Negro Racial Consciousness, the 1920s: Three Harlem Renaissance Authors* (New York: Libra Publishers, 1964).

Mary Campbell et al., *Harlem Renaissance: Art of Black America* (New York: Studio Museum in Harlem, Abrams, 1987).

Abraham Chapman, "The Harlem Renaissance in Literary History," *CLA Journal* 11 (1967), pp. 38–58.

James Lincoln Collier, *Duke Ellington* (New York: Oxford University Press, 1987).

——, *Louis Armstrong: An American Genius* (New York: Oxford University Press, 1983).

Wayne F. Cooper, *Claude McKay: Rebel Sojourner in the Harlem Renaissance* (Baton Rouge: Lousiana State University Press, 1987).

Edmund David Cronon, *Black Moses: The Story of Marcus Garvey and the Universal Negro Improvement Association* (Madison: University of Wisconsin Press, 1955).

Arthur P. Davis, "Growing Up in the Harlem Renaissance, 1920–1935," *Negro American Literature Forum*, Fall 1968, pp. 53–60.

J. Lee Greene, *Time's Unfading Garden: Anne Spencer's Life and Poetry* (Baton Rouge: Louisiana State University Press, 1977).

Richard Hadlock, *Jazz Masters of the Twenties* (New York: Collier, 1974).

Robert E. Hemenway, *Zora Neale Hurston: A Literary Biography* (Champaign-Urbana: University of Illinois Press, 1980).

Frederick J. Hoffman, *The Twenties: American Writing in the Postwar Decade* (New York: Free Press, 1966).

Nathan Huggins, *Harlem Renaissance* (New York: Oxford University Press, 1971).

Langston Hughes, *The Big Sea* (repr. New York: Hill and Wang, 1975), originally published 1940.

Gloria T. Hull, *Color, Sex, and Poetry: Three Women Writers of the Harlem Renaissance* (Bloomington: Indiana University Press, 1987).

James Weldon Johnson, *Along This Way* (New York: Viking Press, 1933).

——, *Black Manhattan* (repr. Salem, N.H.: Ayer Company, 1988), originally published by Alfred Knopf, 1930.

——, *The Book of American Negro Poetry* (repr. New York: Harcourt, Brace, and World, 1958), originally published by Alfred Knopf, 1922.

James Weldon Johnson and J. Rosamond Johnson, *The Books of American Negro Spirituals* (New York: Da Capo Press, 1985), originally published as *The Book of American Negro Spirituals* and *The Second Book of American Negro Spirituals* in 1925 and 1926 respectively.

BIBLIOGRAPHY

Bruce Kellner, *Carl Van Vechten and the Irreverent Decades* (Norman: University of Oklahoma Press, 1968).

——, ed., *The Harlem Renaissance: A Historical Dictionary for the Era* (New York: Methuen, 1984).

——, ed., *"Keep A-Inchin' Along": Selected Writings of Carl Van Vechten About Black Art and Letters* (Westport, Conn.: Greenwood Press, 1979).

Robert T. Kerlin, *Negro Poets and Their Poems* (Washington, D.C.: Associated Publishers, 1923).

Victor A. Kramer, ed., *The Harlem Renaissance Re-examined* (New York: AMS Press, 1987).

Neil Leonard, *Jazz and the White Americans: The Acceptance of a New Art Form* (Chicago: University of Chicago Press, 1962).

Eugene Levy, *James Weldon Johnson: Black Leader, Black Voice* (Chicago: University of Chicago Press, 1973).

David L. Lewis, *When Harlem Was in Vogue* (New York: Oxford University Press, 1989), originally published by Alfred Knopf, 1981.

Sandra Lieb, *Mother of the Blues: A Study of Ma Rainey* (Amherst: University of Massachusetts Press, 1981).

Alain Locke, *The Negro and His Music* (Port Washington, N.Y.: Kennikat Press, 1968), originally published by Associates of Negro Folk Education, 1936.

——, ed., *The New Negro: An Interpretation* (New York: Albert and Charles Boni, 1925).

Carl Lueders, *Carl Van Vechten and the Twenties* (Albuquerque: University of New Mexico Press, 1955).

Claude McKay, *A Long Way from Home* (New York: Arno Press, 1969), originally published by L. Furman, 1937.

——, *Harlem: Negro Metropolis* (New York: Harcourt, Brace, Jovanovich, 1968), originally published by E. P. Dutton, 1940.

Charles H. Nichols, ed., *Arna Bontemps–Langston Hughes Letters, 1925–1967* (New York: Dodd, Mead and Co., 1980).

Kathy J. Ogren, *The Jazz Revolution: Twenties America and the Meaning of Jazz* (New York: Oxford University Press, 1989).

Gilbert Osofsky, *Harlem: the Making of a Ghetto, 1890–1930* (New York: Harper and Row, 1966).

Geoffrey Perrett, *America in the Twenties* (New York: Simon and Schuster, 1982).

Margaret Perry, *The Harlem Renaissance: An Annotated Bibliography and Commentary* (New York: Garland Publishing, 1982).
——, *Silence to the Drums: A Survey of the Literature of the Harlem Renaissance* (Westport, Conn.: Greenwood Press, 1976).
Arnold Rampersad, *The Life of Langston Hughes, Volume 1: 1902–1941* (New York: Oxford University Press, 1986).
Elliott M. Rudwick, *W. E. B. Du Bois, Voice of the Black Protest Movement* (Champaign-Urbana: University of Illinois Press, 1982).
Gunther Schuller, *Early Jazz: Its Roots and Musical Development* (New York: Oxford University Press, 1968).
Charles Scruggs, *The Sage in Harlem: H. L. Mencken and the Black Writers of the 1920s* (Baltimore: Johns Hopkins University Press, 1984).
Amrijit Singh, William S. Shiver, Stanley Brodwin, eds., *The Harlem Renaissance: Revaluations* (New York: Garland Publishing Co., 1989).
Amrijit Singh, *The Novels of the Harlem Renaissance: Twelve Black Writers, 1923–1933* (University Park: Pennsylvania State University Press, 1976).
Wallace Thurman, *Negro Life in New York's Harlem* (Girard, Kans.: Haldemann-Julius, 1928).
William M. Tuttle, *Race Riot: Chicago in the Red Summer of 1919* (New York: Atheneum, 1970).
Jean Wagner, *Black Poets of the Unites States: From Paul Laurence Dunbar to Langston Hughes*, trans. by Kenneth Douglas (Champaign-Urbana: University of Illinois Press, 1973).
Edward E. Waldron, *Walter White and the Harlem Renaissance* (Port Washington, N.Y.: Kennikat Press, 1978).
Newman Ivey White and Walter Clinton Jackson, *An Anthology of Verse by American Negroes* (Durham, N.C.: Trinity College Press, 1924).
Carl D. Wintz, *Black Culture and the Harlem Renaissance* (Houston: Rice University Press, 1988).

Gerald Early is Associate Professor of English and African and Afro-American Studies at Washington University in St. Louis, Missouri. Both a poet and an essayist, he is the author of two books, *The Culture of Bruising: Essays on Literature, Prizefighting, and Modern American Culture* (Ecco Press, 1991) and *Tuxedo Junction: Essays Towards a Cultural Definition of America* (Ecco Press, 1989).